W9-BZT-657

NAPA AND SONOMA

Welcome to Napa and Sonoma

In California's premier wine region, the pleasures of eating and drinking are celebrated daily. It's easy to join in at famous wineries and rising newcomers off country roads, or at trendy in-town tasting rooms. Luxurious inns, hotels, restaurants, and spas abound, yet the natural setting is equally sublime, whether experienced from a canoe on the Russian River or the deck of a winery overlooking endless rows of vines. As you plan your upcoming travels, please confirm that places are still open and let us know when we need to make updates by writing to us at this address: editors@fodors.com.

TOP REASONS TO GO

★ **Fine Wine:** Rutherford Cabernets, Carneros Chardonnays, Russian River Pinots.

★ **Spectacular Food:** Marquee chefs, gourmet groceries, public markets.

★ **Cool Towns:** From chic Healdsburg to laid-back Calistoga, a place to suit every mood.

★ **Spas:** Mud baths, herbal wraps, couples' massages, and more in soothing settings.

★ **Winery Architecture:** Stone classics like Buena Vista, all-glass dazzlers like Hall.

★ **Outdoor Fun:** Biking past bright-green vineyards, hot-air ballooning over golden hills.

Contents

Chapter 1

EXPERIENCE NAPA AND SONOMA

15 ULTIMATE EXPERIENCES

Napa and Sonoma offer terrific experiences that should be on every traveler's list. Here are Fodor's top picks for a memorable trip.

1 Take to the Skies

It's worth waking before sunrise for a hot-air balloon ride over the vineyards. The experience is breathtaking, and oh-so-romantic for couples. Flights end before noon, so you can easily add lunch and wine tasting to the day's activities. *(Ch. 4, 6)*

2 Ogle the Art

Museum-quality artworks enhance a visit at several wineries, but you can also ogle street art and visit artists' studios and arts centers. *(Ch. 4, 5, 6)*

3 Ride the Rails

The romance of the rails and vineyard views make for a crowd-pleasing excursion on the Napa Valley Wine Train, often with winery stops. *(Ch. 4)*

4 Sip Sparkling Wine

A few wineries focus on sparkling wines. Wine making at Schramsberg and Korbel dates back to the 19th century; sip in style at Domaine Carneros, Gloria Ferrer, and Iron Horse. *(Ch. 4, 5, 6)*

5 Paddle a River

Several outfits offer guided or self-guided kayaking or canoe trips on the Napa and Russian rivers. Pack a picnic, and you're ready to go! *(Ch. 4, 6)*

6 Splurge on a Meal

Celebrated chefs operate Wine Country restaurants, often using ingredients grown steps from the kitchen. Food this refined is worth at least one splurge. *(Ch. 4, 5, 6)*

7 Shop Till You Stop

Among the Wine Country's charms is that it's not overrun with cutesy boutiques or chains. Healdsburg earns top honors for its diverse shopping opps. *(Ch. 4, 5, 6)*

8 Play Winemaker

Learn to blend wine at entertaining sessions exploring the winemaker's art. At some wineries you'll even bottle and label your creation to take home. *(Ch. 4, 6)*

9 Sample Spirits

At distillery tasting rooms you can sample spirits and learn about the production process and how it differs from wine and beer making. *(Ch. 4, 5, 6)*

10 Taste on a Hilltop

That Cab or Chard tastes all the better with hilltop valley vistas. In Napa, try Barnett or Pride; in Sonoma, Kunde, Jordan, or Trattore Farms. *(Ch. 4, 5, 6)*

11 Be a Pinot Pilgrim

To get a feel for the climate and terrain that foster world-class Pinot Noir, explore the Carneros District, Russian River Valley, and Sonoma Coast. *(Ch. 4, 5, 6)*

12 Hone Your Skills

Instructors and guest chefs beguile students and visitors during cooking demonstrations at the Culinary Institute of America's CIA at Copia campus. *(Ch. 4)*

13 Luxuriate at a Spa

For pure unadulterated luxuriating, Wine Country spas rank among the world's finest, with the emphasis on wellness as much as working out kinks. *(Ch. 4, 5, 6)*

14 Bike Past Vines

The Wine Country's many valleys make for leisurely guided or self-guided bike rides past gently rolling vineyards and sometimes through them. *(Ch. 4, 5, 6)*

15 Hit the Beach

Windswept, photogenic beaches and dramatically craggy cliffs are the norm along the Sonoma Coast. The drive north from Bodega Bay to Fort Ross is spectacular. *(Ch. 6)*

WHAT'S WHERE

1 Napa Valley. By far the best known of the California wine regions, Napa is home to some of the biggest names in wine, many of which still produce the same bottles of Cabernet Sauvignon that first put the valley on the map. Densely populated with winery after winery, especially along Highway 29 and the Silverado Trail, it's also home to luxury accommodations, some of the country's best restaurants, and spas with deluxe treatments, some incorporating grape seeds and other wine-making by-products.

2 Sonoma Valley and Petaluma. Centered on the historic town of Sonoma, the Sonoma Valley goes easier on the glitz but contains sophisticated wineries and excellent restaurants. Key moments in California and wine-industry history took place here. Part of the Carneros District viticultural area lies within the southern Sonoma Valley. Those who venture into the Carneros and west of the Sonoma Valley into the Petaluma Gap appellation will discover wineries specializing in Pinot

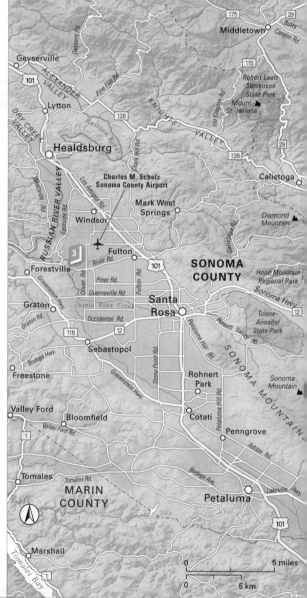

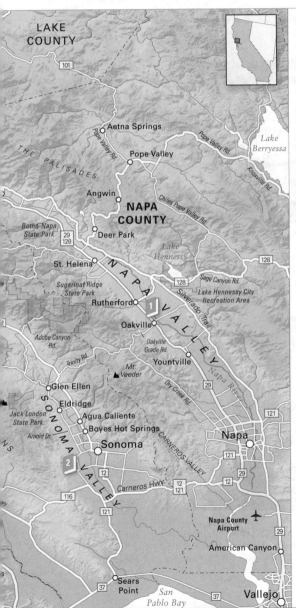

LAKE
COUNTY

101

THE PALISADES

Aetna Springs

Pope Valley Rd.

Pope Valley

Lake
Berryessa

Knoxville Rd.

Angwin

Chiles Pope Valley Rd.

NAPA
COUNTY

Bothe-Napa
State Park

29
128

Deer Park

Lake
Hennessy

St. Helena

128

Sugarloaf Ridge
State Park

128

Sage Canyon Rd.

Lake Hennessy City
Recreation Area

Rutherford

1

NAPA VALLEY

Silverado Trail

Adobe Canyon
Rd.

Oakville

Oakville
Grade Rd.

Trinity Rd.

Mt.
Veeder

Yountville

Napa River

Glen Ellen

Dry Creek Rd.

29

Jack London
State Park

Eldridge

Agua Caliente

Boyes Hot Springs

121

Arnold Dr.

SONOMA VALLEY

CARNEROS VALLEY

Sonoma

Napa

2

12

121

29

116

Carneros Hwy.

12
121

12

121

Napa County
Airport

29

American Canyon

37

Sears
Point

San
Pablo Bay

37

Vallejo

Noir and Chardonnay.
Both grapes thrive in the
comparatively cooler
climate. Farther north,
Cabernet Sauvignon and
other warm-weather
varietals are grown.

**3 Northern Sonoma,
Russian River, and West
County.** Ritzy Healdsburg
is a popular base for
exploring three impor-
tant grape-growing areas:
the Russian River, Dry
Creek, and Alexander
valleys. Everything from
Chardonnay and Pinot
Noir to Cabernet Sauvi-
gnon, Zinfandel, and
Petite Sirah grows here.
In the county's western
parts lie the Sonoma
Coast wineries, beloved
by connoisseurs for
European-style wines
from cool-climate grapes.

What to Eat and Drink in Napa and Sonoma

DAY BOAT SCALLOPS AT VALETTE
Sublime execution and heavenly ingredients—butter, fresh local fennel and leeks, Pernod, fennel pollen, scallops flown in from Maine, caviar, champagne beurre blanc (more butter), and a light, fluffy pastry—make chef Dustin Valette's signature day boat scallops *en croûte* a Healdsburg must-try.

STEAK AND A LIBRARY CAB
Since at least the 1960s, the iconic Wine Country food-wine pairing has been a juicy steak and Cabernet Sauvignon. Maximize your bliss with a Napa Valley Cab from the extensive wine libraries at Cole's (Napa), Perry Lang's (Yountville), Press (above, St. Helena), and Stark's (Santa Rosa).

MAD FRITZ ALE
Master brewer Nile Zacherle and wife Whitney Fisher made a lot of wine for boutique wineries before opening their craft brewery specializing in "origin-specific beers," with each ingredient's source acknowledged on the back label. Tales from a Renaissance-era Aesop's Fables edition provide most of the beers' names and all the front-label illustrations.

DUNGENESS CRAB
Crab season along the Sonoma Coast runs from mid-to-late fall through May. Establishments from seaside shacks to fine-dining spots serve the delectable crustaceans—steamed, as crab cakes and funnel cakes, and in chowder, salads, pasta, and myriad other preparations.

MUSHROOMY MUSHROOM SOUP AT KITCHEN DOOR
"It's so mushroomy, how does he do it?" ask many patrons at star chef Todd Humphries's Kitchen Door in downtown Napa. His soup's secrets of success? A heavy stock, his mushroom combo, and a splash of marsala, says Humphries.

CHARLIE PALMER'S LOBSTER CORN DOG
Chef Charlie Palmer's trademark lobster corn dog is simple in conception—a lump of lobster surrounded by deep-fried cornbread, served on a stick with pickled-ramp remoulade—yet somehow much more than the sum of its parts. Enjoy one at the Archer Hotel's Sky & Vine bar.

SORBET BRUNCH MIMOSA
Brunch isn't brunch at Calistoga's Lovina restaurant without a zesty mimosa with a scoop of seasonal-fruit sorbet. On a sunny day the outdoor patio fronting Lovina's two-story bungalow feels like a backyard party.

Kollar Red Wine Truffle

THOMAS KELLER CUISINE
Dining at Thomas Keller's The French Laundry costs hundreds, but you needn't break the bank to experience his cuisine. The chef's other Yountville restaurants include Ad Hoc (comfort food), Bouchon (French), Bouchon Bakery (fabulous pastries), and La Calenda (Oaxacan). He's also sponsored Burgers & Half Bottles (of wine) pop-ups.

RED WINE TRUFFLES AT KOLLAR CHOCOLATES
Chocolatier Chris Kollar installed an open kitchen in his downtown Yountville shop so patrons could see him and his crew at work, experimenting with new confections or whipping up another batch of red wine truffles, made from Napa Valley Zinfandel.

MODEL BAKERY ENGLISH MUFFINS
The Model Bakery's fluffy, doughy, orgasmically delicious signature baked good seduces on every level. Even Oprah swoons for these muffins, available at the bakery's Napa, Yountville, and St. Helena locations.

Best Bars in Napa and Sonoma

SIGH!

Quotes from Dom Perignon, Coco Chanel, and Churchill extolling champagne's virtues are painted on mirrors at Sigh!, a downtown Sonoma bar devoted to sparkling wine. The cozy, festive space exudes mid-century style. The centerpiece oval bar's taps dispense bubblies from around the world.

DUKE'S SPIRITED COCKTAILS

Happy hour is active in Healdsburg as winery employees unwind and visitors transition from wine-tasting to dining mode. Among the liveliest spots downtown is Duke's, whose elaborate "farm-to-bar" cocktails cleanse weary palates.

THE ROOFTOP

The boutique Harmon Guest House's rooftop bar earns rave reviews for its eco-friendly style and views of downtown Healdsburg and beyond, including 991-foot Fitch Mountain. The specialty cocktail lineup changes regularly to suit the season and complement the seafood-leaning food menu.

ERNIE'S TIN BAR

Roadside Ernie's is as famous for its no-cellphone policy—use your phone, and the next round's on you—as its 20 brews on tap and convivial vibe. The Petaluma watering hole, basically a long narrow bar with a few tables inside and an outdoor patio, shares a corrugated-tin building with a garage. Warning: the dude with the Stetson is as apt to be a millionaire as a ranch hand.

GOOSE & GANDER

A Craftsman bungalow off St. Helena's Main Street houses this popular eatery and its cool basement bar. The low ceiling and subdued lighting add speakeasy appeal G&G comes by honestly: the bungalow's original owner allegedly used the cellar for Prohibition-era bootlegging.

GEYSERVILLE GUN CLUB

Historic, retro, and au courant, this bar occupies a ground-floor sliver of Geyserville's circa-1900 Odd Fellows Hall. Some cocktails change seasonally, with classic Bloody Marys and margaritas among the staples.

EL BARRIO

Guerneville's hole-in-the-wall with south-of-the-border flair specializes in craft cocktails based on tequila and mescal. If you're not sure what to order, La Casa, the house margarita, is a good bet.

Sky & Vine

NAPA PALISADES SALOON

"Be here, drink beer," is the motto of this regular ole place, an excellent downtown Napa spot to throw back a few brews or bourbons and take in the game. Nothing fancy here, just 30-plus craft beers on tap, a full bar, a whiskey bar, and large-screen TVs.

SKY & VINE

The Archer Hotel Napa's sixth-floor rooftop bar seduces with valley views, snappy libations, and snacks and bites from chef Charlie Palmer and crew. If zero proof's your thing, there are always a few delicious and so-good-for-you options. During "reverse happy hour" (a bit before closing except Friday and Saturday), Sky & Vine is almost a bargain.

THE BISTRO AT AUBERGE

In good weather the cocktails at Auberge du Soleil's The Bistro bar pair well with the million-dollar Napa Valley views from the lofty outdoor deck. If a chill's in the air, cozy up to the fireplace inside for a signature margarita or a Basil Limonata (Ketel One Citron Vodka, fresh basil, and lime).

What to Buy in Napa and Sonoma

OLIVE OIL

By tradition dating to antiquity, grapes and olives have supplied two staples of the southern European diet: wine and olive oil. Visitors to several wineries with olive mills, including Petaluma's McEvoy Ranch, can taste and purchase extra virgin oils produced entirely on-site.

POTTERY

For their farm-to-plate cuisine some Wine Country restaurants extend their support of local purveyors to the second part of the equation, serving meals on elegant ceramic dinnerware sometimes crafted within a few miles. Napa Valley artisans of note include Amanda Wright and Richard Carter, both with studios in St. Helena, and Jeff and Sally Manfredi of Calistoga.

WINE GLASSES

High-end wineries take pride in serving wines in high-quality stemware. After a few tastings, you might catch on that the quality and shape of a glass really do enhance wines' aromatics and other attributes. Some winery gift shops sell the brand featured in the tasting room.

FASHION JEWELRY

"Everyday wearable chic" is the goal of many local jewelry artisans, some of whom put a bohemian spin on their output by incorporating leather or oxidized metals. Look for jewelry at winery gift shops and in downtown Sonoma, St. Helena, Healdsburg, Yountville, and Napa.

WINE

Yes, this one is obvious—buy wine in the Wine Country—but perhaps for reasons you haven't considered. Familiar brands have a few widely distributed wines you can easily purchase back home. At the winery, though, the focus will be on higher-quality small-production offerings sold only in the tasting room. Wines in a custom box make an excellent gift for someone back home.

GIFT BOOKS

With their photogenic mountains, valleys, vineyards, and architecture, the Napa Valley and Sonoma County inspire large-format gift books devoted to wine, food, and other topics. Perennial favorites include titles about winery dogs and cats or containing aerial photography.

WINE-BARREL FURNITURE AND ACCESSORIES

What happens to oak barrels after they're used to make wine? Most are sold off, their staves, metal hoops, and lids transformed into Adirondack chairs, barstools, planters, wine racks, lazy Susans, chandeliers, swings, jewelry, and anything else enterprising artisans dream up.

TERROIR-DRIVEN BEAUTY PRODUCTS

"Terroir" is the French term for soil, climate, and related conditions that make a vineyard, and therefore its wines, unique. Several Napa and Sonoma companies apply this concept to sourcing ingredients for beauty and skin-care products found throughout the Wine Country.

ALL-NATURAL SOAPS

The catchy names of Napa Soap Company's all-natural soaps—Cabernet Soapignon, Clean O Noir—reflect their local ingredients, among them grapeseed oil (a wine-making by-product), and sometimes wine itself. Customers swoon over the fragrances. Find them at owner Sheila Rockwood's St. Helena shop at 655 Main Street and elsewhere in Napa and Sonoma.

WINE-BOTTLE CANDLES

Wine bottles are even more ubiquitous than barrels as a wine-making by-product in need of recycling and reuse. Many bottles are indeed recycled, with others finding a second life as water glasses, chandeliers, and vessels for candles. Feast it Forward, in Napa, carries wine-scented candles made from natural soy wax.

Art Lover's Guide to Napa and Sonoma

THE HESS COLLECTION

Artworks by heavy hitters like Robert Rauschenberg fill the Hess Collection's two-floor gallery west of downtown Napa. Swiss-born founder Donald Hess acquired the pieces over several decades. Some tastings involve a guided or self-guided tour.

THE DONUM ESTATE

It's fitting that most of The Donum Estate's three dozen-plus large-scale outdoor sculptures grace the winery's lush vineyards, where the winegrowing team's farming skills yield Pinot Noirs and Chardonnays that are works of art themselves. The visual feast begins with Jaume Plensa's marble *Sanna, Giant Head,* which looms over the driveway leading to the board-and-batten hospitality center, itself a stylish set piece by San Francisco–based architect Matt Hollis. Collection highlights include Chinese artist-activist Ai Weiwei's bronze *Circle of Animals/ Zodiac Heads,* displayed in a grassy meadow. A Louise Bourgeois spider occupies its own indoor pavilion.

HALL ST. HELENA

Lawrence Argent's 35-foot polished-stainless-steel sculpture of a leaping rabbit marks the entrance to Hall St. Helena, which devotes a private tour (reservations required, tasting included) to the contemporary artworks collected by owners Kathryn and Craig Hall. You can view much of the collection before or after a standard tasting or on other tours. Hall is known for Cabernet Sauvignons, a few of which have earned 100-point scores from wine critics.

DI ROSA CENTER FOR CONTEMPORARY ART

The late Rene di Rosa founded this Carneros District art park that focuses on Northern California works from the mid-20th century to the present. Two galleries display some of the permanent collection and host temporary exhibitions, and the Sculpture Meadow and the area around di Rosa's former residence contain outdoor sculptures.

GEYSERVILLE SCULPTURE TRAIL

Enormous sculptures grab the eye north and south of downtown Geyserville. The figurative and abstract artworks change as they're sold or loans expire, but there's always plenty to view. From the south, take U.S. 101's Geyserville/ Highway 128 East exit, turn right, then quickly left, onto Geyserville Avenue. From the north, exit at Canyon Road, turn left, then right, onto the avenue.

RAD NAPA

Full-scale murals adorn warehouses and other structures in Napa courtesy of artists funded by RAD Napa (Rail Arts District Napa). One of the flashiest examples, painted on the two-story CIA at Copia building, was inspired by the culinary gardens out front. Napa Valley Wine Train passengers and hikers and bikers along the Napa Valley Vine Trail have the best views. RAD Napa's website has a touring map.

di Rosa Center for Contemporary Art

HEALDSBURG GALLERIES

Downtown Healdsburg is awash with tasting rooms and fancy eateries, but the arts are an enduring presence as well. Most spaces exhibit contemporary art. The 9,000-square-foot Paul Mahder Gallery, inside a vintage Quonset hut at 222 Healdsburg Avenue, has the largest selection: paintings, sculptures, and works in other media. Gallery Lulo (art, jewelry, design), at 303 Center Street, and Aerena Gallery Healdsburg (painting and sculpture), at 115 Plaza Street, are also worth checking out.

PATRICK AMIOT JUNK ART

All over Sonoma County you'll see the sculptures Sebastopol resident Patrick Amiot fashions out of sheet metal and found objects, rendered all the more whimsical by the wild colors his wife, Brigitte Laurent, paints on them. For the most significant concentration of sculptures, head two blocks west of Main Street to Florence Avenue, where many residents, including the two artists, proudly display the fanciful fabrications.

CA' TOGA GALLERIA D'ARTE

For sheer exuberance it's hard to imagine anything topping Italian artist Carlo Marchiori's storefront Ca' Toga Galleria d'Arte in downtown Calistoga. This place is all about Marchiori's creativity, as expressed in everything from paintings and sculptures to ceramic housewares. Be sure to look up—the ceiling's a trip. The pièce de résistance is the artist's over-the-top Palladian-style villa. Heavy on the trompe l'oeil, it's open for visits on a limited basis.

FRANCIS FORD COPPOLA WINERY

The famous director's Geyserville winery doesn't display much art per se, but its collection contains props and other items related to his films, among them some of late-20th-century cinema's defining works. Two selfie stars are Don Corleone's desk from *The Godfather* and the namesake 1948 vehicle from *Tucker: The Man and His Dream.* Displayed on a car-showroom platform and one of only 51 produced, the auto is worth more than a million dollars. The gallery's supporting cast includes costumes from *Bram Stoker's Dracula,* models from daughter-director Sofia Coppola's films, five FFC Oscars, and hundreds of other items.

Top Napa Wineries

ASHES AND DIAMONDS
Record producer Kashy Khaledi opened this winery whose splashy glass-and-metal tasting space evokes classic mid-century-modern California architecture. In their restrained elegance, the all-Bordeaux wines by two much-heralded pros hark back to 1960s Napa, too.

DOMAINE CARNEROS
The main building of this Napa winery was modeled after an 18th-century French château owned by the Champagne-making Taittinger family, one of whose members selected the site Domaine Carneros now occupies. On a sunny day, the experience of sipping a crisp sparkling wine on the outdoor terrace feels noble indeed.

INGLENOOK
History buffs won't want to miss Inglenook, founded in the 19th century by a Finnish sea captain and rejuvenated over the past several decades by filmmaker Francis Ford Coppola. You can learn all about this fabled property during elegant tastings—or just sip a glass peacefully at a wine bar with a picturesque courtyard.

JOSEPH PHELPS VINEYARDS
There are few more glorious tasting spots in the Napa Valley than the terrace at this St. Helena winery. Phelps is known for its Cabernet Sauvignons and Insignia, a Bordeaux blend. The wine-related seminars here are smart and entertaining.

LARKMEAD
Founded in 1895 but planted to grapes even before that, 150-acre Larkmead is one of the Napa Valley's storied estates. Hosts pour collector-quality Cabernets in a chic barn or outdoors in view of grapevines and the colorful garden.

SCHRAMSBERG
The 19th-century cellars at sparkling-wine producer Schramsberg hold millions of bottles. During a visit you'll learn how the bubblies at this Calistoga mainstay are made using the *méthode traditionelle,* and how the bottles are "riddled" (turned every few days) by hand.

SMITH-MADRONE WINERY
Step back in time at this Spring Mountain winery where two brothers named Smith make wines in a weathered, no-frills redwood barn. Founder Stu has been doing the farming and Charlie has been making the wines for more than four decades at this place with splendid valley views.

STONY HILL VINEYARD
The cellar at this winery on Spring Mountain's eastern slope known for Old World–style white wines looks like something out of *The Hobbit.* The dense woods on the drive up to the winery and the steeply banked vineyards surrounding it reinforce the sense of timeless perfection each bottle expresses.

TREFETHEN FAMILY VINEYARDS
The main tasting space at Trefethen, a three-story wooden former winery building dating to 1886, was completely renovated following the 2014 Napa earthquake. More than a half-century old itself, Trefethen makes Riesling, Chardonnay, and Merlot in addition to Cabernet Sauvignon and a Malbec-oriented red blend.

VGS CHATEAU POTELLE
Small bites from an acclaimed Napa restaurant and Cabernet and other reds made from mountain fruit pair perfectly in Chateau Potelle's whimsically decorated St. Helena bungalow. In good weather, tastings take place under an open-air Moroccan tent. In either setting, owner Jean-Noel Fourmeaux's hospitality shines.

Top Sonoma Wineries

APERTURE CELLARS

In 2009, still in his 20s, celebrated winemaker Jesse Katz started Aperture, whose focus is single-vineyard Cabernets and Bordeaux-style red blends. The architecture of Katz's Russian River Valley tasting room, which opened in 2020, riffs off photography, a nod to his dad and winery partner, Andy Katz, a world-famous photographer.

CHENOWETH WINES

Distinguished producers purchase grapes farmed by the Chenoweth family, whose ancestors settled northwest of Sebastopol in the mid-1800s. Some grapes are held back for the Chenoweth label's Chardonnay, rosé, and Pinot Noir wines. Family members, including winemaker Amy Chenoweth, often conduct the down-home tastings.

THE DONUM ESTATE

Single-vineyard Pinot Noirs exhibiting "power yet elegance" made the reputation of this Carneros District winery also known for smooth, balanced Chardonnays. The three dozen–plus large-scale, museum-quality outdoor sculptures by the likes of Anselm Kiefer add a touch of culture to a visit.

IRON HORSE VINEYARDS

Proof that tasting sparkling wine doesn't have to be stuffy, this winery on the outskirts of Sebastopol pours its selections outdoors, with tremendous views of vine-covered hills that make the top-notch bubblies (and a few still wines) taste even better.

JORDAN VINEYARD AND WINERY

A winery with a knack for discerning hospitality, Jordan produces a single Russian River Valley Chardonnay and an Alexander Valley Cabernet Sauvignon that perennially rank high on lists of best restaurant wines nationwide.

LIMERICK LANE

This winery's tasting room, in a restored stone farm building, is hardly Sonoma County's grandest, but the Zinfandel, Syrah, and Petite Sirah are arguably among the entire state's best. If you're curious about Zinfandel, don't miss Limerick Lane, whose oldest vines date back a century-plus.

RIDGE VINEYARDS

Oenophiles will be familiar with Ridge, which produces some of California's best Cabernet Sauvignon, Chardonnay, and Zinfandel. You can taste wines made from grapes grown here at Ridge's Healdsburg vineyards, and some from its neighbors, along with wines made at its older Santa Cruz Mountains winery.

ROBERT YOUNG ESTATE WINERY

Guests at this longtime grower's hilltop tasting room enjoy views down the Alexander Valley while sipping Chardonnay and other whites and Bordeaux-style reds. The first Youngs settled in Geyserville in 1858; the entire history of local agriculture unfolded on this historic site.

SILVER OAK

"Only one wine can be your best," was cofounder Justin Meyer's rationale for Silver Oak's decision to focus solely on Cabernet. The winery pours its two yearly offerings (one from Napa, the other from Sonoma) in a glass-walled eco-friendly tasting room in the Alexander Valley.

THREE STICKS WINES

The chance to make Pinots and Chardonnays from Three Sticks's prized Durell and Gap's Crown vineyards lured Bob Cabral from his longtime post at an exclusive Sonoma County winery. Guests taste Cabral's gems, made with Ryan Prichard, at the lavishly restored Adobe, west of Sonoma Plaza.

What to Read and Watch

Books

COOKBOOKS

Bouchon Bakery (2012), by Thomas Keller and Sebastien Rouxel. The legendary Keller and his executive pastry chef share recipes that made Yountville's Bouchon Bakery an instant hit.

The Cakebread Cellars American Harvest Cookbook: Celebrating Wine, Food, and Friends in the Napa Valley (2011), by Dolores and Jack Cakebread. This book collects 25 years' worth of recipes from the authors' annual cooking workshops.

The Essential Thomas Keller: The French Laundry Cookbook & Ad Hoc at Home (2010), by Thomas Keller. Recipes inspired by Keller's upscale and down-home Yountville establishments show the chef's range.

Mustards Grill Napa Valley Cookbook (2001), by Cindy Pawlcyn and Brigid Callinan. Pawlcyn describes her iconic eatery as "a cross between a roadside rib joint and a French country restaurant." She shares recipes and expounds on her culinary philosophy.

Plats du Jour: The Girl & the Fig's Journey Through the Seasons in Wine Country (2011), by Sondra Bernstein. The chef behind Sonoma County's two "fig" restaurants reveals her cooking secrets and adapts some of her signature dishes.

Wine Country Women of Sonoma (2020), by Michelle Mandro. In this sequel to a similar large-format photography book about the Napa Valley (2017), winemakers, chefs, executives, and women holding other key positions share insights and recipes.

FICTION

Eight Hundred Grapes (2017), by Laura Dave. At a personal crossroads, the protagonist returns to her family's Sebastopol vineyard as harvest season begins.

Murder Uncorked (2005), Murder by the Glass: A Wine-Lover's Mystery (2006), and Silenced by Syrah (2007), by Michele Scott. Vineyard manager Nikki Sands is the protagonist of this light and humorous mystery series that unfolds in the Napa Valley.

Nose: A Novel (2013), by James Conaway. A fictitious Northern California wine-making region—couldn't be Napa or Sonoma, could it?—is the setting for a mystery.

NONFICTION

Harvests of Joy: How the Good Life Became Great Business (1999), by Robert Mondavi and Paul Chutkow. Wine tycoon Robert Mondavi tells his story.

Hidden History of Napa Valley (2019), by Alexandria Brown. A local historian chronicles the activities and lives of Native Americans, Chinese and Mexican immigrants, African Americans, and other "marginalized people" in the valley.

The House of Mondavi: The Rise and Fall of an American Wine Dynasty (2007), by Julia Flynn Siler. The author ruffled many a Napa feather when she published this tell-all book.

Judgment of Paris: California vs. France and the Historic 1976 Paris Tasting That Revolutionized Wine (2005), by George M. Taber. The journalist who broke the story of the pivotal event analyzes its history and repercussions.

Lost Napa Valley (2021), by Lauren Coodley. With chapters detailing where Napans of yore farmed, worked, lived, played, and shopped, this book fondly recalls the days before the valley became an upscale destination.

Murder & Mayhem in the Napa Valley **(2012), by Todd L. Shulman.** A Napa police officer recounts a century and a half of crime in the land of fine wine.

Napa at Last Light: America's Eden in an Age of Calamity **(2018), by James Conaway.** The author of two previous bestsellers *(Napa,* 1990; *The Far Side of Eden,* 2002) about the Napa Valley reflects on more recent challenges.

Napa County **(2009), by Todd L. Shulman.** Old postcards of Krug, Inglenook, and other historic wineries add visual spice to this county chronicle.

Napa Valley: The Land, the Wine, the People **(2011), by Charles O'Rear.** A former *National Geographic* photographer portrays the valley in this lush book.

Napa Valley Then & Now **(2015), by Kelli A. White.** A well-regarded sommelier's encyclopedic book details the valley's wines, wineries, and history.

The Napa Murder of Anita Fagiani Andrews **(2021), by Raymond A. Guadagni.** The judge in the trial of a downtown Napa bar owner's killer tells the story of the nearly four-decade quest to achieve justice for her.

A New Napa Cuisine **(2014), by Christopher Kostow.** The much-lauded chef of the Restaurant at Meadowood in St. Helena describes his evolution as a chef and his land-focused approach to cooking.

Sonoma Wine and the Story of Buena Vista **(2013), by Charles L. Sullivan.** California's first winery provides the hook for this survey of Sonoma County's wine-making history.

Tangled Vines: Greed, Murder, Obsession, and an Arsonist in the Vineyards of California **(2015), by Frances Dinkelspiel.** Rare vintages by the author's great-great-grandfather were among the 4½ million bottles destroyed in a deliberately set warehouse fire south of Napa.

When the Rivers Ran Red: An Amazing Story of Courage and Triumph in America's Wine Country **(2009), by Vivienne Sosnowski.** The author chronicles the devastating effect of Prohibition on Northern California winemakers.

Movies and TV

Bottle Shock **(2008).** Filmed primarily in the Napa and Sonoma valleys, Randall Miller's fictionalized feature about the 1976 Paris tasting focuses on Calistoga's Chateau Montelena.

Burn Country **(2016).** Sonoma County seems downright sinister (especially at night) in this indie drama about an Afghani exile who becomes a reporter for a local paper and falls into danger pursuing leads on a murder case. Melissa Leo and James Franco are among the stars.

Falcon Crest **(1981–1990).** This soap opera centered on a winery in the fictional "Tuscany Valley" (aka Napa) may not have aged as well as wines made during its era, but it's acquired a nostalgic patina. At its best it's pulpy good fun.

Somm, Somm into the Bottle, Somm 3 **(2012–2018).** The Napa Valley plays a role in each of these documentaries about, respectively, the master sommelier exam, the world of wine through ten bottles, and three influential experts.

Wine Country **(2019).** Napa-Sonoma locations make cameo appearances in this comedy about a 50th-birthday celebration; Amy Poehler directed and co-stars (with Tina Fey).

Kids and Families

The Wine Country isn't a particularly child-oriented destination, so don't expect to find tons of activities organized with kids in mind. That said, you'll find plenty of playgrounds (there's one in Sonoma Plaza, for instance), as well as the occasional family-friendly attraction.

CHOOSING A PLACE TO STAY

If you're traveling with kids, always mention it when making your reservations. Most of the smaller, more romantic inns and bed-and-breakfasts discourage or prohibit children, and those places that do allow them may prefer to put such families in a particular cottage or room so that any noise is less disruptive to other guests. Larger hotels are a mixed bag. Some actively discourage children, whereas others are more welcoming. Of the large, luxurious hotels, the Carneros Resort and Spa tends to be the most child-friendly.

EATING OUT

Unless your kid is a budding Thomas Keller, it's best to call ahead to see if a restaurant can accommodate those under 12 with a special menu. You'll find inexpensive cafés in almost every town, and places like Gott's Roadside, a retro burger stand in St. Helena, are big hits with kids.

FAMILY-FRIENDLY ATTRACTIONS

One especially family-friendly attraction is the Charles M. Schulz Museum in Santa Rosa. Its intelligent exhibits generally appeal to adults; younger kids may or may not enjoy the level of detail. The sure bets for kids are the play area outside and the education room, where they can color, draw, and create their own cartoons. Another place for a family outing, also in Santa Rosa, is Safari West, an African wildlife preserve on 400 acres. The highlight is the two-hour tour of the property in open-air vehicles that sometimes come within a few feet of giraffes, zebras, and other animals. You can spend the night in tent-cabins here. At Sonoma Canopy Tours, north of Occidental, families zipline through the redwoods together. A mile south of Sonoma Plaza, Sonoma TrainTown Railroad dazzles the under-10 set with a 4-mile ride on a quarter-scale train, a petting zoo, and amusement rides.

AT THE WINERIES

Children have become a common sight at many wineries, and well-behaved kids will generally be greeted with a smile. Some wineries offer a small treat—grape juice or another beverage, or sometimes coloring books or a similar distraction.

When booking a tour, ask if kids are allowed (for insurance and other reasons, wineries sometimes prohibit children under a certain age), how long it lasts, and whether there's another tour option that would be more suitable.

A few particularly kid-friendly wineries include Calistoga's Castello di Amorosa (what's not to like about a 107-room medieval castle, complete with a dungeon?) and Yountville's Oasis by Hoopes, whose rescue farm animals and acre-plus organic garden keep kids occupied.

You'll find plenty of kids poolside at the Francis Ford Coppola Winery in Geyserville, and Honig Vineyard & Winery in Rutherford prides itself on making sure kids enjoy a visit as much as their parents do.

Chapter 2

TRAVEL SMART

★ **CAPITAL:**
Sacramento

♔ **POPULATION:**
40.1 million

$ **CURRENCY**
U.S. dollar

☎ **AREA CODE**
707

⚠ **EMERGENCIES:**
911

🚗 **DRIVING**
On the right

⚡ **ELECTRICITY:**
120–240 v/60 cycles; plugs have two or three rectangular prongs

🕓 **TIME:**
Three hours behind New York

🌐 **WEB RESOURCES:**
www.visitnapavalley.com,
www.sonomacounty.com,
www.visitcalifornia.com,
travel.state.gov

Know Before You Go

THE WINE COUNTRY SURVIVED THE FIRES (AGAIN)

Wildfires have disrupted life in Napa and Sonoma several times in the past few years. The dramatic television footage of ravaging flames inevitably leaves some viewers with the impression that the entire Wine Country has been destroyed, but in most cases the conflagrations take place in forested areas away from tourist spots. One notable exception, the Glass Fire of 2020, impacted a few dozen wineries, restaurants, and resorts. Although most businesses had resumed operations by early 2021, in the northern Napa Valley you're apt to notice evidence of the fire's path.

PLAN AHEAD FOR THE FRENCH LAUNDRY

Travel restrictions during 2020 and 2021 made it easier to secure a table at chef Thomas Keller's highly praised restaurant The French Laundry, in Yountville. As normal patterns resume, though, it's expected to remain the Wine Country's hottest (and at a few hundred dollars minimum not counting wine pairings, most expensive) dining ticket. And "ticket" here is literal. When you reserve a table, you're essentially purchasing a seat, as at the theater; if you miss the show, there's no refund. Here's how it works when demand is high: at specific times (often the first or 15th day of a month), the Tock online reservation service releases seats for a group of future dates, usually a month or more. Click the FAQs link on the restaurant's Tock page for the latest on how bookings are being released.

AVOID STICKER SHOCK AT RESTAURANTS

Even if you're not dining at The French Laundry, eating out in Napa and Sonoma can induce sticker shock. There are several ways to avoid this. Have the day's fancy meal at brunch or lunch, when prices tend to be lower. Happy hour, when a restaurant might serve a signature appetizer or a smaller version of a famous plate at a lower price, is another option. Nearly every Wine Country town has a purveyor or two of gourmet food to go, making picnicking in a park or eating back at your lodging a viable strategy, too.

AVOID STICKER SHOCK AT HOTELS

Unlike many other U.S. destinations where rates are highest from Memorial Day to Labor Day, the Wine Country in typical (that is, nonfire) years is the busiest—and most expensive—between September and October, during harvest. Year-round you can save money by traveling midweek, when rates tend to be lower. The shoulder seasons of mid-to-late spring and early November, just after harvest, often bring beautiful weather and more reasonable prices. It's cheaper still in the off-season, from December to March, when, for instance, some hotels with spas offer packages that include massages, mud baths, or other treatments.

HOW TASTING ROOM HOURS WORK

Some wineries welcome walk-ins, but many require an appointment for all visits or ones involving tours or food pairings. It's still possible to visit some tasting rooms on short notice, but keep in mind that unlike at restaurants, you can't pop in three minutes before closing and expect to be served. If you arrive at a tasting room 15 or 20 minutes before closing time, you might receive a courtesy pour and an invitation to return another day for the full experience. If you arrive 5 minutes before closing, you likely won't be served at all.

FEES AND TIPPING

One of the easiest ways to save on tasting fees—two people sharing a tasting—fell out of favor because of COVID-19, but check at visitor centers and lodgings for complimentary or two-for-the-price-of-one passes. Some wineries will waive the charge if you join the wine club, purchase a few bottles, or spend a particular dollar amount, but fees at others are, in industry parlance, "exclusive of purchase." By long-standing tradition, tipping isn't required, and you'll rarely see a jar to prod you, but many winery guests tip out of instinct. Instances when you might consider doing so include when your server has given you a few extra pours or has otherwise provided outstanding service, or when you've received a discount on your purchases.

SONOMA COUNTY IS WORTH IT

The 1976 Judgment of Paris blind tasting of French and California reds and whites sealed the Napa Valley's fame when the all-French judging panel unwittingly awarded top honors in both categories to Napa wineries. Less-known fact: half the grapes in the winning white, a Chardonnay from Calistoga's Chateau Montelena, came from Sonoma County's Bacigalupi Vineyard, among the many clues that the region west of the Napa Valley also produces world-class grapes. If you love Chardonnay and Pinot Noir, you're probably already planning to visit Sonoma County, but Cabernet Sauvignon, Zinfandel, and cool-climate Syrah are among the other stars. With coastal beaches, whale-watching, and parks full of redwoods, there are nonwine diversions, too.

DRIVING AND TRAFFIC

Traffic in Napa and Sonoma is generally a straightforward affair, the critical issue being negotiating rush-hour traffic. The Napa Valley is relatively compact, but there are only two main north–south roads. At rush hour and on weekends, when Bay Area locals descend, you're likely to get caught in traffic, so it's wise to plan your day's last winery stop away from busy Highway 29. In Sonoma County it's best to avoid the U.S. 101 corridor during the morning and evening commutes.

ALTERNATIVES TO DRIVING

Police actively look for signs of driver intoxication, making it wise to have a designated driver, avail yourself of the many driver services and tour-company options, or take Uber or Lyft. If you'll be carless, consider staying in Yountville, downtown Napa, Sonoma, or Healdsburg, all of which have numerous tasting rooms within walking distance of each other. A short walk or bike ride will transport you to the countryside in each of these places.

SHIPPING WINE

Because individual states regulate alcoholic beverages, shipping wine back home can be easy or complicated, depending on where you live. Some states prohibit all direct shipments from wineries. Others allow limited quantities—a certain number of gallons or cases per year—if a winery has purchased a permit to do so. The penalties for noncompliance can be steep: it's a felony, for instance, to ship wines to Utah. Since selling wine is their business, tasting room hosts are well versed in the regulations. If you send wines back home, keep in mind that most states require someone 21 or older to sign for the delivery. Alaska Airlines allows passengers flying out of the Charles M. Schulz Sonoma County Airport (STS) to check up to one case of wine for free.

Getting Here and Around

✈ Air

Nonstop flights from New York to San Francisco take about 6½ hours. Some flights require changing planes, making the total excursion between 8½ and 10 hours.

AIRPORTS

The Wine Country's major gateway is San Francisco International Airport (SFO), 60 miles from the city of Napa and 57 miles from Sonoma. Oakland International Airport (OAK), almost directly across San Francisco Bay, is closer to Napa, 50 miles away. Most visitors choose SFO, though, because it has more daily flights. Another option is to fly into Sacramento International Airport (SMF), about 68 miles from Napa and 76 miles from Sonoma. Wine Country regulars often fly into Santa Rosa's Charles M. Schulz Sonoma County Airport (STS), which receives daily nonstop flights from several western cities. The airport is 15 miles from Healdsburg.

AIRPORT TRANSFERS

Evans Airport Service ($40–$60) is an option for travelers staying in Napa or Yountville. Sonoma County Airport Express (about $40) shuttles passengers to Petaluma and Santa Rosa.

The smallest Uber or Lyft vehicle from SFO costs from $110 to southern Sonoma or Napa and from $130 to Santa Rosa. A private service like Pleasant Limo charges up to $320, depending on how far north you're going.

🚲 Bicycle

Much of the Wine Country is flat. With all the vineyard scenery, if you're fit at all you can spend a great day touring the countryside by bike. Some lodgings provide bicycles free of charge, and you can rent them or book guided tours in Napa, Yountville, St. Helena, and Calistoga; in Sonoma County you'll find rental places in Healdsburg, Santa Rosa, and a few other towns.

🚤 Boat

Except for Napa Valley Gondola's romantic Napa River excursions, there's no real boat service here. You can rent a canoe for a glide along the Russian River and book guided and self-guided kayak tours on the Napa and Russian rivers. The San Francisco Bay Ferry connects San Francisco and the city of Vallejo, where you can board a VINE bus to downtown Napa.

🚌 Bus

The knee-jerk local reaction to the notion of getting to tasting rooms—or the Wine Country—via public transit is that it's impossible or will take forever, but it's definitely possible. Napa, Petaluma, Santa Rosa, and Sonoma are the easiest to visit by bus. Napa and Sonoma both have fairly compact downtowns with numerous tasting rooms, restaurants, and lodgings. VINE buses connect Napa Valley towns; Sonoma County Transit serves its entire county. Golden Gate Transit Bus 101 heads north from San Francisco to Petaluma and Santa Rosa.

🚗 Car

A car is the most convenient way to navigate Napa and Sonoma. If you're flying into the area, it's almost always easiest to pick up a car at the airport. You'll also find rental companies in the larger Wine Country towns. A few rules to note: Smartphone use for any purpose is prohibited, including mapping applications unless the device is mounted to a car's windshield or dashboard and can be activated with a single swipe or finger tap. A right turn after stopping at a red light is legal unless posted otherwise.

PARKING

Parking is rarely a problem, as wineries have ample free lots, as do most hotels (some charge). In some communities, street parking is limited to two or three hours during the day, but municipal lots are usually available for free or at a low rate.

ROAD CONDITIONS

Roads in the Wine Country are generally well maintained and, except on weekdays between 7 and 9:30 am and 4 and 6 pm and on some weekends, scenic and relatively uncrowded.

DRIVER AND CAR SERVICES

Several companies supply designated drivers to operate your rental or personal vehicle for winery visits. The fees are reasonable, and many patrons appreciate the stories and on-the-fly schedule adjustments of a knowledgeable local. Most outfits will provide the car if necessary. Wine Tasting Driver serves Napa and Sonoma.

Another option is a private customized tour in a car, SUV, or van. Perata Luxury Tours allows clients to create their own itineraries or will tailor one to their interests. With Platypus Tours, you can join an existing tour with other guests or book a private one. Both companies have contacts with high-profile and off-the-beaten-path wineries in Napa and Sonoma.

🚗 Ride-Sharing

Lyft and Uber are generally dependable, though rides are sometimes difficult to get after 10 pm or if you're far from one of the towns.

🚕 Taxi

Taxis are nearly extinct in the Wine Country, and the few remaining companies provide so-so service. A better option is to use limousine or car services that charge by the hour or trip. Executive Car Service Napa Valley is a solid Napa outfit. In Sonoma County try Sonoma Sterling Limousines.

🚆 Train

SMART (Sonoma-Marin Area Rail Transit) trains travel between San Rafael in Marin County north to Santa Rosa's Airport, with Sonoma County stops that include Petaluma and downtown Santa Rosa. If you're carless and traveling light, you can take Golden Gate Transit Bus 101 and then a SMART train from San Francisco into Sonoma County. Trains don't run late, though. Napa has no commuter train service, but the Napa Valley Wine Train's historic cars travel between Napa and St. Helena, offering meals, on-board wine tasting, and in some cases winery stops.

Essentials

⚡ Activities

Driving from winery to winery, you may find yourself captivated by the incredible landscape. To experience it up close, hop on a bike, paddle a canoe or a kayak, or hike a trail. Balloon rides depart early in the morning. Packages at bicycle outfitters may include bikes, winery tours, and a guide—or you can rent a bike and head off on your own. The Napa and Russian rivers provide serene settings for canoe and kayaking trips past trees, meadows, vineyards, and small towns. Among the area state parks with hiking trails are Robert Louis Stevenson in the Napa Valley and Jack London and Armstrong Woods in Sonoma County.

🍴 Dining

What It Costs in U.S. Dollars			
$	$$	$$$	$$$$
RESTAURANTS			
under $17	$17–$26	$27–$36	over $36

Top Wine Country chefs tend to apply French and Italian techniques to dishes incorporating fresh, local products. Menus are often vegan- and vegetarian-friendly, with gluten-free options.

DISCOUNTS AND DEALS

Dining out for lunch or brunch can be a cost-effective strategy at pricey restaurants, as can sitting at the bar and ordering appetizers rather than entrées. Some places eliminate corkage fees one night a week or more.

MEALS AND MEALTIMES

Lunch is typically served from 11 or 11:30 to 2:30 or 3, with dinner service starting at 5 or 5:30 and lasting until 9 or 10.

Restaurants that serve breakfast usually open by 7, sometimes earlier, with some serving breakfast through the lunch hour. Most weekend brunches start at 10 or 11 and go at least until 2.

PAYING

In 2020, most restaurants began taking only credit cards and not cash, though some still don't accept one or the other. In most establishments tipping is the norm, but some include the service in the menu price or add it to the bill. *For guidelines on tipping see Tipping, below.*

RESERVATIONS AND DRESS

Where reservations are indicated as essential, book a week or more ahead in summer and early fall. Except as noted in individual listings, dress is informal.

➕ Health/Safety

The Wine Country is a safe place for travelers who observe normal precautions. Most visitors will feel safe walking at night in all the smaller towns. Still, the largest cities, Napa and Santa Rosa, have a few rougher sections (typically far from the tourist spots), so check with a local before wandering in unknown neighborhoods. Car break-ins are not particularly common here, but it's always best to remove valuables from your car, or at least keep them out of sight. Wildfires are a sad recent fact of life. These often take place away from populated areas, but not always: if ordered to evacuate, heed immediately. Queen of the Valley Medical Center (Napa) and Santa Rosa Memorial Hospital have emergency facilities.

COVID-19

COVID-19 brought travel to a virtual standstill for most of 2020 and into 2021, but vaccinations have made travel possible and safe again. However, each destination (and each business within that destination) may have its own requirements and regulation. Travelers should expect to continue to wear a mask in public and obey any other rules.

Given how abruptly travel was curtailed at the onset of the pandemic, it is wise to consider protecting yourself by purchasing a travel insurance policy that will reimburse you for cancellation costs related to COVID-19. Not all travel insurance policies protect against pandemic-related cancellations, so always read the fine print.

🛏 Lodging

Inns and hotels range from low-key to sumptuous, with the broadest selection of moderately priced rooms in Napa, Petaluma, and Santa Rosa. Reservations are a good idea, especially during the fall harvest season and on weekends. Minimum stays of two or three nights are common, though some lodgings are flexible about this in winter. Some places aren't suitable for kids, so ask before you book.

APARTMENT AND HOUSE RENTALS

Although Napa and other cities restrict Airbnb and similar rentals, you'll find listings online for accommodations throughout the Wine Country.

INNS

Many inns occupy historic Victorian-era buildings. When rates include breakfast, the preparations often involve fresh, local produce. Most inns have Wi-Fi, but some may not have air-conditioning—be sure to ask if visiting in July or August, when temperatures can reach 90°F.

HOTELS

Newer hotels tend to have a more modern, streamlined aesthetic and spa-like bathrooms, and many have excellent restaurants. Most hotels have Wi-Fi, sometimes free. Most large properties have pools and fitness rooms; those without usually have arrangements with nearby facilities, sometimes for a fee.

What It Costs in U.S. Dollars			
$	**$$**	**$$$**	**$$$$**
HOTELS			
under $201	$201–$300	$301–$400	over $400

▶ Nightlife

The Wine Country's two largest cities, Santa Rosa and Napa, offer the most in the way of nightlife, with Healdsburg and Petaluma two additional possibilities. Healdsburg has a sophisticated bar scene—and like Napa a popular rooftop hotel bar—though beer lovers might favor the Russian River Brewing Company's original Santa Rosa pub or its full-scale brewpub and beer garden in Windsor (between Santa Rosa and Healdsburg). The beer garden at Lagunitas Brewing Co. in Petaluma is among the other options for a fresh Sonoma County brew (if in Napa, try Stone Brewing Co.). If you're into sparkling wine, Sigh in downtown Sonoma pours an international selection of bubbles.

🎭 Performing Arts

Most A-list talents who perform in the Napa Valley do so as part of one of several festivals, most notably BottleRock Napa Valley (major and indie

Essentials

bands), Festival Napa Valley (opera, theater, dance, and classical music), and the Napa Valley Film Festival (more to promote a film than to perform, but sometimes both). Because of the city of Napa's size and proximity to San Francisco, a few downtown venues, among them Blue Note Napa, attract big-name musical acts. Over in Sonoma County, the Luther Burbank Center for the Arts in Santa Rosa and the Green Music Center in nearby Rohnert Park draw top musicians in all genres and present plays and musicals. Healdsburg's Raven Theater hosts community theater and the home-grown jazz festival.

🛍 Shopping

Fine wine attracts fine everything else—dining, lodging, and spas—and shopping is no exception. Sonoma County's Healdsburg and Sonoma and the Napa Valley's Napa, St. Helena, and Yountville stand out for quality, selection, and their walkable downtowns.

Hands-down the Wine Country's best shopping town, Healdsburg supports establishments selling one-of-a-kind artworks, housewares, and clothing. Heading south 37 miles, in Sonoma, shops and galleries ring its historic plaza and fill adjacent arcades and side streets.

🧳 Packing

You needn't pack anything for a Wine Country excursion you wouldn't include for any other domestic U.S. trip. Dressy-casual attire is the norm at most wineries, restaurants, and accommodations, though except at resorts and fine-dining establishments no one will pay much attention to what you wear. Pack a sweater or light jacket even in

summer—it gets chilly when the fog rolls in. It rarely rains from May through October; the rest of the year an umbrella can come in handy.

💲 Taxes

Sales tax is 7¾%–8¼% in Napa County and 8¼%–9¼% in Sonoma County. The tax on hotel rooms adds 14%–15% to your bill in Sonoma County and 15% in Napa County.

💵 Tipping

Tipping Guidelines for Napa and Sonoma	
Bartender	15%–20%, starting at $1 per drink at casual places
Bellhop	$2–$5 per bag, depending on the level of the hotel
Hotel concierge	$5 or more, if concierge performs a service for you
Hotel doorman, room service, or valet	$3–$5
Hotel maid	$4–$6 a day (either daily or at the end of your stay, in cash)
Tasting-room server	$5–$10 per couple basic tasting, $5–$10 per person hosted seated tasting
Tour guide	10%–15% of the cost of the tour
Waiter	18%–22%, with 20% being the minimum at high-end restaurants; nothing additional if a service charge is added to the bill

On the Calendar

January

Napa Truffle Festival. Chef Ken Frank's passion for truffles is boundless. His La Toque restaurant in Napa is the scene of a fancy dinner, the highlight of this festival that also includes seminars and foraging expeditions. ⊕ *www.napatrufflefestival.com.*

January or February

Winter Wineland. In early winter, wineries in the Alexander, Russian River, and Dry Creek valleys—including many not generally open to the public—host tastings and other events. ⊕ *www.wineroad.com.*

March

Wine Road Barrel Tasting. In early March, northern Sonoma County wineries open their cellars for tastings of wines not yet bottled. ⊕ *www.wineroad.com.*

April

Passport to Dry Creek Valley. Participants at this two-day northern Sonoma County event sample the Zinfandels that made the valley's name, along with wines from the many other varietals that grow here. ⊕ *www.drycreekvalley.org/passport.*

May

BottleRock Napa Valley. Except for 2021, when its promoters moved the event to September, this end-of-May three-day food, wine, and music festival gets summer rolling (and rocking) with acts headlined by the likes of Bruno Mars, the Red Hot Chili Peppers, and Halsey.

Tickets sell out in early January when the lineup is announced. ⊕ *www.bottlerock-napavalley.com.*

July

Festival Napa Valley. This acclaimed mid-July event attracts international opera, theater, dance, and classical-music performers to Castello di Amorosa and other venues. ⊕ *www.festivalnapavalley.org.*

September

Taste of Sonoma. Chefs, grape growers, and winemakers team up to celebrate Sonoma County food and wine on the first Saturday in September. Dozens of wineries and culinary vendors take part. ⊕ *tasteofsonoma.com.*

September–October

Sonoma County Harvest Fair. This three-week festival honors Sonoma agriculture with grape-stomping, wine, and olive-oil competitions, cooking demos, flower and livestock shows, carnival rides, and local entertainers. Grand tastings of award-winning wines and foods take place in early October. ⊠ *Santa Rosa* ⊕ *www.sonomacountyfair.com.*

November

A Wine & Food Affair. For this November event, wineries prepare a favorite recipe and serve it with wine. Participants travel from winery to winery to sample the fare. ⊕ *www.wineroad.com.*

Great Itineraries

First-Timer's Napa Tour

On this two-day Napa Valley survey you'll tour key wineries, taste fine wine, learn some history, and shop and dine. This itinerary is best done from Thursday through Sunday, when all the wineries (which all require an appointment) are open.

DAY 1: HISTORY, TASTING, SHOPPING, DINING

Start your first morning at downtown Napa's **Oxbow Public Market.** Pick up a brew at Ritual Coffee Roasters, or if in need of something more substantial drop by C Casa for tacos, quesadillas, and other gluten-free breakfast items or the nearby Model Bakery for a doughy English muffin. Afterward, tour the culinary garden at the adjacent **CIA at Copia** campus and, if the building's open, pop inside and peruse the Wine Hall of Fame plaques on the ground floor. Inductees include Gustave Niebaum and John Daniel of the day's first stop, Inglenook, and Joseph Phelps, whose namesake winery is an afternoon alternate. The second-floor Chuck Williams Culinary Arts Museum contains kitchen implements dating back more than a century.

From the market drive north on Highway 29 to Rutherford, where film director Francis Ford Coppola spent decades acquiring and restoring **Inglenook,** one of the 19th-century Napa Valley's grand estates. The winery's hosts provide a fascinating overview of area wine making, and the Cabernets, most notably the flagship Rubicon, are superb. If you can't get an appointment at Inglenook, try **Trefethen Family Vineyards.** The main tasting space of this winery founded in 1968 is a wooden winery built in 1886.

Departing Inglenook, continue north 3¾ miles on Highway 29 to St. Helena for lunch at **Farmstead at Long Meadow Ranch,** where many ingredients and some of the wines come from the ranch's properties in Rutherford and elsewhere.

Plan your after-lunch tasting based on your preferences in wine and atmosphere. The Super Tuscan wines at Calistoga's always lively **Castello di Amorosa,** off Highway 29 about 6½ miles north of Farmstead, are as over-the-top as the 107-room structure's medieval-style architecture. More serene in both setting and wines is **Joseph Phelps Vineyards,** off the Silverado Trail about 3 miles from Farmstead. In good weather the St. Helena operation's flagship Terrace Tasting of its collector-worthy wines, including the Cabernet-heavy Insignia Bordeaux red blend, take place alfresco overlooking grapevines and oaks. Reach Phelps from Farmstead by heading north briefly on Highway 29, east on Pope Street, south on the Silverado Trail, and east on Taplin Road.

Check into your St. Helena lodgings—the **Harvest Inn** and **Inn St. Helena,** both on Main Street, are good options. Poke around St. Helena's shops until dinner, perhaps at **Cook St. Helena** or **Goose & Gander.**

DAY 2: TASTINGS, A TOUR, LUNCH, AND A TOAST

If your lodging doesn't serve breakfast, begin your day in downtown St. Helena with a pastry, quiche, or granola parfait at the original **Model Bakery** location or The Station nearby.

After breakfast, drive about 6 miles (south on Highway 29, east on Zinfandel Lane, south on the Silverado Trail, and west on Highway 128, also signed

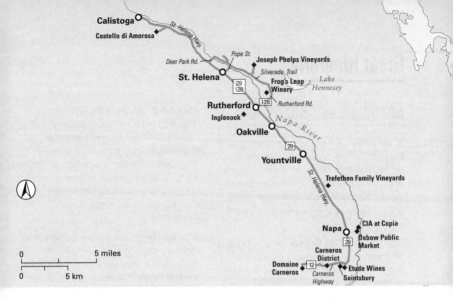

Calistoga
Castello di Amorosa
St. Helena Hwy.
Pope St.
Deer Park Rd.
Joseph Phelps Vineyards
St. Helena
Silverado Trail
Frog's Leap
Winery
Lake Hennessy
29
128
128
Rutherford Rd.
Rutherford
Inglenook
Napa River
Oakville
29
Yountville
St. Helena Hwy.
Trefethen Family Vineyards
CIA at Copia
Napa
29
Oxbow Public Market
Carneros District
Domaine Carneros
12
Carneros Highway
Etude Wines
Saintsbury

0   5 miles
0   5 km

as Conn Creek Road) to **Frog's Leap.** The Rutherford winery's guided tour is educational and entertaining, but you can also taste Sauvignon Blanc, Cabernet Sauvignon, and other wines without the tour.

Spend the afternoon in the Carneros District, known for Chardonnay, Pinot Noir, and sparkling wine. From Frog's Leap, head south on Conn Creek Road and east on Skellenger Lane to the Silverado Trail, where you'll turn south. After about 8 miles, turn west on Oak Knoll Road, which in 2 miles runs into Highway 29. Drive south 7 miles, then turn west on Highway 121 (aka Carneros Highway) for 1¾ miles to reach your lunchtime stop, the **Boon Fly Café.** Part of the Carneros Resort and Spa, the casual café serves fried chicken, gourmet pizzas, and burgers.

From Boon Fly, backtrack ¼ mile east on Highway 121 to Cuttings Wharf Road, which leads south (turn right) to Etude Wines, known for Chardonnay, Pinot Noir, and Cabernet Sauvignon. If you're not hungry, visit Etude first and then stop by Boon Fly for a late lunch—the restaurant serves food all day. Nearby

Saintsbury, where reservations are always required, is another famed Pinot house that merits a visit if you have time.

From Etude (or Boon Fly), continue west on Highway 121 to **Domaine Carneros,** whose stately château was modeled after one in France by the winery's founders, the makers of Taittinger champagne. The original winemaker here is fond of comparing the sophisticated sparkling wines to "Audrey Hepburn in a little black dress." If the weather's fine, sit on the vineyard-view outdoor terrace.

After your tasting, take the scenic route—Old Sonoma Road, north off Highway 121 less than ¼ mile east of Domaine Carneros—to downtown Napa. In town, turn north on Jefferson Street and east on 1st Street. Consider **Angèle** (French), **Compline** (Modern American), or **Zuzu** (Spanish tapas) for dinner.

Great Itineraries

Sonoma Back Roads Tour

Stay strictly rural on this easygoing trek through forests, vineyards, and the occasional meadow. Some of the suggested wineries aren't open one or two days a week, usually Tuesday and Wednesday.

DAY 1: FROM SEBASTOPOL TO FORESTVILLE

Start Day 1 at **The Barlow** food, wine, and art complex in Sebastopol; it's on the north side of Highway 12 two blocks east of Main Street. Have coffee and a pastry at **Taylor Lane Organic Coffee** and mosey around. Most of the shops won't be open yet, but you can catch a whiff of the complex's maker vibe and plot a return visit.

From The Barlow pick up the Gravenstein Highway (also signed as Main Street and Highway 116 just west of The Barlow), heading north 3½ miles to Graton Road and **Dutton-Goldfield Winery.** The winery, a collaboration between a major grape grower, Steve Dutton of Dutton Ranch, and Dan Goldfield, a celebrated winemaker, built its reputation on Chardonnay and Pinot Noir grown in the Russian River Valley and other vineyards that benefit from coastal fog and wind. Dutton-Goldfield also makes a few other whites and reds.

If your tasting goes quickly, you can sample more cool-climate Chardonnays and Pinot Noirs at nearby **Red Car Wines** without even getting into your car—the two spaces share the same parking lot. When you're ready to move on, take Graton Road west half a mile to Graton. Browse the shops and gallery on the hamlet's one-block main drag and have lunch at the **Willow Wood Market Cafe.** The creamy polenta with roasted-vegetable ragout is a signature dish.

After lunch, drive northeast on Ross Road and west on Ross Station Road a total of 3 miles to visit **Iron Horse Vineyards,** known for sparkling wines. The barnlike tasting space has only three walls, providing patrons close-up views of rolling vineyard hills steps away. When needed, the hosts fire up heaters to keep things toasty.

After tasting at Iron Horse, backtrack to Highway 116 and turn north. At Martinelli Road hang a right to reach Forestville's **Hartford Family Winery,** which produces Chardonnay, Pinot Noir, and old-vine Zinfandel.

Splurge on a night's rest at Forestville's **The Farmhouse Inn** and dine at its stellar restaurant. (A less-expensive option: stay in Guerneville at **AutoCamp Russian River** or **boon hotel + spa** and have dinner at **boon eat + drink.**)

DAY 2: HEALDSBURG AND GEYSERVILLE

Have a leisurely breakfast at your lodging or start Day 2 with a stop at **Pascaline Patisserie & Café,** a treat as much for its French-country ambience as the exquisite French pastries. (If you stayed in Guerneville, head downtown to Big Bottom Market.) You can dawdle on weekdays because the first stop, **MacRostie Estate House,** doesn't open until 11 (tastings start at 10 on weekends). From River Road head north on Wohler Road (which begins across from The Farmhouse Inn) and then Westside Road, a 6½-mile drive. Owner Steve MacRostie has grown grapes for decades. His Healdsburg winery sources Chardonnay and Pinot Noir from his vineyards but also many other all-star sites.

After tasting, continue on Westside to West Dry Creek Road, proceed north, and turn east at Lambert Bridge Road, which dead-ends at your next stop, the **Dry Creek General Store,** which opened in 1881. Order inside and have lunch on the covered front porch.

Cabernet is the focus at Geyserville's **Robert Young Estate Winery.** From the general store head south on Dry Creek Road ¾ mile, turning left onto Lytton Springs Road, left again (after 2¾ miles) on Lytton Station Road, left again onto Alexander Valley Road 1½ miles later, and left once more onto Highway 128 after 2 miles. When the highway curves sharply right after about ½-mile, continue straight onto Geysers Road and turn right onto Red Winery Road. The namesake founder has two Chardonnay clones named for him, but the robust Cabernet Sauvignons and other wines from red Bordeaux grapes are the reason to come here—oh yes, and the view down the entire Alexander Valley from the winery's knoll-top hospitality center. (Robert Young is closed on Tuesday; visit **Zialena** instead.)

Departing Robert Young, backtrack to U.S. 101 and head south to Healdsburg. Check out the shops on the streets bordering Healdsburg Plaza, then stop for a cocktail at **Duke's Spirited Cocktails** or the fourth-story rooftop bar of the **Harmon Guest House.** Have dinner with a view at Harmon or walk to nearby **Barndiva** or **Valette.**

Great Itineraries

The Ultimate Wine Trip, 4 Days

On this four-day extravaganza, you'll taste well-known and under-the-radar wines, bed down in plush hotels, and dine at restaurants operated by celebrity chefs. Reservations are required for all winery visits and recommended for dinner.

DAY 1: NORTHERN SONOMA

Begin your tour in **Geyserville,** about 78 miles north of San Francisco off U.S. 101. Get your bearings and smart advice at the small downtown area's **Locals Tasting Room,** which pours the wines of superlative boutique wineries. Have lunch at nearby Diavola or Catelli's, then head south on Geyserville Avenue to the French-style château of Healdsburg's **Jordan Vineyard & Winery.** (After 4 miles on Geyserville Avenue, look for the arrowed Jordan signs instructing you to turn left on Lytton Springs Road, Lytton Station Road, and Alexander Valley Road to reach the winery's yellow entrance.) Jordan produces one Russian River Valley Chardonnay and one Alexander Valley Cabernet Sauvignon each year. Enjoy a 2 pm Library Tasting of the current releases and an older red, then head southwest on Alexander Valley Road and Healdsburg Avenue to **Healdsburg Plaza.**

Explore the shops near the plaza; if you're up for more tasting, Cartograph Wines, a block off the plaza, and Breathless Wines, several blocks away, and are good options. **Hôtel Les Mars** and **Harmon Guest House** are two spots near the plaza to spend the night; stay at the Camellia Inn or River Belle Inn for a more traditional bed-and-breakfast experience, or **Montage Healdsburg** for high design amid 250 acres of vineyards and oaks. The Harmon's rooftop bar is a swank spot for a predinner cocktail before moving on

to a meal at **Bravas Bar de Tapas, Campo Fina,** or **Valette,** all close by. If you're in the mood to splurge, reserve (well in advance) a table at **SingleThread Farms Restaurant,** across from Valette, or at Montage's **Hazel Hill.**

DAY 2: HEALDSBURG AND GLEN ELLEN

Hike in the early morning or midafternoon, whichever suits you best, before or after visiting a few wineries or tasting rooms. If you're an early riser, begin the morning 2¾ miles north of Healdsburg Plaza strolling through part of **Healdsburg Ridge Open Space Preserve.** Wineries dot the Dry Creek Valley countryside, among them **Ridge Vineyards.** After tasting, have lunch in Healdsburg at Costeaux French Bakery, Oakville Grocery, or Willi's Seafood & Raw Bar before heading south on U.S. 101 and east on scenic Highway 12 to the Sonoma Valley town of **Glen Ellen.** If you've already hiked, drop by the tasting room of **Laurel Glen Vineyards** or **Schermeister Winery,** both in or near downtown. **Benziger Family Winery,** on London Ranch Road on the way to **Jack London State Historic Park,** is another good choice. If headed to the park, hike one of the shorter trails and visit the memorabilia-filled museum dedicated to the famous writer, who grew grapes and wrote some of his later works here. Have dinner at **Glen Ellen Star** and stay at the **Olea Hotel** or the **Gaige House + Ryokan.**

DAY 3: NORTHERN NAPA VALLEY

Head east 11 miles from Glen Ellen on Trinity Road, which twists and turns over the Mayacamas Mountains, eventually becoming the Oakville Grade. Unless you're the one driving, bask in the stupendous **Napa Valley** views as you descend into Oakville. At Highway 29, drive 7½ miles north through downtown **St. Helena** to **Charles Krug Winery,** where

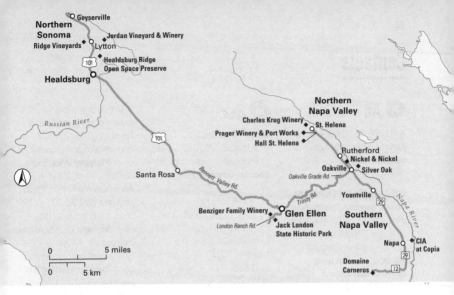

Napa Valley wine making got its start in 1861.

After tasting at Charles Krug, take lunch downtown at **Market** or **Cook St. Helena** and check out Main Street's shops before heading south on Highway 29 to **Hall St. Helena** (high-scoring Cabernets, impressive art collection) or its homey neighbor, **Prager Winery & Port Works.**

When you're done tasting, continue south on Highway 29 to Yountville for more shopping. Start in the north end of town at Restoration Hardware's **RH Yountville** and work your way south on Washington Street, stopping in the middle of town at **The Conservatory** and **Senses by JCB** and anywhere else that catches your eye. **Heron House Yountville,** which pours the Cabernets of nine small producers, carries upscale fashion, art, and household items.

Stay overnight at **Bardessono** or the **North Block Hotel,** both within walking distance of Yountville's famous restaurants. A meal at Thomas Keller's **The French Laundry** is many visitors' holy grail, but dining at **Bistro Jeanty** or Keller's **Bouchon Bistro** will also leave you feeling well served. Head to **Perry Lang's** for steak or chef Michael Chiarello's **Coqueta Napa Valley** for tapas and larger Spanish plates. The specialty cocktails at both are exceptional.

DAY 4: SOUTHERN NAPA VALLEY

Take breakfast at your lodging or Southside Yountville at Stewart Cellars, then head north 3 miles on Highway 29 to **Oakville,** where sipping wine at **Nickel & Nickel** or **Silver Oak** will make clear why collectors covet Oakville Cabernet Sauvignons. Nickel & Nickel is on Highway 29; Silver Oak is east of it on Oakville Cross Road. After your tasting, have a picnic at **Oakville Grocery,** in business on Highway 29 since 1881, or lunch at **Brix Napa Valley** or **Mustards Grill.** You're liable to see winery folk at either Brix or Mustards.

Your meal completed, head south on Highway 29, exiting at 1st Street to visit downtown Napa's **CIA at Copia** food and wine complex (if it's open, don't miss the museum of culinary equipment upstairs). Backtrack on 1st Street to Highway 29 and head south to Highway 121. Turn west to reach the Carneros District, whose **Domaine Carneros** makes French-style sparkling wines. There's hardly a more elegant way to bid a Wine Country adieu than from the château's vineyard-view terrace.

Contacts

Air

AIRLINE SECURITY Transportation Security Administration. ☎ 866/289–9673 ⊕ www.tsa.gov.

INFORMATION Charles M. Schulz Sonoma County Airport. (STS). ✉ 2200 Airport Blvd. ☎ 707/565–7240 ⊕ www.sonomacountyairport.org. **Oakland International Airport.** (OAK). ✉ 1 Airport Dr., Oakland ☎ 510/563–3300 ⊕ www.oaklandairport.com. **Sacramento International Airport.** (SMF). ✉ 6900 Airport Blvd. ☎ 916/929–5411 ⊕ www.sacramento.aero/smf. **San Francisco International Airport.** (SFO). ✉ McDonnell and Links Rds., San Francisco ☎ 800/435–9736, 650/821–8211 ⊕ www.flysfo.com.

AIRLINES Alaska Airlines. ☎ 800/252–7522 ⊕ www.alaskaair.com. **Allegiant.** ☎ 702/505–8888 ⊕ www.allegiantair.com. **American Airlines.** ☎ 800/433–7300 ⊕ www.aa.com. **Sun Country Airlines.** ☎ 651/905–2737 ⊕ www.suncountry.com.

⊕ Boat

San Francisco Bay Ferry. ☎ 707/643–3779, 877/643–3779 ⊕ sanfranciscobayferry.com.

⊕ Bus

Golden Gate Transit. ☎ 415/455–2000 ⊕ www.goldengatetransit.org. **Sonoma County Transit.** ☎ 707/576–7433, 800/345–7433 ⊕ www.sctransit.com. **VINE.** ✉ Soscol Gateway Transit Center, 625 Burnell St., Napa ☎ 707/251–2800, 800/696–6443 ⊕ www.ridethevine.com.

⊕ Car

American Automobile Association. (AAA). ☎ 800/222–4357 ⊕ www.aaa.com. **511 SF Bay Traffic/Transit Alerts.** ⊕ 511.org.

RENTAL AGENCIES Alamo. ☎ 800/462–5266 ⊕ www.alamo.com. **Avis.** ☎ 800/633–3469 ⊕ www.avis.com. **Budget.** ☎ 800/218–7992 ⊕ www.budget.com. **Exotic Car Collection by Enterprise.** ☎ 415/542–6023, 866/458–9227 ⊕ exoticcars.enterprise.com/sanfrancisco. **Hertz.** ☎ 800/654–3131 ⊕ www.hertz.com. **National Car Rental.** ☎ 844/382–6875 ⊕ www.nationalcar.com.

CAR SERVICES AND SHUTTLES Evans Airport Shuttle. ☎ 707/255–1559 ⊕ www.evanstransportation.com. **Executive Car Service Napa Valley.** ☎ 707/479–4247 ⊕ executivecarservice-napa.com. **Perata Luxury Tours.** ☎ 707/227–8271 ⊕ perataluxurycarservices.com. **Platypus Wine Tours.** ☎ 707/253–2723 ⊕ www.platypustours.com. **Pleasant Limo.** ☎ 650/697–9999 ⊕ www.pleasantlimo.com. **Sonoma County Airport Express.** ☎ 707/837–8700 ⊕ www.airportexpressinc.com. **Sonoma Sterling Limousines.** ☎ 707/542–5444 ⊕ sonomasterlinglimo.com. **Wine Tasting Driver.** ☎ 707/681–7050 ⊕ wine-tasting-driver.com.

⊕ Train

Bay Area Rapid Transit. (BART). ☎ 510/465-2278 ⊕ www.bart.gov. **SMART.** (Sonoma-Marin Area Rapid Transit). ☎ 707/794–3330 ⊕ sonomamarintrain.org.

⊕ Health/Safety

Ambulance, fire, police. ☎ 911 emergency. **Queen of the Valley Medical Center.** ✉ 1000 Trancas St., At Villa La., Napa ☎ 707/252–4411 ⊕ www.thequeen.org. **Santa Rosa Memorial Hospital.** ✉ 1165 Montgomery Dr., Off 3rd St., Santa Rosa ☎ 707/546–3210 ⊕ www.stjoesonoma.org.

Chapter 3

VISITING WINERIES AND TASTING ROOMS

3

Whether you're a serious wine collector making your annual pilgrimage to Napa and Sonoma or a newbie who doesn't know the difference between Merlot and Mourvèdre but is eager to learn, you can have a great time touring the Wine Country. Your gateway to the wine world is the tasting room, where staff members—occasionally even the winemaker—are happy to chat with curious guests.

Tasting rooms range from the grand to the humble, offering everything from a few sips of wine to in-depth tours of facilities and vineyards. First-time visitors frequently enjoy the history-oriented focus at Beaulieu, Beringer, Charles Krug, and Inglenook. The environments at some wineries reflect their founders' or current owners' other interests: horses at Nickel & Nickel and Tamber Bey, movie-making at Francis Ford Coppola and Frank Family, contemporary art and architecture at The Donum Estate and Hall St. Helena, and medieval history at the Castello di Amorosa.

To prepare yourself for your winery visits, we've covered the fundamentals: how to taste wine, tasting rooms and what to expect, and the types of tours typically offered by wineries. A list of common tasting terms will help you interpret what your mouth is experiencing as you sip. We've also described the major grape varietals, as well as the specific techniques employed to craft white, red, sparkling, and rosé wines. Because great wines begin in the vineyard, we've included a section on soils, climates, and organic and biodynamic farming methods. A handy Wine Lover's Glossary of terms, from *acidity* to *zymology*, covers ones you may come across in the tasting room or on a tour.

Wine Tasting 101

Don't be intimidated by the esoteric adjectives some wine types toss around as they swirl their glasses. At its core, wine tasting is simply about determining which wines you like best. Nevertheless, knowing a few basic terms and guidelines can make your winery visit more enjoyable. ■ TIP→ **Follow your instincts: there's no right or wrong way to describe wine.**

If you watch the pros, you may notice that they inspect, swirl, and sniff before sipping a wine. Follow their lead and take it slow, involving all your senses as you proceed through the steps outlined below.

USE YOUR EYES

Before you taste it, take a good look at the wine in your glass. Holding the glass by the stem, raise it to the light. Whether it's white, rosé, or red, your wine should be clear, without cloudiness or sediments. Some unfiltered wines may seem cloudy at first, but most clear as the sediments settle.

In natural light, place the glass in front of a white background such as a blank sheet of paper or a tablecloth. **Check the color.** Is it right for the wine? A California white should be golden: straw, medium, or deep, depending on the type. Rich, sweet, dessert wine will have more intense color, but Chardonnay and Sauvignon Blanc will be paler. A rosé should be a clear pink, from pale to deep, without too much red. Reds may lean toward ruby or garnet coloring; some have a purple tinge. They shouldn't be pale (the exception is Pinot Noir, which can be quite pale yet still have character). In any color of wine, a brownish tinge is a flaw that indicates the wine is too old, has been incorrectly stored, or has gone bad.

BREATHE DEEP

After observing the wine, **sniff once or twice** and try to identify its aromas. Then gently move your glass in a circular motion to swirl the wine around. Aerating the wine this way releases more aromas. (It's called "volatilizing the esters," if you're trying to impress someone.) Stick your nose into the glass and take another long sniff. You might pick up the scent of apricots, peaches, ripe melon, and wildflowers in white wine; black pepper, cherry, violets, and cedar in a red. Rosés, made from red-wine grapes, smell something like a red, but in a scaled-back way, with hints of raspberry, strawberry, and sometimes rose petal. You might encounter surprising scents such as leather or graphite, which some people appreciate in certain (generally expensive) red wines.

For the most part, a wine's aroma should be clean and pleasing. If you find a wine's odor unpleasant, there's probably something wrong. A vinegar smell indicates that the wine has started to spoil. A rotten wood or soggy cardboard smell usually means that the cork has gone bad, ruining the wine. It's rare to find these faults in wines poured in the tasting rooms, however, because staffers usually taste from each bottle before pouring from it.

JUST A SIP

Once you've checked its appearance and aroma, **take a sip**—not a swig or a gulp—of the wine. As you sip a wine, **gently swish it around in your mouth**—this releases more aromas for your nose to explore. Do the aroma and the flavor complement each other, improve each other? While moving the wine around in your mouth, think about the way it feels: silky or crisp? Does it coat your tongue or is it thinner? Does it fill your mouth with flavor or is it weak? This combination of weight and intensity is referred to as *body*: a good wine may be light-, medium-, or full-bodied.

The more complex a wine, the more flavors you will detect in the course of tasting. You might experience different things when you first take a sip (*up front*), when you swish (*in the middle* or *midpalate*), and just before you swallow (*at the end* or *back-palate*).

SPIT OR SWALLOW?

You may choose to spit out the wine (into the cup or receptacle provided) or swallow it. The pros typically spit because they want to preserve their palates (and sobriety) for the wines to come, but you'll find that swallowers far outnumber spitters in tasting rooms. Either way, **pay attention to what happens after the wine leaves your mouth**—this is the finish, and it can be spectacular. What sensations stay behind or appear? Does the flavor fade away quickly or linger pleasantly? A long finish is a sign of quality; wine with no perceptible finish is inferior.

Tasting Rooms and Winery Tours

At most wineries you'll have to pay for the privilege of tasting. In the Napa Valley expect to pay $35–$65 for a tasting of current releases and $75–$100 or more for reserve, estate, or library wines. Sonoma County tastings generally cost $20–$40 for the former and $40–$75 for the latter. To experience wine making at its highest level, consider splurging for a special tasting at one winery at least.

For years it was the norm in tasting rooms not to tip, but with today's more personalized service, you might consider doing so. It's not required, though. For a basic tasting, $5 or $10 per couple will suffice; for a hosted seated tasting, $5 or $10 per person, perhaps a little more for extra attention.

Many wineries are open to the public, usually daily from 10 or 11 am to 5 pm. They may close as early as 4 or 4:30, so it's best to get a reasonably early start if you want to fit in more than a few spots. ■TIP➔ **Wineries that allow walk-ins usually stop serving new visitors from 15 to 30 minutes before the posted closing time, so don't expect to skate in at the last moment.**

IN THE TASTING ROOM
In most tasting rooms, the server will provide a list of the wines being poured. The wines will be listed in a suggested tasting order, generally starting with the lightest-bodied whites and progressing to the most intense reds. Dessert wines will come at the end.

If you haven't reserved a set tasting experience—all Cabernets, for example—you may be able to choose several wines from the winery's available lineup. In

Wine Clubs

If several of a winery's offerings appeal to you and you live in a state that allows you to order wines directly from wineries, consider joining its wine club. You'll receive offers for members-only releases, invitations to winery events, and a discount on all your purchases.

either case, if you have a preference for whites or reds, make this known. If possible, the server will adjust the offerings. Many wineries limit the number of pours to four or five, so don't waste a taste on something you know you don't prefer.

Each pour will be about an ounce. If your tasting doesn't involve a food pairing, crackers or breadsticks might be provided; nibble them to clear your palate between selections. If you don't like a wine, or you've tasted enough, don't feel obligated to finish it.

TAKING A TOUR
Even if you're not a devoted wine drinker, seeing how grapes become wine can be fascinating. Tours tend to be most exciting in September and October, when the harvest and crush are underway. Depending on the winery's size, tours range from a few people to large groups and typically last 30 minutes to an hour. ■TIP➔ **Wear comfortable shoes because you might be walking on wet floors or stepping over hoses or other equipment.**

Some winery tours are free, in which case you usually pay a separate fee to taste wine. If you've paid for the tour—often $20–$40—your tasting is usually included in the price.

At large wineries, introductory tours are typically offered several times daily. Less frequent are specialized tours and seminars focusing on growing techniques,

Filmmaker Francis Ford Coppola owns Inglenook, one of the Napa Valley's great wine estates.

sensory evaluation, wine blending, food-and-wine pairing, and related topics. These events typically cost $30–$125.

VISITING SAFELY

Social-distancing, mask-wearing, and other safeguards against the spread of COVID-19 may evolve, but expect adherence to current CDC and California state guidelines. Winery websites usually describe what to expect during a tasting or tour. Call ahead if you have any specific concerns. To maintain proper sanitation and control patron flow, most wineries receive guests by appointment only. Some allow walk-ins space permitting, but many don't. Be aware, too, that many wineries that previously allowed picnicking, guests under age 21, or pets no longer do. Check ahead to avoid disappointment.

Top Varietals

Several dozen grape varietals are grown in Napa and Sonoma, from favorites like Chardonnay and Cabernet Sauvignon to less familiar types like Albariño and Tempranillo. You'll likely come across many of the following varietals as you visit the wineries.

WHITE

Albariño. One of the most popular wine grapes in Spain (it's also a staple of Portuguese wine making), this cool-climate grape creates light, citrusy wines, often with overtones of mango or kiwi.

Chardonnay. A grape originally from relatively cool Burgundy, France, Chardonnay in Napa and Sonoma can be fruit-forward or restrained, buttery or highly acidic, depending on where it's grown, when during harvest it's picked, and the wine-making techniques applied.

From a balloon you'll see how compact the Napa Valley is.

Gewürztraminer. Cooler climes such as the Russian River Valley are great for growing this German-Alsatian grape, which is turned into a boldly perfumed, fruity wine.

Marsanne. A white-wine grape of France's northern Rhône Valley, Marsanne can produce a dry or sweet wine depending on how it is handled.

Pinot Gris. Known in Italy as Pinot Grigio, this varietal in Napa and Sonoma yields a more deeply colored, less acidic wine with medium to full body.

Riesling. Also called White Riesling, this cool-climate German grape has a sweet reputation in America. When made in a dry style, though, it can be crisply refreshing, with lush aromas.

Roussanne. This grape from the Rhône Valley makes a fragrant wine that can achieve a balance of fruitiness and acidity.

Sauvignon Blanc. Hailing from Bordeaux and the Loire Valley, this white grape does very well almost anywhere in Napa and Sonoma. Sauvignon Blancs display a range of personalities, from herbaceous to tropical-fruit.

Viognier. A grape from France's Rhône Valley, Viognier is usually made in a dry style. The best Viogniers often have an intense bouquet.

RED

Barbera. Prevalent in California thanks to 19th-century Italian immigrants, Barbera yields low-tannin, high-acid wines with ample fruit.

Cabernet Franc. Often used in blends to add complexity to Cabernet Sauvignon, this French grape can produce aromatic, soft, and subtle wines.

Cabernet Sauvignon. The king of California reds, this Bordeaux grape is at home in well-drained soils. On its own it can require an extended aging period, so it's often softened with Cabernet Franc, Merlot, and other red varieties for earlier drinking.

Grenache. This Spanish grape, which makes some of the southern Rhône Valley's most distinguished wines, ripens best in hot, dry conditions. Medium-bodied, often light in color, Grenache is sometimes blended with a little Syrah to add tannin and texture.

Merlot. This blue-black Bordeaux varietal makes soft, full-bodied wines. Often fruity, it can be complex even when young.

Mourvèdre. A native of France's Rhône Valley, this grape makes wine that is deeply colored, very dense, and high in alcohol. When young it can seem harsh, but it mellows with aging.

Petite Sirah. A cross between the Rhône grapes Syrah and Peloursin, Petite Sirah, which loves a warm climate, produces a hearty wine.

Pinot Noir. The darling of grape growers in cooler parts of Napa and Sonoma, including the Carneros region and the Russian River Valley, Pinot Noir is also called the "heartbreak grape" because it's hard to cultivate. At its best it has a subtle but addictive earthy quality.

Sangiovese. Dominant in the Chianti region and much of central Italy, Sangiovese can, depending on how it's grown and vinified, be made into vibrant, light- to medium-bodied wines or complex reds.

Syrah. Another big California red, this grape originated in the Rhône Valley. With good tannins it can become a full-bodied, almost smoky beauty.

Tempranillo. The primary varietal in Spain's Rioja region, sturdy Tempranillo makes inky purple wines with a rich texture. Wines from this grape are great on their own but often excel paired with red-meat and game dishes.

Zinfandel. Celebrated as California's own (though it has distant old-world origins), Zinfandel is rich and spicy. Its tannins can make it complex and well suited for aging.

How Wine Is Made

THE CRUSH

Turning grapes into wine generally starts at the **crush pad,** where the grapes are brought in from the vineyards. Good winemakers keep tabs on the fruit throughout the year, but their presence is critical at harvest, when ripeness determines the proper day for picking. Once that day arrives, the crush begins.

Wineries pick grapes by machine or by hand, depending on the terrain and the type of grape. Harvesting often takes place at night with the help of powerful floodlights. Why at night? In addition to it being easier on the workers (daytime temperatures frequently reach 90°F [32°C] or more from August well into October), the fruit-acid content in the grape's pulp and juice peaks in the cool night air. The acids—an essential component during fermentation and aging and an important part of wine's flavor—plummet in the heat of the day.

Grapes arrive at the crush pad in large containers called gondolas. Unless the winemaker intends to ferment the entire clusters, which is generally done only for red wines, they are dropped gently onto a conveyor belt that deposits them into a **stemmer-crusher,** which separates the grapes from their stems. Then the sorting process begins. At most wineries this is done by hand at sorting tables, where workers remove remaining stems and leaves and reject any damaged berries.

Because anything not sorted out will wind up in the fermenting tank, some wineries double or even triple sort to achieve higher quality. Stems, for instance, can add unwanted tannins or, if not sufficiently ripe, "greenness" to a finished wine. On the other hand, winemakers sometimes desire those tannins and allow some stems through. A few high-end wineries use optical grape sorters that scan and assess the fruit.

Berries deemed too small or otherwise defective are whisked away, along with any extraneous vegetal matter.

No matter the process used, the sorted grapes are then ready for transfer to a press or vat. After this step the production process goes one of four ways, depending on whether a white, red, rosé, or sparkling wine is being made.

WHITE WINES

The juice of white-wine grapes first goes to **settling tanks,** where the skins and solids sink to the bottom, separating from the free-run juice on top. The material in the settling tanks still contains a lot of liquid, so after the free-run juice is pumped off, the rest goes into a **press.** By one of several methods, additional liquid is squeezed from the solids. Like the free-run juice, the press juice is usually pumped into a stainless-steel **fermenter.**

During fermentation, yeast feeds on the sugar in the grape juice and converts it to alcohol and carbon dioxide. Wine yeast dies and fermentation naturally stops in two to four weeks, when the alcohol level reaches between 13% and 15% (or sometimes more).

To prevent oxidation that damages wine's color and flavor, winemakers almost always add sulfur dioxide, in the form of sulfites, before fermenting. A winemaker may also encourage **malolactic fermentation** (or simply *malo*) to soften a wine's acidity or deepen its flavor and complexity. This is done either by inoculating the wine with lactic bacteria soon after fermentation begins or right after it ends, or by transferring the new wine to wooden vats that harbor the bacteria.

For richer results, free-run juice from Chardonnay grapes might be fermented in oak barrels. In many cases the barrels used to make white wines, especially Sauvignon Blanc, are older, "neutral" barrels previously used to make other wines. These **neutral barrels** can add

fullness to a wine without adding any wood flavors. In recent years wineries have begun using fermenting tanks made out of concrete. Initially these vessels, some shaped like eggs, others square or cone-shaped, were employed mostly to make white wines, but more wineries are also using them for rosés and reds. Bigger than an oak barrel but smaller than most stainless tanks, the vessels, like barrels, are porous enough to "breathe," but unlike wood don't impart flavors or tannins to wines. The notion of fermenting wines in concrete receptacles may sound newfangled, but their use dates back to the 19th century (and some say even further).

When the wine has finished fermenting, whether in a tank or a barrel, it is generally **racked**—moved into a clean tank or barrel to separate it from any remaining grape solids. Sometimes Chardonnay and special batches of Sauvignon Blanc are left "on the lees"—atop the spent yeast, grape solids, and other matter in the fermenting tank—for an extended period before being racked to pick up extra complexity. Wine may be racked several times as the sediment continues to settle out.

After the first racking the wine may be **filtered** to remove solid particles that can cloud the wine and any stray yeast or bacteria that can spoil it. Some whites are filtered several times before bottling. Most commercial producers filter their wines, but many fine-wine makers don't, as they believe it leads to less complex wines that don't age as well.

White wine may also be **fined** by mixing in a fine clay called bentonite, albumen from egg whites, or other agents to absorb substances that can cloud the wine. As with filtering, the process is more common with ordinary table wines than with fine wines.

New wine is stored in stainless-steel, wood (predominantly oak), or concrete containers to rest and develop before bottling. This stage, called **maturation** or **aging,** may last anywhere from a few months to more than a year. Barrel rooms are kept dark to protect the wine from both light and heat, either of which can be damaging. Some wineries keep their wines in air-conditioned rooms or warehouses; others use long, tunnel-like caves bored into hillsides, where the wine remains at a constant temperature.

Before bottling (sometimes earlier), winemakers typically blend two or more wine batches to balance flavor. **Blending** provides an extra chance to create a perfect single-varietal wine or combine several varietals that complement each other. To highlight the attributes of grapes from a single vineyard, a winemaker might forgo blending.

If wine is aged for any length of time before bottling, it may be racked and perhaps filtered several times. Once it is bottled, the wine is stored for **bottle aging** in a cool, dark space. In a few months most white wines will be ready for release.

RED WINES

Red-wine production differs slightly from that of white wine. Red-wine grapes are crushed in the same way, but the juice is not separated from the grape skins and pulp before fermentation. This is what gives red wine its color and flavor. After crushing, the red-wine **must**—the thick slurry of juice, pulp, and skins—is fermented in vats. The juice is "left on the skins" from a few days to a few weeks. The length of time depends on the grape type and how much color and flavor the winemaker wants to extract.

Fermentation also extracts chemical compounds such as **tannins** from the skins and seeds, making red wines more robust than whites. In a red designed for drinking soon after bottling, tannin levels are kept down; they should have a greater presence in wine meant for aging. In a young red not ready for drinking, tannins feel dry or coarse in your mouth, but they soften over time. A wine with well-balanced tannins will maintain its fruitiness and backbone as its flavor develops. Without adequate tannins and acidity, a wine will not age well.

Creating the **oak barrels** that age the wine is a craft in its own right. At Demptos Napa Cooperage, a French-owned company that employs French barrel-making techniques, the process involves several elaborate production phases. Oak staves are formed into the shape of a barrel using metal bands, and then the rough edges of the bound planks are smoothed. Finally, the barrels are toasted (exposed to fire) to give the oak its characteristic flavor, which will be imparted to the wine over time. Depending on the winemaker's preferences and goals, a barrel might have a "light," "medium," or "heavy" toast.

At the end of fermentation, the free-run wine is drained off. The grape skins and pulp are sent to a press, where the remaining liquid is extracted. As with white wines, the winemaker may blend a little of the press wine into the free-run wine to add complexity. Otherwise, the press juice goes into bulk wine—the lower-quality, less expensive stuff.

Next up is **oak-barrel aging,** which takes from a half year to a year or longer. Oak, like grapes, contains natural tannins, and the wine extracts these tannins from the barrels. The wood also has countless tiny pores through which water slowly evaporates, making the wine more concentrated. To ensure the aging wine does not oxidize, the barrels are regularly **topped off** with wine from the same vintage, reducing oxygen exposure.

How to Read a Wine Label

A wine's label will tell you a lot about what's inside. To decode the details, look for the following information:

■ **Alcohol content:** In most cases, U.S. law requires wineries to list the alcohol content, which typically hovers around 13% or 14%, though big reds like Zinfandel can soar to 16% or more.

■ **Appellation:** At least 85% of the grapes must have come from the AVA (American Viticultural Area) listed on the bottle. A bottle that says "Mt. Veeder," for example, contains mostly grapes grown in the compact Mt. Veeder appellation, but if the label says "California," the grapes could be from anywhere in the state.

■ **Estate or Estate Grown:** Wines with this label must be made entirely of grapes grown on land owned or farmed by the winery.

■ **Reserve:** An inexact term meaning "special" (and therefore usually costing more), *reserve* can refer to how or where the grapes were grown, how the wine was made, or how long it was aged.

■ **Varietal:** If the label lists a single grape type, it means that at least 75% of the wine's grapes are of that varietal. If no grape is named, the wine is likely a blend of different types.

■ **Vineyard name:** If the label lists a vineyard, at least 95% of the grapes must have been harvested there.

■ **Vintage:** If a year appears on the label, at least 95% of the grapes were harvested that year (85% for wines not designated with an AVA). If no vintage is listed, the grapes may come from more than one year's harvest.

New, or virgin, oak barrels impart the most tannins to a wine. With each successive use the tannins are diminished, until the barrel is said to be "neutral." Depending on the varietal, winemakers might blend juice aged in virgin oak barrels with juice aged in neutral barrels. In the tasting room you may hear, for instance, that a Pinot Noir was aged in 30% new oak and 70% two-year-old oak, meaning that the bulk of the wine was aged in oak used for two previous agings.

SPARKLING WINES

Despite the mystique surrounding them, sparkling wines are nothing more or less than wines in which carbon dioxide is suspended, making them bubbly. Good sparkling wine will always be fairly expensive because a great deal of work goes into making it.

White sparkling wines can be made from either white or red grapes. In France, champagne is traditionally made from Chardonnay, Pinot Meunier, and Pinot Noir. That's mostly the case in Napa and Sonoma, though fewer sparklers have Pinot Meunier.

The freshly pressed juice and pulp, or must, is **fermented with special yeasts** that preserve the characteristic fruit flavor of the grape variety used. Before bottling, this finished "still" wine (without bubbles) is mixed with a *liqueur de tirage,* a blend of wine, sugar, and yeast. This mixture causes the wine to ferment again—in the bottle, where it stays for up to 12 weeks. **Carbon dioxide,** a by-product of fermentation, is produced and trapped in the bottle, where it dissolves into the wine (instead of escaping into the air, as happens during fermentation in barrel, vat, or tank). This captive carbon dioxide transforms a still wine into a sparkler.

New bottles of sparkling wine are stored on their sides. The wine now ages *sur lie,* or "on the lees" (the dead yeast cells and other deposits trapped in the bottle). This aging process enriches the wine's texture and increases the complexity of its bouquet. The amount of time spent sur lie relates directly to its quality: the longer the aging, the more complex the wine.

The lees must be removed from the bottle before a sparkling wine can be enjoyed. This is achieved in a process whose first step is called **riddling.** In the past, each bottle, head tilted slightly downward, was placed in a riddling rack, an A-frame with many holes of bottle-neck size. Riddlers gave each bottle a slight shake and a downward turn—every day, if possible. This continued for six weeks, until each bottle rested upside down in the hole and the sediment had collected in the neck. Today most sparkling wines are riddled in ingeniously designed machines called gyro palettes, which can handle 500 or more bottles at a time, though at a few wineries, such as Schramsberg, the work is still done by hand.

After riddling, the bottles are **disgorged.** The upside-down bottles are placed in a very cold solution, freezing the sediments in a block that attaches itself to the crown cap that seals the bottle. The cap and frozen plug are removed, and the bottle is topped off with a wine-and-sugar mixture called **dosage** and recorked with the traditional champagne cork. The dosage ultimately determines the sparkler's sweetness.

Most sparkling wines are not vintage dated but are *assembled* (the term sparkling-wine makers use instead of *blended*) to create a **cuvée,** a mix of different wines and sometimes different vintages consistent with the house style. Nevertheless, sparkling wines may be vintage dated in particularly great years.

Sparkling wine may also be made by time- and cost-saving bulk methods. In the **Charmat process,** invented by Eugene Charmat early in the 20th century, the secondary fermentation takes place in large tanks rather than individual bottles. Basically, each tank is treated as one huge bottle. This comes at a price: although the sparkling wine may be ready in as little as a month, it has neither the complexity nor the bubble quality of traditional sparklers.

ROSÉ WINES

Rosé or blush wines come from red-wine grapes, but the juicy pulp is left on the skins for a matter of hours—typically from 12 to 36—rather than days. When the winemaker decides that the juice has reached the desired color, it is drained off and filtered. Yeast is added, and the juice is left to ferment. Because the juice stays on the skins for a shorter time, fewer tannins are leached from them, and the resulting wine is not as full flavored as a red.

The range of tastes and textures is remarkable. Rosé of Cabernet Sauvignon, for instance, can have a velvety and almost savory taste, while rosé of Pinot Noir or Syrah might have a crisp and mineral taste.

Grape Growing: The Basics

Most kinds of wine grapes are touchy. If the weather is too hot, they can produce too much sugar and not enough acid, resulting in overly alcoholic wines. Too cool and they won't ripen properly, and some will develop an unpleasant vegetal taste. And rain at the wrong time of year

Pinot Noir and Chardonnay are widely grown in the Russian River Valley.

can wreak havoc on vineyards, causing grapes to rot on the vine. These and many other conditions must be just right to coax the best out of persnickety wine grapes, and Napa and Sonoma have that magical combination of sun, rain, fog, slope, and soil that allows many varieties of wine grape to thrive.

APPELLATIONS: LOCATION, LOCATION, LOCATION

Winemakers generally agree that despite the high-tech equipment at their disposal, wine is made in the vineyard. This emphasis on *terroir* (a French term that encompasses a region's soil, climate, and overall growing conditions) reflects a belief that what happens before grapes are crushed determines a wine's quality.

In the United States, the Alcohol and Tobacco Tax and Trade Bureau (TTB) designates **appellations of origin** based on political boundaries or unique soil, climate, or other characteristics. California, for instance, is an appellation, as are Napa and Sonoma counties. More

significantly to wine lovers, the TTB can designate a unique grape-growing region as an American Viticultural Area (AVA), more commonly called an appellation. Whether the appellation of origin is based on politics or terroir, it refers to the source of a wine's grapes, not to where it was made.

Many appellations are renowned for particular wines. The Napa Valley is known for Cabernet Sauvignon, for example, the Russian River Valley for Chardonnay and Pinot Noir, and the Dry Creek Valley for Zinfandel. As of early 2021, the Napa Valley contained 16 subappellations and Sonoma County 18, with a 19th, the West Sonoma Coast AVA, expecting approval before year's end. Wineries can indicate the appellation or AVA on a bottle's label only if 85% of the grapes were grown within it.

What makes things a little confusing is that appellations often overlap, allowing for increased levels of specificity. The Napa Valley AVA is, of course, part of the

California appellation, but the Napa Valley AVA is itself divided into 16 smaller sub-appellations, the Oakville and Rutherford AVAs being among the most famous of these. Another well-known AVA, Los Carneros, overlaps Napa and Sonoma counties, and there are even subappel-lations within subappellations. Sonoma County's Russian River Valley AVA, for example, contains the smaller Green Valley of the Russian River Valley AVA. The latter earned status as a separate viticultural area because of its soils and a climate cooler and foggier than much of the Russian River Valley.

GEOLOGY 101

"Site trumps everything," says longtime Frank Family Vineyards winemaker Todd Graff, by which he means that the specific land where vines grow is more significant than grape clones, farming techniques, and even wine making. In other words, geology matters. Grape-vines are among the few plants that give their best fruit when grown in poor, rocky soil. On the other hand, they don't like wet feet: the ideal vineyard soil is easily permeable by water for good drainage.

Grape varieties thrive in different types of soil. For instance, Cabernet Sauvignon does best in well-drained, gravelly soil. If it's too wet or contains too much heavy clay or organic matter, the soil will give the wine an obnoxious vegetative quality. Merlot, however, can grow in soil with more clay and still be made into rich, delicious wine. Chardonnay likes well-drained vineyards but will also take heavy soil.

Napa Valley and Sonoma County soils are dizzyingly diverse, which helps account for the inordinate variety of grapes grown here. Some soils are composed of dense, heavy, sedimentary clays washed from the mountains; others are very rocky clays, loams, or silts of alluvial fans. These fertile, well-drained soils cover the valley floors in large swaths of the two regions. In all there are about 60 soil types in the Napa Valley and Sonoma County.

DOWN ON THE FARM

Much like a fruit or nut orchard, a vine-yard can produce excellent grapes for decades—with varietals like Zinfandel even a century or more—if given the proper attention. The growing cycle starts in winter, when the vines are bare and dormant. While the plants rest, the grower works to enrich the soil and repair the trellising system (if there is one) that holds up the vines. This is when **pruning** takes place to regulate the vine's growth and the crop size.

In spring the soil is aerated by plowing or other methods, and new vines go in. The grower trains established vines so they grow, with or without trellising, in the shape most beneficial for the grapes. **Bud break** occurs when the first bits of green emerge from the vines, and a pale green veil appears over the winter's gray-black vineyards. A late frost can be devastating at this time of year. Springtime brings the flowering of the vines, when clusters of tiny green blossoms appear, followed by **fruit set,** when grapes form from the blossoms.

As the vineyards turn luxuriant and leafy in summer, more pruning, along with leaf pulling, keeps foliage in check so the vine directs nutrients to the grapes, and so the sun can reach the fruit. As summer advances, during what's known as **veraison** (pronounced "vuh-ray-SAHN"), grapes begin to change color from green to yellow (for most whites) or purple (for reds). Before or after veraison (sometimes both), the grower will **"drop fruit,"** cutting off some clusters so the remaining grapes intensify in flavor.

Fall is the busiest season in the vineyard. Growers and winemakers carefully monitor grape ripeness, sometimes with equipment that tests sugar and acid

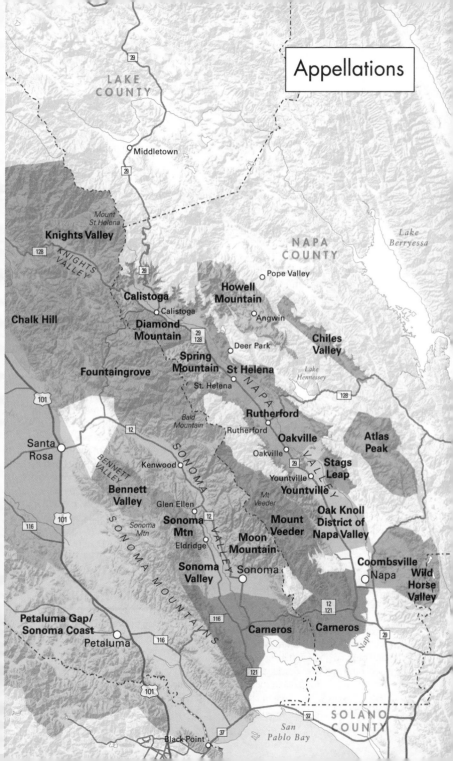

Appellations

LAKE COUNTY

Middletown

Mount St Helena

Knights Valley

KNIGHTS VALLEY

Chalk Hill

Calistoga

Calistoga

Diamond Mountain

Fountaingrove

Spring Mountain

St Helena

St. Helena

Bald Mountain

Santa Rosa

BENNETT VALLEY

Kenwood

SONOMA VALLEY

Bennett Valley

Glen Ellen

Sonoma Mtn

Eldridge

Sonoma Valley

Sonoma Mtn

SONOMA MOUNTAINS

Petaluma Gap/ Sonoma Coast

Petaluma

Black Point

NAPA COUNTY

Lake Berryessa

Pope Valley

Howell Mountain

Angwin

Chiles Valley

Deer Park

Lake Hennessey

NAPA VALLEY

Rutherford

Rutherford

Oakville

Oakville

Atlas Peak

Stags Leap

Yountville

Yountville

Mt Veeder

Mount Veeder

Moon Mountain

Oak Knoll District of Napa Valley

Sonoma

Coombsville

Napa

Wild Horse Valley

Carneros

Carneros

Napa

San Pablo Bay

SOLANO COUNTY

levels and sometimes simply by tasting them. As soon as the grapes are ripe, **harvest** begins. In Napa and Sonoma this generally starts in August and continues into November. Once grapes are ripe, picking must be done as quickly as possible, within just a day or two, to prevent the grapes from passing their peak. Most grapes are harvested mechanically, but some are picked by hand. After harvest, the vines start to regenerate for the next year.

Many wineries purchase at least some of their fruit. Some negotiate contracts, often long-term, that allow the winery a say in farming decisions. This way, the winemaker can control the consistency and quality of the grapes, just as if they came from the winery's vineyard. Some wineries buy from several growers, and many growers sell to more than one winery.

ORGANIC AND BIODYNAMIC

If, as many grape growers insist, a wine is only as good as the vineyard it comes from, those who have adopted organic and biodynamic agricultural methods may be on to something. But when using terms like *organic* and *biodynamic,* what do vintners mean? It boils down to a rejection of chemical fertilizers, pesticides, and fungicides. Biodynamic farmers also reject these artificial agents, and their vineyard maintenance often involves metaphysical principles as well.

Even rarer than wines produced from organically grown grapes are completely organic wines. For a wine to be certified as organic, not only do the grapes have to come from organic vineyards, but the processing must use a minimum of chemical additives and no added sulfites. (Remember that some wines made from certified organic grapes still contain naturally occurring sulfites.) Some winemakers argue that it is impossible to make outstanding wine without using additives like sulfur dioxide, an antioxidant that

protects the wine's color, aroma, flavor, and longevity. Very few producers make completely organic wine.

Biodynamic farmers view the land as a living, self-sustaining organism requiring a healthy, unified ecosystem to thrive. To nurture the soil, for instance, vineyard workers spray specially formulated herbal "teas" (the ingredients include yarrow, dandelion, valerian, and stinging nettle flowers) onto compost spread in the fields. Grazing animals such as sheep maintain the ground cover between the vines (and the animals' manure provides natural fertilizer). Natural predators, among them insect-eating bats, control pests that might damage the crop. Biodynamic farmers believe that the movements of the sun and the moon influence plant development, so astronomical calendars play a role in the timing of many vineyard activities.

At its most elevated level, the biodynamic philosophy recognizes a farm as a metaphysical entity requiring its human inhabitants not merely to tend it but to form a spiritual bond with it. Other organic farmers share this notion in theory, even if their methods sometimes diverge. Among wineries whose practices have been certified organic are Hall St. Helena in the Napa Valley and Preston Family Winery in Northern Sonoma County. The Napa Valley's Robert Sinskey Vineyards is certified organic and biodynamic, as is the Sonoma Valley's Benziger Family Winery.

Wine Lover's Glossary

Wine making and tasting require specialized vocabularies. Some words are merely show-off jargon, but many are specific and helpful.

Acidity. A wine's tartness, derived from grapes' fruit acids. These stabilize a wine (i.e., preserve its character), balance its sweetness, and bring out its flavors. Tartaric acid is the primary acid in wine, but malic, lactic, and citric acids also occur.

Aging. The process by which some wines improve over time, becoming smoother and more complex. Wine is often aged in oak vats or barrels, slowly interacting with the air through the wood's pores. Sometimes wine is cellared for bottle aging.

Alcohol. Ethyl alcohol is a colorless, volatile, pungent spirit that gives wine its stimulating effect and some of its flavor. Alcohol also acts as a preservative, stabilizing the wine and allowing it to age.

American Viticultural Area (AVA). More commonly termed an *appellation*. A region with unique soil, climate, and other conditions can be designated an AVA by the Alcohol and Tobacco Tax and Trade Bureau. When a label lists an AVA—Napa Valley or Mt. Veeder, for example—at least 85% of the grapes used to make the wine must come from that AVA.

Ampelography. The science of identifying varietals by their leaves, grapevines, and, more recently, DNA.

Appellation. *See American Viticultural Area.*

Aroma. The scent of young wine derived from the fresh fruit. It diminishes with fermentation and is replaced by a more complex bouquet as the wine ages. The term may also describe particular fruity odors in a wine, such as black cherry, green olive, ripe raspberry, or apple.

Balance. A quality of wine in which all desirable elements (fruit, acid, tannin) are present in the proper proportion.

Barrel fermenting. The fermenting of wine in small oak or other barrels instead of large tanks or vats. This method keeps grape lots separate before wine blending. The cost of oak barrels makes this method expensive.

Biodynamic. An approach to agriculture that regards the land as a living thing; it incorporates organic farming techniques and the use of the astronomical calendar to cultivate a healthy balance in the vineyard ecosystem.

Blanc de blancs. Sparkling or still white wine made solely from white grapes.

Blanc de noirs. White wine made with red grapes by removing the skins during crush. Some sparkling whites, for example, are made with red Pinot Noir grapes.

Blending. The mixing of several wines to create one of greater complexity or appeal, as when a heavy wine is blended with a lighter one to make a more approachable medium-bodied wine.

Body. The wine's heft or density as experienced by the palate. *See also Mouthfeel.*

Bordeaux blend. A red wine blended from varietals native to France's Bordeaux region. The primary ones are Cabernet Sauvignon, Cabernet Franc, Malbec, Merlot, and Petit Verdot.

Bouquet. The odors a mature wine gives off when opened. They should be pleasantly complex and hint at the wine's grape variety, origin, age, and quality.

Brix. A method of telling whether grapes are ready for picking by measuring their sugars.

Brut. French term for the driest category of sparkling wine. *See also Demi-sec, Sec.*

Cellaring. Storage of wine in bottles for aging. The bottles are laid on their sides to keep the corks moist and prevent air leakage that would spoil the wine.

Champagne. The northernmost wine district of France, where the world's only genuine champagne is made. The term is often used loosely in America to denote sparkling wines.

3

Visiting Wineries and Tasting Rooms WINE LOVER'S GLOSSARY

Cloudiness. The presence of particles that do not settle out of a wine, causing it to look and taste dusty or muddy.

Cluster. A single bunch of grapes.

Complexity. The qualities of good wine that provide a multilayered sensory experience to the drinker. Balanced flavors, harmonious aromas or bouquet, and a long finish are components of complexity.

Cork taint. Describes wine that is flawed by the musty, wet-cardboard flavor imparted by cork mold, technically known as TCA, or 2,4,6-Trichloroanisole.

Crush. American term for the harvest season. Also refers to the year's crop of grapes crushed for wine.

Cuvée. Generally a sparkling wine, but sometimes a still wine, that is a blend of different wines and sometimes different vintages.

Decant. To pour a wine from its bottle into another container to expose it to air or eliminate sediment. Decanting for sediment pours out the clear wine and leaves the residue behind in the original bottle.

Demi-sec. French term that translates as "half-dry." It is applied to sweet wines that contain 3.5%–5% sugar.

Dessert wines. Sweet wines that are big in flavor and aroma. Some are relatively low in alcohol; others, such as port-style wines, are fortified with brandy or another spirit and may be 17%–21% alcohol.

Dry. Having very little sweetness or residual sugar. Most wines are dry, although some whites, such as Rieslings, are made to be "off-dry," meaning "on the sweet side."

Estate bottled. A wine entirely made by one winery at a single facility. In general the grapes come from the vineyards the winery owns or farms within the same appellation (which must be printed on the label).

Fermentation. The biochemical process by which grape juice becomes wine. Enzymes generated by yeast cells convert grape sugars into alcohol and carbon dioxide. Fermentation stops when either the sugar is depleted and the yeast starves or when high alcohol levels kill the yeast.

Filtering, Filtration. A purification process in which wine is pumped through filters to rid it of suspended particles.

Fining. A method of clarifying wine by adding egg whites, bentonite (a type of clay), or other substances to a barrel. Most wine meant for everyday drinking is fined; however, better wines are fined less often.

Finish. The flavors that remain in the mouth after swallowing wine. Good wine has a long finish with complex flavors and aromas.

Flight. A few wines—usually from three to five—selected for tasting together.

Fortification. Adding brandy or another spirit to wine to stop fermentation and increase the alcohol level, as with port-style dessert wines.

Fruity. Having aromatic nuances of fresh fruit, such as fig, raspberry, or apple. Fruitiness, a sign of quality in young wines, is replaced by bouquet in aged wines.

Late harvest. Wine made from grapes harvested later in the season than the main lot and thus higher in sugar levels. Many dessert wines are late harvest.

Lees. The spent yeast, grape solids, and tartrates that drop to the bottom of the barrel or tank as wine ages. Wine, particularly white wine, gains complexity when it is left on the lees for a time.

Library wine. An older vintage than the winery's current releases.

Malolactic fermentation. A secondary fermentation, aka *ML* or *malo*, that changes harsh malic acid into softer lactic acid and carbon dioxide. Wine is sometimes inoculated with lactic bacteria or placed in wooden containers harboring the bacteria to enhance this process.

Meritage. A trademarked name for American Bordeaux-style white and red blends.

Méthode champenoise. The traditional, time-consuming method of making sparkling wines by fermenting them in individual bottles. By agreement with the European Union, sparkling wines made in California this way are labeled *méthode traditionelle*.

Mouthfeel. Literally, the way wine feels in the mouth.

Neutral oak. The wood of older barrels or vats that no longer pass much flavor or tannin to the wine stored within.

New oak. The wood of a fresh barrel or vat that has not previously been used to ferment or age wine. It can impart desirable flavors and enhance a wine's complexity, but if used to excess it can overpower a wine's true character.

Nonvintage. A blend of wines from different years. Nonvintage wines have no date on their labels.

Nose. The overall fragrance (aroma or bouquet) a wine gives off.

Oaky. A vanilla-woody flavor that develops when wine ages in oak barrels. Leave a wine too long in a new oak barrel, and that oaky taste overpowers the other flavors.

Organic viticulture. The technique of growing grapes without the use of chemical fertilizers, pesticides, or fungicides.

Oxidation. Undesirable flavor and color changes to juice or wine caused by too much contact with the air, either during processing or because of a leaky barrel or cork.

pH. Technical term for a measure of acidity. It is a reverse measure: the lower the pH level, the higher the acidity, with the most desirable level between 3.2 and 3.5.

Phylloxera. A disease caused by the root louse *Phylloxera vastatrix*, which attacks and ultimately destroys vines' roots.

Residual sugar. The natural sugar left in a wine after fermentation, which converts sugar into alcohol. In general, the higher the sugar levels, the sweeter the wine.

Rhône blend. A wine made from grapes hailing from France's Rhône Valley, such as Grenache, Syrah, and Mourvèdre.

Rosé. Pink wine, usually made from red-wine grapes (of any variety). The juice is left on the skins only long enough to give it a tinge of color.

Sec. French for "dry." The term is generally applied within the sparkling or sweet categories, indicating the wine has 1.7%–3.5% residual sugar. Sec is drier than demi-sec but not as dry as brut.

Sediment. Dissolved or suspended solids that drop out of most red wines as they age in the bottle, thus clarifying their appearance, flavors, and aromas. Sediment is not a defect in old wine or unfiltered new wine.

Sparkling wines. Wines in which carbon dioxide is dissolved, making them bubbly. Examples are French champagne, Italian prosecco, and Spanish cava.

Sugar. Source of grapes' natural sweetness. When yeast feeds on sugar, it produces alcohol and carbon dioxide. The higher the grape's sugar content, the higher the wine's potential alcohol level or sweetness.

Sulfites. Compounds of sulfur dioxide almost always added before fermentation to prevent oxidation and kill bacteria and wild yeasts that can cause off-flavors.

3

Visiting Wineries and Tasting Rooms WINE LOVER'S GLOSSARY

Sustainable viticulture. Farming that aims to bring the vineyard into harmony with the environment. Organic and other techniques are used to minimize agricultural impact and promote biodiversity.

Table wine. Any wine that has at least 7% but not more than 14% alcohol by volume. The term doesn't necessarily imply anything about the wine's quality or price—both super-premium and jug wines can be labeled as table wine.

Tannins. You can tell when they're there, but their origins are still a mystery. These natural grape compounds produce a sensation of drying or astringency in the mouth and throat. Tannins settle out as wine ages; they're a big player in many red wines.

Tartaric acid, Tartrates. The principal acid of wine. Crystalline tartrates form on the insides of vats or barrels and sometimes in the bottle or on the cork. They look like tiny shards of glass but are not harmful.

Terroir. French for "soil." Typically used to describe the soil and climate conditions that influence the quality and characteristics of grapes and wine.

Varietal. A grape type. According to U.S. law, at least 75% of a wine must come from a particular grape to be labeled with a varietal name.

Veraison. The time during the ripening process when grapes change their color from green to red or yellow and sugar levels rise.

Vertical tasting. A tasting of several vintages of the same wine.

Vintage. A given year's grape harvest. A vintage date (e.g., 2020) on a label indicates the year the wine's grapes were harvested rather than the year the wine was bottled.

Yeast. A minute, single-celled fungus that germinates and multiplies rapidly as it feeds on sugar with the help of enzymes, creating alcohol and releasing carbon dioxide in the process of fermentation.

Zymology. The science of fermentation.

Chapter 4

NAPA VALLEY

4

👁 Sights   🍴 Restaurants   🏨 Hotels   🛍 Shopping   🍸 Nightlife

★★★★★   ★★★★★   ★★★★★   ★★★★☆   ★★★☆☆

WELCOME TO NAPA VALLEY

TOP REASONS TO GO

★ **Wine tasting:** Whether you're on a pilgrimage to famous Cabernet houses or searching for hidden-gem wineries and obscure varietals, the valley supplies plenty of both.

★ **Fine dining:** It might sound like hype, but a meal at one of the valley's top-tier restaurants can be a revelation—about the level of artistry intuitive chefs can achieve and how successfully quality wines pair with food.

★ **Art and architecture:** Several wineries are owned by art collectors whose holdings grace indoor and outdoor spaces, and the valley contains remarkable specimens of winery architecture.

★ **Spa treatments:** Work-hard, play-hard types and inveterate sybarites flock to spas for pampering.

★ **Balloon rides:** By the dawn's early light, hot-air balloons soar over the vineyards, a magical sight from the ground and even more thrilling from above.

1 Napa. The valley's largest town has plenty of wineries and tasting rooms, and downtown has evolved into a shopping and fine-dining haven.

2 Yountville. Find several must-visit restaurants, a well-groomed main street, and downtown tasting rooms; most of Yountville's wineries are to the east, with a few to the north and south.

3 Oakville. With a population of less than 100, this town is all about its mostly Cabernet vineyards.

4 Rutherford. "It takes Rutherford dust to grow great Cabernet," a legendary winemaker once said, and with several dozen wineries in this appellation, there are plenty of opportunities to ponder what this means.

5 St. Helena. Genteel St. Helena's Main Street evokes images of classic Americana; its wineries range from valley stalwarts Beringer and Charles Krug to boutique wineries in the hills.

6 Calistoga. This spa town still has its Old West–style false fronts, but it's now also home to luxurious lodgings and spas with 21st-century panache.

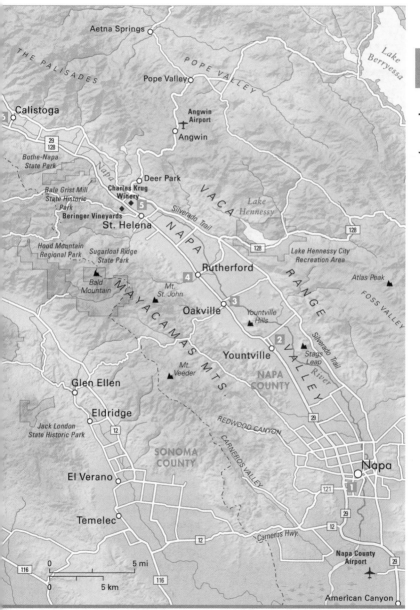

With more than 500 wineries and many of the industry's biggest brands, the Napa Valley is the Wine Country's star. Napa, the largest town, lures visitors with cultural attractions and (relatively) reasonably priced lodgings. A bit north, compact Yountville is packed with top-notch restaurants and hotels, and Oakville and Rutherford are extolled for their Cabernet Sauvignon–friendly soils. Beyond them, St. Helena teems with boutiques and wineries, and casual Calistoga, known for its spas, feels like an Old West frontier town, albeit one with luxury resorts.

The Napa Valley contains only about an eighth of the acreage planted in Bordeaux, but past volcanic and other seismic activity have bequeathed the valley diverse soils and microclimates that provide winemakers with the raw materials to craft wines of consistently high quality. More land is devoted to Cabernet Sauvignon and Chardonnay than any other varietals, but Cabernet Franc, Merlot, Pinot Noir, Petite Sirah, Sauvignon Blanc, Syrah, Zinfandel, and other wines are also made here. In terms of output, though, the valley's reputation far exceeds the mere 4% of California's total wine-grape harvest it represents.

So what makes the Napa Valley one of the state's top tourist destinations and a playground for San Francisco Bay Area residents? For one thing, variety: for every blockbuster winery whose name you'll recognize from the shelves of wine stores and the pages of *Wine Spectator*—Robert Mondavi, Beringer, and Caymus, to name a very few—you'll also find lower-profile operations that will warmly invite you into their modest tasting rooms. The local viticulture has in turn inspired a passion for food, and several marquee chefs have solidified the valley's position as one of the country's great restaurant destinations. You'll also get a glimpse of California's history, from wine cellars dating back to the late 1800s to the flurry of Steamboat Gothic architecture dressing up Calistoga. Binding all these temptations together is the sheer scenic beauty of the place. Much of Napa Valley's landscape unspools in orderly, densely planted rows of vines. Even the climate cooperates, as the warm summer days and refreshingly cool evenings so favorable for grape growing also make fine weather for traveling.

MAJOR REGIONS

The Napa Valley has 16 American Viticultural Areas (see Appellations, below) but practically speaking can be divided into its southern and northern parts. The southern Napa Valley encompasses the relatively cooler grape-growing areas and the towns of Napa and Yountville, along with slightly warmer Oakville. The northern Napa Valley begins around Rutherford and continues north to even hotter St. Helena and Calistoga.

Planning

When to Go

The Napa Valley is a year-round destination whose charms vary depending on the season. Watching a rainy winter day's misty fog rising off dark, gnarly grapevines, for example, can be just as captivating as witnessing a summer sunset backlighting flourishing vineyard rows. Because the Napa Valley is the most-visited Wine Country locale, summers draw hordes of tourists, making late spring and early fall, when it's less crowded and temperatures are often cooler, among the best times to come. Harvesttime—from August into November, depending on the grape type and the year's weather—is the best time to visit to see wine making in action. Weekends can be busy year-round. To avoid heavy traffic on summer weekends, it almost always works best to arrive by midmorning, especially if you need to be back in San Francisco by early evening.

Getting Here and Around

BUS

VINE buses, which pick up passengers from the BART (Bay Area Rapid Transit) El Cerrito Del Norte station and the Vallejo Ferry Terminal, run between Napa and Calistoga, with one stop or more in Yountville, Oakville, Rutherford, St. Helena, and Calistoga. Buses don't operate on all routes on Sunday (sometimes Saturday). *For more information about arriving by bus, see the Bus section in the Travel Smart chapter.*

CONTACT VINE. ☎ *707/251–2800, 800/696–6443* ⊕ *www.ridethevine.com.*

CAR

Traveling by car is the most convenient way to tour the Napa Valley. In normal traffic both of the main routes from San Francisco will get you here in about an hour. You can head north across the Golden Gate Bridge and U.S. 101, east on Highway 37 and then Highway 121, and north on Highway 29; or east across the San Francisco–Oakland Bay Bridge and north on Interstate 80, west on Highway 37, and north on Highway 29.

Highway 29 can become congested, especially on summer weekends. Traffic can be slow in St. Helena during morning and afternoon rush hours. You might find slightly less traffic on the Silverado Trail, which roughly parallels Highway 29 between Napa and Calistoga. Every few miles, cross streets connect the two highways like rungs on a ladder, making it easy to cross from one to the other.

■ TIP→ **Although the Silverado Trail can get busy in the late afternoon, it's often a better option than Highway 29 if you're traveling between, say, St. Helena or Calistoga and the city of Napa.**

For information about car services and limos, see Getting Here and Around in the Travel Smart chapter.

4

Napa Valley PLANNING

Restaurants

Dining out is one of the deep pleasures of a Napa Valley visit. Cuisine here tends to focus on seasonal produce, some of it from gardens the restaurants maintain themselves, and many chefs endeavor to source their proteins locally, too. The French Laundry, La Toque, Bouchon Bistro, Bistro Jeanty, Press, Solbar, and the Restaurant at Auberge du Soleil often appear at the top of visitors' agendas, and rightfully so: in addition to stellar cuisine they all have sommeliers or waiters capable of helping you select wines that will enhance your enjoyment of your meal immeasurably, and the level of service matches the food and surroundings. Another dozen restaurants provide experiences nearly on a par with those at the above establishments. *Restaurant reviews have been shortened. For full information, visit Fodors.com.*

Hotels

With the price of accommodations at high-end inns and hotels *starting* at $900 or $1,000 a night, when it comes to Napa Valley lodging the question seems to be how much are you willing to pay? If you have the means, you can ensconce yourself between plush linens at exclusive hillside retreats with fancy architecture and even fancier amenities, and you're more or less guaranteed to have a fine time. As with Napa Valley restaurants, though, the decor and amenities the most stylish hotels and inns provide have upped the ante for all hoteliers and innkeepers, so even if you're on a budget you can live well. Many smaller inns and hotels and even the motels provide pleasant stays for a fairly reasonable price. The main problem with these establishments is that they can book up quickly, so if you're visiting between late May and October, it's wise to reserve your room as far ahead as possible. *Hotel*

reviews have been shortened. For full information, visit Fodors.com.

What It Costs in U.S. Dollars			
$	$$	$$$	$$$$
RESTAURANTS			
under $17	$17–$26	$27–$36	over $36
HOTELS			
under $201	$201–$300	$301–$400	over $400

Planning Your Time

First things first: even in a month it's impossible to "do" the Napa Valley—there are simply too many wineries here. Many visitors find that tasting at three or at most four a day and spending quality time at each of them, with a leisurely lunch to rest the palate, is preferable to cramming in as many visits as possible. You can, of course, add variety with a spa treatment (these can take up to a half day), a balloon ride (expect to rise early and finish in the late morning), shopping, or a bicycle ride.

You can maximize your time touring wineries with a few simple strategies. If you'll be visiting a big operation such as Mondavi, Beringer, or Castello di Amorosa, try to schedule that stop early in the day and then smaller wineries after lunch; you're less likely to be held up by the crowds that way. Even during the week in summertime, the afternoon traffic on Highway 29 can be heavy, so after 3 pm try to avoid wineries along this stretch. Plan your visits to wineries on or just off the Silverado Trail for later in the day, though even there you might find the going slow heading south from Rutherford.

The town of Napa is the valley's most affordable base, and it's especially convenient if most of your touring will be in the southern half. If you'll be dining a lot in Yountville, staying there is a good idea because you can walk or take the Yountville Trolley back to your lodging. Calistoga is the most affordable base in the northern Napa Valley, though it's not always convenient for touring southern Napa wineries.

Visitor Information

CONTACT Visit Napa Valley. ☎ *707/226–5813* ⊕ *www.visitnapavalley.com.*

Appellations

Nearly all of Napa County, which stretches from the Mayacamas Mountains in the west to Lake Berryessa in the east, makes up the Napa Valley American Viticultural Area (AVA). This region is divided into many smaller AVAs, or subappellations, each with unique characteristics.

Los Carneros AVA stretches west from the Napa River, across the southern Napa Valley, and into the southern Sonoma Valley. Pinot Noir and Chardonnay are the main grapes grown in this cool, windswept region just north of San Pablo Bay, but Merlot, Syrah, and, in the warmer portions, Cabernet Sauvignon, also do well here. Pinot Noir and Chardonnay are also the stars of the **Wild Horse Valley AVA.** East of the Carneros, it's the valley's coolest subappellation. Four of the subappellations north of the Carneros District—Oak Knoll, Oakville, Rutherford, and St. Helena—stretch clear across the valley floor. Chilled by coastal fog, the **Oak Knoll District of Napa Valley AVA** has some of the coolest temperatures. The **Oakville AVA,** just north of Yountville, is studded with big-name wineries such as Robert Mondavi and Silver Oak and awe-inspiring boutique labels, among them the superexclusive Screaming Eagle. Oakville's gravelly, well-drained soil is especially good for Cabernet Sauvignon.

A sunny climate and well-drained soil make **Rutherford AVA** one of the best locations for Cabernet Sauvignon in California, if not the world. North of Rutherford, the **St. Helena AVA** is one of Napa's toastiest, as the slopes surrounding the narrow valley reflect the sun's heat. Bordeaux varietals are the most popular grapes grown here—particularly Cabernet Sauvignon, but also Merlot. Just north, at the foot of Mt. St. Helena, is the **Calistoga AVA**; Cabernet Sauvignon does well here, as do Zinfandel, Petite Sirah, and Charbono (aka "Calistoga's cult grape").

The **Stags Leap District AVA,** a small section of the valley's eastern floor and hillsides, is marked by steep volcanic palisades. As with the neighboring **Yountville AVA,** Cabernet Sauvignon and Merlot are by far the favored grapes. In both subappellations, cool evening breezes encourage a long growing season and intense fruit flavors. Some describe the resulting wines as "rock soft" or an "iron fist in a velvet glove." Also on the valley's eastern edge is the **Coombsville AVA.** Cabernet Sauvignon grows on the western-facing slopes of the Vaca Mountains, with Merlot, Chardonnay, Syrah, and Pinot Noir more prevalent in the cooler lower elevations.

The **Mt. Veeder, Spring Mountain,** and **Diamond Mountain District AVAs,** stretching south to north amid the Mayacamas Mountains to the valley's west, and the **Atlas Peak, Chiles Valley,** and **Howell Mountain AVAs,** east across the valley within the Vaca Mountains, each demonstrate how stressing out grapevines can yield outstanding results. The big winner is Cabernet Sauvignon, which loves this type of terrain. Many of the vineyards on these slopes are so steep that they must be tilled and harvested by hand.

The valley's great variety of climates and soils explains why vintners here can make so many different wines, and so well, in a relatively compact region.

Napa

46 miles northeast of San Francisco.

After many years as a blue-collar burg detached from the Wine Country scene, the Napa Valley's largest town (population about 80,000) has evolved into its shining star. Masaharu Morimoto, Charlie Palmer, and other chefs of note operate restaurants here, and swank hotels and resorts can be found downtown and beyond. A walkway that follows the Napa River has made downtown more pedestrian-friendly, and the Oxbow Public Market, a complex of high-end food purveyors, is popular with locals and tourists.

The market is named for the nearby oxbow bend in the Napa River, a bit north of where Napa was founded in 1848. The first wood-frame building was a saloon, and the downtown area still projects an old-river-town vibe. Many Victorian houses have survived, some as bed-and-breakfast inns, and in the heart of downtown older buildings like the 1879 Italianate-style Napa Courthouse at 825 Brown Street have been preserved. The courthouse was among the numerous structures damaged during a magnitude 6.0 earthquake in 2014.

Napans are rightly proud of how the city responded to the quake and subsequent challenges—wildfires, fire-related power outages, and of course COVID-19—with support instantly materializing for first responders, healthcare workers, stranded visitors, and fellow citizens in need. One cause for celebration in 2020 was the debut of a dozen-plus new shops and services in the First Street Napa complex surrounding the five-story Archer Hotel Napa, whose rooftop bar affords splendid southern Napa Valley views.

■TIP→ **If based in Napa, in addition to exploring the wineries amid the surrounding countryside, plan on spending at least a half day strolling downtown.**

Getting Here and Around

To get to downtown Napa from Highway 29, take the 1st Street exit and follow the signs. Most of downtown's sights and many of its restaurants are clustered in an easily walkable area around Main Street (you'll find street parking and garages nearby). Outside downtown, most wineries with Napa addresses are on or just off Highway 29 or the parallel Silverado Trail, the exception being the ones in the Carneros District or Mt. Veeder AVA. Most of these are on or just off Highway 121. VINE buses serve downtown Napa and adjacent locales.

Visitor Information

CONTACTS Do Napa. ☎ *707/257–0322* ⊕ *www.donapa.com.* **Napa Valley Welcome Center.** ✉ *1300 1st St., Suite 313 ✛ At Franklin St.* ☎ *707/251–5895, 855/847–6272* ⊕ *www.visitnapavalley. com.*

◉ Sights

Artesa Vineyards & Winery
WINERY/DISTILLERY | From a distance the modern, minimalist architecture of Artesa blends harmoniously with the surrounding Carneros landscape, but up close its pools, fountains, and large outdoor sculptures make their own impression. As might be expected in this region, Chardonnay and Pinot Noir from estate and sourced grapes predominate, but the winery also produces Albariño and sparkling wine, plus reds that include Cabernet Sauvignon, Merlot, and Tempranillo. By appointment you can sample them, some paired with food, while enjoying views of estate and neighboring vineyards and, on a clear day, San Francisco. ■TIP→ **Guests on Friday and weekend vineyard hikes sip wines where their grapes grew.** ✉ *1345 Henry Rd. ✛ Off Old Sonoma Rd. and Dealy La.*

Top Tastings

Classic Cabs

Joseph Phelps Vineyards, St. Helena. Tastings of Phelps's Cabernet Sauvignon and flagship Insignia Bordeaux-style blend unfold like everything else here: with class, grace, and precision—an apt description of the wines themselves.

Silver Oak, Oakville. The sole wine Silver Oak produces is a Cabernet Sauvignon hosts pour in a stone building constructed of materials from a 19th-century flour mill.

Setting

Hall St. Helena. A glass-walled tasting area perched over the vineyards provides a dramatic setting for sampling award-winning Cabernets.

Oasis by Hoopes, Yountville. A second-generation vintner expands the tasting-room paradigm with this family- and dog-friendly space anchored by an organic garden and adjacent corral for gotta-love-'em rescue animals. The wine's good, too.

Quixote Winery, Napa. An eccentric structure by a world-famous European architect and Cabernets and Petite Sirahs overseen by elite consultant Philippe Melka make for a memorable outing at this Stags Leap District winery.

Schweiger Vineyards, St. Helena. The northern Napa Valley views from this winery atop Spring Mountain never fail to astonish; neither does the Schweiger family's hospitality.

Food Pairing

Theorem Vineyards, Calistoga. A local caterer prepares the app-sized bites that are paired with Sauvignon Blanc, Merlot, Syrah, and Cabernet Sauvignon at this Diamond Mountain winery with vineyard and Mt. St. Helena views.

VGS Chateau Potelle, St. Helena. Sophisticated whimsy is on full display at this bungalowlike space where wines are paired exceedingly well with a top chef's small bites.

Old-School Charm

Prager Winery & Port Works, St. Helena. Drift back in time at this homey, family-run operation specializing in fortified wines.

Tres Sabores, St. Helena. Tastings are low-key and fun at owner-winemaker Julie Johnson's down-home ranch, one of the Napa Valley's first with certified organic vineyards.

☎ *707/224–1668* ⊕ *www.artesawinery. com* 🍷 *Tastings from $45, tour $75.*

⭐ **Ashes & Diamonds**

WINERY/DISTILLERY | Barbara Bestor's sleek white design for this appointment-only winery's glass-and-metal tasting space evokes mid-century modern architecture and with it the era and wines predating the Napa Valley's rise to prominence. Two much-heralded pros lead the wine-making team assembled by record producer Kashy Khaledi: Steve Matthiasson, known for his classic, restrained style and attention to viticultural detail, and Diana Snowden Seysses, who draws on experiences in Burgundy, Provence, and California. Bordeaux varietals are the focus, most notably Cabernet Sauvignon and Cabernet Franc but also the white blend of Sauvignon Blanc and Sémillon and even the rosé (of Cabernet Franc). With a label designer who was also responsible for a Jay-Z album cover and

The château at Domaine Carneros sits high on a hill.

interiors that recall the *Mad Men* in the Palm Springs story arc, the pitch seems unabashedly intended to millennials, but the wines, low in alcohol and with high acidity (good for aging the wines), enchant connoisseurs of all stripes. ⊠ *4130 Howard La.* ⊕ *Off Hwy. 29* ☏ *707/666–4777* ⊕ *ashesdiamonds.com* ▣ *Tastings from $75.*

Bouchaine Vineyards

WINERY/DISTILLERY | Tranquil Bouchaine lies just north of San Pablo Bay's tidal sloughs—to appreciate the off-the-beaten-path setting, step outside the semicircular hilltop tasting room and scan the skies for hawks and golden eagles soaring above the vineyards. The alternately breezy and foggy weather in this part of the Carneros works well for Pinot Noir and Chardonnay. These account for most of the wines, but also look for Riesling and Cabernet Sauvignon. Sip current releases in the garden or tour the vineyard before tasting. ⊠ *1075 Buchli Station Rd.* ⊕ *Off Duhig Rd., south of Hwy. 121*

☏ *707/252–9065* ⊕ *www.bouchaine.com* ▣ *Tasting $25, tour and tasting $75.*

CIA at Copia

COLLEGE | Full-fledged foodies and the merely curious achieve gastronomical bliss at the Culinary Institute of America's Oxbow District campus, its facade brightened by a wraparound mural inspired by the colorful garden that fronts the facility. When everything's going full tilt, you could easily spend a few hours dining at the indoor and outdoor restaurants; checking out the shop, themed exhibitions, and Vintners Hall of Fame wall; or attending (book ahead) classes and demonstrations. If it's open, head upstairs to the Chuck Williams Culinary Arts Museum. Named for the Williams-Sonoma kitchenwares founder, it holds a fascinating collection of cooking, baking, and other food-related tools, tableware, gizmos, and gadgets, some dating back more than a century. ⊠ *500 1st St.* ⊕ *Near McKinstry St.* ☏ *707/967–2500* ⊕ *www.ciaatcopia.com* ▣ *Facility/ museum free, class/demo fees vary.*

Clos Du Val

WINERY/DISTILLERY | Searching in the early 1970s for the best non-European site to grow Cabernet Sauvignon, this French-owned outfit's founding winemaker selected land now called Hirondelle Vineyard. He chose well: Clos Du Val built its reputation on its intense estate Cabernet, made with the Stags Leap District vineyard's fruit. Grapes for the much-praised Three Graces Bordeaux-style red blend also come from Hirondelle, the French word for "swallow," a bird species prevalent here. Guests sample these wines plus Sauvignon Blanc, Chardonnay, Pinot Noir, Merlot, and sometimes others in a glass-fronted vineyard's-edge hospitality center (reservations required, same-day visits possible). In good weather, hosts retract the windows, transforming the tasting room, its flashy interiors by St. Helena–based designer Erin Martin, and its patio into a unified space. ⊠ 5330 Silverado Trail ⊹ Near Capps Dr. ☎ 707/261–5212 ⊕ www.closduval.com ⊠ Tastings from $50.

Darioush

WINERY/DISTILLERY | The visitor center at Darioush is unlike any other in the valley: 16 freestanding, sand-colored columns loom in front of a travertine building whose exuberant architecture recalls the ancient Persian capital Persepolis. Exceptional hospitality and well-balanced wines from southern Napa Valley grapes are the winery's hallmarks. The signature Napa Valley Cabernet Sauvignon and other bottlings combine grapes grown high on Mt. Veeder with valley-floor fruit, the former providing tannins and structure, the latter mellower, savory notes. Viognier, Chardonnay, Merlot, Shiraz, and the Duel Cab-Shiraz blend are among other possible pours here. All visits are by appointment, best made at least a day or two ahead. ⊠ 4240 Silverado Trail ⊹ Near Shady Oaks Dr. ☎ 707/257–2345 ⊕ www.darioush.com ⊠ Tastings from $65.

di Rosa Center for Contemporary Art

MUSEUM | The late Rene di Rosa assembled an extensive collection of artworks created by Northern California artists from the 1960s to the present, displaying them on this 217-acre Carneros District property surrounded by Chardonnay and Pinot Noir vineyards. Two galleries at opposite ends of a 35-acre lake show works from the collection and host temporary exhibitions; the Sculpture Meadow behind the second gallery holds a few dozen large outdoor pieces. As 2021 dawned, the di Rosa, which was closed for most of 2020, planned to reopen with exhibitions assembled by guest curators. ⊠ 5200 Sonoma Hwy./Hwy. 121 ⊹ Near Duhig Rd. ☎ 707/226–5991 ⊕ www.dirosaart.org ⊠ $20 ☉ Closed most weekdays.

★ Domaine Carneros

WINERY/DISTILLERY | A visit to this majestic château is an opulent way to enjoy the Carneros District—especially in fine weather, when the vineyard views are spectacular. The château was modeled after an 18th-century French mansion owned by the Taittinger family. Carved into the hillside beneath the winery, the cellars produce sparkling wines reminiscent of those made by Taittinger, using only Los Carneros AVA grapes. Enjoy flights of sparkling wine or Pinot Noir with cheese and charcuterie plates, caviar, or smoked salmon. Tastings are by appointment only. ⊠ 1240 Duhig Rd. ⊹ At Hwy. 121 ☎ 707/257–0101, 800/716–2788 Ext. 150 ⊕ www.domainecarneros.com ⊠ Tastings from $40.

Etude Wines

WINERY/DISTILLERY | You're apt to see or hear hawks, egrets, Canada geese, and other wildlife on the grounds of Etude, known for sophisticated Pinot Noirs. Although the winery and its light-filled tasting room are in Napa County, the grapes for its flagship Carneros Estate Pinot Noir come from the Sonoma portion of Los Carneros, as do those for the

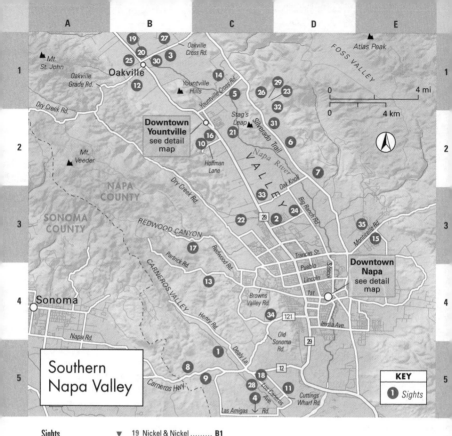

Southern Napa Valley

KEY

1 Sights

At di Rosa, the art treasures can be found indoors and out.

rarer Heirloom Carneros Pinot Noir. Long-time winemaker Jon Priest also excels at single-vineyard Napa Valley Cabernets. In good weather, hosts pour Priest's reds, plus Chardonnay, Pinot Gris, and a few others, on the patio outside the contemporary tasting room. ⊠ *1250 Cuttings Wharf Rd. ✛ 1 mile south of Hwy. 121* ☎ *707/257–5782* ⊕ *www.etudewines. com* ✉ *Tastings from $30* ☉ *Closed Tues. and Wed.*

★ Fontanella Family Winery

WINERY/DISTILLERY | Six miles from the downtown Napa whirl, husband-and-wife Jeff and Karen Fontanella's hillside spread seems a world apart. In addition to his formal studies, Jeff learned about wine making at three prestigious wineries before he and Karen, a lawyer, established their own operation on 81 south-facing Mt. Veeder acres. The couple braved an economic recession, an earthquake, and wildfires in the first decade but emerged tougher, if no less gracious to guests lucky enough to find themselves tasting Chardonnay,

Zinfandel, and Cabernet Sauvignon on the patio here. Tastings often end with a Zinfandel-based port-style wine. With the barnlike production facility in the foreground and nearby Cabernet vines ringing a large irrigation pond, the setting represents the very picture of Napa Valley life many visitors imagine. ■**TIP**→ **If offered the chance to stroll the estate, take it—the views south to San Francisco and east to Atlas Peak reward the exertion.** ⊠ *1721 Partrick Rd. ✛ 1st St. to Browns Valley Rd. west of Hwy. 29* ☎ *707/252–1017* ⊕ *www.fontanellawinery.com* ✉ *Tasting $45.*

Gordon Huether Studio

MUSEUM | Local multimedia artist Gordon Huether has made a name for himself at home and internationally with his large-scale sculptures and installations. His Napa 9/11 Memorial anchors a section of Main Street downtown, across the street his music-inspired wall installations pep up the Blue Note Napa jazz club, and his sculpture of the late vintner Robert Mondavi and his wife, Margrit,

Both the art and the wine inspire at the Hess Collection.

sits atop the CIA at Copia building in the Oxbow District. To view scale models of his latest projects and glimpse his staff (and sometimes the artist himself) at work, make a weekday appointment to visit his studio, 3 miles north of downtown. ⊠ *1821 Monticello Rd.* ✛ *Near Atlas Peak Rd.* ☎ *707/255–5954* ⊕ *www. gordonhuether.com* ✉ *Free* ☉ *Closed weekends.*

Hess Collection

WINERY/DISTILLERY | About 9 miles northwest of Napa, up a winding road ascending Mt. Veeder, this winery is a delightful discovery. The limestone structure, rustic from the outside but modern and airy within, contains Swiss founder Donald Hess's world-class art collection, including large-scale works by contemporary artists such as Andy Goldsworthy, Anselm Kiefer, and Robert Rauschenberg. Cabernet Sauvignon and Chardonnay are strengths, along with small-lot reds (Petite Sirah, Pinot Noir, Syrah, and blends). All visits are by appointment. ■**TIP**➔ **Guided or self-guided gallery tours**

are part of most tastings. ⊠ *4411 Redwood Rd.* ✛ *West off Hwy. 29 at Trancas St./ Redwood Rd. exit* ☎ *707/255–1144* ⊕ *www.hesscollection.com* ✉ *Tastings from $45.*

Hyde Estate Winery

WINERY/DISTILLERY | Dubbed "the wise man of Carneros" by *Wine Spectator* magazine, winegrower Larry Hyde began farming grapes in the southern Napa Valley in 1979. For years his fruit has gone into the high-scoring vineyard-designate Chardonnays of posh labels like Massican, DuMol, and Kistler, and Chardonnays and Pinot Noirs for Patz & Hall. With this exalted a pedigree—experts consider Hyde Vineyard not merely among California's finest vineyards but also the world—it was only a matter of time before wines bearing Hyde's name would debut. Pinot came first (2009) followed by Chardonnay (2012), and later Viognier, Sauvignon Blanc, Merlot, and Syrah. In 2017 Hyde and his son, Chris, opened a winery and appointment-only tasting room in the Carneros. When much of the valley is roasting during midsummer heat waves, San Pablo Bay breezes keep patio patrons here blessedly cool. ✉ *1044 Los Carneros Ave.* ✛ *At Carneros Highway (121/12)* ☎ *707/265–7626* ⊕ *www.hydew-ines.com* 🍷 *Tasting $75.*

John Anthony Vineyards Tasting Room

WINERY/DISTILLERY | Cabernet Sauvignon from Coombsville and Oak Knoll, two southern Napa Valley appellations, is the specialty of John Anthony Truchard, who presents his wines by the glass, flight, or bottle at a storefront tasting room in downtown Napa. As a farmer Truchard emphasizes matching the right varietal and clone, or variant of it, to the right vineyard. Having done so, he creates only 100% single-varietal wines—no blending of Cabernet with Merlot, for instance—meant to be "as beautiful as the vineyards they come from." The Syrah also stands out among the reds. La Dame Michele, a sparkling wine, and the Church Vineyard Sauvignon Blanc are lighter wines to seek out. ✉ *Andaz Napa, 1440 1st St.* ✛ *At Franklin St.* ☎ *707/265–7711* ⊕ *www.johnanthonyvineyards.com* 🍷 *Tastings from $30.*

Mark Herold Wines

WINERY/DISTILLERY | Several years after selling his cult brand Merus, Pana-ma-born Mark Herold emerged with a namesake line of collector-quality Cabernet Sauvignons from the Atlas Peak, Coombsvillle, and Oakville AVAs. Herold also makes Uproar, a Cabernet blend from those three areas that astounds for its intense flavors and relatively accessible price. At the winemaker's Oxbow District storefront, where a wall sculpture of a hot-rod-green marlin surrounded by white lilies sets a peppy tone, you can sample four Cabernets at an Appellation Series tasting. The introductory Herold Highlights often begins with a Sauvignon Blanc and a Chardonnay (sometimes a dry rosé of Cabernet) before sips of Uproar and one of the appellation Cabs. All visits are by appointment, with last-minute ones often possible. ✉ *710 1st St.* ✛ *At McKinstry St.* ☎ *707/256–3111* ⊕ *www.markheroldwines.com* 🍷 *Tastings $35–$75.*

★ Mayacamas Downtown

WINERY/DISTILLERY | Cabernets from Mayacamas Vineyards placed second and fifth respectively on *Wine Spectator* magazine's 2019 and 2020 "Top 100" lists of the world's best wines, two accolades among many for this winery founded atop Mt. Veeder in 1889. One of Napa's leading viticulturists, Annie Favia farms the organic vineyards, elevation 2,000-plus feet, without irrigation; her husband, Andy Favia, is the consulting winemaker. The grapes for the Chardon-nay come from 40-year-old vines. Aged in mostly neutral (previously used) French oak barrels to accentuate mountain minerality, the wine is a Napa Valley marvel. The Cabernet Sauvignon ages for three years, spending part of the time in oak barrels more than a century old. Erin Martin, a Napa Valley resident with a hip international reputation, designed the light-filled storefront tasting space. ■ TIP→ **Experiencing these magnificent wines at this downtown tasting room may entice you to visit the estate.** ✉ *First Street Napa, 1256 1st St.* ✛ *At Randolph St.* ☎ *707/294–1433* ⊕ *www.mayacamas. com* 🍷 *Tastings from $35* ⊗ *Closed Mon. and Tues.*

Napa Valley Distillery

WINERY/DISTILLERY | Entertaining educators keep the proceedings light and lively at this distillery, which bills itself as Napa's first since Prohibition. NVD makes gin, rum, whiskey, and the flagship grape-based vodka, along with brandies and barrel-aged bottled cocktails that include Manhattans (the top seller), mai tais, and negronis. Lesson number one at visits, always by appointment, is how to prop-erly sip spirits (spoiler: don't swirl your glass as you would with wine). ■ TIP→ **If you just want to sample the wares, the distillery operates a tasting bar at Oxbow**

Napa Valley Wine Train passengers get up-close vineyard views from vintage railcars.

Public Market. ⊠ *2485 Stockton St.* ✚ *Off California Blvd.* ☎ *707/265–6272* ⊕ *www. napadistillery.com* 🎟 *Tastings $30* 🕐 *Closed Tues. and Wed.*

Napa Valley Wine Train
TOUR—SIGHT | Guests on this Napa Valley fixture ride the same 150-year-old rail corridor along which trains once transported passengers as far north as Calistoga's spas. The rolling stock includes restored Pullman cars and a two-story Vista Dome coach with a curved glass roof. The train travels a leisurely, scenic route between Napa and St. Helena. Patrons on some tours enjoy a multicourse meal and tastings at one or more wineries. Some rides involve no winery stops, and themed trips are occasionally scheduled. ■ TIP→ **It's best to make this trip during the day, when you can enjoy the vineyard views.** ⊠ *1275 McKinstry St.* ✚ *Off 1st St.* ☎ *707/253–2111, 800/427–4124* ⊕ *www. winetrain.com* 🎟 *From $160.*

★ O'Brien Estate
WINERY/DISTILLERY | Barb and Bart O'Brien live on and operate this 40-acre Oak Knoll District estate, where in good weather guests sip wines at an outdoor tasting area adjoining the vineyard that produces the fruit for them. It's a singular setting to enjoy Merlot, Cabernet Sauvignon, Bordeaux-style red blends, Sauvignon Blanc, and Chardonnay wines that indeed merit the mid-90s (sometimes higher) scores they garner from critics. Club members snap up most of the bottlings, with the rest sold at intimate tastings (reservations are required; book well ahead). All visits include vineyard and winery tours and an account of Barb and Bart's inspiring path to winery ownership. ■ TIP→ **The superb wines and genial hosts make a stop here the highlight of many a Wine Country vacation.** ⊠ *1200 Orchard Ave.* ✚ *Off Solano Ave.* ☎ *707/252–8463* ⊕ *www.obrienestate.com* 🎟 *Tasting $55.*

★ Oxbow Public Market
MARKET | The 40,000-square-foot market's two dozen stands provide an introduction to Northern California's diverse artisanal food products. Swoon over decadent charcuterie at the Fatted Calf (great

sandwiches, too), slurp oysters at Hog Island, enjoy empanadas at El Porteño, or chow down on vegetarian, duck, or salmon tacos at C Casa. Sample wine (and cheese) at the Oxbow Cheese & Wine Merchant, ales at Fieldwork Brewing's taproom, and barrel-aged cocktails at the Napa Valley Distillery. The owner of Kara's Cupcakes operates the adjacent Bar Lucia for (mostly) sparkling wines and rosés. Napa Bookmine is among the few nonfood vendors here. ■TIP→ **Five Dot Ranch and Cookhouse sells quality steaks and other meat to go; if you don't mind eating at the counter, you can order from the small menu and dine on the spot.** ⊠ *610 and 644 1st St.* ✛ *At McKinstry St.* ⊕ *www. oxbowpublicmarket.com.*

★ Quixote Winery

WINERY/DISTILLERY | Extravagance infuses this boutique Stags Leap District operation, most notably in its architecture but also in the Petite Sirahs and Cabernets. Founder Carl Doumani spent years wooing the Austria-born architect Friedensreich Hundertwasser, whose sensibility has been compared to Antoni Gaudí's, to design the winery and production facility. Per Hundertwasser's insistence on replicating natural forms, the sod-roofed structure, clad in red brick and colorful ceramic tiles and topped with a gold onion dome, has no straight lines. Under new ownership, Philippe Melka became the consulting winemaker in 2016, his rich, velvety style a complement to the ebullient setting. Winery visits are by appointment only. ⊠ *6126 Silverado Trail* ✛ *¾ mile south of Yountville Cross Rd.* ☎ *707/944–2659* ⊕ *quixotewinery.com* 🥂 *Tastings from $60.*

RAD Napa (*Rail Arts District Napa*)

PUBLIC ART | An ambitious beautification project also promoting democracy in art, outdoor wellness, and a few other ideals, RAD Napa commissions artists to paint murals on buildings, fences, and utility boxes along or near downtown Napa's railroad tracks. Sculptures and other installations are also involved. Many of the outdoor artworks can be viewed along the Napa Valley Vine Trail pedestrian and biking path or aboard the Napa Valley Wine Train. ■TIP→ **Download a walking map on RAD Napa's website.** ⊠ *Napa* ☎ *707/501–5355* ⊕ *www.radnapa.org.*

RiverHouse by Bespoke Collection

WINERY/DISTILLERY | Commune with artworks by modern and contemporary masters at this tasting room operated by Aerena Galleries, where hosts pour wines from two labels—Aerena Wines and Blackbird Vineyards—both crafted by Aaron Pott and Kyle Mizuno. Grapes for the Aerena wines, among them Chardonnay, rosé, and Cabernet Sauvignon, come from several appellations, with the ones for Blackbird strictly Napa Valley. Smooth yet complex "Right Bank" Bordeaux reds emphasizing Merlot and Cabernet Franc are Blackbird's calling card. Tastings take place inside the high-ceilinged, vaguely industrial-loft gallery space or on the riverfront patio just outside. ⊠ *604 Main St.* ✛ *At 5th St.* ☎ *707/252–4440* ⊕ *riverhouse.bespokecollection.com* 🥂 *Tastings from $40* ☉ *Closed Mon.–Wed.*

★ Robert Biale Vineyards

WINERY/DISTILLERY | Here's a surprise: a highly respected Napa Valley winery that doesn't sell a lick of Cabernet. Zinfandel from heritage vineyards, some with vines more than 100 years old, holds the spotlight, with luscious Petite Sirahs in supporting roles. Nearly every pour comes with a fascinating backstory, starting with the flagship Black Chicken Zinfandel. In the 1940s, the Biale family sold eggs, walnuts, and other farm staples, with bootleg Zinfandel a lucrative sideline. Because neighbors could eavesdrop on party-line phone conversations, "black chicken" became code for a jug of Zin. These days the wines are produced on the up-and-up by valley native Tres Goetting, whose vineyard and cellar choices bring out the best in two unsung varietals. The 10-acre property's

The Paris Wine Tasting of 1976

The event that changed the California wine industry forever took place half a world away, in Paris. To celebrate the American Bicentennial, Steven Spurrier, a British wine merchant, sponsored a comparative blind tasting of California Cabernet Sauvignon and Chardonnay wines against Bordeaux Cabernet blends and French white Burgundies. The tasters were French and included journalists and producers.

And the Winners Were...
The 1973 Stag's Leap Wine Cellars Cabernet Sauvignon came in first among the reds, and the 1973 Chateau Montelena Chardonnay edged out the French and other California whites. The so-called Judgment of Paris stunned the wine establishment, as it was the first serious challenge to French wines supremacy. When the shouting died down, the rush was on. Tourists and winemakers streamed into the Napa Valley and interest grew so strong it helped revitalize Sonoma County's wine industry.

open-air tasting setting—a stone's throw from Zinfandel vines, with far-off views of two mountain ranges—has a back-porch feel. Visits are by appointment; call ahead for same-day. ⊠ *4038 Big Ranch Rd., at Salvador Ave.* ☎ *707/257–7555* ⊕ *biale. com* ☕ *Tastings from $35.*

Saintsbury
WINERY/DISTILLERY | In 1981, when Saintsbury released its first Pinot Noir, the Carneros District had yet to earn its reputation as a setting in which the often finicky varietal could prosper. This pioneer helped disprove the conventional wisdom that only the French could produce great Pinot Noir; with their subtlety and balance Saintsbury's wines continue to please. In recent years the winery has expanded its reach to the Green Valley of the Russian River Valley, the Sonoma Coast, and Mendocino County's Anderson Valley with equally impressive results. Named for the English author and critic George Saintsbury (he wrote *Notes on a Cellar-Book*), this unpretentious operation also makes Chardonnay. Visits are by appointment only. ■TIP→ **When the weather cooperates, tastings take place in a rose garden.**

⊠ *1500 Los Carneros Ave.* ⊹ *South off Hwy. 121 and east (left) on Withers Rd. for entrance* ☎ *707/252–0592* ⊕ *www. saintsbury.com* ☕ *Tastings from $40.*

★ Shafer Vineyards
WINERY/DISTILLERY | Its Hillside Select Cabernet Sauvignon has long been one of the Napa Valley's most sought-after bottlings, and Shafer conducts small appointment-only tastings in a hospitality space with views of the rugged Stags Leap District incline where the prized wine's grapes grow. Sessions, expected to resume in late 2021, usually start with the Red Shoulder Ranch Carneros Chardonnay, followed by TD-9 (a Merlot-based Bordeaux blend), the One Point Five 100% Cabernet Sauvignon, and Relentless (a Syrah–Petite Sirah blend), concluding with the 100% Cabernet Hillside Select. Expertly farmed and masterfully balanced, these collector-quality wines deserve the high praise they receive. ⊠ *6154 Silverado Trail* ⊹ *¾ mile south of Yountville Cross Rd.* ☎ *707/944–2877* ⊕ *www.shafervineyards.com* ☕ *Tasting $85* ⊗ *Closed weekends.*

Stag's Leap Wine Cellars

WINERY/DISTILLERY | A 1973 Stag's Leap Wine Cellars S.L.V. Cabernet Sauvignon put this winery and the Napa Valley on the enological map by placing first in the famous Judgment of Paris tasting of 1976. The grapes for that wine came from a vineyard visible from the stone-and-glass Fay Outlook & Visitor Center, which has broad views of a second fabled Cabernet vineyard (Fay) and the promontory that gives both the winery and the Stags Leap District AVA their names. The top-of-the-line Cabernets from these vineyards are poured at appointment-only tastings (call ahead for same-day visits), some of which include perceptive food pairings by the winery's executive chef. ■ TIP➔ **When the weather's right, two patios with the same views as the tasting room fill up quickly.** ✉ *5766 Silverado Trail* ✚ *At Wappo Hill Rd.* ☎ *707/261–6410* ⊕ *www.stagsleapwinecellars.com* 🍷 *Tastings from $50.*

Stags' Leap Winery

WINERY/DISTILLERY | A must for history buffs, this winery in a bowl-shaped micro valley at the base of the Stags Leap Palisades dates to 1893. Three years earlier, its original owners erected the Manor House, which reopened in 2016 after the restoration of its castlelike stone facade and redwood-paneled interior. The home, whose open-air porch seems out of a flapper-era movie set, hosts seated tastings of the refined wines of Bordeaux-born Christophe Paubert. Estate Cabernet Sauvignons, Merlot, and Petite Sirah, one bottling of the last varietal from vines planted in 1929, are the calling cards. Paubert also makes Malbec, along with Viognier, Chardonnay, and rosé. Some tastings take place on the porch, others inside; all require an appointment best made a day or more ahead. ✉ *6150 Silverado Trail* ✚ *¾ mile south of Yountville Cross Rd.* ☎ *707/257–5790* ⊕ *stagsleap.com* 🍷 *Tastings from $75* ⊗ *Closed Tues. and Wed.*

St. Clair Brown Winery & Brewery

WINERY/DISTILLERY | Tastings at this women-en-run "urban winery" and nanobrewery a few blocks north of downtown unfold in a colorful culinary garden. Winemaker Elaine St. Clair, well regarded for stints at Domaine Carneros and Black Stallion, produces elegant wines—crisp yet complex whites and smooth, French-style reds whose stars include Cabernet Sauvignon and Syrah. While pursuing her wine-making degree, St. Clair also studied brewing; a few of her light-, medium-, and full-bodied brews are always on tap. You can taste the wines or beers solo or enjoy them paired with appetizers that might include a selection of cheeses or addictive almonds roasted with rosemary, lemon zest, and lemon olive oil. ■ TIP➔ **The tasting garden, anchored by an intimate, light-filled greenhouse, stays open until 8 pm on Friday and Saturday.** ✉ *816 Vallejo St.* ✚ *Off Soscol Ave.* ☎ *707/255–5591* ⊕ *www.stclairbrown.com* 🍷 *Tastings $18 beer, wine from $40* ⊗ *Closed Mon.–Wed.*

Studio by Feast it Forward

WINERY/DISTILLERY | Fans of the online Feast it Forward lifestyle network flock to its brick-and-mortar location in downtown Napa to experience food, wine, and entertainment with a philanthropic component—at least 5% of the proceeds goes to charity. On any given day, tastings of impressive boutique wines might be taking place downstairs, a sommelier-taught class upstairs, and a musician or other performer mesmerizing millennials in the covered, open-air performance space out back. The upbeat vibe, good intentions, high-quality food and kitchenware products, and well-curated events make this Oxbow District space worth investigating. ✉ *1031 McKinstry St.* ✚ *Near 1st St.* ☎ *707/819–2403* ⊕ *www.feastitforward.com* 🍷 *Tastings from $25* ⊗ *Closed Wed.*

★ Trefethen Family Vineyards

WINERY/DISTILLERY | Superior estate Chardonnay, Dry Riesling, Cabernet Sauvignon, Merlot, Pinot Noir, and the Malbec-heavy Dragon's Tooth blend are the trademarks of this family-run winery founded in 1968. To find out how well Trefethen wines age, book a reserve tasting, which includes pours of limited-release wines and one or two older vintages. The terra-cotta-color historic winery on-site, built in 1886, was designed with a gravity-flow system, with the third story for crushing, the second for fermenting the resulting juice, and the first for aging. The wooden building suffered severe damage in the 2014 Napa earthquake but after extensive renovations, it reopened as the main tasting room. The early-1900s Arts and Crafts–style Villa, situated amid gardens, hosts reserve and elevated tastings. All visits require a reservation. ⊠ *1160 Oak Knoll Ave.* ✛ *Off Hwy. 29* ☎ *707/255–7700* ⊕ *www. trefethen.com* ✎ *Tastings from $30.*

Truchard Vineyards

WINERY/DISTILLERY | Diversity is the name of the game at this family-owned winery on prime acreage amid the Carneros District's rolling hills. High-profile Napa Valley wineries purchase most of the grapes grown here, but some of the best are held back for estate-only wines—the Chardonnays and Pinot Noirs the region is known for, along with Roussanne, Zinfandel, Merlot, Syrah, Cabernet Sauvignon, and a few others. You must call ahead to taste, but a casual experience tailored to your interests awaits if you do. The included tour takes in the vineyards and the wine cave. ■ **TIP→ Climb the small hill near the winery for a photo-op view of the pond and pen of Angora goats over the ridge.** ⊠ *3234 Old Sonoma Rd.* ✛ *Off Hwy. 121* ☎ *707/253–7153* ⊕ *www.truchardvineyards.com* ✎ *Tasting $40* ☽ *Closed weekends (check website for Sat.).*

Village at Vista Collina Tasting Rooms

WINERY/DISTILLERY | Guests at Vista Collina and across-the-street sister resort Meritage have easy access to nine tasting rooms providing a Wine Country sampler all in one courtyard. Three to seek out are **Cornerstone Cellars** and **Jason by Pahlmeyer** for classic Napa Cabs and **Mi Sueño Winery,** whose Mexico-born founders' American-dream story is as compelling as their extensive offerings. Also of interest is **Anarchist,** where the wines' names (e.g., Rosé Against the Machine) are as catchy as their grape and flavor combinations. Anarchist also pours the more straightforward wines of **The Foundry** (same owners and winemaker), a custom small-lot winery with access to top vineyard sites. In its space the **Foley Food & Wine Society** showcases five California brands, including Merus and Chalk Hill. If after a few tastings your palate needs cleansing, repair to **Napa Smith Brewery** for a lager or two. ⊠ *850 Bordeaux Way* ✛ *4 miles south of downtown, west off Hwy. 221 on Napa Valley Corporate Dr.* ⊕ *villagenapavalley.com* ✎ *Tasting fees vary.*

Whetstone Wine Cellars

WINERY/DISTILLERY | Hamden McIntyre, whose other Napa Valley wineries include the majestic Inglenook in Rutherford and Greystone (now the Culinary Institute of America) in St. Helena, designed this boutique appointment-only winery's less showy yet still princely 1885 château. The French-style stone structure's tree-shaded front lawn is a civilized spot to enjoy by-the-glass or bottle service. Pinot Noir, Syrah, and Viognier are winemaker Jamey Whetstone's specialties. The influence of his mentor Larry Turley, known for velvety Zinfandels, is most evident in the Pinot and the Syrah, but their élan is Whetstone's alone. ⊠ *1075 Atlas Peak Rd.* ✛ *Off Monticello Rd.* ☎ *707/254–0600* ⊕ *www.whetstonewinecellars.com* ✎ *Tastings from $20 a glass.*

🍴 Restaurants

Angèle

$$$ | **FRENCH** | A vaulted wood-beamed ceiling and paper-topped tables set the scene for romance at this softly lit French bistro inside an 1890s boathouse. Look for clever variations on classic dishes such as croque monsieur (grilled Parisian ham and Gruyère) and Niçoise salad for lunch, with veal sweetbreads and, in season, steamed mussels with white wine–and–saffron broth for dinner. **Known for:** classic bistro cuisine; romantic setting; outdoor seating under bright-yellow umbrellas. [$] *Average main: $33* ✉ *540 Main St.* ✣ *At 5th St.* ☎ *707/252–8115* 🌐 *www.angelerestaurant.com.*

Avow Napa

$$ | **MODERN AMERICAN** | The rooftop's the draw at this three-level brick-walled bar and restaurant opened by vintner Joseph Wagner, who grew up working at his family's Caymus Vineyards before starting Belle Glos Pinot Noir and other brands on his own. Small plates might include oysters on the half shell and crab funnel cake, but it's worth staying for dinner and items like rabbit gnocchi or diver scallops with grits, and always the Avow bone-marrow burger. **Known for:** international wines and beers; carved-wood first-floor bar; affiliated Quilt & Co. tasting room next door for Wagner's small-lot wines. [$] *Average main: $24* ✉ *813 Main St.* ✣ *At Third St.* ☎ *707/203–8900* 🌐 *avownapa.com.*

★ **Bistro Don Giovanni**

$$$ | **ITALIAN** | After a brief absence, longtime executive chef Scott Warner returned to this Cal-Italian bistro with a new title: chef partner with beloved proprietor Giovanni Scala, who opened the boisterous roadhouse in the mid-1990s. Regulars still favor the fritto misto (deep-fried calamari, onions, fennel, and rock shrimp), spinach ravioli with lemon-cream or tomato sauce, slow-braised lamb shank, and wood-fired pizzas. **Known for:** patio and garden dining; specialty cocktails and aperitifs; many wines by the glass. [$] *Average main: $30* ✉ *4110 Howard La.* ✣ *5 miles north of downtown Napa off Hwy. 29* ☎ *707/224–3300* 🌐 *www.bistrodongiovanni.com.*

The Boon Fly Café

$$ | **MODERN AMERICAN** | This small spot that melds rural charm with industrial chic serves updated American classics such as fried chicken (free-range in this case), burgers (with Kobe beef), and pork chops (with lush tomato fondue). The flatbreads, including a smoked salmon one made with fromage blanc, Parmesan, lemon crème fraîche, and capers, are worth a try. **Known for:** open all day; signature breakfast doughnuts; excellent cocktails and wines by the glass. [$] *Average main: $22* ✉ *Carneros Resort and Spa, 4048 Sonoma Hwy.* ☎ *707/299–4870* 🌐 *www.boonflycafe.com.*

Bounty Hunter Wine Bar & Smokin' BBQ

$$ | **AMERICAN** | Every dish on the small menu at this wine store, wine bar, and restaurant is a standout, including the pulled-pork and beef-brisket sandwiches served with three types of barbecue sauce, the meltingly tender St. Louis–style ribs, and the signature beer-can chicken (only Tecate will do). The space is whimsically rustic, with stuffed-game trophies mounted on the wall and leather saddles used as seats at a couple of tables. **Known for:** lively atmosphere; combo plates; sides and sauces. [$] *Average main: $18* ✉ *975 1st St.* ✣ *Near Main St.* ☎ *707/226–3976* 🌐 *www.bountyhunterwinebar.com.*

Carpe Diem Wine Bar

$$$ | **MODERN AMERICAN** | Patrons at this restaurant's sociable happy hour wash down nibbles such as truffle popcorn, tacos, and harissa-spiced house fries with draft-beer and weekly wine specials. Those who remain for dinner graze on steak tartare, brick-oven flatbreads topped with roasted wild mushrooms, and larger plates that include an ostrich

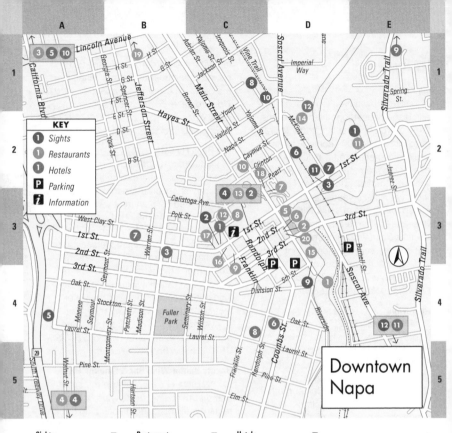

Downtown Napa

burger smothered in triple-cream Brie. **Known for:** small plates; artisanal cheeses and charcuterie; good selection of wines and draft beers. $ *Average main: $28* ✉ *1001 2nd St.* ✛ *At Brown St.* ☎ *707/224–0800* ⊕ *carpediemnapa.com* ◷ *Closed Sun. No lunch.*

Cole's Chop House
$$$$ | **STEAKHOUSE** | When only a thick, flawlessly cooked New York or porterhouse (dry-aged by the eminent Allen Brothers of Chicago) will do, this steak house inside an 1886 stone building is just the ticket. New Zealand lamb chops are the nonbeef favorite, with oysters Rockefeller, beef carpaccio, and creamed spinach among the options for starters and sides. **Known for:** large outdoor patio; borderline-epic wine list; whiskey flights. $ *Average main: $49* ✉ *1122 Main St.* ✛ *At Pearl St.* ☎ *707/224–6328* ⊕ *www. coleschophouse.com* ◷ *No lunch.*

★ Compline
$$$ | **MODERN AMERICAN** | The full name of this enterprise put together by master sommelier Matt Stamp and restaurant wine vet Ryan Stetins is Compline Wine Bar, Restaurant, and Merchant, and indeed you can just sip wine or purchase it here. The place evolved into a hot spot, though, for its youthful vibe and eclectic small and large plates that might include shrimp lumpia (essentially a type of fried spring roll) and citrus-brined chicken but always the Compline burger, best enjoyed with duck-fat fries—and, per Stamp, champagne. **Known for:** upbeat vibe; pastas and vegetarian dishes; by-the-glass wines. $ *Average main: $29* ✉ *1300 1st St., Suite 312* ☎ *707/492– 8150* ⊕ *complinewine.com* ◷ *Closed Tues.*

Grace's Table
$$ | **ECLECTIC** | A dependable, varied menu makes this modest corner restaurant occupying a brick-and-glass storefront many Napans' go-to choice for a simple meal. Fish tacos and iron-skillet corn bread with lavender honey and butter show up at all hours, with buttermilk pancakes and chilaquiles scrambled eggs among the brunch staples and cassoulet and roasted young chicken popular for dinner. **Known for:** congenial staffers; good beers on tap; eclectic menu focusing on France, Italy, and the Americas. $ *Average main: $26* ✉ *1400 2nd St.* ✛ *At Franklin St.* ☎ *707/226–6200* ⊕ *www.gracestable.net.*

Gran Eléctrica
$$ | **MEXICAN** | A neon sign toward the back of Gran Eléctrica translates to "badass bar," but the same goes for the restaurant and its piquant lineup of *botanas* (snacks), tacos, salads, entrées, and sides. Ceviche, fish or carnitas tacos, the chile relleno, and duck-confit mole are among the year-round favorites, with dishes like grilled street-style corn with chipotle mayo appearing in-season. **Known for:** zippy decor; outdoor patio; tequila and mezcal cocktails. $ *Average main: $21* ✉ *1313 Main St.* ✛ *Near Clinton St.* ☎ *707/258–1313* ⊕ *www. granelectrica.com/about-napa* ◷ *Closed Mon. and Tues. No lunch.*

Grove at Copia
$$ | **MODERN AMERICAN** | From a perch high above the olive grove that gives the Culinary Institute of America's outdoor restaurant its name, a larger-than-life sculpture of Robert Mondavi and his wife Margrit (by Gordon Huether) offers a wine toast to diners grazing on comfort-oriented plates whose oh-so-fresh ingredients come mainly from the surrounding culinary garden. The setting, which includes a boccie court, is as splendid as the cuisine. **Known for:** seasonal cocktails inspired by garden; Napa and Sonoma wines; adjacent Restaurant at CIA Copia for indoor dining. $ *Average main: $22* ✉ *500 1st St.* ✛ *Near McKinstry St.* ☎ *707/967–2555* ⊕ *www. ciaatcopia.com/grove* ◷ *Hrs vary; call or check website.*

Kenzo

$$$$ | JAPANESE | From the limestone floor to the cedar walls and cypress tabletops, most of the materials used to build this downtown Napa restaurant specializing in seasonally changing multicourse *kaiseki* meals were imported from Japan, as was the ceramic dinnerware. Delicate preparations of eel, abalone, bluefin tuna, and slow-roasted Wagyu tenderloin are typical of the offerings on the prix-fixe menu, which also includes impeccably fresh, artistically presented sashimi and sushi courses. **Known for:** spare aesthetic; delicate preparations; wine and sake selection. $ *Average main: $225* ⊠ *1339 Pearl St., at Franklin St.* ☎ *707/294–2049* ⊕ *kenzonapa.com* ☉ *Closed Mon. No lunch.*

Kitchen Door

$$ | ECLECTIC | Todd Humphries has overseen swank Manhattan, San Francisco, and Napa Valley kitchens, but for his casual restaurant, scheduled to reopen on 1st Street in late 2021, he set more modest goals, focusing on multicultural comfort cuisine. The signature dishes include a silky cream of mushroom soup whose triumph lies in its magical stock and soupçon of marsala, with pizzas and flatbreads, chicken pho, rice bowls, Niman Ranch burgers, and duck banh mi sandwiches (go for the voluptuous duck jus add on) among the other customer favorites. **Known for:** multicultural comfort cuisine; river-view patio; weekend brunch. $ *Average main: $19* ⊠ *1300 1st St., Suite 272* ⊹ *Near Clay St.* ☎ *707/226–1560* ⊕ *www.kitchendoornapa.com.*

★ La Toque

$$$$ | MODERN AMERICAN | Chef Ken Frank's La Toque is the complete package: his imaginative French-inspired cuisine, served in a formal dining space, is complemented by a wine lineup that consistently earns the restaurant a coveted *Wine Spectator* Grand Award. Ingredients appearing on the prix-fixe multicourse tasting menu often include caviar, sea scallops, squab, and lamb saddle, in dishes prepared and seasoned to pair with wines jointly chosen by the chefs and master sommelier. **Known for:** chef's tasting menu (á la carte also possible); astute wine pairings; vegetarian tasting menu. $ *Average main: $150* ⊠ *Westin Verasa Napa, 1314 McKinstry St.* ⊹ *Off Soscol Ave.* ☎ *707/257–5157* ⊕ *www.latoque.com* ☉ *Closed Mon. and Tues. No lunch.*

Morimoto Napa

$$$$ | JAPANESE | *Iron Chef* star Masaharu Morimoto is the big name behind this downtown Napa restaurant where everything is delightfully over the top, including the desserts. Organic materials such as twisting grapevines above the bar and rough-hewn wooden tables seem simultaneously earthy and modern, creating a fitting setting for the gorgeously plated Japanese fare, from straightforward sashimi to more elaborate seafood, chicken, pork, and beef entrées. **Known for:** theatrical ambience; gorgeous plating; cocktail and sake menu. $ *Average main: $42* ⊠ *610 Main St.* ⊹ *At 5th St.* ☎ *707/252–1600* ⊕ *www.morimotonapa.com.*

Oenotri

$$ | ITALIAN | Often spotted at local farmers' markets and his restaurant's gardens, Oenotri's ebullient chef-owner and Napa native Tyler Rodde is ever on the lookout for fresh produce to incorporate into his rustic southern-Italian cuisine. His restaurant, a brick-walled contemporary space with tall windows and wooden tables, is a lively spot to sample house-made salumi and pastas, thin-crust pizzas, and entrées that might include seared fresh fish or grilled skirt steak. **Known for:** lively atmosphere; Margherita pizza with San Marzano tomatoes; desserts with flair. $ *Average main: $26* ⊠ *1425 1st St.* ⊹ *At Franklin St.* ☎ *707/252–1022* ⊕ *www.oenotri.com.*

Tarla Mediterranean Grill

$$$ | **MEDITERRANEAN** | You can build a meal at Tarla by combining traditional Mediterranean mezes (small plates)— stuffed grape leaves with fresh tzatziki, perhaps, and spanakopita—with contemporary creations such as burrata stone-fruit salad. Entrées include updates of moussaka and other Turkish and Greek standards, along with fancifully modern items like beef short ribs braised with a pomegranate-wine sauce. **Known for:** sidewalk seating; updates of Turkish and Greek standards; multiple gluten-free options. $ *Average main: $28* ⊠ *Andaz Napa, 1480 1st St.* ✛ *At School St.* ☎ *707/255–5599* ⊕ *www.tarlagrill.com.*

★ Torc

$$$ | **MODERN AMERICAN** | *Torc* means "wild boar" in an early Celtic dialect, and owner-chef Sean O'Toole, who formerly helmed kitchens at top Manhattan, San Francisco, and Yountville establishments, occasionally incorporates the restaurant's namesake beast into his eclectic offerings. A recent menu featured baked-stuffed Maine lobster, nettle risotto, three hand-cut pasta dishes, and pork-belly with pole beans, all prepared by O'Toole and his team with style and precision. **Known for:** gracious service; specialty cocktails; Bengali sweet-potato pakora and deviled-egg appetizers. $ *Average main: $36* ⊠ *1140 Main St.* ✛ *At Pearl St.* ☎ *707/252–3292* ⊕ *www. torcnapa.com* ✚ *Closed Sun. and Mon.*

Yak & Yeti

$ | **NEPALESE** | The strip-mall location next to a pizza-chain franchise couldn't be more modest, but the chef—a Himalayan Sherpa—at this restaurant serving Nepalese, Tibetan, and Indian cuisine is a charmer, and his dishes are flavor revelations. *Pakoras* (fritters), samosas, daal soup, and steamed dumplings all make excellent starters, with meat and vegetable curries, and sizzling tandoori platters among the mains. **Known for:** many vegetarian options; good choice for

lunch; reasonable food, beer, and wine prices. $ *Average main: $16* ⊠ *3150B Jefferson St.* ✛ *At Sheridan Dr., 2 miles north of downtown* ☎ *707/666–2475* ⊕ *yakandyetinapa.com.*

★ ZuZu

$$$ | **SPANISH** | At festive ZuZu the focus is on cold and hot tapas, paella, and other Spanish favorites often downed with cava or sangria. Regulars revere the paella, made with Spanish *bomba* rice, and small plates that might include garlic shrimp, jamón Ibérico, lamb chops with Moroccan barbecue glaze, and white anchovies with sliced egg and rémoulade on grilled bread. **Known for:** singular flavors and spicing; Spanish jazz on the stereo; sister restaurant La Taberna three doors south for beer, wine, and bar bites. $ *Average main: $32* ⊠ *829 Main St.* ✛ *Near 3rd St.* ☎ *707/224–8555* ⊕ *www. zuzunapa.com* ✚ *Closed Mon. and Tues.*

Hotels

Andaz Napa

$$$ | **HOTEL** | Part of the Hyatt family, this boutique hotel with an urban-hip vibe has spacious guest rooms with white-marble bathrooms stocked with high-quality products. **Pros:** casual-chic feel; proximity to downtown restaurants, theaters, and tasting rooms; cheery, attentive service. **Cons:** unremarkable views from some rooms; expensive on weekends in high season; some room show wear and tear. $ *Rooms from: $304* ⊠ *1450 1st St.* ☎ *707/687–1234* ⊕ *andaznapa.com* ⇨ *141 rooms* ⦿ *No meals.*

★ Archer Hotel Napa

$$$ | **HOTEL** | Ideal for travelers seeking design pizzazz, a see-and-be-seen atmosphere, and first-class amenities, this five-story downtown Napa property fuses New York City chic and Las Vegas glamour. **Pros:** restaurants and room service by chef Charlie Palmer; Sky & Vine rooftop bar; great views from upper-floor rooms (especially south and west). **Cons:**

not particularly rustic; expensive in high season; occasional service, hospitality lapses. $ *Rooms from: $324* ✉ *1230 1st St.* ☎ *707/690–9800, 855/200–9052* ⊕ *archerhotel.com/napa* ⤵ *183 rooms* ⊙ *No meals.*

Blackbird Inn and Finch Guest House

$$ | B&B/INN | Arts and Crafts style infuses the 1902 Blackbird Inn, from the lobby's fieldstone fireplace and lamps casting a warm glow over the impressive wooden staircase to the guest rooms' period-accurate, locally crafted oak beds and matching night tables. **Pros:** enthusiastic hosts; convenient to downtown; Victorian style in adjacent Finch house. **Cons:** per website "not an appropriate lodging for children"; some rooms are on the small side; street noise in rooms on Blackbird building's west side. $ *Rooms from: $205* ✉ *1755 1st St.* ☎ *707/226–2450* ⊕ *www.blackbirdinnnapa.com* ⤵ *12 rooms* ⊙ *Free breakfast.*

★ Carneros Resort and Spa

$$$$ | RESORT | A winning combination of glamour, service, and pastoral seclusion makes this resort with freestanding board-and-batten cottages the perfect getaway for active lovebirds or families and groups seeking to unwind. **Pros:** cottages have lots of privacy; beautiful views from hilltop pool and hot tub; heaters on private patios. **Cons:** long drive to upvalley destinations; least expensive accommodations pick up highway noise; pricey pretty much year-round. $ *Rooms from: $749* ✉ *4048 Sonoma Hwy./Hwy. 121* ☎ *707/299–4900, 888/400–9000* ⊕ *www.carnerosresort.com* ⤵ *100 rooms* ⊙ *No meals.*

Cottages of Napa Valley

$$$ | B&B/INN | Although most of the accommodations here date from the 1920s—when they rented for $5 *a month* (imagine that)—contemporary design touches and amenities, plush new furnishings, up-to-date bathrooms, and attentive service ensure a cozy, 21st-century experience. **Pros:** private porches and patios; basket of Bouchon pastries each morning; kitchen with utensils in each cottage. **Cons:** hum of highway traffic; extra-person charge for children under 12; weekend minimum-stay requirement. $ *Rooms from: $385* ✉ *1012 Darms La.* ☎ *707/252–7810* ⊕ *www.napacottages. com* ⤵ *9 cottages* ⊙ *Free breakfast.*

The George

$$ | B&B/INN | Tall palms tower over this gracefully restored three-story boutique inn, an elaborate 1891 Queen Anne–style structure, once dubbed "the handsomest house in town." Opened in 2021, the property is decorated in a palette of soft whites, grays, and occasional browns, and the guest rooms contain custom-made beds with plush headboards outfitted with top-of-the-line mattresses and bedding. **Pros:** period character with contemporary style; in a quiet neighborhood but only a few blocks from downtown; high ceilings add to feeling of spaciousness. **Cons:** first-come first serve on-site parking (though ample street spaces in vicinity); no elevator (but one ground-floor ADA room); staff on-site for limited hours. $ *Rooms from: $280* ✉ *492 Randolph St.* ☎ *707/681–1433* ⊕ *www.thegeorgenapa.com* ⤵ *9 rooms* ⊙ *Free breakfast.*

★ The Inn on First

$$ | B&B/INN | Guests gush over the hospitality at this inn where the painstakingly restored 1905 mansion facing 1st Street contains five rooms, with five additional accommodations, all suites, in a building behind a secluded patio and garden. **Pros:** full gourmet breakfast by hosts-with-the-most owners; gas fireplaces and whirlpool tubs in all rooms; away from downtown but not too far. **Cons:** no TVs; owners "respectfully request no children"; lacks pool, fitness center, and other amenities of larger properties. $ *Rooms from: $225* ✉ *1938 1st St.* ☎ *707/253–1331* ⊕ *www.theinnonfirst. com* ⤵ *10 rooms* ⊙ *Free breakfast.*

★ Inn on Randolph

$$$ | B&B/INN | A few calm blocks from the downtown action on a nearly 1-acre lot with landscaped gardens, the Inn on Randolph—with a Gothic Revival–style main house and its five guest rooms plus five historic cottages out back—is a sophisticated haven celebrated for its gourmet gluten-free breakfasts and snacks. **Pros:** quiet residential neighborhood; spa tubs in cottages and two main-house rooms; romantic setting. **Cons:** a bit of a walk from downtown; expensive in-season; weekend minimum-stay requirement. $ *Rooms from: $339* ⊠ *411 Randolph St.* ☎ *707/257–2886* ⊕ *www. innonrandolph.com* ⇆ *10 rooms* ⦿ *Free breakfast.*

Milliken Creek Inn

$$$ | B&B/INN | The chic rooms at this romantic inn take a page from the stylebook of British-colonial Asia, and the intimate lobby's terrace overlooks a lush lawn and the Napa River. **Pros:** countryside feeling but 1 mile from Oxbow Public Market area; serene spa; breakfast delivered to your room or elsewhere on the beautiful grounds. **Cons:** expensive in-season; road noise audible in outdoor areas; no pool, fitness center, or bar. $ *Rooms from: $349* ⊠ *1815 Silverado Trail* ☎ *707/255–1197* ⊕ *www.millikencreekinn.com* ⇆ *14 rooms* ⦿ *Free breakfast.*

Senza Hotel

$$$ | HOTEL | Exterior fountains, gallery-quality outdoor sculptures, and rows of grapevines signal the Wine Country–chic aspirations of this boutique hotel that the owners of Hall Wines operate. **Pros:** high-style fixtures; fireplaces in all rooms; elegant atmosphere. **Cons:** just off highway; 5-mile drive to downtown Napa or Yountville; some bathrooms have no tub. $ *Rooms from: $399* ⊠ *4066 Howard La.* ☎ *707/253–0337* ⊕ *www. senzahotel.com* ⇆ *43 rooms* ⦿ *Free breakfast.*

Vista Collina Resort

$$$ | HOTEL | This contemporary resort's shops, restaurants, tasting rooms, and event spaces—not to mention the adjacent industrial park and much larger affiliated Meritage Resort & Spa across the street—evoke suburbia as much as the Wine Country. **Pros:** resort trappings at not unreasonable cost; room service; pool and entertainment amenities. **Cons:** seems like it could be anywhere; resort fee; 4 miles south of downtown (must drive to visit anything off-property). $ *Rooms from: $336* ⊠ *850 Bordeaux Way* ☎ *707/251–3060, 888/965–7090* ⊕ *www.vistacollina.com* ⇆ *145 rooms* ⦿ *No meals.*

Westin Verasa Napa

$$$ | HOTEL | Near the Napa Valley Wine Train depot and Oxbow Public Market, this spacious mostly suites resort is soothing and sophisticated, particularly in the guest quarters, where pristine white bedding plays well off the warm earth tones of the other contemporary furnishings. **Pros:** woodsy Napa River setting but close to town; many rooms with well-equipped kitchenettes (some full kitchens); destination La Toque restaurant. **Cons:** amenities fee; slightly corporate feel; new wing construction may begin in 2021 (if true, ask for a room away from it). $ *Rooms from: $310* ⊠ *1314 McKinstry St.* ☎ *707/257–1800, 888/627–7169* ⊕ *www.westinnapa.com* ⇆ *180 rooms* ⦿ *No meals.*

ⓨ Nightlife

Blue Note Napa

MUSIC CLUBS | The famed New York jazz room's intimate West Coast club hosts national headliners such as Kenny Garrett, KT Tunstall, and Jody Watley. There's a full bar, and you can order a meal or small bites from the kitchen. The larger JaM Cellars Ballroom upstairs books similar artists. ⊠ *Napa Valley Opera House, 1030 Main St.* ✛ *At 1st St.* ☎ *707/880–2300* ⊕ *www.bluenotenapa.com.*

Cadet Wine + Beer Bar

WINE BARS—NIGHTLIFE | Cadet plays things urban-style cool with a long bar, high-top tables, and a low-lit, generally loungelike feel. When they opened their bar, the two owners described their outlook as "unabashedly pro-California," but their wine-and-beer lineup circles the globe. The crowd here is youngish, the vibe festive. ⊠ *930 Franklin St.* ✢ *At end of pedestrian alley between 1st and 2nd Sts.* ☎ *707/224–4400* ⊕ *www.cadetbeerand-winebar.com* ☞ *Closed Mon. and Tues.*

Stone Brewing Napa

BREWPUBS/BEER GARDENS | Southern California–based Stone Brewing transformed a long-abandoned 1877 Italian Renaissance–style structure into an energetic two-story brew pub and restaurant. The beers and ales, some made on-site, run the gamut from extremely light to a stout so dark and sultry it could substitute for espresso. The large outdoor patio, the place to be if the weather's right, looks west across the Napa River to Main Street and beyond. ⊠ *930 3rd St.* ✢ *At Soscol Ave.* ☎ *707/252–2337* ⊕ *www.stonebrewing.com/visit/outposts/napa.*

🎭 Performing Arts

JaM Cellars Ballroom

MUSIC | Upstairs from the Blue Note Napa jazz club, this larger venue inside the 1880 Napa Valley Opera House books acts like Chris Botti year-round and hosts some of the hottest aftershow events of the BottleRock Napa Valley music festival. ⊠ *1030 Main St., at 1st St.* ☎ *707/880–2300* ⊕ *www.jamcellarsballroom.com.*

Uptown Theatre

MUSIC | At 860 seats, this art deco former movie house attracts performers like Ziggy Marley, Lyle Lovett, Roseanne Cash, Napa Valley resident Boz Scaggs, and others. ⊠ *1350 3rd St.* ✢ *At Franklin St.* ☎ *707/259–0123* ⊕ *www.uptowntheatrenapa.com.*

🛍 Shopping

BOOKS

Copperfield's Books

BOOKS/STATIONERY | Check the Napa page on this indie chain's website for local authors' readings and signings while you're in town. ⊠ *First Street Napa, 1300 1st St., Suite 398* ✢ *At Franklin St.* ☎ *707/252–8002* ⊕ *www.copperfields-books.com/napa.*

Napa Bookmine

BOOKS/STATIONERY | An indie shop with additional locations in the Oxbow Public Market and St. Helena, Napa Bookmine sells current magazines and new and used books and hosts author events. Specialties include children's and teen titles, travel books, and works by local writers. ⊠ *964 Pearl St.* ✢ *Near Main St.* ☎ *707/265–8131* ⊕ *www.napabookmine.com.*

HOUSEHOLD ITEMS

Makers Market

HOUSEHOLD ITEMS/FURNITURE | Wine Country and San Francisco Bay Area artisans are represented at this downtown store that sells jewelry, home decor, apothecary, and many other handcrafted items revealing "the soul or the mark of a proud maker." ⊠ *First Street Napa, 1300 1st St., Suite 301* ☎ *707/637–4637* ⊕ *makersmarket.us.*

SHOPPING CENTERS, MALLS

First Street Napa

SHOPPING CENTERS/MALLS | The Archer Hotel Napa anchors this open-air downtown complex of mostly ground-level restaurants, tasting rooms, and national (Anthropologie, Lululemon) and homegrown (Bennington Napa Valley, Habituate Lifestyle + Interiors, Napa Stäk) design, clothing, housewares, and culinary shops. Copperfield's Books and the Visit Napa Valley Welcome Center are also here, along with Milo and Friends for pet necessities and accessories. ⊠ *1300 1st St.* ✢ *Between Franklin and Coombs Sts.* ☎ *707/257–6900* ⊕ *www.firststreet-napa.com.*

Musical performances and other events take place at CIA at Copia's outdoor amphitheater.

🏃 Activities

Enjoy Napa Valley

KAYAKING | Napa native Justin Perkins leads a history-oriented Napa River kayak tour that passes by downtown sights. On the easy paddle, Perkins points out the wildlife and regales participants with amusingly salacious tales of Napa's river-town past. ✉ *Main Street Boat Dock, 680 Main St.* ✛ *Riverfront Promenade south of 3rd St. Bridge* ☎ *707/227–7364* ⊕ *enjoy-napa-valley.com* ✉ *$71.*

Napa Valley Bike Shop

BICYCLING | This outfit that rents bikes is near the Napa Valley Vine Trail and another trail that follows the Napa River. Staffers will help with guided trips booked through the affiliated Napa Valley Bike Tours in Yountville. ■ **TIP→ The shop has an excellent map of Napa bike trails for all abilities.** ✉ *950 Pearl St.* ✛ *At West St.* ☎ *707/251–8687* ⊕ *www.napavalleybiketours.com* ☞ *Rentals from $35, tours from $124.*

Napa Valley Gondola

TOUR—SPORTS | Rides in authentic gondolas that seat up to six depart from downtown Napa's municipal dock. You'll never mistake the Napa River for the Grand Canal, but on a sunny day this is a diverting excursion that often includes a serenade. ✉ *Main Street Boat Dock, 680 Main St.* ✛ *Riverfront Promenade, south of 3rd St. Bridge* ☎ *707/373–2100* ⊕ *napavalleygondola.com* ☞ *From $145 (up to 6 people).*

SPAS

Rooftop Spa by Francis & Alexander

FITNESS/HEALTH CLUBS | Two consultants who manage several Wine Country resorts' spas developed the earth-friendly, sustainable treatments at the Archer Hotel Napa's rooftop facility. The duo's highly skilled practitioners employ the latest relaxation and rejuvenation treatments, some involving CBD. Wine Country Road Trip for 2 aims to replicate a Napa-Sonoma spa excursion with Calistoga mud and body oils produced in both counties. Hotel accommodations in

Few experiences are as exhilarating yet serene as an early-morning balloon ride above the vineyards.

the Archer's Den category are designed for in-room sessions, including one for couples involving side-by-side massages and a "sensual dice game." ✉ *Archer Hotel Napa, 1230 1st St.* ✛ *At Franklin St.* ☎ *707/240–2942* ⊕ *archerhotel.com/napa/ rooftop-spa* ✆ *Treatments from $99.*

Yountville

9 miles north of downtown Napa; 9 miles south of St. Helena.

Yountville (population about 3,000) is something like Disneyland for food lovers. It all started with Thomas Keller's The French Laundry, one of the best restaurants in the United States. Keller is also behind a few other Yountville enterprises—a French bistro, a bakery, American and Oaxacan restaurants, and a food-oriented boutique among them. And that's only the tip of the iceberg: you could stay here several days and not exhaust all the options in this tiny town with an outsize culinary reputation.

Yountville is full of small inns and luxurious hotels catering to those who prefer to walk rather than drive to their lodgings after dinner. Although visitors use Yountville as a home base, touring Napa Valley wineries by day and returning to dine, you could easily while away a few hours downtown, wandering through the shops on or just off Washington Street, or visiting the many tasting rooms. The Yountville Chamber of Commerce, on the southern end of town across from Hotel Villagio, has maps with wine-tasting and history walks.

The town is named for George C. Yount, who in 1836 received the first of several large Napa Valley land grants from the Mexican government. Yount is credited with planting the valley's first vinifera grapevines in 1838. The vines are long gone, but wisps of Yountville's 19th-century past bleed through, most notably along Washington Street, where a restaurant at 6525 Washington occupies the red-brick former train depot, and shops and restaurants west of it inhabit the former Groezinger Winery, established in 1870.

Getting Here and Around

If you're traveling north from Napa on Highway 29, take the Yountville/Veterans Home exit, make a right on California Drive and a left onto Washington Street. Traveling south on Highway 29, turn left onto Madison Street and right onto Washington Street. Nearly all of Yountville's businesses and restaurants are clustered along a 1-mile stretch of Washington Street. Yountville Cross Road connects downtown Yountville to the Silverado Trail, where you'll find several wineries. VINE buses serve Yountville. The Yountville Trolley circles the downtown area and hits a few spots beyond.

CONTACT Yountville Trolley. ☎ 707/312–1509 (or download the Ride the Vine smartphone app) ⊕ www.ridethevine. com/yountville-trolley.

Visitor Information

CONTACT Yountville Chamber Of Commerce. ⊠ 6484 Washington St. ✛ At Oak Circle ☎ 707/944–0904 ⊕ yountville.com.

◉ Sights

★ Cliff Lede Vineyards

WINERY/DISTILLERY | Inspired by his passion for classic rock, owner and construction magnate Cliff Lede named the blocks in his Stags Leap District vineyard after hits by the Grateful Dead and other bands. Rock memorabilia and contemporary art like Jim Dine's outdoor sculpture *Twin 6′ Hearts,* a magnet for the Instagram set, are two other Lede obsessions. The vibe at his efficient, high-tech winery is anything but laid-back, however. Cutting-edge agricultural and enological science informs the vineyard management and wine making here. Lede produces Sauvignon Blanc, Cabernet Sauvignon, and Bordeaux-style red blends; tastings often include a Chardonnay, Pinot Gris, or Pinot Noir from sister

winery FEL. All the wines are well crafted, though the Cabs really rock. ⊠ 1473 Yountville Cross Rd. ✛ Off Silverado Trail ☎ 707/944–8642 ⊕ cliffledevineyards. com ⊠ Tastings from $60 (sometimes $40 for weekend garden tastings).

Domaine Chandon

WINERY/DISTILLERY | On a knoll shaded by ancient oak trees, this French-owned maker of sparkling wines claims one of Yountville's prime pieces of real estate. Chandon is best known for bubbles, but the still wines—among them Cabernet Sauvignon, Chardonnay, and Pinot Noir—also warrant a try. You can sip by the flight or glass and order cheese or small bites. Bottle service is available, and when the weather's good, tables and cabanas are set up outside. Some tastings are designed for romance. ⊠ 1 California Dr. ✛ Off Hwy. 29 ☎ 707/204–7530 ⊕ www.chandon.com ⊠ Tastings from $15.

★ Elyse Winery

WINERY/DISTILLERY | One of his colleagues likens Elyse's winemaker, Russell Bevan, to "a water witch without the walking stick" for his ability to assess a vineyard's weather, soil, and vine positioning and intuit how particular viticultural techniques will affect wines' flavors. Bevan farms judiciously during the growing season, striving later in the cellar to preserve what nature and his efforts have yielded rather than rely on heavy manipulation. Under previous owners for three-plus decades (until 2018), Elyse became known for single-vineyard Zinfandels and Cabernet Sauvignons, with Merlot, Petite Sirah, and red blends other strong suits. A country lane edged by vines leads to this unassuming winery, whose tastings, often outdoors, have a backyard-casual feel. ■TIP→ **Costing much less than the average Napa Valley Cab, Elyse's Holbrook Mitchell Cabernet Sauvignon holds its own against peers priced appreciably higher.** ⊠ 2100 Hoffman La., Napa ✛ 1¾ miles south of central Yountville, off Hwy. 29 or

Domaine Chandon claims a prime piece of real estate.

Solano Ave. ☎ 707/944–2900 ⊕ elysewinery.com ⌧ Tastings from $50.

Goosecross Cellars

WINERY/DISTILLERY | Large retractable west-facing windows in this boutique winery's barnlike tasting space open up behind the bar to views of Cabernet vines—in fine weather, guests on the outdoor deck can practically touch them. Farther in the distance lie the Mayacamas Mountains. Goosecross makes Chardonnay and Pinot Noir from Carneros grapes, but the soul of this cordial operation is its 12-acre State Lane Vineyard, the 9.2 planted acres mostly Cabernet Sauvignon and Merlot with some Cabernet Franc, Malbec, and Petit Verdot. The State Lane Cabernet and Merlot are the stars, along with the Holly's Block 100% Cab and the Aeros Bordeaux-style blend of the vineyard's best grapes. The last two aren't always poured, but the intentionally big Branta red wine (the blend changes with each vintage), a crowd-pleaser, usually is. Visits to Goosecross are by appointment only. ⌧ 1119 State La. ✛ Off Yountville Cross Rd. ☎ 707/944–1986 ⊕ www. goosecross.com ⌧ Tasting $50.

Handwritten Wines

WINERY/DISTILLERY | Handcrafted, 100% Cabernet Sauvignons from hillside and mountain vineyards 2 acres or smaller are this boutique winery's emphasis, with the wines from Mt. Veeder, Rutherford, and Calistoga often among the best. The lineup also includes Sauvignon Blanc and Chardonnay, along with a Pinot Noir from Santa Barbara County's Sta. Rita Hills AVA. Guests at appointment-only seated tastings sip either in a light-filled upscale-rustic space clad in reclaimed redwood wine-barrel staves or in the open-air courtyard the structure surrounds. ⌧ 6494 Washington St. ✛ Near Oak Circle ☎ 707/944–8524 ⊕ www. handwrittenwines.com ⌧ Tastings from $40.

★ Heron House Yountville

WINERY/DISTILLERY | Nine family-owned wineries specializing in small-batch Cabernet Sauvignon showcase their output at this southern Yountville tasting space that doubles as a boutique for contemporary art, fashion accessories, and household items. Several heavy-duty Napa names are involved, starting with Richard Steltzner, who began growing grapes here in 1965. His daughter, Allison, Heron House's founder, represents his Steltzner Vineyards and her Bench Vineyards, and well-known vintners and winemakers are behind the other operations: Eponymous, Hobel, Lindstrom, Myriad, Perchance, Switchback Ridge, and Zeitgeist. The wineries also make whites, rosés, and other reds. Tasting fees vary depending on the flight, which hosts are happy to adjust to match guests' preferences. Visits are by appointment, but walk-ins are accommodated when possible. ■TIP➔ The King of Kings Cabernet Experience suits collectors and Napa Valley Cab lovers eager to up their game. ⊠ 6484 Washington St., Suite G ✛ At Oak Circle ☎ 707/947–7039 ⊕ heronhouseyountville. com ☕ Tastings $65–$125 ⊗ Closed Tues. and Wed.

Hill Family Estate Winery

WINERY/DISTILLERY | Doug Hill has farmed grapes for prominent Napa Valley wineries for years, but at the urging of his son, Ryan, the family began bottling its own Merlot, Cabernet Sauvignon, and other wines. Crafted by Alison Doran, a protégé of the late Napa winemaker André Tchelistcheff, these are refined reds you can sample, along with whites that include Albariño and Chardonnay, on a 7½-acre estate. Alfresco tastings take advantage of classic valley views—vineyards and the board-and-batten winery building up close, the Mayacamas Mountains farther west. Appointment-only visits are limited to a few guests per day, but the family also operates a tasting salon less than a mile away in downtown Yountville. ■TIP➔ Ask about seasonal tours (with tasting) of a "secret garden" that grows produce for The French Laundry and other top restaurants. ⊠ 6155 Solano Ave., Napa ✛ Near Hoffman La.

☎ 707/944–9580 ⊕ www.hillfamilyestate. com ☕ Tastings from $35 downtown, $50 at winery.

JCB Tasting Salon

WINERY/DISTILLERY | Mirrors and gleaming surfaces abound in this eye-catching ode to indulgence named for its French owner, Jean-Charles Boisset (JCB). The JCB label first made its mark with sparkling wine, Chardonnay, and Pinot Noir, with Cabernet Sauvignon a more recent strong suit. In addition to providing a plush setting for sampling his wines, Boisset's downtown Yountville tasting space is also a showcase for home decor items from the likes of Lalique and Baccarat. JCB exceeds the salon's flamboyance a few steps away in a rococo-on-steroids (in a fun way) wine bar and lounge, swathed in white with ruby-red accents, where wines are served by the glass or bottle. ⊠ 6505 Washington St. ✛ At Mulberry St. ☎ 707/934–8237 ⊕ jcbcollection.com/visit ☕ Tastings $50–$65 ⊗ Closed Tues. and Wed.

Napa Valley Vine Trail

TRAIL | Dedicated locals conceived this multipurpose walking, biking, and jogging path they hope will eventually run 47 miles from below Napa, north through the Napa Valley to Calistoga. As 2021 dawned, 12½ miles had been completed, with the most trafficked, largely flat, section following the Napa Valley Wine Train's tracks for 8¾ miles between Yountville and downtown Napa. Vineyard views predominate in the Yountville portion, giving way in Napa to the RAD Napa (Rail Arts District Napa) murals that grace warehouse walls and utility boxes. Markers let trailgoers know where they are, and interpretive signs convey a bit of history. ■TIP➔ Napa Valley Bike Tours, with shops near the trail in Napa and Yountville, rents helmets and bikes. ✛ Trailheads in Yountville at Hwy. 29 and Madison St., in Napa west of Soscol Ave. and Vallejo St. ☎ 707/252–3547 ⊕ www.vinetrail.org.

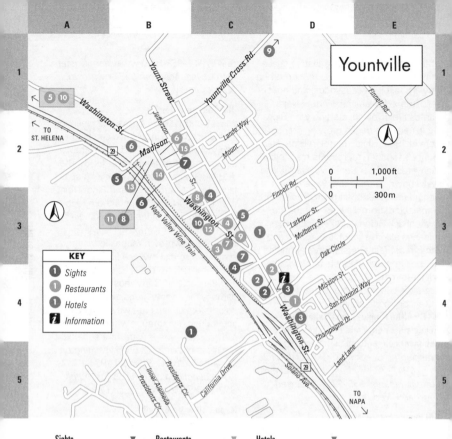

Yountville

KEY

- 1 Sights
- 1 Restaurants
- 1 Hotels
- i Information

0 ——— 1,000ft
0 ——— 300m

TO ST. HELENA

TO NAPA

★ Oasis by Hoopes

WINERY/DISTILLERY | Vineyards surround the walk-through organic garden and corral for rescue animals that anchor second-generation vintner Lindsay Hoopes's playfully pastoral, cool-bordering-on-chic wine venue. In conceiving this family- and dog-friendly outdoor-oriented spot—with ample patio and garden seating, an Airstream trailer Instagrammers love, and even a tent—Hoopes aimed to expand the notion of what a Napa Valley wine tasting can entail. To that end, each group or solo visitor pays a table charge the hosts apply to bottles purchased for sipping on-site or later. If you prefer a traditional flight, the fee can go toward that, too. Lindsay's father started Hoopes Vineyard in the 1980s, selling his Oakville AVA Cabernet Sauvignon grapes to A-list producers before starting his boutique label in 1999. The lineup now includes Sauvignon Blanc, Chardonnay, rosé, Merlot, and Syrah. Most are gems, particularly two Oakville Cabs and a Howell Mountain Merlot. ✉ *6204 Washington St.* ✛ *1 mile south of downtown* ☎ *707/944–1869* ⊕ *hoopesvineyard.com/oasis-by-hoopes* 🍷 *Tastings from $75.*

RH Wine Vault

WINERY/DISTILLERY | Gargantuan crystal chandeliers, century-old olive trees, and strategically placed water features provide visual and aural continuity at Restoration Hardware's quadruple-threat food, wine, art, and design compound. An all-day café fronts two steel, glass, and concrete home-furnishings galleries, with a bluestone walkway connecting them to a reboot of the former Ma(i)sonry wine salon here. Centered around a two-story 1904 manor house constructed from Napa River stone, it remains an excellent spot to learn about small-lot Napa and Sonoma wines, served by the glass, flight, or bottle. Collector-revered labels like Corison, Fisher, Lail, Matthiasson, Melka, and Spottswoode are all represented, the wines in good weather poured in "outdoor living rooms" behind the stone structure. Oozing RH fabulousness as it does, the Wine Vault can feel like a scene on a busy day, but the wines are the real deal. All tastings are by appointment. ✉ *6725 Washington St.* ✛ *At Pedroni St.* ☎ *707/339–4654* ⊕ *www.restorationhardware.com* 🍷 *Tastings from $50.*

Robert Sinskey Vineyards

WINERY/DISTILLERY | Although the winery produces a Stags Leap Cabernet Sauvignon (SLD Estate), two Bordeaux-style red blends (Marcien and POV), and white wines, Sinskey is best known for its intense, brambly Carneros District Pinot Noirs. All the grapes are grown in organic, certified biodynamic vineyards. The influence of Robert's wife, Maria Helm Sinskey—a chef and cookbook author and the winery's culinary director—is evident during the tastings, all of which are accompanied by at least a few bites of food. The elevated Terroir Tasting explores the winery's land and farming practices. Chef's Table takes in the winery's culinary gardens and ends with a seated wine-and-food pairing. All visits require an appointment, wisely made a day or two ahead. ✉ *6320 Silverado Trail, Napa* ✛ *At Yountville Cross Rd.* ☎ *707/944–9090* ⊕ *www.robertsinskey.com* 🍷 *Tastings $40–$175.*

Stewart Cellars

WINERY/DISTILLERY | Three stone structures meant to mimic Scottish ruins coaxed into modernity form this complex that includes public and private tasting spaces, a bright outdoor patio, and an independently run café. The attention to detail in the ensemble's design mirrors that of the wines, whose grapes come from coveted sources, most notably all six Beckstoffer Heritage Vineyards, among the Napa Valley's most historic sites for Cabernet Sauvignon. Although the Nomad Collection sextet of Cabs is the focus, winemaker Blair Guthrie also makes Sauvignon Blanc, Chardonnay, rosé, and Pinot Noir. Visits are by appointment, but except for Nomad tastings, walk-ins are usually accommodated. ■ TIP→ **On sunny days Stewart Cellars is a good stop around lunchtime, when you can order a meal from the café and a glass of wine from the tasting room—for permitting reasons this must be done separately—and enjoy them on the patio.** ✉ *6752 Washington St.* ✥ *Near Pedroni St.* ☎ *707/963–9160* 🌐 *www.stewartcellars.com* 🎫 *Tastings from $30.*

🍴 Restaurants

Ad Hoc

$$$$ | **MODERN AMERICAN** | At this low-key dining room with zinc-top tables and wine served in tumblers, superstar chef Thomas Keller offers a single, fixed-price, nightly menu that might include smoked beef short ribs with creamy herb rice and charred broccolini or sesame chicken with radish kimchi and fried rice. Ad Hoc also serves a small but decadent Sunday brunch, and Keller's Addendum annex, in a separate small building behind the restaurant, sells boxed lunches to go (including moist buttermilk fried chicken) from Thursday to Saturday except in winter. **Known for:** casual cuisine at great prices for a Thomas Keller restaurant; don't-miss buttermilk-fried-chicken night; Burgers & Half Bottles (of wine) pop-up. [$] *Average main: $56* ✉ *6476 Washington St.* ✥ *At Oak Circle* ☎ *707/944–2487* 🌐 *www.thomaskeller.com/adhoc* ⏲ *Closed Tues. and Wed.; no lunch Mon. and Thurs.* ☞ *Check website or call a day ahead for next day's menu.*

★ Bistro Jeanty

$$$ | **FRENCH** | Escargots, cassoulet, *steak au poivre* (pepper steak), and other French classics are prepared with the utmost precision inside this tan-brick country bistro whose flower-filled window boxes, extra-wide shutters, and red-and-white-striped awning hint at the Old World flair and joie de vivre that infuse the place. Regulars often start with the rich tomato soup in a flaky puff pastry before proceeding to sole meunière or coq au vin, completing the French sojourn with a lemon meringue tart or other authentic dessert. **Known for:** traditional preparations; oh-so-French atmosphere; patio seating. [$] *Average main: $30* ✉ *6510 Washington St.* ✥ *At Mulberry St.* ☎ *707/944–0103* 🌐 *www.bistrojeanty.com.*

Bottega

$$$ | **ITALIAN** | At his softly lit, exposed-redbrick downtown trattoria, which occupies sections of the 19th-century former Groezinger Winery, chef Michael Chiarello (Food Network, etcetera) and his team transform local ingredients into regional Italian cuisine. Seasonally changing plates—perhaps ricotta gnocchi with tomato sauce or smoked/braised short rib in espresso *agrodolce* (sweet-and-sour sauce) served with creamy ancient-grain polenta—show the chef at his most rustic yet sophisticated. **Known for:** romantic setting; gluten-free items; Italian and California wines. [$] *Average main: $28* ✉ *6525 Washington St.* ✥ *Near Mulberry St.* ☎ *707/945–1050* 🌐 *www.bottegnapavalley.com* ⏲ *Closed Mon.*

★ Bouchon Bistro

$$$ | **FRENCH** | The team that created The French Laundry is also behind this place, where everything—the zinc-topped bar, antique sconces, suave waitstaff, and traditional French onion soup—could have come straight from a Parisian bistro. Pan-seared rib eye with béarnaise and mussels steamed with white wine, saffron, and Dijon mustard—both served with crispy, addictive fries—are among the perfectly executed entrées. **Known for:** bistro classics; raw bar; Bouchon Bakery next door. [$] *Average main: $35* ✉ *6534 Washington St.* ✥ *Near Humboldt St.* ☎ *707/944–8037* 🌐 *thomaskeller.com/bouchonyountville.*

Brix Napa Valley

$$$ | **MODERN AMERICAN** | A southern Napa Valley roadside stop for specialty

cocktails, casual lunches, and evening fine dining, Brix shares ownership with Kelleher Family Vineyards, whose Cabernet Sauvignon grapevines surround the restaurant on three sides. King salmon, juicy Brix burgers, house-made pasta, and risotto appear on both the lunch and dinner menus, with prime rib and fried chicken the crowd-pleasers on Sunday and Wednesday nights respectively. **Known for:** verdant outdoor dining areas; Napa/Sonoma–centric wine list with older-vintage surprises; Sunday brunch. $ *Average main: $33* ✉ *7377 St. Helena Hwy., Napa* ✛ *1½ miles north of Yountville* ☎ *707/944–2749* ⊕ *www.brix.com* ⊘ *Closed Mon. and Tues. early Nov.–Feb.*

Ciccio

$$ | **MODERN ITALIAN** | The ranch of Ciccio's owners, Frank and Karen Altamura, supplies some of the vegetables and herbs for the modern Italian cuisine prepared in the open kitchen of this remodeled former grocery store. Seasonal growing cycles dictate the menu, with fried-seafood appetizers (calamari, perhaps, or softshell crabs), a few pasta dishes, herb-crusted fish, and several pizzas among the likely offerings. **Known for:** Negroni bar; pizzas' flavorful cheeses; mostly Napa Valley wines, some from owners' winery. $ *Average main: $23* ✉ *6770 Washington St.* ✛ *At Madison St.* ☎ *707/945–1000* ⊕ *www.ciccionapavalley.com* ⊘ *Closed Mon. and Tues. No lunch.*

Coqueta Napa Valley

$$$ | **SPANISH** | From *pintxos* (small plates) and paellas to Iberian cheeses and fish *a la plancha* (flat-grilled), the chefs at this Wine Country offspring of Michael Chiarello's successful San Francisco restaurant Coqueta reimagine Spanish classics with a 21st-century farm-to-table sensibility. The frenetic pace in the flame-happy open kitchen, inside Yountville's redbrick former railroad depot, keeps the mood lively in the relatively small dining space, with the vibe on the patio out back even

more so. **Known for:** sensual flavors; dynamic spicing; seasonal cocktails inspired by Spain and the Napa Valley. $ *Average main: $32* ✉ *6525 Washington St.* ✛ *Near Yount St.* ☎ *707/244–4350* ⊕ *www.coquetanv.com/home* ⊘ *Closed Tues. and Wed.*

★ The French Laundry

$$$$ | **AMERICAN** | An old stone building laced with ivy houses chef Thomas Keller's destination restaurant. Some courses on the two prix-fixe menus, one of which highlights vegetables, rely on luxe ingredients such as *calotte* (cap of the rib eye); others take humble elements like carrots or fava beans and elevate them to art. **Known for:** signature starter "oysters and pearls"; sea urchin, black truffles, and other "supplements"; superior wine list. $ *Average main: $350* ✉ *6640 Washington St.* ✛ *At Creek St.* ☎ *707/944–2380* ⊕ *www.frenchlaundry.com* ⊘ *No lunch Mon.–Thurs.* ⌂ *Jacket required* ☞ *Reservations essential wks ahead.*

La Calenda

$$ | **MEXICAN** | A few steps south of his Bouchon Bistro, chef Thomas Keller opened this ivy-covered restaurant serving Oaxacan-inspired Mexican cuisine. The decor inside is airily upscale casual, though on sunny days most patrons head to the streetside patio to dine on dishes like tacos *al pastor* (with slow-grilled pork), chicken enchiladas with mole, and *pescado zarandeado verde* (grilled marinated fish with green salsa). **Known for:** house margarita; churros with dulce de leche for dessert; patio people-watching. $ *Average main: $21* ✉ *6518 Washington St.* ✛ *At Yount St.* ☎ *833/682–8226* ⊕ *www.lacalendamex.com.*

Mustards Grill

$$$ | **AMERICAN** | Cindy Pawlcyn's Mustards Grill fills day and night with fans of her hearty cuisine, equal parts updated renditions of traditional American dishes—what Pawlcyn dubs "deluxe truck

stop classics"—and fanciful contemporary fare. Barbecued baby back pork ribs and a lemon-lime tart piled high with brown-sugar meringue fall squarely in the first category, and sweet corn tamales with tomatillo-avocado salsa and wild mushrooms represent the latter. **Known for:** roadhouse setting; convivial mood; hoppin' bar. $ Average main: $30 ⊠ 7399 St. Helena Hwy./Hwy. 29, Napa ✚ 1 mile north of Yountville ☎ 707/944–2424 ⊕ www.mustardsgrill.com.

North Block

$$$ | MODERN AMERICAN | In his California debut, chef Nick Tamburo, previously of two Manhattan locations of celeb chef David Chang's Momofuku, prepares farm-to-table cuisine with intriguing flavors and ingredients. A recent starter paired oro blanco (a grapefruitlike citrus) and ever-so-thinly sliced kohlrabi (a type of turnip) spiced to marvelous effect with the mildly minty Japanese herb shiso, the chef's artistry repeating itself on the menu's wood-fired pizzas and fish and meat entrées. **Known for:** courtyard patio seating; cocktails and wine list; atmospheric interior. $ Average main: $35 ⊠ North Block Hotel, 6757 Washington St. ✚ Near Madison St. ☎ 707/944–8080 ⊕ www.northblockhotel.com/dining.

★ Perry Lang's

$$$$ | STEAKHOUSE | An 1870 redbrick former mansion holds this contemporary chophouse whose art-deco accents recall an old-school gentlemen's club—the kind of place to order a stiff cocktail, a wedge salad topped with thick maple-glazed bacon, and a dry-aged rib eye or tomahawk. Chef Adam Perry Lang, a grilling and barbecue artiste, seduces patrons with culinary drama and hand-tooled steak knives so exquisite it's a felony to swipe them, delivering the goods with an experience that satisfies appetite and soul. **Known for:** St. Louis pork ribs with peach barbecue sauce; Cabernet bone-marrow jus and béarnaise and horseradish sauces for steaks; potent craft cocktails. $ Average main: $40 ⊠ 6539 Washington St. ✚ Just south of Vintage House ☎ 707/945–4522 ⊕ perrylangs.com ⊘ No lunch.

R+D Kitchen

$$ | ECLECTIC | As the name suggests, the chefs at this restaurant with an expansive patio often packed on weekends are willing to experiment, starting with sushi plates that include spicy hiramasa (yellowtail kingfish) rolls topped with rainbow-trout caviar. Among the items served at both lunch and dinner are rotisserie chicken, the buttermilk fried-chicken sandwich topped with Swiss, and a slow-roasted pork sandwich served with coleslaw. **Known for:** good value; cheerful staff; Dip Duo (guacamole and pimento cheese with chips) on patio bar menu. $ Average main: $25 ⊠ 6795 Washington St. ✚ At Madison St. ☎ 707/945–0920 ⊕ rd-kitchen.com/locations/yountville.

RH Yountville Restaurant

$$$ | MODERN AMERICAN | Crystal chandeliers and fountains worthy of a French château supply the pizzazz at Restoration Hardware's streetside café, and the all-day menu's starters (charcuterie, shrimp cocktail, crispy artichoke), salads, and mains (from a burger modeled on one from Chicago's Au Cheval restaurant to delicate Atlantic sole in brown butter) easily live up to it. The prosciutto is flown in from Parma and the burrata from Puglia, the greens are ever-so-fresh, and the plating impresses. **Known for:** streetside patio; shaved rib-eye sandwich; Bellini with prosecco and peach purée. $ Average main: $32 ⊠ 6725 Washington St. ✚ At Pedroni St. ☎ 707/339–4654 ⊕ www.restorationhardware.com.

Southside Yountville at Stewart Cellars

$ | MODERN AMERICAN | Comfort food for breakfast and lunch never looked as pretty as it does at the Yountville outpost of local-fave Southside Napa. The Latin-tinged California cuisine changes with the season but might include stone-fruit and ricotta toast for breakfast and shrimp ceviche tostadas for lunch. **Known for:** buttermilk biscuits and chorizo-sausage gravy; wine available (separately) from tasting room; healthful items like "superfood" and protein bowls. [$] *Average main: $14* ✉ *6752 Washington St.* ✥ *Near Pedroni St.* ☎ *707/947–7120* 🌐 *www.southsidenapa.com/southside-yountville* ⏲ *No dinner.*

Hotels

★ Bardessono

$$$$ | **RESORT** | Tranquility and luxury with a low carbon footprint are among the goals of this ultragreen wood, steel, and glass resortlike property in downtown Yountville, but there's nothing spartan about the accommodations, arranged around four landscaped courtyards. **Pros:** large rooftop lap pool; in-room spa treatments; three luxury villas for extra privacy. **Cons:** expensive year-round; limited view from some rooms; a bit of street traffic on hotel's west side. [$] *Rooms from: $750* ✉ *6526 Yount St.* ☎ *707/204–6000, 855/232–0450* 🌐 *www.bardessono.com* 🛏 *65 rooms* 🍴 *No meals.*

Hotel Villagio

$$$$ | **RESORT** | At this slick yet inviting downtown haven of tranquility, the streamlined furnishings, subdued color schemes, and high ceilings create a sense of spaciousness in the rooms and suites, each of which has a wood-burning fireplace and a balcony or patio. **Pros:** central location; steps from restaurants and tasting rooms; 13,000-square-foot spa. **Cons:** staff could be more solicitous; highway noise audible from some rooms on property's west side; expensive on weekends in high season. [$] *Rooms from: $475* ✉ *6481 Washington St.* ☎ *707/927–1991, 800/351–1133* 🌐 *www.villagio.com* 🛏 *113 rooms* 🍴 *Free breakfast.*

Hotel Yountville

$$$$ | **HOTEL** | The landscaped woodsy setting, resortlike pool area, and exclusive yet casual ambience of the Hotel Yountville attract travelers wanting to get away from it all yet still be close—but not too close—to fine dining and tasting rooms. **Pros:** chic rooms; close to Yountville fine dining; high ceilings in upper-floor rooms. **Cons:** occasional service lapses that are unusual at this price point; expensive in high season; minimum-stay requirement some weekends. [$] *Rooms from: $550* ✉ *6462 Washington St.* ☎ *707/967–7900, 855/232–0452* 🌐 *www.hotelyountville.com* 🛏 *80 rooms* 🍴 *No meals.*

★ Lavender Inn

$$$ | **B&B/INN** | Travelers looking for personalized service from innkeepers who take the trouble to learn guests' names and preferences will enjoy this intimate inn just off Yountville's main drag. **Pros:** on-site free bike rental; use of pool at nearby sister property; personalized service. **Cons:** hard to book in high season; lacks amenities of larger properties; not sceney enough for some guests. [$] *Rooms from: $349* ✉ *2020 Webber St.* ☎ *707/944–1388* 🌐 *www.lavendernapa.com* 🛏 *9 rooms* 🍴 *Free breakfast.*

Maison Fleurie

$$ | **B&B/INN** | A stay at this comfortable, reasonably priced inn, said to be the oldest hotel in the Napa Valley, places you within walking distance of Yountville's fine restaurants. **Pros:** smallest rooms a bargain; outdoor hot tub and pool; free bike rental. **Cons:** lacks amenities of a full-service hotel; some rooms pick up noise from nearby Bouchon Bakery; hard to book in high season. [$] *Rooms from: $229* ✉ *6529 Yount St.* ☎ *707/944–2056* 🌐 *www.maisonfleurienapa.com* 🛏 *13 rooms* 🍴 *Free breakfast.*

Napa Valley Lodge

$$ | **HOTEL** | Clean rooms in a convenient motel-style setting draw travelers willing to pay more than at comparable lodgings in the city of Napa to be within walking distance of Yountville's tasting rooms, restaurants, and shops. **Pros:** well maintained rooms; vineyard-view rooms

on north and west sides; large pool area. **Cons:** no elevator; nice enough but lacks panache; pricey on weekends in high season. $ *Rooms from: $285* ✉ *2230 Madison St.* ☎ *707/944–2468, 888/944–3545* ⊕ *www.napavalleylodge.com* ⤶ *55 rooms* ❍❘ *Free breakfast.*

Napa Valley Railway Inn

$$ | HOTEL | Budget-minded travelers and those with kids appreciate these basic accommodations—inside actual railcars—just steps from Yountville's best restaurants. **Pros:** central location; quaint appeal; semi-reasonable rates. **Cons:** office is sometimes unstaffed; sells out quickly in high season; lacks pool, fitness center, and other amenities. $ *Rooms from: $245* ✉ *6523 Washington St.* ☎ *707/944–2000* ⊕ *www.napavalleyrail-wayinn.com* ⤶ *9 rooms* ❍❘ *No meals.*

★ North Block Hotel

$$$$ | HOTEL | A two-story boutique property near downtown Yountville's northern edge, the North Block attracts sophisticated travelers who appreciate the clever but unpretentious style and offhand luxury. **Pros:** extremely comforta-ble beds; personalized service; spacious bathrooms. **Cons:** outdoor areas get some traffic noise; weekend minimum-stay requirement; rates soar on high-sea-son weekends. $ *Rooms from: $540* ✉ *6757 Washington St.* ☎ *707/944–8080* ⊕ *northblockhotel.com* ⤶ *20 rooms* ❍❘ *No meals.*

★ Poetry Inn

$$$$ | B&B/INN | All the rooms at this splurge-worthy hillside retreat have full vistas of the lower Napa Valley from their westward-facing balconies; indoors the comfortably chic decor and amenities that include a private spa and a fully stocked wine cellar only add to the pleas-ure of a stay. **Pros:** valley views; discreet, polished service; gourmet breakfasts. **Cons:** expensive pretty much year-round; party types might find atmosphere too low-key; shops and restaurants 3 miles away. $ *Rooms from: $1300* ✉ *6380*

Silverado Trail ☎ *707/944–0646* ⊕ *poetry-inn.com* ⤶ *5 rooms* ❍❘ *Free breakfast.*

Vintage House

$$$$ | RESORT | Part of the 22-acre Estate Yountville complex—other sections include sister lodging Hotel Villagio, the 13,000-square-foot Spa at the Estate, and shops and restaurants—this downtown hotel consists of two-story brick buildings along verdant landscaped paths shaded by mature trees. **Pros:** aesthetically pleasing accommodations; private patios and balconies; secluded feeling yet near shops, tasting rooms, and restaurants. **Cons:** highway noise audible in some exterior rooms; very expensive on summer and fall weekends; weekend minimum-stay requirement. $ *Rooms from: $429* ✉ *6541 Washington St.* ☎ *707/944–1112, 877/351–1153* ⊕ *www.vintagehouse.com* ⤶ *80 rooms* ❍❘ *Free breakfast.*

🛍 Shopping

CLOTHING

The Conservatory

CLOTHING | The New York City–based lifestyle company's heavily curated "considered luxury" comes in the form of clothing, accessories, and decor and well-being items created by small, quality-oriented brands for a discerning clientele. Local products include Vintner's Daughter Active Botanical Serum face oil, whose adherents swear nearly stops time. ✉ *6540 Washington St.* ✛ *Near Humboldt St.* ☎ *707/415–5015* ⊕ *thecon-servatorynyc.com/pages/napa-store.*

FOOD AND WINE

Kelly's Filling Station and Wine Shop

CONVENIENCE/GENERAL STORES | The fuel is more than petrol at this gas station–convenience store whose design recalls the heyday of Route 66 travel. The shop inside sells top-rated wines, hot dogs, fresh scones from nearby R+D Kitchen, gourmet chocolates, and (in summer) ice cream. Gas up, grab some picnic items, order coffee, espresso, or a cool drink to go, and be ever-so-merrily on your way. ⊠ *6795 Washington St.* ✛ *At Madison St.* ☎ *707/944–8165.*

Kollar Chocolates

FOOD/CANDY | The aromas alone will lure you into this shop selling artisanal European-style chocolates created on-site. The imaginative truffles, many incorporating local ingredients, include lavender with dark chocolate and fennel pollen with milk chocolate. ⊠ *The Estate Yountville, 6525 Washington St., 1st Floor* ☎ *707/738–6750* ⊕ *www.kollarchocolates.com.*

 Activities

Balloons Above the Valley

BALLOONING | This company's personable and professional pilots make outings a delight. Hosts pick up guests at their lodgings and return them when the flight is over. ⊠ *Napa* ☎ *707/253–2222, 800/464–6824* ⊕ *www.balloonrides.com* 🖅 *From $300 (per person, two-person minimum; discount for additional guests).*

Napa Valley Aloft

BALLOONING | Passengers soar over the Napa Valley in balloons that launch from downtown Yountville. Flights are from 40 minutes to an hour-plus, depending on the wind speed, with the entire experience taking from three to four hours. ⊠ *The Estate Yountville, 6525 Washington St.* ✛ *Near Mulberry St.* ☎ *707/944–4400, 855/944–4408* ⊕ *www.nvaloft.com* 🖅 *$250 per person.*

Napa Valley Bike Tours

BICYCLING | With dozens of wineries within 5 miles, this shop makes a fine starting point for guided and self-guided vineyard and wine-tasting excursions. Rental bikes are also available. ⊠ *6500 Washington St.* ✛ *At Mulberry St.* ☎ *707/251–8687* ⊕ *www.napavalleybiketours.com* 🖅 *From $124 (½-day guided tour).*

SPAS
B Spa

FITNESS/HEALTH CLUBS | Many of this spa's patrons are Bardessono Hotel guests who take their treatments in their rooms' large, customized bathrooms—all of them equipped with concealed massage tables—but the main facility is open to nonguests as well. An in-room treatment favored by couples starts with massages in front of the fireplace and ends with a bath and sparkling wine. The two-hour Yountville Signature Experience, which can be enjoyed in-room or at the spa, begins with a shea-butter-enriched sugar scrub, followed by a Chardonnay grape-seed oil massage and a hydrating hair-and-scalp treatment. The spa engages massage therapists skilled in Swedish, Thai, and other techniques. In addition to massages, the services include facials and other skin-care treatments. ⊠ *Bardessono Hotel, 6526 Yount St.* ✛ *At Mulberry St.* ☎ *707/204–6050* ⊕ *www. bardessono.com/spa* 🖅 *Treatments from $165.*

The Spa at The Estate

FITNESS/HEALTH CLUBS | The joint 13,000-square-foot facility of Vintage House and the Hotel Villagio is a five-minute walk from the former's lobby, even less from the latter's. Private spa suites are popular with couples, who enjoy the separate relaxation areas, indoor and outdoor fireplaces, steam showers, saunas, and extra-large tubs. Many treatments involve Omorovicza products based on Hungarian thermal waters and minerals. For a quick uplift, book 20 minutes in the spa's oxygen chair, designed to optimize breathing and promote relaxation. Facials, lip plumping, and massages are among the other à la carte services. The ground-floor retail area, open to the public, is well stocked with beauty products. ⊠ *The Estate Yountville, 6481 Washington St.* ✛ *At Oak Circle* ☎ *707/948–5050* ⊕ *www.villagio.com/spa* 🖅 *Treatments from $85.*

Oakville

2 miles northwest of Yountville.

Barely a blip on the landscape as you drive north on Highway 29, Oakville is marked mainly by its grocery store, but the town's small size belies the big splash it makes in the wine-making world. Slightly warmer than Yountville and Carneros to the south, but a few degrees cooler than Rutherford and St. Helena to the north, the Oakville area benefits from gravelly, well-drained soil. This allows roots to go deep—sometimes more than 100 feet—so that the vines produce intensely flavored fruit. Cabernet Sauvignon from the most famous vineyard here, To Kalon, at the base of the Mayacamas range, goes into many top-rated wines from winemakers throughout the valley. Big-name wineries within this appellation include Silver Oak, Far Niente, and Robert Mondavi.

Getting Here and Around

If you're driving along Highway 29, you'll know you've reached Oakville when you see the Oakville Grocery on the east side of the road. Here the Oakville Cross Road provides access to the Silverado Trail (head east). Oakville wineries are scattered along Highway 29, Oakville Cross Road, and the Silverado Trail in roughly equal measure.

You can reach Oakville from the town of Glen Ellen in Sonoma County by heading east on Trinity Road from Highway 12. The twisting route, along the mountain range that divides Napa and Sonoma counties, eventually becomes the Oakville Grade. The views of both valleys on this drive are breathtaking, though the continual curves make it unsuitable for those who suffer from motion sickness. VINE buses serve Oakville.

◉ Sights

B Cellars

WINERY/DISTILLERY | The chefs take center stage in the open-hearth kitchen of this boutique winery's hospitality house, and with good reason: creating food-friendly wines is B Cellars's raison d'être. Visits to the Oakville facility—all steel beams, corrugated metal, and plate glass yet remarkably cozy—often begin with a tour of the winery's culinary garden and vineyard, with a pause for sips of wine still aging in barrel. A seated tasting of finished wines paired with small bites follows the tour. Kirk Venge, whose fruit-forward style suits the winery's food-oriented approach, crafts red and white blends and single-vineyard Cabernets from estate fruit and grapes from Beckstoffer and other noteworthy vineyards. All visits are strictly by appointment. ✉ 703 Oakville Cross Rd. ⊹ West of Silverado Trail ☎ 707/709–8787 ⊕ www.bcellars. com ☎ Tastings from $80 ⊗ Closed Tues. and Wed.

Far Niente

WINERY/DISTILLERY | Hamden McIntyre, a prominent winery architect of his era also responsible for Inglenook and what's now the Culinary Institute of America at Greystone, designed the centerpiece 1885 stone winery here. Abandoned in the wake of Prohibition and only revived beginning in 1979, Far Niente now ranks as one of the Napa Valley's most beautiful properties. Guests participating in the Estate Tasting learn some of this history while sipping the flagship wines, a Chardonnay and a Cabernet Sauvignon blend, along with Russian River Valley Pinot Noir from the affiliated EnRoute label and Dolce, a late-harvest Sémillon and Sauvignon Blanc wine. The Extended Estate Tasting takes in the winery and its aging caves, while the Library Wine Tasting compares older vintages. ✉ 1350 Acacia Dr. ⊹ Off Oakville Grade Rd. ☎ 707/944–2861 ⊕ www.farniente.com ☎ Tastings from $80.

Far Niente ages its Cabernets and Chardonnays in 40,000 square feet of caves.

★ Nickel & Nickel

WINERY/DISTILLERY | A corral out front, antique barns, and a farm-style windmill add horse-country flair to this winery renowned for its smooth, almost sensual, single-vineyard Cabernet Sauvignons. Some of the best derive from the home-base Oakville AVA, in particular the John C. Sullenger Vineyard, which surrounds the property's 1884 Queen Anne residence. Cabernets from other Napa Valley appellations supply the contrast. For the splurge Terroir Tasting, hosts introduce eight Cabernets, paired with artisanal cheeses and charcuterie, describing how each vineyard's distinctive soils and microclimates influence the finished product. Two other tastings explore similar issues less comprehensively. ■TIP→ **Cabernet lovers won't want to miss this sister winery to elegant Far Niente.** ⊠ *8164 St. Helena Hwy./ Hwy. 129 ✛ North of Oakville Cross Rd.* ☎ *707/967–9600* ⊕ *www.nickelandnickel. com* ⊠ *Tastings $80–$150.*

Oakville Wine Merchant

WINERY/DISTILLERY | Survey the Napa Valley under Baccarat crystal chandeliers at this combination wine bar and museum next to Oakville Grocery. After purchasing a payment card, guests proceed on their own or guided by hosts to wine dispensers. In 2-, 4-, or 6-ounce pours you can sample, say, Cabernets from a single AVA, or perhaps compare ones from several subappellations. The museum's displays about wine making and the valley include intriguing farm implements like "soil injectors" formerly used to blast insecticides into the soil. ■TIP→ **You don't need to taste to tour the free museum.** ⊠ *7856 St. Helena Hwy./Hwy. 29 ✛ At Oakville Cross Rd.* ☎ *707/948–6099* ⊕ *1881napa.com* ⊠ *Tastings from $20.*

Robert Mondavi Winery

WINERY/DISTILLERY | Arguably the most influential participant in the Napa Valley's rise to international prominence, the late Robert Mondavi established his namesake winery in the 1960s after losing a battle with his brother over the direction

Oakville's Nickel & Nickel pairs horse-country flair with single-vineyard Cabernets.

of their family's Charles Krug Winery. In an era when tasting rooms were mostly downscale affairs, Mondavi commissioned architect Cliff May to create a grand Mission-style space to receive visitors. May's design still resonates, the graceful central arch framing the lawn and the vineyard behind, inviting a stroll under the arcades. The Estate Tour & Tasting and Vintner's Tasting provide an introduction to the winery, its portfolio, and Mondavi's life. Another offering focuses on whites and caviar, with a third involving Cabernet Sauvignon from the Mondavi section of the famed To Kalon Vineyard. All visits require a reservation, with last-minute requests often granted. ⊠ *7801 St. Helena Hwy./Hwy. 29* ☎ *888/766–6328* ⊕ *www.robertmondaviwinery.com* ⌕ *Tastings and tours from $40.*

Saddleback Cellars

WINERY/DISTILLERY | A short drive down a country lane leads to this winery whose founder, Nils Venge, made history as the first U.S. winemaker to earn a 100-point score. The wine that earned Venge this distinction was a Cabernet Sauvignon for nearby Groth. He makes two Cabs for his own label, along with Pinot Blanc, Sangiovese, Zinfandel, Malbec, and several others guests sample by appointment at vineyard's-edge picnic tables. Compared to its tonier Oakville neighbors, Saddleback's presentation is decidedly retro, but the stories, wines, and mountain views east and west cast a memorable spell. ⊠ *7802 Money Rd.* ⊹ *Off Oakville Cross Rd* ☎ *707/944–1305* ⊕ *www.saddlebackcellars.com* ⌕ *Tasting $30.*

★ Silver Oak

WINERY/DISTILLERY | The first review of this winery's Napa Valley Cabernet Sauvignon declared the debut 1972 vintage not all that good and, at $6 a bottle, overpriced. Oops. The celebrated Bordeaux-style Cabernet blend, still the only Napa Valley wine bearing its winery's label each year, evolved into a cult favorite, and founders Ray Duncan and Justin Meyer received worldwide recognition for their signature use of exclusively American oak to age the wines. At the Oakville tasting room, constructed out of reclaimed stone and other materials from a 19th-century Kansas flour mill, the Silver Oak Tasting includes sips of the current Napa Valley vintage, its counterpart from Silver Oak's Alexander Valley operation in Sonoma County, and a library wine. Hosts of vertical tastings pour six Cabernet vintages. All visits require an appointment. ✉ *915 Oakville Cross Rd.* ✣ *Off Hwy. 29* ☎ *707/942–7022* 🌐 *www.silveroak.com* 🎟 *Tastings $40–$85.*

🍴 Restaurants

Oakville Grocery
$ | DELI | Built in 1881 as a general store, Oakville Grocery carries high-end groceries and prepared foods. On summer weekends, customers stocking up on picnic provisions—meats, cheeses, breads, pizzas, and gourmet sandwiches—pack the place, but during the week it serves as a mellow pit stop to sip an espresso out front, picnic out back, or taste wines at Oakville Wine Merchant next door. **Known for:** breakfast quiches, scones, muffins; BLTA and chicken Gruyère sandwiches; lots of Napa and Sonoma wines. [$] *Average main: $14* ✉ *7856 St. Helena Hwy./Hwy. 29* ✣ *At Oakville Cross Rd.* ☎ *707/944–8802* 🌐 *www.oakvillegrocery.com.*

Rutherford

2 miles northwest of Oakville.

The spot where Highway 29 meets Rutherford Road in the tiny community of Rutherford may well be the most significant wine-related intersection in the United States. With its singular microclimate and soil, Rutherford is an important viticultural center, with more big-name wineries than you can shake a corkscrew at, including Beaulieu, Inglenook, Mumm Napa, and St. Supéry.

Cabernet Sauvignon is king here. The soil is ideal for those vines, and since this part of the valley gets plenty of sun, the grapes develop intense flavors. Legendary winemaker André Tchelistcheff's famous claim that "it takes Rutherford dust to grow great Cabernet" is quoted by just about every area winery that produces the stuff. That "dust," courtesy of the region's primarily gravel, sand, and loam soils, imparts faint chocolaty notes you may detect in the reds.

Getting Here and Around

Wineries line Highway 29 and parallel Silverado Trail north and south of Rutherford Road/Conn Creek Road, which connects the two roads. VINE buses serve Rutherford.

Visitor Information

CONTACT Rutherford Dust Society. ☎ *707/987–9821* 🌐 *www.rutherforddust.org.*

👁 Sights

Beaulieu Vineyard
WINERY/DISTILLERY | The influential André Tchelistcheff (1901–1994), who helped define the California style of wine making, worked his magic here for many years. BV, founded in 1900 by Georges de Latour and his wife, Fernande, makes several widely distributed wines, but others are produced in small lots and are available only at the winery. The most famous of these is the Georges de Latour Private Reserve Cabernet Sauvignon, first crafted in the late 1930s. All visits require a reservation. **■ TIP→ Book a Cabernet Collector Tasting ($50) to sample current and older Cabernet Sauvignons and the most recent Georges de Latour vintage.**

Prohibition and Depression

The National Prohibition Act, which passed in 1919 under the popular name of the Volstead Act, had far-reaching effects on California wineries. Prohibition forced many to shut down altogether, but some, particularly Napa operations such as Beaulieu Vineyard, Beringer, and (on the St. Helena site now occupied by the Culinary Institute of America) the Christian Brothers, stayed in business by making sacramental wines. Others took advantage of the exception permitting home wine making and sold grapes and in some cases do-it-yourself kits with "warnings" about the steps that would result in grape juice turning into wine. A few wineries kept their inventories in bond, storing their wine in warehouses certified by the Department of Internal Revenue and guaranteed secure by bonding agencies. Magically, wine flowed out the back doors of the bonded warehouses into barrels and jugs brought by customers, and just as magically it seemed to replenish itself. Now and then a revenuer would crack down, but enforcement was lax at best.

Struggle and Survival
Prohibition, which ended in 1933, did less damage in the Napa Valley, where grapes thrive but fruit trees grow poorly on the rocky and gravelly slopes, benchlands, and alluvial fans, than it did in Sonoma County, where plum, walnut, and other orchards had replaced many vineyards. Fewer Napa growers had been able to convert to other crops, and more had been able to survive with sacramental wine, so more vineyards could be brought back to fine-wine production after repeal. Several major wineries survived Prohibition, including Inglenook and Charles Krug (acquired in the 1940s by the Cesare Mondavi family), which made very good wines during this period. Nevertheless, the wine industry struggled well into the 1960s to regain its customer base.

✉ 1960 St. Helena Hwy./Hwy. 29 ✛ At Hwy. 128 ☏ 707/257–5749 ⊕ www.bvwines.com ✉ Tastings from $50 ☉ Closed Mon.–Wed. (but check).

Cakebread Cellars
WINERY/DISTILLERY | Jack and Dolores Cakebread were among the wave of early-1970s vintners whose efforts raised the Napa Valley's wine-making profile and initiated what became known as the Wine Country lifestyle. The revamped tasting experiences at a redwood-lined hospitality center that opened in 2019 updated that lifestyle to contemporary sensibilities while still honoring the winery's history. Chardonnay and Cabernet Sauvignon helped establish the company, which makes so many other wines—among them Sauvignon Blanc, rosé, Merlot, Pinot Noir, Syrah, and sundry red blends—that you can opt for an all-reds or all-whites tasting. All visits are by appointment. ■ TIP→ The Cakebread Classic survey of current releases provides a good introduction; for a deeper dive, book one of the wine-and-food pairings or the library tasting of older vintages. ✉ 8300 St. Helena Hwy./Hwy. 29 ☏ 707/963–5222 for info, 800/588–0298 for reservations ⊕ www.cakebread.com ✉ Tastings from $30.

Caymus Vineyards
WINERY/DISTILLERY | This winery's Special Selection Cabernet Sauvignon twice won *Wine Spectator* wine of the year. In good weather you can sample the latest

vintage and a few other wines outdoors in a landscaped area in front of the tasting room. Chuck Wagner started making wine on this property in 1972 and still oversees Caymus production. His children craft wines for other brands within the Wagner Family of Wine portfolio, including oaked and unoaked Mer Soleil Chardonnays, a Pinot Noir, Conundrum white and red blends, Red Schooner Malbec, and Emmolo Sauvignon Blanc and Merlot. All Caymus visits require an appointment. ⊠ *8700 Conn Creek Rd.* ⊹ *Off Rutherford Rd.* ☎ *707/967–3010* ⊕ *www.caymus.com* ⊠ *Tasting $50.*

Elizabeth Spencer Winery

WINERY/DISTILLERY | Although its first vintage (1998) debuted long after those of neighbors Inglenook and Beaulieu, this winery lays claim to a slice of Rutherford history: guests gain entry to the courtyard tasting area via the town's 1872 redbrick former post office. Varietal and geographical variety is a primary goal, with Cabernet Sauvignon, Grenache, Merlot, Pinot Noir, and Syrah among the reds produced from Napa, Sonoma, and Mendocino county grapes. Whites include Chardonnay, Pinot Blanc, and Sauvignon Blanc. Tastings, all seated, require an appointment. ⊠ *1165 Rutherford Rd.* ⊹ *At Hwy. 29* ☎ *707/963–6067* ⊕ *www.elizabethspencerwinery.com* ⊠ *Tastings $40–$65* ⊙ *Closed Mon. and Tues.*

★ Frog's Leap

WINERY/DISTILLERY | If you're a novice, the tour at eco-friendly Frog's Leap is a fun way to begin your education. Conducted by hosts with a sense of humor, the tour stops by a barn built in 1884, 5 acres of organic gardens, and a frog pond topped with lily pads. The winery produced its first vintage, small batches of Sauvignon Blanc and Zinfandel, in 1981, adding Chardonnay and Cabernet Sauvignon the next year. These days Chenin Blanc is another white, with Merlot, Petite Sirah, and the Heritage Blend of classic Napa

Valley varietals among the other reds. All visits require a reservation. ■ T I P → **The tour is recommended, but you can forgo it and taste on a garden-view porch.** ⊠ *8815 Conn Creek Rd.* ☎ *707/963–4704* ⊕ *www.frogsleap.com* ⊠ *Tastings $45–$95, tour and tasting $75.*

Honig Vineyard & Winery

WINERY/DISTILLERY | **FAMILY** | Sustainable farming is the big story at this family-run winery. When offered, the absorbing Eco-Tour and Tasting focuses on the Honig family's environmentally friendly farming and production methods, which include using biodiesel to fuel the tractors, monitoring water use in the vineyard and winery, and generating power with solar panels. Bluebirds, hawks, and owls patrol for insects, rodents, and other pests; trained golden retrievers spot vine-damaging mealybugs early, eliminating the need for heavy pesticides. Known for Sauvignon Blanc and Cabernet Sauvignon, the Honigs also make rosé of Cabernet and late-harvest Sauvignon Blanc. All tastings are by appointment. ⊠ *850 Rutherford Rd.* ⊹ *Near Conn Creek Rd.* ☎ *800/929–2217* ⊕ *www.honigwine.com* ⊠ *Tastings from $30.*

★ Inglenook

WINERY/DISTILLERY | *Wine Enthusiast* magazine bestowed a lifetime-achievement award on vintner-filmmaker Francis Ford Coppola, whose wine-world contributions include resurrecting the historic Inglenook estate. Over the decades he reunited the original property acquired by Inglenook founder Gustave Niebaum, remodeled Niebaum's ivy-covered 1880s château, and purchased the rights to the Inglenook name. The winery's place in Napa Valley history is among the topics discussed at tastings, some of which involve cheese, charcuterie, or other wine-food pairings. Most sessions see a pour of the signature Rubicon wine, a Cabernet Sauvignon–based blend. All visits require an appointment; call the winery or check at the visitor center for

4

Napa Valley

RUTHERFORD

same-day. ■TIP➔ **In lieu of a tasting, you can book a table at The Bistro, a wine bar with a picturesque courtyard, to sip wine by the glass or bottle.** ✉ *1991 St. Helena Hwy./Hwy. 29 ✛ At Hwy.128* ☎ *707/968–1100* ⊕ *www.inglenook.com* 🍷 *Tastings from $60* ⊘ *Closed Mon.–Wed.*

Mumm Napa

WINERY/DISTILLERY | When Champagne Mumm of France set about establishing a California sparkling-wine outpost, its winemaker chose the Napa Valley, where today the winery sources grapes from more than 50 local producers. Made in the *méthode traditionelle* style from Chardonnay, Pinot Noir, Pinot Meunier, and occasionally Pinot Gris, the wines are all fermented in the bottle. Most guests enjoy them alfresco, by the glass or flight, on a patio above the surrounding vineyards or one at eye level. Book an Oak Terrace Tasting to sample top-of-the-line cuvées under the sprawling branches of a blue oak nearly two centuries old. Tasting is by appointment only. ✉ *8445 Silverado Trail ✛ 1 mile south of Rutherford Cross Rd.* ☎ *707/967–7700* ⊕ *www. mummnapa.com* 🍷 *Tastings $40–$75.*

Piña Napa Valley

WINERY/DISTILLERY | The Piña family, whose Napa Valley heritage dates from the 1850s, is known locally as much for its first-rate vineyard-management company as its modest winery that specializes in single-vineyard, 100% Cabernet Sauvignon. Winemaker Anna Monticelli crafts these robust Cabs from mostly hillside fruit, all estate grown. Though she doesn't blend in other varietals, commonly done to soften Cabernet, the winery doesn't release its wines until age has mellowed them. If he's not busy elsewhere, Larry Piña, the genial managing partner and among his family's seventh generation involved in the wine business, often drops by during tastings. All require an appointment, with same-day guests accommodated when possible (but call ahead). ✉ *8060 Silverado Trail ✛ 0.2 miles*

north of Skellenger La. ☎ *707/738–9328* ⊕ *pinanapavalley.com* 🍷 *Tasting $20* ⊘ *Closed Tues. and Wed.*

Round Pond Estate

FARM/RANCH | Sophisticated wines come from Round Pond, but the estate also produces premium olive oils, most from olives grown and crushed on the property. Guests participating in the olive oil tasting, held across the street from the winery, pass through the high-tech olive mill and sample the aromatic oils, both alone and with house-made red-wine vinegars. Hosts at the winery tasting room pour Round Pond's well-rounded red and other wines. The flagship Estate Cabernet Sauvignon has the structure and heft of the classic 1970s Rutherford Cabs but acknowledges 21st-century palates with smoother, if still sturdy, tannins. Tastings, some of which involve food, are by appointment only (24–48 hours in advance). ■TIP➔ **The full Il Pranzo lunch incorporates products made and produce grown on-site, as does the Sunday brunch.** ✉ *875 Rutherford Rd. ✛ Near Conn Creek Rd.* ☎ *707/302–2575* ⊕ *www. roundpond.com* 🍷 *Tastings from $40.*

Sequoia Grove

WINERY/DISTILLERY | Sequoias shade the outdoor areas and century-old barn of this winery acclaimed for its single-vineyard Cabernet Sauvignons. Their fruit comes from two estate properties in Rutherford plus sourced grapes from that appellation and several other valley-floor and mountain AVAs. Sequoia Grove also makes Sauvignon Blanc, Cabernet Franc, Syrah, and a few others. A current-release tasting might include a single-vineyard Cab, but for a sense of how variations in terrain and microclimate influence Cabernet, choose the Single Vineyard experience. All visits require an appointment. ■TIP➔ **A Taste for Cabernet, a seminar that provides sometimes surprising insights into what foods best complement Cabernet Sauvignon, is worth considering if it's offered.** ✉ *8338 St.*

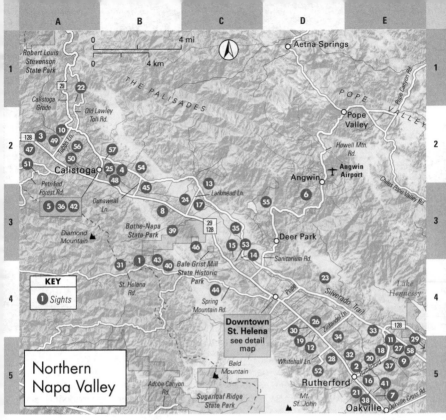

Northern Napa Valley

Round Pond Estate makes sophisticated wines and extra-virgin olive oils.

Helena Hwy./Hwy. 29 ✛ Near Bella Oaks La. ☎ 707/944–2945, 800/851–7841 ⊕ www.sequoiagrove.com ✉ Tastings from $30.

St. Supéry Estate Vineyards & Winery

WINERY/DISTILLERY | The French fashion company Chanel purchased St. Supéry in 2015, adding further glamour to this winery whose Rutherford vineyards surround its immaculate hospitality center and production facility. St. Supéry makes two widely distributed wines, a Sauvignon Blanc and a Cabernet Sauvignon, but most tastings revolve around limited-production efforts from the Rutherford property and the 1,500-acre Dollarhide Ranch on Howell Mountain. Hosts tailor sessions to guests' preferences, pouring, for instance, all whites or all reds. One of the latter tastings explores valley-floor and mountain Cabernet Sauvignon, another that varietal and four other Bordeaux grapes, Cabernet Franc, Malbec, Merlot, and Petit Verdot. Among the specialized experiences at this enthusiastic proponent of wine education, look

for the return of Aromatherapy with a Corkscrew, which involves blind sniffing and tasting to learn how to identify citrus, tropical, and other aromas in wines. ✉ 8440 St. Helena Hwy./Hwy. 29 ✛ Near Manley La. ☎ 707/963–4507 ⊕ www. stsupery.com ✉ Tastings from $40 ⊙ Closed Tues.

ZD Wines

WINERY/DISTILLERY | Founded in 1969 and still run by the same family, this winery specializing in Chardonnay, Pinot Noir, and Cabernet Sauvignon is respected for its organic practices, local philanthropy, and Abacus blend. Made "solera-style," Abacus contains wine from every ZD Reserve Cabernet Sauvignon vintage since 1992. The Chardonnay and Pinot Noir come from a Carneros property, the Cabernet from the winery's Rutherford estate, where the wines are made and presented to the public. Appointment-only tastings (same-day often possible) take place in a second-floor space with broad valley views west to the Mayacamas Mountains. For an introduction to ZD and its wine-making philosophy, book a current-release flight. Barrel tastings, small bites, and small-batch reserve wines are all part of the Abacus Experience, which concludes with a current and older Abacus blend. ✉ *8383 Silverado Trail* ☎ *800/487–7757* 🌐 *www.zdwines.com* 🎫 *Tastings from $40.*

🍴 Restaurants

La Luna Market & Taqueria

$ | **MEXICAN** | The burritos, tacos, and quesadillas at this peppy if unassuming pit stop will fill you up before wine tasting or help absorb what you've imbibed. The super burrito laden with cheese, beans, sour cream, guacamole, and your choice of meat—winery workers swear by the crispy carnitas—provides a day's fuel in itself; for breakfast (before 11) there's a burrito with eggs, your choice of meat, and potatoes, beans, and salsa. **Known for:** vegetarian variations with chiles rellenos; homemade-tortilla nachos; outdoor seating. [$] *Average main: $10* ✉ *1153 Rutherford Rd.* ✥ *Off Hwy. 29* ☎ *707/963–3211* 🌐 *www.lalunamarket.com* 🕒 *No dinner.*

★ **Restaurant at Auberge du Soleil**

$$$$ | **MODERN AMERICAN** | Possibly the most romantic roost for brunch or dinner in all the Wine Country is a terrace seat at the Auberge du Soleil resort's illustrious restaurant, and the Mediterranean-inflected cuisine more than matches the dramatic vineyard views. The prix-fixe dinner menu (three or four courses), which relies mainly on local produce, might include caviar or diver scallop starters, delicately prepared fish or vegetable middle-course options, and mains like prime beef pavé with béarnaise, spiced lamb loin, or Japanese Wagyu. **Known for:** polished service; comprehensive wine list; special-occasion feel. [$] *Average main: $135* ✉ *Auberge du Soleil, 180 Rutherford Hill Rd.* ✥ *Off Silverado Trail* ☎ *707/963–1211, 800/348–5406* 🌐 *www.aubergedusoleil.com.*

Rutherford Grill

$$$ | **AMERICAN** | Dark-wood walls, subdued lighting, and red-leather banquettes make for a perpetually clubby mood at this Rutherford hangout where the patio, popular for its bar, fireplace, and rocking chairs, opens for full meal service or drinks and appetizers when the weather's right. Many entrées—steaks, burgers, fish, rotisserie chicken, and barbecued pork ribs—emerge from an oak-fired grill operated by master technicians. **Known for:** iron-skillet corn bread direct from the oven; signature French dip sandwich and grilled jumbo artichokes; reasonably priced wine list with rarities. [$] *Average main: $29* ✉ *1180 Rutherford Rd.* ✥ *At Hwy. 29* ☎ *707/963–1792* 🌐 *www.rutherfordgrill.com.*

🛏 Hotels

★ **Auberge du Soleil**

$$$$ | **RESORT** | Taking a cue from the olive-tree-studded landscape, this hotel with a renowned restaurant and spa cultivates a luxurious look that blends French and California style. **Pros:** stunning valley views; spectacular pool and spa areas; Deluxe-category suites fit for a superstar. **Cons:** stratospheric prices; least expensive rooms get some noise from the bar and restaurant; weekend minimum-stay requirement. [$] *Rooms from: $925* ✉ *180 Rutherford Hill Rd.* ☎ *707/963–1211, 800/348–5406* 🌐 *www.aubergedusoleil.com* 🛏 *52 rooms* 🍽 *Free breakfast.*

★ **Rancho Caymus Inn**

$$$ | **HOTEL** | A romantic hacienda-away-from-home that off-season may well be the Napa Valley's best value in its price range, this upscale-contemporary boutique hotel near Inglenook and the Rutherford Grill contains rooms whose decor and artworks evoke the area's Mexican heritage. **Pros:** courtyard pool area; smallest rooms are 400 square feet, with several 600 or more; well-trained staff. **Cons:** all rooms have only showers (albeit nice ones); king beds in

all rooms (no sofa beds, though a few rollaways available); no spa or fitness center. [$] *Rooms from: $396* ✉ *1140 Rutherford Rd.* ☎ *707/200–9300* 🌐 *www.ranchocaymusinn.com* 🛏 *26 rooms* 🍴 *Free breakfast.*

St. Helena

2 miles northwest of Rutherford.

Downtown St. Helena is the very picture of good living in the Wine Country: sycamore trees arch over Main Street (Highway 29), where visitors flit between boutiques, cafés, and storefront tasting rooms housed in sun-faded redbrick buildings. The genteel district pulls in rafts of tourists during the day, though like most Wine Country towns St. Helena more or less rolls up the sidewalks after dark.

The Napa Valley floor narrows between the Mayacamas and Vaca mountains around St. Helena. The slopes reflect heat onto the vineyards below, and since there's less fog and wind, things get pretty toasty. This is one of the valley's hottest AVAs, with midsummer temperatures often reaching the mid-90s. Bordeaux varietals predominate—mainly Cabernet Sauvignon but also Merlot, Cabernet Franc, and Sauvignon Blanc. High-profile wineries bearing a St. Helena address abound, with Beringer, Charles Krug, and Ehlers Estate among the ones whose stories begin in the 19th century. The successes of relatively more recent arrivals such as Stony Hill, Rombauer, Duckhorn, Hall, Phelps, and a few dozen others have only added to the town's enological cachet.

Getting Here and Around

Highway 29 in downtown St. Helena is called Main Street, with many shops and restaurants between Pope and Adams streets. Wineries are found north and south of downtown along Highway 29 and the Silverado Trail, but some of the less touristy and more scenic spots are east of the trail on Howell Mountain and northwest of downtown on Spring Mountain. VINE buses stop along Main Street.

Visitor Information

CONTACT St. Helena Chamber of Commerce. ✉ *1320A Main St.* ✣ *Near Hunt Ave.* ☎ *707/963–4456* 🌐 *www.sthelena.com.*

👁 Sights

Barnett Vineyards

WINERY/DISTILLERY | Spring Mountain Road winds past oaks and madrones and, in springtime, sprays of wildflowers to this winery's lofty east-facing hillside setting. Most tastings are held outside to take advantage of views across the northern Napa Valley rivaling those from a balloon. Barnett's winemaker, David Tate, makes restrained, beautifully balanced wines: Cabernet Sauvignon, Cabernet Franc, and Merlot from the steeply terraced mountain estate and Chardonnay and Pinot Noir sourced from prestigious vineyards. Quietly dazzling, the wines will draw your attention from those vistas. Tastings are by appointment. ✉ *4070 Spring Mountain Rd.* ✣ *At Napa–Sonoma county line* ☎ *707/963–7075* 🌐 *www.barnettvineyards.com* 🎫 *Tasting $80.*

Beringer Vineyards

WINERY/DISTILLERY | Brothers Frederick and Jacob Beringer opened the winery that still bears their name in 1876. One of California's earliest bonded wineries, it's the oldest one in the Napa Valley never to have missed a vintage—no mean feat, given Prohibition. Reserve tastings of a limited release Chardonnay, a few big Cabernets, and a Sauterne-style dessert wine take place on the veranda (also inside when possible) at Frederick's grand Rhine House Mansion, built in 1884 and surrounded by mature landscaped gardens. Beringer is known for several widely distributed wines, but many poured here are winery exclusives. Visits require a reservation; same-day guests are accommodated if possible. ⊠ *2000 Main St./Hwy. 29* ⚜ *Near Pratt Ave.* ☎ *707/963–8989* ⊕ *www.beringer. com* 🍷 *Tastings from $35.*

CADE Estate Winery

WINERY/DISTILLERY | On a clear day, the views from this Howell Mountain winery's hospitality center and gravel patio—complete with infinity waterfall and Robinia shade trees—stretch south down the valley to Carneros. The exceptional tableau befits the collector-worthy Cabernets created by a team deservedly proud of its eco-friendly farming and production practices. Winemaker Danielle Cyrot's attention to detail begins in the vineyard and continues in the cellar, where she uses five dozen barrel types from two dozen coopers to bring out the best in the frisky (as in highly tannic) mountain fruit. The Signature CADE Estate Experience, conducted by polished, well-informed hosts, begins with two Sauvignon Blancs, followed by three Cabernets. All visits are by appointment, best made at least a day or two ahead. ⊠ *360 Howell Mountain Rd. S, Angwin* ⚜ *From Silverado Trail, head northeast on Deer Park Rd.* ☎ *707/965–2746* ⊕ *www. cadewinery.com* 🍷 *Tasting $80.*

Charles Krug Winery

WINERY/DISTILLERY | A historically sensitive renovation of its 1874 Redwood Cellar Building transformed the former production facility of the Napa Valley's oldest winery into an epic hospitality center. Charles Krug, a Prussian immigrant, established the winery in 1861 and ran it until his death in 1892. Italian immigrants Cesare Mondavi and his wife, Rosa, purchased Charles Krug in 1943, operating it with their sons Peter and Robert (who later opened his own winery). Still run by Peter's family, Charles Krug specializes in small-lot Yountville and Howell Mountain Cabernet Sauvignons plus Sauvignon Blanc, Chardonnay, Merlot, and Pinot Noir. All visits are by appointment. ⊠ *2800 Main St./Hwy. 29* ⚜ *Across from Culinary Institute of America* ☎ *707/967–2229* ⊕ *www.charleskrug.com* 🍷 *Tasting $45, tour $75 (includes tasting).*

Clif Family Tasting Room

WINERY/DISTILLERY | Cyclists swarm to the tasting room of Gary Erickson and Kit Crawford, best known for the Clif energy bar, a staple of many a pedaling adventure. Cycling trips through Italian wine country inspired the couple to establish a Howell Mountain winery and organic farm whose bounty they share at some of this merry hangout's tastings. The estate Cabernets show winemaker Laura Barrett at her most nuanced, but she crafts whites, a rosé of Grenache, and reds for all palates. ■ TIP→ **The Tour de St. Helena Bike Rental with Tasting begins with coffee and a Clif Bar, followed by biking, window shopping, and a well-earned wine tasting.** ⊠ *709 Main St./Hwy. 29* ⚜ *At Vidovich La.* ☎ *707/968–0625* ⊕ *www.cliffamily.com* 🍷 *Tasting $50* ⊙ *Closed Mon. and Tues.*

Conn Creek Winery

WINERY/DISTILLERY | The grapes for this winery's Cabernet Sauvignons come from most of the Napa Valley's 16 subappellations. To provide insight into the factors winemakers consider when crafting a Bordeaux-style red, Conn Creek developed the Barrel Blending Experience. An affable educator supplies the lowdown on basics like the characteristics of five Bordeaux varietals and how variations in soils and microclimates of valley-floor and mountain vineyards affect tannin structure. Armed with this information, participants set about blending, bottling, corking, and labeling a wine to take home. Even among friends, the competition to produce a successful blend is sometimes intense. Trivia: Koerner Rombauer, who later founded the famous Chardonnay house bearing his

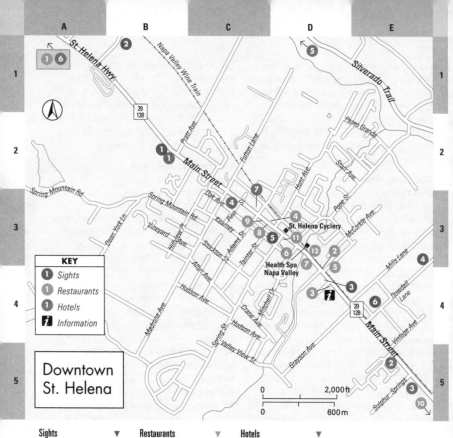

Downtown
St. Helena

Sights ▼

1 Beringer Vineyards..... **B2**
2 Charles Krug Winery ... **B1**
3 Clif Family
   Tasting Room............ **D4**
4 Crocker & Starr **E3**
5 Lang & Reed
   Napa Valley............. **D3**
6 VGS Chateau Potelle **E4**

Restaurants ▼

1 Brasswood Bar +
   Bakery + Kitchen **A1**
2 The Charter Oak **D3**
3 Clif Family Bruschetteria
   Food Truck............... **D4**
4 Cook St. Helena.......... **C3**
5 Farmstead at
   Long Meadow Ranch .. **D3**
6 Goose & Gander **D3**
7 Gott's Roadside **D3**
8 Market **C3**
9 Model Bakery............ **C3**
10 Press **E5**
11 The Station **D3**
12 Tra Vigne Pizzeria
   and Restaurant.......... **D3**

Hotels ▼

1 Alila Napa Valley........ **B2**
2 El Bonita Motel........... **E5**
3 Harvest Inn **E5**
4 Inn St. Helena **C3**
5 Meadowood
   Napa Valley............. **D1**
6 Wine Country Inn **A1**
7 Wydown Hotel **C3**

name, got his Napa Valley wine-making start as a Conn Creek partner. ■TIP→ **The blending seminar ($125) is great fun.** ⊠ *8711 Silverado Trail* ⊹ *At Hwy. 128* 🕾 *707/968–2669* ⊕ *www.conncreek.com* 🍷 *Tastings from $40* ⊘ *Closed Tues. and Wed.*

★ Corison Winery

WINERY/DISTILLERY | Respected for three 100% Cabernet Sauvignons, Corison Winery harks back to simpler days, with tastings either amid oak barrels inside an unadorned, barnlike facility or alfresco in view of the half century–old Kronos Vineyard. The straightforward approach suits the style of Cathy Corison. One of post-1960s Napa Valley's first women owner-winemakers, she eschews blending because she believes her sunny St. Helena AVA vineyards (and other selected sites) can ripen Cabernet better than anywhere else in the world. Critics tend to agree with her approach, often waxing ecstatic about these classic wines. Discovery tastings, a showcase of current releases—and always a Cabernet—begin with a brief look at Kronos. Library tastings, which start with a winery and vineyard tour, include recent releases and older vintages that together illustrate Corison's consistency as a winemaker and how gracefully her wines mature. Tastings by appointment. ⊠ *987 St. Helena Hwy.* ⊹ *At Stice La.* 🕾 *707/963–0826* ⊕ *www.corison.com* 🍷 *Tastings from $55.*

Crocker & Starr

WINERY/DISTILLERY | Cabernet Sauvignons expressing "power and elegance" and "a deep sense of place" are the main event at this winery jointly owned by businessman Charlie Crocker and founding winemaker Pam Starr. Head winemaker Evyn Cameron also crafts Sauvignon Blanc, Cabernet Franc, and Malbec, along with the Bridesmaid series Sauvignon Blanc and a Cabernet Franc–dominant red blend. Crocker & Starr was established in 1997, but James Dowdell, a St. Helena wine pioneer, planted grapes

and built a winery and a brandy facility on this land in the late 1800s. Hosts at appointment-only tastings (same-day sometimes possible) recount the Dowdell family's story at an experience that includes a brief foray into the vineyards and a peek at the winery followed by a seated tasting in an arbor. There's also a cheese-and-charcuterie pairing. ⊠ *700 Dowdell La.* ⊹ *¼-mile east of Hwy. 29* 🕾 *707/967–9111* ⊕ *www.crockerstarr. com* 🍷 *Tastings $55–$100.*

Duckhorn Vineyards

WINERY/DISTILLERY | Merlot's moment in the sun may have passed, but you wouldn't know it at Duckhorn, whose Three Palms Merlot was crowned wine of the year by *Wine Spectator* magazine in 2017. Duckhorn also makes Cabernet Sauvignon, Cabernet Franc, Chardonnay, Sauvignon Blanc, and a few other wines you can sip in the airy, high-ceilinged tasting room or on a fetching wraparound porch overlooking carefully tended vines. "Elevated" experiences, some not offered daily, include a tasting of estate and single-vineyard wines and private hosted tastings guests can customize to suit their preferences. All visits are by appointment. ⊠ *1000 Lodi La.* ⊹ *At Silverado Trail N* 🕾 *707/963–7108* ⊕ *www. duckhorn.com* 🍷 *Tastings from $40.*

Ehlers Estate

WINERY/DISTILLERY | New and old blend seamlessly at this winery whose 1886 tasting room's contemporary furnishings benefit from the gravitas and sense of history the original stone walls and exposed redwood beams impart. The wine-making team crafts complex Cabernet Sauvignon and other Bordeaux-style wines from 100% organically and biodynamically farmed estate grapes. Seated, appointment-only tastings, one of current releases, the other solely of Cabernets, focus on the growing practices and the winery's fascinating history, including Prohibition hijinks and the property's late-20th-century revival by a dynamic

French couple. ⊠ 3222 Ehlers La. ✛ At Hwy. 29 ☎ 707/963–5972 ⊕ www.ehlersestate.com ⊒ Tastings from $50.

Hall St. Helena

WINERY/DISTILLERY | The Cabernet Sauvignons produced here are works of art born of the latest in organic-farming science and wine-making technology. A glass-walled tasting room allows guests to see some of the high-tech equipment winemaker Megan Gunderson employs to craft wines that also include Merlot, Cabernet Franc, and Sauvignon Blanc. Looking westward from the second-floor tasting area, rows of neatly spaced Cabernet vines capture the eye, beyond them the tree-studded Mayacamas Mountains. Hard to miss as you arrive along Highway 29, Lawrence Argent's 35-foot-tall *Bunny Foo Foo,* a stainless-steel sculpture of a rabbit leaping out of the vineyard, is one of many museum-quality artworks on display at appointment-only Hall (call for sameday). ■TIP➔ **Sister winery Hall Rutherford hosts an exclusive wine-and-food pairing atop a Rutherford hillside.** ⊠ 401 St. Helena Hwy./Hwy. 29 ✛ Near White La. ☎ 707/967–2626 ⊕ www.hallwines.com ⊒ Tastings from $40.

★ Joseph Phelps Vineyards

WINERY/DISTILLERY | An appointment is required for tastings at the winery started by the late Joseph Phelps, but it's worth the effort—all the more so after an inspired renovation of the main redwood structure, a classic of 1970s Northern California architecture. Phelps produces very fine whites, along with Pinot Noir from its Sonoma Coast vineyards, but the blockbusters are the Bordeaux reds, particularly the Cabernet Sauvignons and Insignia, a luscious-yet-subtle Cab-dominant blend. Insignia, which often receives high-90s scores from respected wine publications, is always among the current releases poured at the one-hour seated Terrace Tasting overlooking grapevines and oaks. Several other experiences involve food pairings; participants in the blending seminar mix the varietals that go into Insignia. ⊠ 200 Taplin Rd. ✛ Off Silverado Trail ☎ 707/963–2745, 800/707–5789 ⊕ www.josephphelps. com ⊒ Tastings from $90.

Lang & Reed Napa Valley

WINERY/DISTILLERY | Playful labels by artist Jeanne Greco, whose past clients include Aerosmith, Mattel (for Barbie), and the post office, are the first indication that something offbeat is afoot at Lang & Reed. The second: the wines themselves. In the land of Chardonnay, Sauvignon Blanc, and Cabernet Sauvignon, husband-wife owners John and Tracey Skupny focus on Cabernet Franc and Chenin Blanc. In making the Cab Francs, John strives for wines "delicious and fruity but not simple." He succeeds. Son Reed Skupny's worldwide quest for wine knowledge found him in the Loire Valley, eventually becoming obsessed with crafting noteworthy Chenin Blanc. His Chenins, clean on the palate with pleasing acidity, achieve his objective. Named for him and a brother, Lang & Reed pours its wines in an 1880s bungalow, sometimes on the front porch. A block from Main Street, the casual setting evokes the slower-paced Napa of yore. ⊠ 1200 Oak Ave. ✛ At Spring St. ☎ 707/963–7547 ⊕ langandreed.com ⊒ Tastings from $35.

Louis M. Martini Winery

WINERY/DISTILLERY | A 100-point score for its Lot No. 1 Cabernet Sauvignon and a snappy renovation of the original 1933 winery added 21st-century luster to this operation whose namesake was a founding Napa Valley Vintners member. Established well before the valley's preoccupation with Cabernet Sauvignon took hold, Martini also makes Sauvignon Blanc, Bordeaux-style red blends, Cabernet Franc, Merlot, Malbec, Muscat, Petite Sirah, Zinfandel, and dessert wines. A basic tasting includes a few of these, and as with other experiences you can add a food pairing. The Heritage Lounge tasting of small-lot wines is highly recommended. Fun fact: 10 of the St. Helena AVA acres the winery occupies cost Louis M. a whopping $3,000 (total) in 1933. ⊠ *254 St. Helena Hwy. S* ✛ *At Chaix La.* ☎ *707/968–3362* ⊕ *www.louismartini. com* ⟋ *Tastings $30–$250.*

Pestoni Family Estate Winery

WINERY/DISTILLERY | A 19th-century wine-bottling contraption, a Prohibition-era safe with tales to tell, and photos and documents spanning five generations enhance a visit to this winery run by the descendants of Albino Pestoni, their Swiss-Italian forebear. Pourers share the Pestoni story while dispensing wines made from grapes grown in choice vineyards the family has acquired over the decades. The Howell Mountain Merlots and Cabernet Sauvignons at Legacy tastings always stand out. Heritage tastings of current releases often include Sauvignon Blanc, Sangiovese, and Cabernet grown on the Pestonis' Rutherford Bench property. The 1892 Field Blend from Lake County heirloom grapes—Zinfandel, Cabernet, and Petite Sirah—commemorates the year Albino entered the wine business. ■TIP➔ **After a tasting, guests are welcome to picnic in the winery's tree-shaded pavilion.** ⊠ *1673 St. Helena Hwy. S/Hwy. 29* ✛ *Near Galleron Rd.* ☎ *707/963–0544* ⊕ *www.pestonifamily. com* ⟋ *Tastings from $35.*

Prager Winery & Port Works

WINERY/DISTILLERY | "If door is locked, ring bell," reads a sign outside the weathered-redwood tasting shack at this family-run winery known for red, white, and tawny ports. The sign, the bell, and the thousands of dollar bills tacked to the walls and ceilings inside are your first indications that you're drifting back in time with the old-school Pragers, who have been making regular and fortified wines in St. Helena since the late 1970s. Five members of the second generation, along with two spouses,

run this homespun operation founded by Jim and Imogene Prager. In addition to ports the winery makes Petite Sirah and Sweet Claire, a late-harvest Riesling dessert wine. Some tastings take place in a garden outside the tasting room or on the crush pad. ⊠ *1281 Lewelling La.* ✛ *Off Hwy. 29* ☎ *707/963–7678* ⊕ *www. pragerport.com* ⟋ *Tastings $40 (includes glass).*

★ Pride Mountain Vineyards

WINERY/DISTILLERY | This winery 2,200 feet up Spring Mountain straddles Napa and Sonoma counties, confusing enough for visitors but even more complicated for the wine-making staff: government regulations require separate wineries and paperwork for each side of the property. It's one of several Pride Mountain quirks, but winemaker Sally Johnson's "big red wines," including a Cabernet Sauvignon that earned 100-point scores from a major wine critic two years in a row, are serious business. On a visit, by appointment only, you can learn about the farming and cellar strategies behind Pride's acclaimed Cabs (the winery also produces Syrah, a Cab-like Merlot, Viognier, and Chardonnay among others). ■TIP➔ **The views here are knock-your-socks-off gorgeous.** ⊠ *4026 Spring Mountain Rd.* ✛ *Off St. Helena Rd. (extension of Spring Mountain Rd. in Sonoma County)* ☎ *707/963–4949* ⊕ *www.pridewines. com* ⟋ *Tastings $30–$90* ☾ *Closed Tues.*

The Prisoner Wine Company

WINERY/DISTILLERY | The iconoclastic brand opened an industrial-chic space with interiors by the wildly original Napa-based designer Richard Von Saal to showcase its flagship The Prisoner red blend. "Getting the varietals to play together" is winemaker Chrissy Wittmann's mission with that wine (Zinfandel, Cabernet Sauvignon, Petite Sirah, Syrah, Charbono) and siblings like the Blindfold white (Chardonnay plus Rhône and other varietals). The Line-up Tasting of current releases unfolds either

Tastings in Raymond's atmospheric Barrel Cellar include wines that are still aging.

in the Tasting Lounge (more hip hotel bar than traditional tasting room) or outside in the casual open-air The Yard. When offered, The Makery Experience (indoors) involves boldly flavored plates that pair well with Wittman's fruit-forward wines. The Prisoner's tasting space is quite the party, for which a reservation is required. ⊠ *1178 Galleron Rd.* ✛ *At Hwy. 29* ☎ *707/967–3823, 877/283–5934* ⊕ *www. theprisonerwinecompany.com* ☏ *Tastings from $45.*

★ Quintessa

WINERY/DISTILLERY | The enduring beauty of this 280-acre estate reveals itself most vividly atop an oak-laced vineyard's-edge ridge with views across much of the Rutherford appellation. Fortunately for guests, many tastings take place here, some at open-air seating areas, others in steel, glass, and stone pavilions that open or close to the elements as needed. This land was a cattle ranch until the current owners purchased it in 1989, convinced it could produce collector-worthy wines. Time has proven them correct,

as the single Bordeaux-style red blend made each vintage, aged in caves dug deep into the hillside, annually garners mid- to high-90s scores from top critics. Tastings, strictly by appointment, start with the Illumination Sauvignon Blanc and include at least one library (older) vintage for comparison. ⊠ *1601 Silverado Trail S* ✛ *¼ mile north of Hwy. 128* ☎ *707/286–2730* ⊕ *www.quintessa.com* ☏ *Tastings from $125* ⊙ *Closed Tues. and Wed.*

Raymond Vineyards

WINERY/DISTILLERY | All the world's a stage to Jean-Charles Boisset, Raymond's charismatic owner—even his vineyards, where his five-act Theater of Nature includes a series of gardens and displays that explain biodynamic agriculture. The theatrics continue indoors in the disco-dazzling Crystal Cellar tasting room (chandeliers and other accoutrements by Baccarat), along with several additional spaces, some sedate and others equally expressive. Despite goosing up the glamour—gal pals out for a fun afternoon love this place—Boisset and winemaker Stephanie Putnam have continued the winery's tradition of producing reasonably priced premium wines. The Cabernet Sauvignons and Merlots often surprise. All visits are by appointment. ⊠ *849 Zinfandel La.* ✛ *Off Hwy. 29* ☎ *707/963–3141* ⊕ *www.raymondvineyards.com* ⊜ *Tastings from $25.*

Rombauer Vineyards

WINERY/DISTILLERY | Irma S. Rombauer, the great-aunt of winery founder Koerner Rombauer (who passed away in 2018) defined generations of American home cuisine with her best-selling book *The Joy of Cooking,* but he laid claim to a similar triumph. "Iconic" is an adjective often associated with Rombauer Chardonnays, particularly the flagship Carneros bottling. Although often described simply as "buttery," at their best the wines express equal parts ripeness, acidity, and creaminess, with vanilla accents courtesy of skillful oak aging. Most guests book a full tasting—Rombauer also makes Sauvignon Blanc, Zinfandel, Cabernet Sauvignon, Merlot, and dessert wines—but it's also possible to sip by the glass, on the vineyard-view porch or while strolling the landscaped grounds. In either case you'll need a reservation (call for same-day visits). ⊠ *3522 Silverado Trail N* ✛ *¾ mile north of Glass Mountain Rd.* ☎ *866/280–2582* ⊕ *rombauer.com* ⊜ *Tastings from $13 glass, $20 flight.*

★ Schweiger Vineyards

WINERY/DISTILLERY | Trying to sell his wife, Sally, on his late-1970s notion of planting a vineyard on their woodsy Spring Mountain property, contractor Fred Schweiger assured her, "It'll just be a hobby." Over time that hobby evolved into the lifestyle the family now shares with guests at its indoor and outdoor tasting spaces, whose gasp-worthy elevation-2,000-feet views include some of the original vines and extend across the Napa Valley to Howell Mountain. One of Fred's mentors advised him to plant the "king and queen of grapes," Chardonnay and Cabernet Sauvignon. For a decade the family sold all the fruit, but in 1994 son Andy began making wines bearing the Schweiger name, eventually adding Sauvignon Blanc, more Bordeaux reds, and two port-style dessert wines. ■ **TIP→ For an exhilarating and educational spin through the vines, some on steeply terraced slopes, book (May–September) the All-Terrain Vineyard Experience, led by either Fred or Andy.** ⊠ *4015 Spring Mountain Rd.* ✛ *500 feet from Sonoma County line* ☎ *707/963–4882* ⊕ *www.schweigervineyards.com* ⊗ *Tastings from $50.*

★ Smith-Madrone Vineyards & Winery

WINERY/DISTILLERY | For a glimpse of the Napa Valley before things got precious, head up Spring Mountain to the vineyard Stu Smith purchased in 1970 and still farms. His low-tech winery is a family affair: brother Charlie has made Smith-Madrone's critically acclaimed wines for more than four decades, and son Sam is Charlie's assistant. Blissfully informal tastings of Chardonnay, Cabernet Sauvignon, and Riesling take place by appointment four days a week in a weather-worn no-frills redwood barn. Charlie mostly lets the grapes do the talking, but profound wisdom underlies his restraint: these food-friendly wines are marvels of acidity, minerality, but most of all flavor. The 2020 Glass Fire burned much of the 200-acre property's forest perimeter, but the winery and the vineyards remain as before, as does the view across the valley to Howell Mountain. ⊠ *4022 Spring Mountain Rd.* ✛ *Near Napa/Sonoma county line* ☎ *707/963–2283* ⊕ *www.smithmadrone.com* ⊜ *Tastings from $35* ⊗ *Closed Sun., Tues., and Thurs.*

Spring Mountain Vineyard

WINERY/DISTILLERY | Until the 2020 Glass Fire swept through this historic property, tales hosts shared revolved around the estate's illustrious past, but these days the topics also include heroism and resilience. Although several 19th-century buildings perished, the longtime vineyard manager helped save the 1885 Miravalle mansion (famous for a star turn in TV's *Falcon Crest)* even as his own home on-site burned to the ground. He fought as well to preserve the vineyard, most of which survived, as did caves holding many previous vintages. Spring Mountain produces Chardonnay, Sauvignon Blanc, and Pinot Noir, but the calling cards are the Estate Cabernet Sauvignon and signature Elivette Bordeaux-style blend, both bold and robust, reflecting their mountain origin. Despite its brush with disaster, the winery, whose renaissance began soon after the flames receded, remains worth a visit (appointment required) for its wines, views, and staff's courtly hospitality. ⊠ *2805 Spring Mountain Rd.* ⊹ *Off Madrona Ave.* ☎ *707/967–4188* ⊕ *www.springmountainvineyard. com* ⊠ *Tastings from $45.*

★ Stony Hill Vineyard

WINERY/DISTILLERY | An ageless wonder whose Old World–style Chardonnays sommeliers love, Stony Hill was founded by the late Fred and Eleanor McCrea. During World War II the couple purchased a 160-acre goat farm on Spring Mountain's eastern slope, first planting grapevines, some still bearing fruit, in 1948. Private tastings (reservations required) emphasize whites—Stony Hill also produces dry Gewürztraminer and White Riesling, and in some years Semillon du Soleil, a dessert wine from grapes dried in the sun after harvesting to increase their sugars—with a leaner-than-average Cabernet Sauvignon the heaviest offering. Tastings indoors or (usually) out, take advantage of the property's views east to Howell Mountain. In late 2020 the winery changed hands for the second time in two years. The new owners, whose portfolio includes other Napa Valley heritage wineries, vowed to maintain the place's original spirit and wine-making style. ⊠ *3331 St. Helena Hwy. N* ⊹ *Near Bale Grist Mill* ☎ *707/963–2636* ⊕ *stonyhillvineyard.com* ⊠ *Tasting $75.*

★ Tres Sabores Winery

WINERY/DISTILLERY | A long, narrow lane with two sharp bends leads to splendidly workaday Tres Sabores, where the sight of sheep, golden retrievers, guinea hens, pomegranate and other trees and plants, a slew of birds and bees, and a heaping compost pile reinforce a simple point: despite the Napa Valley's penchant for glamour this is, first and foremost, farm country. Owner-winemaker Julie Johnson specializes in single-vineyard wines that include Cabernet Sauvignon and Zinfandel from estate-grown certified-or-ganic Rutherford bench vines. She also excels with Petite Sirah from dry-farmed Calistoga fruit, Sauvignon Blanc, and the zippy ¿Por Qué No? (Why not?) red blend. *Tres sabores* is Spanish for "three flavors," which to Johnson represents the land, her vines, and, as she puts it, "the spirit of the company around the table." Tastings by appointment only are informal and usually held outside. ⊠ *1620 S. Whitehall La.* ⊹ *West of Hwy. 29* ☎ *707/967–8027* ⊕ *www.tressabores. com* ⊠ *Tasting $50.*

Trinchero Napa Valley

WINERY/DISTILLERY | Sipping this winery's Malbec or Forté red Bordeaux blend, it seems inconceivable that last century's White Zinfandel craze made possible these willfully tannic wines. Over the years, the Trinchero family, owners of Sutter Home, which invented White Zin and stills sells millions of bottles annually, assembled a quality portfolio of estate vineyards whose grapes go into wines that truly live up to the term "terroir-driven." The wowsers include the Single Vineyard Collection reds—several Cabs, two Petit Verdots, two Malbecs, and a Merlot and a Petite Sirah—most from the Napa Valley's Atlas Peak, Calistoga, Mt. Veeder, and St. Helena subappellations. All are served either in an elegant, exuberant tasting room designed by St.

Helena's internationally acclaimed Erin Martin or in several outdoor spaces. All tastings require a reservation. ✉ *3070 St. Helena Hwy. N* ✣ *Near Ehlers La.* ☎ *707/963–1160* 🌐 *www.trincheronapavalley.com* 🎫 *Tastings from $35.*

★ VGS Chateau Potelle

WINERY/DISTILLERY | Sophisticated whimsy is on full display at the Chateau Potelle tasting room. Jean-Noel Fourmeaux, its bon vivant owner, fashioned this jewel of a space out of a nondescript 1950s bungalow south of downtown St. Helena. The residence, decorated with contemporary art (some wine-themed) and the Moroccan-tented outdoor patio are the scene of leisurely paced, sit-down, appointment-only tastings, some accompanied by gourmet bites from Napa's La Toque restaurant. Fourmeaux prefers fruit grown at higher elevations because he believes the extended ripening time grapes require in a cooler environment produces more complex and flavorful wines. His Cabernet Sauvignon, Syrah, and other reds support this thesis. The Chardonnay stars among the whites. **■ TIP→ Be sure to ask what "VGS" stands for.** ✉ *1200 Dowdell La.* ✣ *At Hwy. 29* ☎ *707/255–9440* 🌐 *www.vgschateaupotelle.com* 🎫 *Tastings from $50* 🕒 *Closed Mon. and Tues.*

Viader Vineyards & Winery

WINERY/DISTILLERY | On a 92-acre Howell Mountain property with valley views west to the Mayacamas range, this boutique winery was established in 1986. Founder Delia Viader bucked conventional wisdom by planting her vines vertically down a 32% slope instead of terracing them horizontally. Her three principle red blends, these days assembled by her son Alan, are similarly atypical in that they're not, per Delia, "trying to hijack your palate with high tannins or alcohol." Smooth and supple yet intense and aromatic, the wines are the product of tender yet exacting farming and wine-making processes. A curving knoll of oaks, madrones, and manzanitas separating the two vineyard sections holds the winery and nearby tasting room. The vistas from the latter and its terrace are as alluring as the much-sought-after wines. Visits to Viader are strictly by appointment, preferably made at least a day or two ahead. ✉ *1120 Deer Park Rd., Deer Park* ✣ *3 miles northeast off Silverado Trail* ☎ *707/963–3816* 🌐 *viader.com* 🕒 *Tasting $100.*

🍴 Restaurants

Brasswood Bar + Bakery + Kitchen

$$$ | ITALIAN | After Napa Valley fixture Tra Vigne lost its lease, many staffers regrouped a few miles north at the restaurant (the titular Kitchen) of the Brasswood complex, which also includes a bakery, shops, and a wine-tasting room. Along with dishes developed for the new location, chef David Nuno incorporates Tra Vigne favorites such as mozzarella-stuffed *arancini* (rice balls) into his Mediterranean-leaning menu. **Known for:** mostly Napa-Sonoma wine list; no corkage on first bottle; Tra Vigne favorites. [$] *Average main: $31* ✉ *3111 St. Helena Hwy. N* ✣ *Near Ehlers La.* ☎ *707/968–5434* 🌐 *www.brasswood.com.*

The Charter Oak

$$$ | MODERN AMERICAN | Christopher Kostow's reputation rests on his swoon-worthy haute cuisine for The Restaurant at Meadowood, but he and his Charter Oak team adopt a more straightforward approach—fewer ingredients chosen for maximum effect—at this high-ceilinged, brown-brick downtown restaurant. On the ever-evolving menu this strategy might translate into dishes like celery-leaf chicken with preserved lemon, herbs, and pan drippings, and red kuri squash with caramelized koji and goat cheese (or just go for the droolworthy cheeseburger and thick fries). **Known for:** exceedingly fresh produce from nearby Meadowood farm; patio dining in brick courtyard; top chef's affordable cuisine. [$] *Average main: $29*

✉ *1050 Charter Oak Ave., at Hwy. 29* ☎ *707/302–6996* 🌐 *www.thecharteroak.com* 🕑 *No lunch Mon. and Tues.*

Clif Family Bruschetteria Food Truck
$ | **ITALIAN** | Although it ventures out for special events, this walk-up food truck serving Italian-inflected fast food has a steady gig outside the Clif Family Tasting Room. From 11 am to 6 or 6:30 pm order salads, panini, Moroccan street food, organic rotisserie chicken, or a tomato, mushroom, pork, or other bruschetta to go or, hopefully by the second half of 2021, to enjoy on the tasting room's back patio as before. **Known for:** soups and salads; many organic ingredients; Wednesday's international street food menu. [$] *Average main: $14* ✉ *709 Main St./Hwy. 29* ✣ *At Vidovich La.* ☎ *707/968–0625 for tasting room* 🌐 *cliffamily.com/visit/daily-food-truck-menu* 🕑 *Closed Mon. and Tues. No dinner.*

★ **Cook St. Helena**
$$ | **ITALIAN** | A curved marble bar spotlit by contemporary art-glass pendants adds a touch of style to this downtown restaurant whose northern Italian cuisine pleases with understated sophistication. Mussels with house-made sausage in a spicy tomato broth, chopped salad with pancetta and pecorino, and the daily changing risotto are among the dishes regulars revere. **Known for:** top-quality ingredients; reasonably priced local and international wines; intimate dining. [$] *Average main: $26* ✉ *1310 Main St.* ✣ *Near Hunt Ave.* ☎ *707/963–7088* 🌐 *www.cooksthelena.com* 🕑 *Closed weekends (check website for updates).*

★ **Farmstead at Long Meadow Ranch**
$$$ | **MODERN AMERICAN** | In a high-ceilinged former barn with plenty of outside seating, Farmstead revolves around an open kitchen whose chefs prepare meals with grass-fed beef and lamb, fruits and vegetables, and eggs, olive oil, wine, honey, and other ingredients from nearby Long Meadow Ranch. Entrées might include wood-grilled trout with fennel, mushroom, onion, and bacon-mustard vinaigrette; caramelized beets with goat cheese; or a wood-grilled heritage pork chop with jalapeño grits. **Known for:** Tuesday fried-chicken night; house-made charcuterie; on-site general store, café, and Long Meadow Wines tasting space. [$] *Average main: $27* ✉ *738 Main St.* ✣ *At Charter Oak Ave.* ☎ *707/963–4555* 🌐 *www.longmeadowranch.com/eat-drink/restaurant.*

Goose & Gander
$$$ | **MODERN AMERICAN** | A Craftsman bungalow whose 1920s owner reportedly used the cellar for bootlegging during Prohibition houses this restaurant where the pairing of food and drink is as likely to involve a craft cocktail as a sommelier-selected wine. Main courses such as brick-cooked chicken, a heritage-pork burger, and dry-aged New York steak with black-lime and pink-peppercorn butter follow starters that might include blistered Brussels sprouts and roasted octopus. **Known for:** intimate main dining room with fireplace; alfresco patio dining; basement bar among Napa's best watering holes. [$] *Average main: $31* ✉ *1245 Spring St.* ✣ *At Oak St.* ☎ *707/967–8779* 🌐 *www.goosegander.com* 🕑 *No lunch.*

Gott's Roadside
$ | **AMERICAN** | A 1950s-style outdoor hamburger stand goes upscale at this spot whose customers brave long lines to order breakfast sandwiches, juicy burgers, root-beer floats, and garlic fries. Choices not available a half century ago include ahi tuna and Impossible burgers and kale and Vietnamese chicken salads. **Known for:** tasty 21st-century diner cuisine; shaded picnic tables (arrive early or late for lunch to get one); second branch at Napa's Oxbow Public Market. [$] *Average main: $14* ✉ *933 Main St./Hwy. 29* ✣ *Near Charter Oak Ave.* ☎ *707/963–3486* 🌐 *www.gotts.com* ☞ *Reservations not accepted.*

Long Meadow Ranch's St. Helena compound includes a general store, a café, and Farmstead restaurant.

Market

$$$ | **AMERICAN** | Ernesto Martinez, this understated eatery's Mexico City–born chef and co-owner, often puts a Latin spin on farm-to-table American classics. Although he plays things straight with the Caesar salad, fish-and-chips, and braised short ribs, the fried chicken comes with cheddar-jalapeño corn bread, and the fried calamari owes its piquancy to the accompanying peppers, nopales cactus, chipotle aioli, and avocado tomatillo sauce. **Known for:** free corkage; Wine Bubbles & Bites happy hour 3–5; Sunday brunch. $ *Average main: $29* ⌧ *1347 Main St.* ✛ *Near Hunt Ave.* ☎ *707/963–3799* ⊕ *marketsthelena.com* ⊘ *Closed Sun. and Mon. (but check).*

Model Bakery

$ | **BAKERY** | Thanks to multiple plugs by Oprah, each day's fresh batch of English muffins here sells out quickly, but the scones, croissants, breads, and other baked goods also inspire. Breakfast brings pastries and sandwiches with scrambled eggs, cheddar, and bacon between a buttermilk biscuit; the lunch menu expands to include soups, salads, pizzas, and more sandwiches—turkey focaccia, ciabatta chicken-Asiago panini, and vegan veggies among them. **Known for:** signature English muffins; people-watching at outdoor tables; second Oxbow market location. $ *Average main: $12* ⌧ *1357 Main St.* ✛ *Near Adams Ave.* ☎ *707/963–8192* ⊕ *www.themodelbakery.com* ⊘ *No dinner.*

★ Press

$$$$ | **MODERN AMERICAN** | For years this cavernous restaurant with a contempo-barn interior and wraparound patio steps from neighboring vineyards was northern Napans' preferred stop for a top-shelf cocktail, grass-fed dry-aged steak, and high-90s-scoring local Cabernet. It still is, but since arriving in 2019, chef Philip Tessier, formerly of Yountville's The French Laundry and Bouchon Bistro and New York City's Le Bernardin, has expanded the menu to include more refined preparations, much of whose produce is grown nearby. **Known for:**

extensive wine cellar; impressive cocktails; casual-chic ambience. $ *Average main: $45* ✉ *587 St. Helena Hwy./Hwy. 29* ✛ *At White La.* ☎ *707/967–0550* ⊕ *www.pressnapavalley.com* ☾ *No lunch Mon.–Thurs.*

The Station

$ | **AMERICAN** | Joel Gott of nearby Gott's Roadside purchased a downtown gas station and kept the pumps humming, spiffing up the interior retro-style and adding shaded outdoor seating. Start the day with quiche, a chipotle-bacon and egg biscuit, or a breakfast bun with ham and sweet-potato gratin, or drop by for lunch wraps, grain bowls, salads, and sandwiches. **Known for:** morning pastries; grab-and-go items; reasonably priced "Lunch Bag" sandwich, chips, cookie, and bottled water combos. $ *Average main: $13* ✉ *1153 Main St.* ✛ *At Spring St.* ☎ *707/963–3356* ⊕ *www.stationsh. com* ☾ *No dinner.*

Tra Vigne Pizzeria and Restaurant

$$ | **PIZZA** | Crisp, thin-crust Neapolitan-style pizzas—among them the unusual Positano, with sautéed shrimp, crescenza cheese, and fried lemons—are the specialties of this family-friendly offshoot of the famous, now departed, Tra Vigne restaurant. Hand-pulled mozzarella and a few other beloved Tra Vigne dishes are on the menu, along with the salads, pizzas, and pastas. **Known for:** well-priced oysters at happy hour (4–6); relaxed atmosphere; create-your-own-pizza option. $ *Average main: $18* ✉ *1016 Main St.* ✛ *At Charter Oak Ave.* ☎ *707/967–9999* ⊕ *www.pizzeriatravigne.com.*

 Hotels

Alila Napa Valley

$$$$ | **HOTEL** | An upscale-casual ultra-contemporary adults-only resort formerly known as Las Alcobas Napa Valley but as of 2021 in the Hyatt Alila brand's fold, this hillside beauty sits adjacent to Beringer Vineyards six blocks north of Main Street shopping and dining. **Pros:** vineyard views from most rooms; Acacia House restaurant; pool, spa, and fitness center. **Cons:** expensive much of the year; per website no children under age 18 permitted; no self-parking. $ *Rooms from: $700* ✉ *1915 Main St.* ☎ *707/963–7000* ⊕ *www.alilanapavalley.com* ⇋ *68 rooms* ◉ *No meals.*

El Bonita Motel

$ | **HOTEL** | A classic 1950s-style neon sign marks the driveway to this well-run roadside motel that—when it isn't sold out—offers great value to budget-minded travelers. **Pros:** cheerful rooms; family-friendly; microwaves and mini-refrigerators. **Cons:** noise issues in roadside and ground-floor rooms; expensive on high-season weekends; lacks amenities of fancier properties. $ *Rooms from: $160* ✉ *195 Main St./Hwy. 29* ☎ *707/963–3216* ⊕ *www.elbonita.com* ⇋ *52 rooms* ◉ *Free breakfast.*

Harvest Inn

$$$ | **HOTEL** | Although this inn sits just off Highway 29, its patrons remain mostly above the fray, strolling 8 acres of gardens, enjoying views of the vineyards adjoining the property, partaking in spa services, and drifting to sleep in beds adorned with fancy linens and down pillows. **Pros:** garden setting; spacious rooms; near choice wineries, restaurants, and shops. **Cons:** some lower-price rooms lack elegance; high weekend rates; occasional service lapses. $ *Rooms from: $359* ✉ *1 Main St.* ☎ *707/963–9463* ⊕ *www.harvestinn.com* ⇋ *81 rooms* ◉ *No meals.*

Inn St. Helena

$$$ | **B&B/INN** | A large room at this spiffed-up downtown St. Helena inn is named for author Ambrose Bierce *(The Devil's Dictionary),* who lived in the main Victorian structure in the early 1900s, but sensitive hospitality and modern amenities are what make a stay worth writing home about. **Pros:** aim-to-please staff and

owner; outdoor porch and swing; convenient to shops, tasting rooms, restaurants. **Cons:** no pool, gym, room service, or other typical amenities; two-night minimum on weekends (three with Monday holiday); per website "children 16 and older are welcome". ⑤ *Rooms from: $309* ✉ *1515 Main St.* ☎ *707/963–3003* ⊕ *www.innsthelena.com* �“ *8 rooms* ⦶ *Free breakfast.*

Meadowood Napa Valley
$$$$ | RESORT | This elite 250-acre resort's celebrated restaurant and more than half its accommodations were destroyed in the 2020 Glass Fire, but the spa, pools, tennis courts, fitness center, and a fair number of cottages in one part survived and are set to reopen in late summer 2021, with reconstruction in other areas not expected to affect the guest experience. **Pros:** scrupulously maintained rooms; all-organic spa; gracious service. **Cons:** still recovering from fire; far from downtown St. Helena; weekend minimum-stay requirement. ⑤ *Rooms from: $825* ✉ *900 Meadowood La.* ☎ *707/963–3646, 866/987–8212* ⊕ *www.meadowood.com* �“ *31 rooms* ⦶ *No meals.*

Wine Country Inn
$$$ | B&B/INN | Vineyards flank the three buildings, containing 24 rooms, and five cottages of this pastoral retreat, where blue oaks, maytens, and olive trees provide shade, and gardens feature lantana (small butterflies love it) and lavender. **Pros:** staff excels at anticipating guests' needs; good-size swimming pool; vineyard views from most rooms. **Cons:** some rooms let in noise from neighbors; expensive in high season; weekend minimum-stay requirement. ⑤ *Rooms from: $329* ✉ *1152 Lodi La.* ✛ *East of Hwy. 29* ☎ *707/963–7077, 888/465–4608* ⊕ *www.winecountryinn.com* �“ *29 rooms* ⦶ *Free breakfast.*

★ Wydown Hotel
$$$ | HOTEL | This smart boutique hotel near downtown shopping and dining delivers comfort with a heavy dose of style: the storefront lobby's high ceiling and earth tones, punctuated by rich-hued splashes of color, hint at the relaxed grandeur owner-hotelier Mark Hoffmeister and his design team achieved in the rooms upstairs. **Pros:** well run; eclectic decor; downtown location. **Cons:** lacks the amenities of larger properties; large corner rooms pick up some street noise; two-night minimum on weekends. ⑤ *Rooms from: $339* ✉ *1424 Main St.* ☎ *707/963–5100* ⊕ *www.wydownhotel.com* �“ *12 rooms* ⦶ *No meals.*

▼ Nightlife

Cameo Cinema
FILM | The art nouveau Cameo Cinema, built in 1913 and now beautifully restored, screens first-run and art-house movies and occasionally hosts live performances. ✉ *1340 Main St.* ✛ *Near Hunt Ave.* ☎ *707/963–9779* ⊕ *www.cameocinema.com.*

The Saint
WINE BARS—NIGHTLIFE | This high-ceilinged downtown wine bar benefits from the grandeur and gravitas of its setting inside a stone-walled late-19th-century former bank. Lit by chandeliers and decked out in contemporary style with plush sofas and chairs and Lucite stools at the bar, it's a classy, loungelike space to expand your enological horizons. ✉ *1351 Main St.* ✛ *Near Adams St.* ☎ *707/302–5130* ⊕ *www.thesaintnapavalley.com* ☞ *Closed Mon.–Wed. (but check).*

● Shopping

ART GALLERIES
Caldwell Snyder
ART GALLERIES | Inside the Star Building (1900), this gallery exhibits contemporary American, European, and Latin American paintings and sculptures. ✉ *1328 Main St.* ✛ *Near Hunt Ave.* ☎ *707/200–5050* ⊕ *www.caldwellsnyder.com.*

BOOKS

Main Street Bookmine

BOOKS/STATIONERY | St. Helena's treasured Main Street Books was headed for closure when the folks behind Napa Bookmine in downtown Napa rescued the indie. The tiny shop's specialties include Napa and Sonoma titles. ⊠ *1315 Main St.* ✛ *Near Hunt Ave.* ☎ *707/963–1338* ⊕ *napabookmine.com* ☾ *Closed Sun.*

CLOTHING

★ Pearl Wonderful Clothing

CLOTHING | Sweet Pearl carries the latest in women's fashions, in a space that makes dramatic use of the section of the historic stone building the shop occupies. Celebs find bags, shoes, jewelry, and outfits here—and you might, too. ⊠ *1219C Main St.* ☎ *707/963–3236* ⊕ *pearlwonderfulclothing.com.*

FOOD AND WINE

Gary's Wine & Marketplace

FOOD/CANDY | Gary Fisch owns four New Jersey stores selling gourmet groceries and international wines but has such a soft spot for the Napa Valley that when the Dean & DeLuca chain abandoned this location, he swooped in and set up shop. The wine selection is as good as ever, and the prepared foods and deli items will ensure you'll picnic in style. ⊠ *607 St. Helena Hwy./Hwy. 29* ✛ *At White La.* ☎ *707/531–7660* ⊕ *garyswine.com/napa-valley.*

Woodhouse Chocolate

FOOD/CANDY | Elaborate confections made on the premises are displayed like miniature works of art at this shop that resembles an 18th-century Parisian salon. ⊠ *1367 Main St.* ✛ *At Adams St.* ☎ *707/963–8413, 800/966–3468* ⊕ *www.woodhousechocolate.com.*

HOUSEHOLD ITEMS

Acres Home and Garden

HOUSEHOLD ITEMS/FURNITURE | Part general store, part gift shop, Acres sells bulbs, gardening implements, and home decor items "for the well-tended life." Bucking a brick-and-mortar retail trend, the smart shop doubled in size in late 2020. ⊠ *1219 Main St.* ✛ *Near Spring St.* ☎ *707/967–1142* ⊕ *www.acreshomeandgarden.com.*

🏃 Activities

BICYCLING

St. Helena Cyclery

SPORTS—SIGHT | Rent hybrid and road bikes by the hour or day at this shop that has a useful "Where to Ride" page on its website (see the About tab). ⊠ *1156 Main St.* ✛ *At Spring St.* ☎ *707/963–7736* ⊕ *www.sthelenacyclery.com* 🖃 *From $15 per hr, $45 per day.*

SPAS

Health Spa Napa Valley

FITNESS/HEALTH CLUBS | The focus at this local favorite is on health, wellness, and fitness, so there are personal trainers offering advice and an outdoor lap pool in addition to the extensive regimen of massages and body treatments. The Harvest Mud Wrap, for which clients are slathered with grape-seed mud and French clay, is a more indulgent, less messy alternative to a traditional mud bath. Afterward you can take advantage of the sauna, hot tub, and eucalyptus steam rooms. ■TIP➔ **Longtime patrons book treatments before noon to take advantage of the all-day access.** ⊠ *1030 Main St.* ✛ *At Pope St.* ☎ *707/967–8800* ⊕ *healthspanapavalley.com* 🖃 *Treatments from $20.*

Calistoga

3 miles northwest of St. Helena.

The false-fronted shops, 19th-century buildings, and unpretentious tasting rooms lining the main drag of Lincoln Avenue give Calistoga a slightly rough-and-tumble feel that's unique in the Napa Valley. With Mt. St. Helena rising to the north and visible from downtown, Calistoga looks a bit like a cattle town tucked into a remote mountain valley.

In 1859 Sam Brannan—Mormon missionary, entrepreneur, and vineyard developer—learned about a place in the upper Napa Valley, called Agua Caliente by settlers, that was peppered with hot springs and even had its own "Old Faithful" geyser. He snapped up 2,000 acres of prime property and laid out a resort. Planning a place that would rival New York's famous Saratoga Hot Springs, he built an elegant hotel, bathhouses, cottages, stables, an observatory, and a distillery (the last a questionable choice for a Mormon missionary). Brannan's gamble didn't pay off as he'd hoped, but Californians kept coming to "take the waters," supporting small hotels and bathhouses built wherever a hot spring bubbled to the surface. In the 21st century Calistoga began to get back to its roots, with luxury properties like Solage (2007) springing up and Indian Springs and other old standbys getting a sprucing up. The trend continued in 2021 with the opening of the Four Seasons Resort and Residences Napa Valley and a total makeover of Dr. Wilkinson's. (In 1952 the latter advertised "The Works"—mud and steam baths and a blanket wrap followed by a massage—for a whopping $3.50, a sum that even adjusted for inflation wouldn't come close to covering the current charges.) At the Brannan Cottage Inn *(see Hotels, p. 139)*, you can spend a night in part of the only Sam Brannan cottage still on its original site.

Getting Here and Around

To get here from St. Helena or anywhere else farther south, take Highway 29 north and then turn right on Lincoln Avenue. Alternatively, you can head north on Silverado Trail and turn left on Lincoln. VINE buses serve Calistoga.

Visitor Information

CONTACT Visit Calistoga. ✉ *1133 Washington St.* ✛ *Near Lincoln Ave.* ☎ *707/942–6333* ⊕ *www.visitcalistoga.com.*

◉ Sights

Bennett Lane Winery
WINERY/DISTILLERY | Winemaker Rob Hunter of Bennett Lane strives "to create the greatest Cabernet Sauvignon in the world." At this appointment-only winery's tastefully casual salon in the far northern Napa Valley you can find out how close he and his team come. Although known for valley-floor Cabernet, Bennett Lane also produces Merlot and the Maximus Red Feasting Wine, a Cab-heavy red blend nicely priced considering the quality. On the lighter side there's often sparkling wine, Chardonnay, and the Maximus White Feasting Wine blend. The basic flight surveys current-release whites and reds. There's also a Cab-focused offering. Most tastings take place in a garden whose pergola frames vineyard and Calistoga Palisades views. ✉ *3340 Hwy. 128* ✛ *3 miles north of downtown* ☎ *707/942–6684* ⊕ *www. bennettlane.com* ▦ *Tastings from $25.*

Brian Arden Wines
WINERY/DISTILLERY | This winery with a contemporary stone, glass, and metal facility across from the Four Seasons resort takes its name from its son (Brian Harlan) and father (Arden Harlan) vintners. Brian, who makes the wines, has early memories of a 19th-century Lake County Zinfandel vineyard his family still farms, but his passion for the grape grew out of wine-related work in the restaurant industry. Wines to look for include Chardonnay, Cabernet Franc, Sangiovese, Zinfandel from the family ranch, and a blend called B.A. Red that changes each vintage. Guests sip these wines and a few others in the tasting room or on an outdoor patio, both with Calistoga

Palisades views. ⊠ *331 Silverado Trail* ✛ *Near Rosedale Rd.* ☎ *707/942–4767* ⊕ *www.brianardenwines.com* ☞ *Tastings from $30* ◔ *Closed Mon. and Tues.*

Castello di Amorosa

WINERY/DISTILLERY | An astounding medieval structure complete with drawbridge and moat, chapel, stables, and secret passageways, the Castello commands Diamond Mountain's lower eastern slope. Some of the 107 rooms contain artist Fabio Sanzogni's replicas of 13th-century frescoes (cheekily signed with his website address), and the dungeon has an iron maiden from Nuremberg, Germany. You must pay for a tour, when offered, to see most of Dario Sattui's extensive eight-level property, though with general admission you'll have access to part of the complex. Bottlings of note include several Italian-style wines, including La Castellana, a robust "super Tuscan" blend of Cabernet Sauvignon, Sangiovese, and Merlot; and Il Barone, a deliberately big Cab primarily of Rutherford grapes. All visits are by appointment. ⊠ *4045 N. St. Helena Hwy./Hwy. 29* ✛ *Near Maple La.* ☎ *707/967–6272* ⊕ *www.castellodiamorosa.com* ☞ *Check with winery for tasting and tour prices.*

Ca' Toga Galleria d'Arte

MUSEUM | The boundless wit, whimsy, and creativity of the Venetian-born Carlo Marchiori, this gallery's owner-artist, finds expression in paintings, watercolors, ceramics, sculptures, and other artworks. Marchiori often draws on mythology and folktales for his inspiration. A stop at this magical gallery might inspire you to tour Villa Ca' Toga, the artist's fanciful Palladian home, a tromp-l'oeil tour de force open for tours from May through October on Saturday morning only, by appointment. ⊠ *1206 Cedar St.* ✛ *Near Lincoln Ave.* ☎ *707/942–3900* ⊕ *www.catoga.com* ◔ *Closed Tues. and Wed.*

Chateau Montelena

WINERY/DISTILLERY | Set amid a bucolic northern Calistoga landscape, this winery helped establish the Napa Valley's reputation for high-quality wine making. At the pivotal Paris tasting of 1976, the Chateau Montelena 1973 Chardonnay took first place, beating out four white Burgundies from France and five other California Chardonnays, an event immortalized in the 2008 movie *Bottle Shock*. A 21st-century Napa Valley Chardonnay is always part of A Taste of Montelena—the winery also makes Sauvignon Blanc, Riesling, a fine estate Zinfandel, and Cabernet Sauvignon—or you can opt for the Montelena Estate Collection tasting of Cabernets from several vintages. When tours are offered, there's one that takes in the grounds and covers the history of this stately property whose stone winery building was erected in 1888. All visits require a reservation. ⊠ *1429 Tubbs La.* ✛ *Off Hwy. 29* ☎ *707/942–5105* ⊕ *www.montelena.com* ☞ *Tastings from $40.*

Davis Estates

WINERY/DISTILLERY | Owners Mike and Sandy Davis transformed a ramshackle property into a plush winery whose predominantly Bordeaux-style wines live up to the magnificent setting. In fashioning the couple's haute-rustic appointment-only hospitality center, the celebrated Wine Country architect Howard Backen incorporated cedar, walnut, and other woods. In fine weather, many guests sit on the open-air terrace's huge swinging sofas, enjoying broad valley views while tasting wines by Cary Gott. The winemaker, who counts Ram's Gate and Round Pond among previous clients, makes Sauvignon Blanc and Chardonnay whites, with Pinot Noir, Merlot, Cabernet Franc, Petit Verdot, and Cabs and Cab-heavy blends among the reds. The wines can be paired with small bites by Mark Caldwell, the executive chef. Tastings are by appointment only. ⊠ *4060 Silverado Trail N* ✛ *At Larkmead La.* ☎ *707/942–0700* ⊕ *www.davisestates.com* ☞ *Tastings from $75.*

The astounding Castello di Amorosa has 107 rooms.

Frank Family Vineyards

WINERY/DISTILLERY | As a former Disney film and television executive, Rich Frank knows a thing or two about entertainment, and it shows in the chipper atmosphere that prevails in the winery's bright-yellow Craftsman-style tasting room. The site's wine-making history dates from the 19th century, and portions of an original 1884 structure, reclad in stone in 1906, remain standing today. From 1952 until 1990, Hanns Kornell made sparkling wines on this site. Frank Family makes sparklers itself, but the high-profile wines are the Carneros Chardonnay and several Cabernet Sauvignons, particularly the Rutherford Reserve and the Winston Hill red blend. Tastings are sit-down affairs, indoors, on the back veranda, or under 100-year-old elms. Reservations are required. ⊠ *1091 Larkmead La.* ⊹ *Off Hwy. 29* ☏ *707/942–0859* ⊕ *www.frankfamilyvineyards.com* ▱ *Tastings from $50.*

Jericho Canyon Vineyard

WINERY/DISTILLERY | The grapes at family-owned Jericho Canyon grow on hillsides that slope as much as 55 degrees. The rocky, volcanic soils of this former cattle ranch yield intensely flavored berries that winemaker Nicholas Bleecher, the son of the founders, transforms in consultation with blending specialist Michel Rolland into the flagship Jericho Canyon Cabernet Sauvignon and other wines. The nuances of sustainable farming in this challenging environment are among the topics covered during tastings. All visits, customized based on guests' interests, are by appointment only. ⊠ *3322 Old Lawley Toll Rd.* ⊹ *Off Hwy. 29* ☏ *707/331–9076* ⊕ *jerichocanyonvineyard.com* ▱ *Tastings from $75.*

★ Larkmead

WINERY/DISTILLERY | Founded in 1895 but planted with grapes even before that by San Francisco's free-spirited Lillie Hitchcock Coit, Larkmead was named by her for the meadowlarks that once flitted through the northern Napa Valley.

Intuitive artistry informs everything that unfolds on the 150-acre estate, from the vineyards and colorful gardens to the barn-chic interior design, five-star hospitality, and artworks by Kate Solari Baker, whose parents purchased Larkmead in 1948. Winemaker Dan Petroski describes the diverse soils here as "a 'snapshot' of the entire Napa Valley" and the reason why the winery's three top-of-the-line Cabernets taste so different despite their grapes growing in some cases mere yards from each other. Most tastings include a brief tour that passes by a 3-acre vineyard Petroski planted to research alternative varietals and viticulture to cope with climate change. ⊠ *1100 Larkmead La.* ✛ *Off Hwy. 29* ☎ *707/942–0167* ⊕ *www.larkmead.com* ⌫ *Tastings from $70* ⊗ *Closed Tues. and Wed.*

Lola Wines

WINERY/DISTILLERY | A winery with personality galore, Lola earns plaudits from critics for owner-winemaker Seth Cripe's accessible, unconventional wines. The Chardonnay, Chenin Blanc, Malvasia Bianca, and Riesling whites favor acidity and "unripeness" over bombastic flavors, and the rosé of Pinot Noir and the reds share this succulent trait. Cripe, who also runs a lucrative side business selling bottarga (fish roe) to fine-dining icons like The French Laundry, presents his wines—with partner in love and business Rafaela Costa—at a redbrick 1892 former home a few blocks from the center of town. Its fenced-in patio and the by-the-glass and bottle options invite lingering. As for the flights, one showcases the Chardonnay and a few Pinot Noirs, the other the remaining whites plus Zinfandel and Cabernet. ⊠ *916 Foothill Blvd.* ✛ *At Pine St. south of Lincoln Ave.* ☎ *707/342–0623* ⊕ *www.lolawines.com* ⌫ *Tastings from $12 glass, $30 flight* ⊗ *Closed Tues. and Wed.*

Romeo Vineyards & Cellars

WINERY/DISTILLERY | Redwoods and cedars tower over the jolly downtown Calistoga garden patio of this under-the-radar producer of Bordeaux-varietal wines. Alison Doran, whose first wine-making gig was working as a harvest intern in the 1970s for André Tchelistcheff, the premier California winemaker of his era, extracts rich flavors from grapes grown a few miles away in Romeo's half-century-old southern Calistoga vineyard. The Napa Valley Cabernet is a bona fide bargain for the quality; the Malbec and Petit Verdot are also strong suits, as are the Sauvignon Blanc and Petit Verdot rosé. ⊠ *1224 Lincoln Ave.* ✛ *At Cedar St.* ☎ *707/942–8239* ⊕ *www.romeovineyards.com* ⌫ *Tastings from $20* ⊗ *Closed Tues. and Wed. (check website in summer).*

★ Schramsberg

WINERY/DISTILLERY | On a Diamond Mountain site the German-born Jacob Schram planted to grapes in the early 1860s, Schramsberg pours its esteemed *méthode traditionnelle* (aka *méthode champenoise*) sparkling wines. Author Robert Louis Stevenson was among Schram's early visitors. After the vintner's death in 1905 the winery closed and fell into disrepair, but in 1965 Jack and Jamie Davies purchased the 200-acre Schramsberg property and began restoring its buildings and caves. Chinese laborers dug some of the latter in the 1870s. In the 1990s, the family set about replanting the vineyard to Cabernet Sauvignon and other Bordeaux varietals for the Davies Vineyards label's still red wines. Tastings at Schramsberg can include pours of only sparkling wines, only still wines, or a combination of the two. All visits are by appointment. ⊠ *1400 Schramsberg Rd.* ✛ *Off Hwy. 29* ☎ *707/942–4558, 800/877–3623* ⊕ *www.schramsberg.com* ⌫ *Tastings from $50.*

Sharpsteen Museum of Calistoga History

MUSEUM | Walt Disney animator Ben Sharpsteen, who retired to Calistoga, founded this humble museum whose centerpiece is an intricate diorama depicting the Calistoga Hot Springs Resort during its 19th-century heyday. A restored cottage from the resort, moved to this site, sits next door to the museum, worth a peek if it's open. A permanent exhibit focuses on Sharpsteen's animation career. ⊠ *1311 Washington St.* ⊹ *At 1st St.* ☎ *707/942–5911* ⊕ *www. sharpsteenmuseum.org* ⊠ *$3.*

Sterling Vineyards

WINERY/DISTILLERY | **FAMILY** | An aerial tram whisks guests to this hillside winery with sweeping Napa Valley views. Appointment-only Sterling, which suffered damage during the 2020 wildfires and closed down for several months, is known for Chardonnay and a few other whites (including sparkling wine), along with Cabernet Sauvignon, several other single-varietal reds, and a few blends. ■ TIP→ **For a more fulfilling visit, skip the basic tasting of current releases, opting instead for one of the experiences showcasing upper-tier wines.** ⊠ *1111 Dunaweal La.* ⊹ *Off Hwy. 29* ☎ *707/942–3300, 800/726–6136* ⊕ *www.sterlingvineyards.com* ⊠ *Tastings from $40 (includes tram ride).*

Storybook Mountain Vineyards

WINERY/DISTILLERY | Tucked into a rock face in the Mayacamas range, this winery established in 1976 occupies a picture-perfect site with rows of vines rising steeply in dramatic tiers. Zinfandel is king—there's even a dry Zin Gris rosé. Visits, all by appointment, usually begin with a short walk up the hillside and a visit to the atmospheric aging caves, parts of which have the same rough-hewn look as they did when Chinese laborers dug them by hand in the late 1880s. Jerry Seps, who started Storybook with his wife, Sigrid, continues to make the wines, these days with their daughter, Colleen. ⊠ *3835 Hwy. 128* ⊹ *4 miles northwest of town* ☎ *707/942– 5310* ⊕ *www.storybookwines.com* ⊠ *Tasting and tour $35.*

T-Vine Winery

WINERY/DISTILLERY | Robust reds are the draws at this winery that provides a break from Cabernet with Zinfandels, a Grenache, and wines from less familiar varietals like Carignane and Charbono. Winemaker Bertus van Zyl punches up the Grenache with a year in 50% new French oak, producing a more tannic wine than one usually expects of this grape. Though reds are the focus, van Zyl also makes two whites, one heavy on the old-vine Gewürztraminer, the other Vermentino based. Although many of the wines derive from Northern California legacy vineyards, they're poured in a barn-moderne tasting room whose tall plateglass windows and outdoor patio have views east to the Calistoga Palisades. Guests need an appointment, with same-day visits often possible. ⊠ *810 Foothill Blvd./Hwy. 29* ⊹ *Near Lincoln Ave.* ☎ *707/942–1543* ⊕ *www. tvinewinery.com* ⊠ *Tasting $25.*

Tamber Bey Vineyards

WINERY/DISTILLERY | Endurance riders Barry and Jennifer Waitte share their passion for horses and wine at their glam-rustic winery north of Calistoga. Their 22-acre Sundance Ranch remains a working equestrian facility, but the site has been revamped to include a state-of-the-art winery with separate fermenting tanks for grapes from Tamber Bey's vineyards in Yountville, Oakville, and elsewhere. The winemakers produce Chardonnay, Sauvignon Blanc, and Pinot Noir, but the showstoppers are several subtly powerful reds, including the flagship Oakville Cabernet Sauvignon and a Yountville Merlot. The top-selling wine, Rabicano, is a Cabernet Sauvignon-heavy Bordeaux-style blend. Visits here require an appointment. ⊠ *1251 Tubbs La.* ⊹ *At Myrtledale Rd.* ☎ *707/942–2100* ⊕ *www. tamberbey.com* ⊠ *Tastings from $45.*

Tedeschi Family Winery

WINERY/DISTILLERY | Time-travel back to the days when the Napa Valley "lifestyle" revolved around a family rolling up its collective sleeves to grow grapes, make wines, and pour them at a slab of wood held up by used oak barrels. The first Tedeschi arrived in the valley in 1919 from Pisa, Italy, and the grandparents of the current winemaker, Mario, and general manager, his amiable brother Emilio, purchased the Calistoga property, then an orchard, in the 1950s. Mario makes the Estate Cabernet from an acre of grapes grown on-site, with fruit for Sauvignon Blanc, Merlot, Petite Sirah, and other wines coming from Napa Valley and Sonoma County sources. ■TIP→ **An appointment to taste is required, but it's possible to make one same-day (just call ahead).** ⊠ *2779 Grant St., Napa* ✛ *At Greenwood Ave.* ☎ *707/337–6835* ⊕ *www.tedeschifamilywinery.com* ⊠ *Tastings from $25.*

★ Theorem Vineyards

WINERY/DISTILLERY | The sought-after consultant Thomas Rivers Brown oversees the collector-quality Cabernets of this winery on Diamond Mountain's northern slope. The Voir Dire Cabernet Sauvignon (one owner practices law), Theorem's layered and silky flagship, comes from the property's oldest vines. Younger plantings produce fruit for the friskier Hawk's Prey Cab and mellifluous Merlot, with Chardonnay, Sauvignon Blanc, and Syrah coming from a high-elevation estate in Sonoma County's Moon Mountain appellation. Private appointment-only tastings, some accompanied by catered bites that illustrate (and then some) the wines' food-friendliness, often unfold on a patio with vineyard views in one direction and Mt. St. Helena in the other. Brown and his team create the wines inside a contemporary high-tech facility. Two restored structures nearby, one Calistoga's former schoolhouse, the other a residence erected by a San Francisco surgeon, date to the 19th century. ■TIP→ **It's best to book** tastings a few days ahead. ⊠ *255 Petrified Forest Rd.* ✛ *1¼ miles west of Hwy. 128* ☎ *707/942–4254* ⊕ *www.theoremvineyards.com* ⊠ *Tastings from $100.*

★ Tom Eddy Winery

WINERY/DISTILLERY | If you miss the driveway to Tom and Kerry Eddy's hillside slice of paradise, you'll soon find yourself in Sonoma County—their tree-studded 22-acre property, home to deer, wild turkeys, and a red-shouldered hawk, is that far north. Tom, the winemaker, and Kerry, a sommelier and talented sculptor (look for her works in the wine-aging cave), pour their wines by appointment only. Except for the estate Kerry's Vineyard Cabernet Sauvignon, they're made from grapes sourced from as near as Calistoga and, in the case of the Sauvignon Blanc, as far away as New Zealand. A past president of the Calistoga Winegrowers Association and a winery and wine-making consultant, Tom also makes other Cabernets, along with Chardonnay, Grenache Blanc, rosé of Pinot Noir, Pinot Noir, and Malbec. A visit here is enchanting. ⊠ *3870 Hwy. 128* ✛ *4¼ miles north of downtown* ☎ *707/942–4267* ⊕ *tomeddywinery.com* ⊠ *Tastings from $75* ⊘ *Closed Sun.*

Venge Vineyards

WINERY/DISTILLERY | As the son of Nils Venge, the first winemaker to earn a 100-point score from the wine critic Robert Parker, Kirk Venge had a hard act to follow. Now a consultant to exclusive wineries himself, Kirk is an acknowledged master of fruit-forward but balanced Cabernet-heavy Bordeaux-style blends. At his casual ranch-house tasting room, flights that might include Sauvignon Blanc, Chardonnay, Merlot, Zinfandel, or Syrah set the stage for the Cabernet Sauvignon. With its views of the estate Bone Ash Vineyard and, west across the valley, Diamond Mountain, the ranch house's porch would make for a magical perch even if Venge's wines weren't treasures themselves. Tastings are by appointment only, with same-day visits unlikely. ✉ *4708 Silverado Trail* ✣ *1½ miles south of downtown, near Dunaweal La.* ☎ *707/942–9100* 🌐 *www.vengevineyards.com* 🎟 *Tastings from $45* ⏲ *Closed Mon. and Tues. Reservations recommended 3–4 wks in advance for weekend visits.*

★ **Vincent Arroyo Winery**
WINERY/DISTILLERY | Fans of this down-home winery's flagship Petite Sirah snap it up so quickly that visitors to the plywood-paneled tasting room have to buy "futures" of wines still aging in barrels. The same holds true for the other small-lot wines. Vincent Arroyo, namesake original owner and winemaker, quit his mechanical engineering career in the 1970s to become a farmer, replacing a prune orchard with Petite Sirah and Cabernet Sauvignon, and these days Zinfandel, the winery's top sellers. Later came more acreage and other varietals, including Merlot, Tempranillo, Sangiovese, and Chardonnay—all dry-farmed. These days Vince's daughter, Adrian, and her husband, Matthew Moye (the current winemaker), own and run the winery. The presentation here, experienced by appointment only, is charmingly old-school, with Arroyo, Adrian, and Moye often on hand. ✉ *2361 Greenwood Ave.* ✣ *Off Hwy. 29* ☎ *707/942–6995* 🌐 *www.vincentarroyo.com* 🎟 *Tasting $20.*

Von Strasser Family of Wines
WINERY/DISTILLERY | Winemaker Rudy von Strasser's namesake single-vineyard Diamond Mountain Cabernet Sauvignons earned decades of acclaim and high-90s scores, so to some insiders it seemed an odd match when he acquired Lava Vine Winery, a valley-floor establishment known for its partylike atmosphere and eclectic wine roster. Von Strasser, though, welcomed the opportunity to extend his range: for Lava Vine he produces Sauvignon Blanc, Grüner Veltliner, Grenache, Petite Sirah, and anything else that captures his fancy. Tastings take place in or just outside a barnlike space whose hip-rustic touches include slatted bucket chandeliers that throw off spiffy light patterns. Reservations are required, but walk-ins are welcomed when possible. ✉ *965 Silverado Trail N* ✣ *Near Brannan St.* ☎ *707/942–9500* 🌐 *vonstrasser.com* 🎟 *Tastings from $25.*

🍴 Restaurants

Amaro Italian Kitchen
$$ | ITALIAN | What began as a lockdown-era pop-up at this softly lit space off the Mount View Hotel's lobby struck such a chord it became a permanent fixture. The chefs prepare seasonal country-style Italian cuisine centered on, says the owner, "pizzas and what you miss from your Nonna (grandmother)," with the latter items including pasta dishes and mains like artichoke risotto, lasagna with beef-and-pork Bolognese, and sausage and roasted peppers served with creamy polenta. **Known for:** antipasti selections; Italo-centric wine list; patio dining beside hotel. [$] *Average main: $24* ✉ *Mount View Hotel & Spa, 1457 Lincoln Ave.* ✣ *Near Fair Way* ☎ *707/942–5938* 🌐 *www.amarocalistoga.com* ⏲ *No lunch.*

Buster's Southern BarBeQue & Bakery
$ | BARBECUE | A roadside stand at the west end of Calistoga's downtown, Buster's lives up to its name with Louisiana-style barbecue basics, sweet-potato pies, and corn bread muffins. Local-fave sandwiches at lunch include the tri-tip, spicy hot links, and pulled pork, with tri-tip and pork or beef ribs the hits at dinner. **Known for:** mild and searing hot sauces; slaw, baked beans, and other sides; outdoor dining areas. [$] *Average main: $15* ✉ *1207 Foothill Blvd./Hwy. 29* ✣ *At Lincoln Ave.* ☎ *707/942–5605* 🌐 *www.busterssouthernbbq.com* ☞ *Closes in early evening (6 or 7 in winter, 7 or 8 in summer).*

Cafe Sarafornia

$ | **AMERICAN** | Longtime upvalley restaurateurs run this down-home diner whose efficient chefs churn out comfort food with a touch more flair than the zingy Cal-hippie decor might lead you to expect. Huevos rancheros and other egg dishes top the breakfast (until 2:30 closing) menu along with blintzes, pancakes, waffles, French toast, and vegetarian and corned-beef hash; burgers (beef, fish, or black bean), tuna melts, sandwiches, wraps, and several salads headline at lunch, with sides that include crispy-golden onion rings. **Known for:** huge portions; create-your-own omelets and egg scrambles; cakes and deep-dish pies. [$] *Average main: $13* ✉ *1413 Lincoln Ave.* ✥ *At Washington St.* ☎ *707/942–0555* 🌐 *cafesarafornia.com* 🕓 *No dinner.*

Calistoga Inn Restaurant & Brewery

$$ | **AMERICAN** | When the weather's nice, the inn's outdoor patio and beer garden edging the Napa River are swell places to hang out and sip some microbrews. Among the beer-friendly dishes, the garlic-crusted calamari appetizer and the country paella entrée stand out, along with several pizzas, the burger topped with Tillamook cheddar and applewood-smoked bacon, and (for lunch) the Reuben with ale-braised corned beef. **Known for:** comfort food; kid-friendly patio; ales and beers. [$] *Average main: $24* ✉ *1250 Lincoln Ave.* ✥ *At Cedar St.* ☎ *707/942–4101* 🌐 *www.calistogainn.com.*

Evangeline

$$ | **MODERN AMERICAN** | The gas-lamp-style lighting fixtures, charcoal-black hues, and bistro cuisine at Evangeline evoke old New Orleans with a California twist. The chefs put a jaunty spin on dishes that might include shrimp étouffée, duck confit, or steak frites; the elaborate weekend brunch, with *pamplemousse* (grapefruit) mimosas an acerbic intro to everything from beet toast and smoked salmon to eggs Benedict, is an upvalley favorite. **Known for:** outdoor courtyard; palate-cleansing Sazeracs; gumbo ya-ya and addictive fried pickles. [$] *Average main: $26* ✉ *1226 Washington St.* ✥ *Near Lincoln Ave.* ☎ *707/341–3131* 🌐 *www.evangelinenapa.com* 🕓 *No lunch weekdays.*

★ **Lovina**

$$$ | **MODERN AMERICAN** | A vintage-style neon sign outside this bungalow restaurant announces "Great Food," and the chefs deliver with imaginative, well-plated dishes served on two floors or a streetside patio that in good weather is especially festive during weekend brunch. Entrée staples on the seasonally changing menu include cioppino and slow-roasted half-chicken, with heirloom-tomato gazpacho a summer starter and chicken-dumpling soup its warming winter counterpart. **Known for:** imaginative cuisine; weekend brunch scene; Wine Wednesdays no corkage, discounts on wine list. [$] *Average main: $34* ✉ *1107 Cedar St.* ✥ *At Lincoln Ave.* ☎ *707/942–6500* 🌐 *www.lovinacalistoga.com* 🕓 *No lunch weekdays.*

Sam's Social Club

$$$ | **MODERN AMERICAN** | Tourists, locals, and spa guests—some of the latter in bathrobes after treatments—assemble inside this resort restaurant or on its extensive patio for breakfast, lunch, bar snacks, or dinner. Lunch options include thin-crust pizzas, sandwiches, an aged-cheddar burger, and entrées such as chicken paillard, with the burger reappearing for dinner along with pan-seared fish, rib-eye steak frites, and similar fare. **Known for:** casual atmosphere; cocktail-friendly starters; hearty salads. [$] *Average main: $31* ✉ *Indian Springs Resort and Spa, 1712 Lincoln Ave.* ✥ *At Wappo Ave.* ☎ *707/942–4969* 🌐 *www.samssocialclub.com.*

★ **Solbar**

$$$$ | **MODERN AMERICAN** | The restaurant at Solage attracts the resort's clientele, upvalley locals, and guests of nearby

All three accommodations at the Bungalows at Calistoga have fully equipped kitchens.

lodgings for sophisticated farm-to-table cuisine served in the high-ceilinged dining area or alfresco on a sprawling patio warmed by shapely heaters and a mesmerizing fire pit. Dishes on the lighter side might include house-made pasta or well-executed sole, with duck breast, crispy pork, or prime New York steak among the heartier options. **Known for:** artisanal cocktails; festive patio; Sunday brunch. [$] *Average main: $40* ✉ *Solage, 755 Silverado Trail* ✥ *At Rosedale Rd.* ☎ *866/942–7442* 🌐 *solage.aubergeresorts.com/dine.*

Sushi Mambo

$$ | **JAPANESE** | Preparations are traditional and unconventional at this sushi and country-Japanese restaurant whose owner vows diners will not leave hungry. The menu's diversity might daunt you into sticking to the familiar, but don't overlook offbeat items like the Fungus Among Us (tempura mushrooms stuffed with spicy tuna), Batman Roll (eel and cream cheese), and Hottie (deep-fried panko shrimp with spicy tuna). **Known for:** upbeat vibe; offbeat items; vegetarian options. [$] *Average main: $23* ✉ *1631 Lincoln Ave.* ✥ *At Wappo Ave.* ☎ *707/942–4699* 🌐 *www.napasushi.com* ⏲ *Closed Tues.*

🛏 Hotels

★ **Brannan Cottage Inn**

$$$ | **B&B/INN** | Stained oak floors, wainscoting, and retro bathroom fixtures recall Victorian times at this small inn whose centerpiece is an 1860s cottage from Calistoga's original spa era. **Pros:** short walk from downtown; helpful staff; Sam's General Store for coffee and light meals. **Cons:** noise from neighbors can be heard in some rooms; showers but no bathtubs in some rooms; lacks pool and other amenities of larger properties. [$] *Rooms from: $309* ✉ *109 Wappo Ave.* ✥ *At Lincoln Ave.* ☎ *707/942–4200* 🌐 *www.brannancottageinn.com* 🛏 *6 rooms* 🍴 *Free breakfast.*

Embrace Calistoga's many repeat visitors appreciate the attentive owners and full breakfasts.

Bungalows at Calistoga

$$$ | **B&B/INN** | The owners of these spacious (584–889 square-foot) contemporary bungalows aim to provide guests with an upscale, up-to-date home away from home, with fireplaces, outdoor patios and dining areas, wireless and streaming-service connectivity, fully stocked kitchens (complete with utensils plus dishwashers, refrigerators, and microwaves), and washers and dryers. **Pros:** contemporary style; five-minute walk to downtown Calistoga; rates include up to four guests. **Cons:** lacks room service and other hotel amenities; no pool or fitness center; two-night minimum. $ *Rooms from: $375* ✉ *207 Wappo Ave.* ☎ *707/341–6544* ⊕ *thebungalowsatcalistoga.com* 🛏 *3 bungalows* ⦿ *No meals.*

Calistoga Motor Lodge

$$ | **HOTEL** | **FAMILY** | A 1947 roadside motel renovated in midcentury-modern style, the family-friendly (and in most rooms dog-friendly) Calistoga Motor Lodge recalls the past while simultaneously escorting its guests into a pleasant and reasonably affordable present. **Pros:** 10-minute walk to downtown shops and restaurants; three mineral pools; additional rooms at sister property Dr. Wilkinson's. **Cons:** streetside rooms pick up traffic noise (ask for a room in back); rooms have showers with rain heads but no tubs; pool area feels crowded when motel is full. $ *Rooms from: $249* ✉ *1880 Lincoln Ave.* ☎ *707/942–0991* ⊕ *www.calistogamotorlodgeandspa.com* 🛏 *62 rooms* ⦿ *No meals.*

Cottage Grove Inn

$$ | **B&B/INN** | A long driveway lined with freestanding, elm-shaded cottages with rocking chairs on their porches looks a bit like Main Street USA, but inside each skylighted building you'll find all the perks necessary for a romantic weekend getaway. **Pros:** spacious cottages; hideaway feel; huge bathtubs. **Cons:** no pool; some rooms pick up street noise; weekend minimum-stay requirement. $ *Rooms from: $269* ✉ *1711 Lincoln Ave.*

☎ 707/942–8400, 800/799–2284 ⊕ www.cottagegrove.com ⇗ 16 cottages ⓘ No meals.

Dr. Wilkinson's Backyard Resort & Mineral Springs

$$$ | HOTEL | In 2021 new owners transformed this Calistoga mainstay into a playfully retro mid-century-style resort with all the mod cons a 21st-century guest in need of rejuvenation requires, most notably the slightly kitschy spa, relaxing heated mineral pools, and the House of Better restaurant serving an acclaimed San Francisco chef's healthful "booster foods." Natural wood and soft browns and whites predominate in the guest rooms, whose bright-orange and aqua-blue accents supply vintage verve. **Pros:** easy walk to shops, restaurants, and tasting rooms; twin bunks in family rooms; king suites with all-access Pelotons. **Cons:** some rooms pick up street noise; no room service; kitschy aesthetic may not work for some guests. $ Rooms from: $399 ⊠ 1507 Lincoln Ave. ☎ 707/942–4102 ⊕ www.drwilkinson.com ⇗ 50 rooms ⓘ No meals.

★ Embrace Calistoga

$$$ | B&B/INN | Extravagant hospitality defines the Napa Valley's luxury properties, but Embrace Calistoga takes the prize in the "small lodging" category. **Pros:** attentive owners; marvelous breakfasts; restaurants, tasting rooms, and shopping within walking distance. **Cons:** light hum of street traffic; no pool or spa; two-night minimum some weekends. $ Rooms from: $309 ⊠ 1139 Lincoln Ave. ☎ 707/942–9797 ⊕ embracecalistoga.com ⇗ 5 rooms ⓘ Free breakfast.

Four Seasons Resort and Residences Napa Valley

$$$$ | RESORT | Opened in 2021, this suave luxury resort entices high rollers with farmhouse-eclectic interiors and amenities that include a spa, a destination restaurant, two pools, 7-plus acres of vines, and a working winery. **Pros:** estate villa and one-bedroom suites offer maximum luxury and privacy; destination restaurant Truss; on-site vineyard and winery. **Cons:** expensive year-round; casual-chic yet may feel too formal for some guests; minimum two-night weekend requirement. $ Rooms from: $1400 ⊠ 400 Silverado Trail N ☎ 707/709–2100, 800/819–5053 for reservations ⊕ www.fourseasons.com/napavalley ⇗ 83 rooms ⓘ No meals.

★ Francis House

$$$$ | B&B/INN | Built in 1886 of locally quarried tufa, abandoned for half a century but gloriously restored, the Second Empire–style Francis House opened in 2018 as a five-room luxury inn having already won a prestigious award for historic preservation. **Pros:** ultrachic style evokes the past but feels utterly contemporary; full gourmet breakfast outdoors or in light-filled dining area; pool and lawn area in back. **Cons:** pricey for Calistoga (but less costly than the plushest resorts); more for romantic getaways than family adventures; weekend minimum-stay requirement. $ Rooms from: $473 ⊠ 1403 Myrtle St. ☎ 707/341–3536 ⊕ thefrancishouse.com ⇗ 5 rooms ⓘ Free breakfast.

Indian Springs Calistoga

$$$ | RESORT | Palm-studded Indian Springs—operating as a spa since 1862—ably splits the difference between laid-back and chic in accommodations that include lodge rooms, suites, cottages, stand-alone bungalows, and two houses. **Pros:** palm-studded grounds with outdoor seating areas; on-site Sam's Social Club restaurant; enormous mineral pool. **Cons:** lodge rooms are small; many rooms have showers but no tubs; two-night minimum on weekends (three with Monday holiday). $ Rooms from: $309 ⊠ 1712 Lincoln Ave. ☎ 707/709–8139 ⊕ www.indianspringscalistoga.com ⇗ 113 rooms ⓘ No meals.

Meadowlark Country House & Resort

$$$ | B&B/INN | Two charming European gents run this informal yet sophisticated inn on 20 wooded acres 1½ miles north of downtown. **Pros:** tasty breakfasts; many repeat customers; per website "hetero-, bi-, gay-, and naturist-friendly". **Cons:** clothing-optional pool policy isn't for everyone; one room has a shower but no tub; maximum occupancy in most rooms is two. $ *Rooms from: $310* ✉ *601 Petrified Forest Rd.* ☎ *707/942–5651* ⊕ *www.meadowlarkinn.com* ⤴ *10 rooms* ⓘ *Free breakfast.*

★ Solage

$$$$ | RESORT | The aesthetic at this 22-acre property, where health and wellness are priorities, is Napa Valley barn meets San Francisco loft: guest rooms have high ceilings, sleek contemporary furniture, all-natural fabrics in soothingly muted colors, and an outdoor patio. **Pros:** great service; complimentary bikes; separate pools for kids and adults. **Cons:** vibe might not suit everyone; longish walk from some lodgings to spa and fitness center; expensive in-season. $ *Rooms from: $749* ✉ *755 Silverado Trail* ☎ *866/942–7442, 707/226–0800* ⊕ *www.solagecalistoga.com* ⤴ *89 rooms* ⓘ *No meals.*

Activities

SPAS

Baths at Roman Spa

FITNESS/HEALTH CLUBS | Dispensing with high design and highfalutin treatments, this down-to-earth spa delivers the basics at reasonable prices. The signature treatment consists of mud and mineral baths followed by a full-body massage of 45 or 75 minutes. You can also book these treatments à la carte, along with aromatherapy and Reiki sessions and CBD massages. ■ TIP→ **Not all Calistoga spas have rooms for couples, but this one does.** ✉ *Roman Spa Hot Springs*

Resort, 1300 Washington St. ⊕ *At 1st St.* ☎ *707/942–2122, 800/404–4772* ⊕ *romanspahotsprings.com/spa* ✉ *Treatments $85–$199.*

Indian Springs Spa

FITNESS/HEALTH CLUBS | Even before Sam Brannan constructed a spa on this site in the 1860s, the Wappo Indians built sweat lodges over its thermal geysers. Treatments include a Calistoga-classic, pure volcanic-ash mud bath followed by a mineral bath, after which clients are wrapped in a flannel blanket for a 15-minute cool-down session or until called for a massage if they've booked one. Oxygen-infusion facials are another specialty. Before or following a treatment, guests unwind at the serene Buddha Pool, fed by one of the property's four geysers. ✉ *1712 Lincoln Ave.* ⊕ *At Wappo Ave.* ☎ *707/942–4913* ⊕ *indianspringscalistoga.com/spa-overview* ✉ *Treatments from $95.*

★ Spa Solage

FITNESS/HEALTH CLUBS | This 20,000-square-foot eco-conscious spa reinvented the traditional Calistoga mud-and-mineral-water regimen with the hour-long "Mudslide." The three-part treatment includes a mud body mask applied in a heated lounge, a soak in a thermal bath, and a power nap in a sound-vibration chair. The mud here, less gloppy than at other resorts, is a mix of clay, volcanic ash, and essential oils. Traditional spa services—combination Shiatsu-Swedish and other massages, foot reflexology, facials, and waxes—are available, as are yoga and wellness sessions. ✉ *755 Silverado Trail* ⊕ *At Rosedale Rd.* ☎ *707/226–0825* ⊕ *solage.aubergeresorts.com/spa* ✉ *Treatments from $110.*

SONOMA VALLEY AND PETALUMA

☉ Sights	🍴 Restaurants	🛏 Hotels	🛍 Shopping	🍸 Nightlife
★★★★★	★★★★☆	★★★★☆	★★★☆☆	★★★☆☆

144

WELCOME TO
SONOMA VALLEY AND PETALUMA

TOP REASONS
TO GO

★ **California and wine history:** Sonoma's mission and nearby sites shine a light on California's history; at Buena Vista you can explore the wine industry's roots.

★ **Literary trails:** Work off the wine and fine cuisine—and just enjoy the scenery—while hiking the trails of Jack London State Park, which contains the ruins of London's Wolf House.

★ **Peaceful Glen Ellen:** As writers from Jack London to M. F. K. Fisher discovered, peaceful Glen Ellen is a good place to decompress and tap into one's creativity. (Though Hunter S. Thompson found it too sedate.)

★ **Seated Pinot Noir tastings:** Blue Farm, Sojourn, the Donum Estate, and other wineries host seated tastings of high-quality Pinots from Los Carneros and beyond.

★ **Wineries with a view:** The views from the outdoor tasting spaces at McEvoy Ranch, Ram's Gate, and Kunde encourage lingering over a glass of your favorite varietal.

1 Sonoma. The Wine Country's oldest town has it all: fine dining, historical sites, and wineries from down-home to high style. Much of the activity takes place around Sonoma Plaza, where in 1846 some American settlers declared independence from Mexico and established the California Republic. The republic only lasted a month, but during the next decade, Count Agoston Haraszthy laid the foundation for modern California wine making.

2 Glen Ellen. Sonoma Creek snakes through Glen Ellen's tiny "downtown." The lodgings here are small, and the town, home to Jack London State Park, has retained its rural character.

3 Kenwood. St. Francis and a few other name wineries straddle Highway 12 in Kenwood, whose vague center lies about 5 miles north of Glen Ellen.

4 Petaluma. This southern Sonoma County town's agricultural roots stretch back to the mid-1830s; the 2018 approval of the Petaluma Gap AVA recognized the area's potential for grape growing, especially Pinot Noir and Chardonnay.

The birthplace of modern California wine making, the Sonoma Valley seduces with its unpretentious attitude and pastoral landscape. Tasting rooms, restaurants, and historical sites abound near Sonoma Plaza. Beyond downtown Sonoma, wineries and attractions are spread out along gently winding roads.

Sonoma County's half of the Carneros District lies within Sonoma Valley, whose other towns of note include Glen Ellen and Kenwood. To Sonoma Valley's west, bustling Petaluma has in recent years come into its own as a Wine Country destination. A walkable downtown, burgeoning dining scene, and relatively inexpensive lodgings add to its allure.

Sonoma Valley tasting rooms are often less crowded than those in Napa or northern Sonoma County, especially midweek, and the vibe here, though sophisticated, is less sceney. That's not to suggest that the Sonoma Valley is undiscovered territory. On the contrary, along Highway 12, the main corridor through the Sonoma Valley, you'll spot classy inns, restaurants, and spas in addition to wineries. In high season Glen Ellen and Kenwood are filled with well-heeled wine buffs, and the best restaurants can be crowded.

The historic Sonoma Valley towns offer glimpses of the past. Sonoma, with its tree-filled central plaza, is rich with 19th-century buildings. Two names pop up on many plaques affixed to them: General Mariano Guadalupe Vallejo, who in the 1830s and 1840s was Mexico's highest-ranking military officer in these

parts, and Count Agoston Haraszthy, who opened Buena Vista Winery in 1857. Glen Ellen, meanwhile, has a special connection with the author Jack London. Kenwood claims a more recent distinction: in 1999 a winery here was the first in Sonoma County to earn a wine of the year award from *Wine Spectator* magazine, one of several signs that Sonoma Valley wine making had come of age.

Bounded by the Mayacamas Mountains on the east and Sonoma Mountain on the west, this scenic valley extends north from San Pablo Bay nearly 20 miles to the eastern outskirts of Santa Rosa. The varied terrain, soils, and climate—cooler in the south because of the bay influence and hotter toward the north—allow grape growers to raise cool-weather varietals such as Chardonnay and Pinot Noir as well as Cabernet Sauvignon and other heat-seeking grapes.

In 1836 General Vallejo established the Rancho de Petaluma as an agricultural concern. The oldest surviving structure, the Petaluma Adobe, is now a state park. The surrounding land is still primarily used for farming, some of it grapes.

MAJOR REGIONS

The Sonoma Valley lies north of San Pablo Bay, itself an extension of the larger San Francisco Bay. The largest town, Sonoma, about 41 miles north of San Francisco's Golden Gate Bridge, is bisected by Highway 12, which continues north to Glen Ellen and Kenwood. About 44,500 people live in the Sonoma Valley: 11,000 in Sonoma proper, with another 24,200 within the town's orbit; Glen Ellen has about 730 residents, Kenwood a little more than 1,000. West of the Sonoma Valley in southern Sonoma County—a straight shot north from the Golden Gate Bridge—U.S. 101 bisects Petaluma, with 62,500 residents the county's second-largest city after Santa Rosa.

Planning

When to Go

The best time to visit the Sonoma Valley is between late spring and early fall, when the weather is warm and wineries bustle with activity. September and October, when grape harvesting and crushing are in full swing, are the busiest months. At this time—and on all summer weekends—lodging prices tend to be at their highest. Tasting rooms throughout the Sonoma Valley are generally not too crowded during the week, even in high season, except perhaps on holiday Mondays.

Getting Here and Around

BUS

Sonoma Transit buses provide service within Sonoma and Petaluma and to Glen Ellen and Kenwood. *For more information about arriving by bus, see the Bus section in the Travel Smart chapter. For more information about local bus service, see the Bus sections for the individual towns in this chapter.*

CAR

Traveling by car is the easiest way to tour the Sonoma Valley. Highway 12, also called the Sonoma Highway, is the main thoroughfare through the valley, running north–south through Sonoma, Glen Ellen, and Kenwood into Santa Rosa. Arnold Drive heads north from Highway 121 in southern Sonoma to Glen Ellen. On the north side of town it reconnects with (and dead-ends at) Highway 12. A turn left (north) leads to Kenwood. You can access Petaluma, which lies southwest of Sonoma, off U.S. 101.

From San Francisco: To get to the Sonoma Valley from San Francisco, travel north on U.S. 101 to the Highway 37 turnoff (Exit 460A), driving east for about 7 miles to Highway 121, the main route through the Carneros District. Highway 12 leads north from Highway 121 into the town of Sonoma. For Petaluma, continue on U.S. 101 to Kastania Road (Exit 472A), turn right and then quickly left, and follow signs on Petaluma Boulevard South to downtown.

From the Napa Valley: To reach the Sonoma Valley from Napa, turn west off Highway 29 onto Highway 121/12 and drive north on Highway 12 when it splits off from Highway 121. For Petaluma, turn west off Highway 12 onto Watmaugh Road 2 miles before Sonoma Plaza and follow Highway 116 west; for Sonoma, continue north on Highway 12, by this time signed as Broadway. A more adventurous route (not for the carsick) leads west over the Mayacamas range on highly scenic—but slow and winding—Oakville Grade Road, which turns into Trinity Road before it reaches Highway 12 in Glen Ellen. If coming to the Sonoma Valley from Calistoga, travel north a few miles on Highway 128 and then west on Petrified Forest Road and later Calistoga Road to reach Highway 12 in Santa Rosa. From there, head south into the valley.

Avoiding confusion: In the Carneros District, Highway 121 is signposted as Carneros Highway, Sonoma Highway (the parts coinciding with Highway 12), and Arnold Drive. It's all the same road.

Restaurants

Fine dining in the Sonoma Valley, for many years low-key, received a jolt of high style as two hotel restaurants south of Sonoma Plaza—Layla at MacArthur Place and Wit & Wisdom at the Lodge at Sonoma—waltzed onto the scene in 2019 and 2020 respectively. Stalwarts like Cafe La Haye, the Girl and the Fig, and LaSalette in Sonoma continue to turn out thoughtful, complex cuisine emphasizing locally produced meat, fish, cheese, vegetables, and fruit. Glen Ellen Star is its town's must-do, but you can't go wrong at any of the fine-dining restaurants here. In Kenwood, Salt & Stone serves bistro favorites; New Orleans inspires Tips Roadside's menu. Petaluma's restaurant scene is centered downtown. Central Market for Cal-Med is a longtime star.

Hotels

Sonoma has the valley's most varied accommodations, with motels and small inns, vacation condos, and boutique hotels. Small inns are the norm in Glen Ellen and Kenwood. Spa lovers have two high-end choices at either end of the valley: the large and splashy Fairmont Sonoma Mission Inn & Spa in Sonoma and the Mediterranean-style Kenwood Inn and Spa in Kenwood. Chain motels predominate in Petaluma, though the Hampton Inn here is inside a former silk mill.

For weekend stays it's wise to book ahead from late May through October. Most small lodgings require a two-night minimum stay on weekends at this time, three if Monday is a holiday.

What It Costs in U.S. Dollars			
$	$$	$$$	$$$$
RESTAURANTS			
under $17	$17–$26	$27–$36	over $36
HOTELS			
under $201	$201–$300	$301–$400	over $400

Planning Your Time

You can hit Sonoma Valley's highlights in a day or two—a half or a full day exploring western Carneros District wineries and some in Sonoma proper, and the same amount of time to check out Glen Ellen and Kenwood. Traffic usually isn't an issue, except on Highway 12 north of Sonoma Plaza and the intersection of Highways 116 and 121 during the morning and afternoon commutes. It takes at least half a day to get to know Petaluma.

Many valley wineries receive visitors by appointment only. On weekdays at some you may be able to reserve a space on short notice, but for weekend visits, especially during the summer and early fall, booking ahead is essential even when food pairings (which wineries need time to plan for) are not involved.

Visitor Information

CONTACTS Sonoma Valley Visitors Bureau.
✉ Sonoma Plaza, 453 1st St. E, Sonoma ☎ 707/996–1090 ⊕ www.sonomavalley. com.

Appellations

Although Sonoma *County* is a vast growing region that encompasses several different appellations, the much smaller Sonoma *Valley*, at the southern end of Sonoma County, is comparatively compact. It consists mostly of the **Sonoma**

Top Tastings 👁

Setting

Blue Farm Wines, Sonoma. A few miles south of Sonoma Plaza, Chardonnay and Pinot Noir winegrower Anne Moller-Racke's idyllic 13-acre estate, complete with rose garden and aging pepper tree, recalls old Sonoma.

The Donum Estate, Sonoma. Known for Pinot Noirs displaying both power and elegance, Donum pours its wines in a hilltop tasting room whose views include museum-quality outdoor sculptures.

McEvoy Ranch, Petaluma. The bucolic ranch's Taste of the Season—a wine flight (Chardonnay, Pinot Noir, Syrah, others) served with artisanal cheeses, charcuterie, and seasonal edibles—unfolds on a pond's-edge flagstone patio.

History

Bedrock Wine Co., Sonoma. Zinfandel and other varietals grown in heritage vineyards are Bedrock's passion. A famous Civil War general once owned Bedrock's estate vineyard; the wines are poured a few miles away at his former in-town dwelling.

Benziger Family Winery, Glen Ellen. At tastings and on the tram tour here, you'll learn about the deep commitment of Sonoma County's first certified biodynamic winery and earth-friendly farming.

Buena Vista Winery, Sonoma. The restoration of a 19th-century wine-making structure revived interest in Sonoma's oldest winery, founded in 1857.

Food Pairing

St. Francis Winery, Kenwood. The five petite plates of this famous winery's executive chef pair well with its Zins, Cabs, and other wines.

Just Plain Fun

Jeff Cohn Cellars, Sonoma. A whiz with Rhône-style wines, the wisecracking Jeff Cohn also makes critically acclaimed Zinfandel and Petite Sirah, both of which he strives not to make "over-the-freakin'-top."

Valley AVA, which stretches northwest from San Pablo Bay toward Santa Rosa. The weather and soils here are unusually diverse. Pinot Noir and Chardonnay vineyards are most likely to be found in the AVA's southernmost parts, the sections cooled by fog from San Pablo Bay. (This part of the Sonoma Valley AVA overlaps with the Sonoma County portions of **Los Carneros AVA.**) Zinfandel, Cabernet Sauvignon, and Sauvignon Blanc are more plentiful farther north, near Glen Ellen and Kenwood, both of which in summer tend to be a few degrees warmer than the southern Sonoma Valley.

The **Sonoma Mountain AVA** rises west of Glen Ellen on the Sonoma Valley AVA's western border. Benefiting from a sunny location and rocky soil, the vineyards here produce deep-rooted vines and intensely flavored grapes that are made into complex red wines, often Cabernet Sauvignon. Opposite Sonoma Mountain southeast across the Sonoma Valley lies the **Moon Mountain District Sonoma County AVA.** On the Mayacamas range's western slopes, this sliver due west of the Napa Valley's Mt. Veeder subappellation contains some of California's oldest Zinfandel and Cabernet Sauvignon vines. Steep terrain and rocky soils result in smaller berries relative to valley-floor vines, and the higher skin-to-juice ratio yields intense flavor.

Portions of the **Sonoma Coast AVA** overlap Los Carneros and the Sonoma Valley. The tiny **Bennett Valley AVA,** also part of the Sonoma Valley AVA, falls within the city of Santa Rosa *(see Chapter 6)*. West of the Sonoma Valley AVA and approved in 2018 is the **Petaluma Gap AVA,** whose name references a break in the Coast Range that permits cooling Pacific Ocean fog and wind to flow through. Except for a wee bit that edges into Marin County, this subappellation lies within the Sonoma Coast AVA.

Sonoma

14 miles west of Napa; 45 miles northeast of San Francisco.

One of the few towns in the valley with multiple attractions unrelated to food and wine, Sonoma has plenty to keep you busy for a couple of hours before you head out to the wineries. And you needn't leave town to taste wine: about three dozen tasting rooms do business on or near Sonoma Plaza.

The valley's cultural center, Sonoma, founded in 1835 when California was still part of Mexico, is built around tree-filled Sonoma Plaza. If you arrive from the south, on Broadway (Highway 12), you'll be retracing the last stretch of what long ago was California's most important road—El Camino Real, or "the royal road," the only overland route through the state. During California's Spanish and Mexican periods, it ran past all of the state's 21 missions, beginning at San Diego de Alcalá (1769) and ending at Mission San Francisco Solano (1823). This last mission still sits in the center of Sonoma.

Getting Here and Around

Highway 12 from the south (San Francisco) or north (Santa Rosa) is the main route into Sonoma. North from Highway 121 to Sonoma Plaza the road is also called Broadway. There are two- and three-hour unmetered parking spaces around the plaza, and free all-day parking can be found a block or two off the plaza. Once you've parked, a pleasant stroll takes you past many of the town's restaurants, shops, and tasting rooms. High-profile and boutique wineries can be found a mile or so east; arrow-shaped signs on East Spain Street and East Napa Street will direct you.

Sonoma Transit buses connect Sonoma with other Sonoma County towns.

◉ Sights

Anaba Wines

WINERY/DISTILLERY | Reprising the greatest hits of Burgundy (Chardonnay, Pinot Noir) and the Rhône (Grenache, Mourvèdre, Syrah, Viognier), Anaba hosts guests in a whitewashed board-and-batten hospitality center whose breezeway frames windswept Coast Range views to the west. When John Sweazey founded Anaba in 2006, he named it for the Carneros District's up-sweeping anabatic winds, a few years later installing a turbine to harness them for electricity. When planning the hospitality center and adjacent production facility, both completed in 2019, Sweazey and son John Michael continued the alternative-energy commitment by ordering solar panels that, supplemented by the turbine, supply the winery's power. Lower on the radar than many of its Carneros peers, appointment-only Anaba receives high marks from critics for its wines, particularly the Wildcat Mountain Pinot Noir, Bismark Syrah, and Lando Late Harvest Viognier. For their quality, they're quite reasonably priced. ✉ *62 Bonneau Rd.*

Wine-Making Pioneer 👁

Born in Hungary, Count Agoston Haraszthy—though of his native land's aristocracy, his noble title was self-awarded—arrived in Sonoma in 1857 and set out to make fine wine commercially. He planted European vinifera varietals rather than mission grapes (varietals brought to the Americas by Spanish missionaries) and founded Buena Vista Winery the year he arrived. Bucking custom, Haraszthy grew grapes on dry hillsides instead of in the wetter lowlands, his accomplishment demonstrating that Sonoma's climate was sufficiently moist to sustain vines without irrigation.

Adaptable Zinfandel

Despite producing inferior wines, the prolific mission grapes were preferred by California growers over better varieties of French, German, and Italian vinifera grapes through the 1860s and into the 1870s. But Haraszthy's success had begun to make an impression. A new red-wine grape, Zinfandel, was becoming popular, both because it made excellent Claret (as good red wine was then called) and because it had adapted to the area's climate.

Balance Lost

By this time, however, Haraszthy had disappeared, literally, from the scene. After a business setback during the 1860s, the count lost control of Buena Vista and ventured to Nicaragua to restore his fortune in the sugar and rum industries. While crossing a stream infested with alligators, the count lost his balance and plunged into the water below. The body of modern California wine making's first promoter and pioneer was never recovered.

⚓ At intersection of Hwys. 116 and 121 ☎ 707/996–4188 ⊕ www.anabawines. com ⊠ Tastings from $35.

⭐ Bedrock Wine Co.

WINERY/DISTILLERY | Zinfandel and other varietals grown in heritage vineyards throughout California are the focus of Bedrock, a young winery whose backstory involves several historical figures. Tastings take place in a home east of Sonoma Plaza owned in the 1850s by General Joseph Hooker. By coincidence, Hooker planted grapes at what's now the estate Bedrock Vineyard a few miles away. General William Tecumseh Sherman was his partner in the vineyard (a spat over it affected their Civil War interactions), which newspaper magnate William Randolph Hearst's father, George, replanted in the late 1880s. Some Hearst vines still produce grapes, whose current owner-winemaker, Morgan Twain-Peterson, learned about Zinfandel from his dad, Ravenswood founder Joel Peterson. Twain-Peterson's bottlings, many of them field blends containing multiple varietals grown and fermented together, are as richly textured as his winery's prehistory. ⊠ General Joseph Hooker House, 414 1st St. E ⚓ Near E. Spain St. ☎ 707/343–1478 ⊕ www.bedrockwineco. com ⊠ Tastings from $30 ⊘ Closed Mon. and Tues.

⭐ Blue Farm Wines

WINERY/DISTILLERY | Anne Moller-Racke, founder of the Pinot Noir powerhouse the Donum Estate and its president for nearly two decades, established this smaller label also devoted to serious Chardonnay and Pinot Noir. Moller-Racke, who describes herself as a winegrower in the French vigneron tradition that places agriculture at the pinnacle of wine making, practices "precision farming" to produce the best possible fruit. Hosts of private tastings at her 13-acre estate explain her philosophy and the five Sonoma County appellations where she cultivates grapes. Anchored by a circa-1880 Victorian and adjacent pump house, the former horse farm is now planted to 7 acres of grapes. Near the residence, a formidable century-old pepper tree and a rose garden with dozens of varieties catch the eye, the Mayacamas Mountains supplying the idyllic setting's backdrop. The appointment-only winery requests prospective guests inquire about visits at least 48 hours in advance. ✉ *San Luis Rd., Off Hwy. 12* ☎ *707/721–6773* ⊕ *bluefarmwines.com* 🍷 *Tasting $55* ⊗ *Closed weekends.*

Buena Vista Winery

WINERY/DISTILLERY | A local actor in top hat and 19th-century garb often greets guests as Count Agoston Haraszthy at this entertaining homage to the birthplace of modern California wine making. Haraszthy's rehabilitated former press house (used for pressing grapes into wine), completed in 1864, is the architectural focal point, with photos, banners, plaques, and artifacts providing historical context. Chardonnay, Pinot Noir, and several red blends are the strong suits among the two-dozen-plus wines produced. During appointment-only visits (walk-ins sometimes possible), you can taste some of them solo or preorder a box lunch from the affiliated Oakville Grocery. ✉ *18000 Old Winery Rd.* ✚ *Off E. Napa St.* ☎ *800/926–1266* ⊕ *www. buenavistawinery.com* 🍷 *Tastings from $20.*

Corner 103

WINERY/DISTILLERY | After leading an effort to revive a troubled local winery, Lloyd Davis, an African-American financier and oenophile, turned his attention to a new passion: making the experience of learning about wine and food-wine pairings less daunting. To that end he opened a light-filled space, diagonally across from Sonoma Plaza, for tastings of Sonoma County wines usually paired with cheeses or other pertinent bites. The lineup includes a Brut Rosé sparkler, Chardonnay and Marsanne-Roussanne whites, a rosé of Pinot Noir, and several reds. Corner 103's welcoming atmosphere, which earned it the top slot on USA Today's Best Tasting Room list for 2020, makes it an excellent choice for wine novices seeking to expand their knowledge. Visits are by appointment only, though hosts usually accommodate drop-ins seeking wine-only tastings. ✉ *103 W. Napa St.* ✚ *At 1st St. W* ☎ *707/931–6141* ⊕ *www.corner103.com* 🍷 *Tastings from $20.*

★ The Donum Estate

WINERY/DISTILLERY | The wine-making team of this prominent Chardonnay and Pinot Noir producer prizes viticulture— selecting vineyards with superior soils and microclimates, planting compatible clones, then farming with rigor—over wine-making wizardry. The Donum Estate, whose white board-and-batten tasting room affords guests hilltop views of Los Carneros, San Pablo Bay, and beyond, farms two vineyards surrounding the structure, one in the Russian River Valley, and another in Mendocino County's Anderson Valley. All the wines exhibit the "power yet elegance" that sealed the winery's fame in the 2000s. Tastings are by appointment only. Forty large-scale museum-quality contemporary sculptures placed amid the vines, including works by Ai Weiwei, Lynda Benglis, Louise Bourgeois, Keith Haring, and Anselm Kiefer, add a touch of high culture to a visit here. ■**TIP**➜ **The winery sometimes offers an invigorating 1½-hour guided stroll past the artworks without the tasting.** ✉ *24500 Ramal Rd.* ✚ *Off Hwy. 121/12* ☎ *707/732–2200* ⊕ *www.thedonumestate.com* 🍷 *Tastings from $75.*

Gloria Ferrer Caves and Vineyards

WINERY/DISTILLERY | On a clear day this Spanish hacienda–style winery's Vista Terrace lives up to its name as guests at seated tastings sip delicate sparkling wines while taking in views of gently rolling Carneros hills and beyond them San Pablo Bay. The Chardonnay and Pinot Noir grapes from the vineyards in the foreground are the product of old-world wine-making knowledge—generations of the founding Ferrer family made cava in Spain—but also contemporary soil management techniques and clonal research. Hosts well-acquainted with the winery's sustainability practices and history as the Carneros District's first sparkling-wine house serve the wines accompanied by food that varies from cheese and charcuterie to caviar or a full lunch. All visits are by appointment. ∎ TIP→ **For the cheese-and-charcuterie option you can upgrade from the standard flight, which includes still wines, to an all-bubbles one.** ⊠ 23555 Carneros Hwy./Hwy. 121 ☎ 707/933–1917 ⊕ www.gloriaferrer.com ⌲ Tastings from $55.

Gundlach Bundschu

WINERY/DISTILLERY | "Gun lock bun shoe" gets you close to pronouncing this winery's name correctly, though everyone here shortens it to Gun Bun. The Bundschu family, which has owned most of this property since 1858, still uses parts of an 1870 stone winery for production. Reds from estate grapes include Cabernet Franc, Cabernet Sauvignon, Merlot, and a Bordeaux-style blend of each vintage's best fruit. Gewürztraminer, Chardonnay, and two rosés are also in the mix. You can sample five estate wines in a courtyard with views of vineyards and a pond. For a more comprehensive experience, book a Pinzgauer vehicle vineyard tour or a Heritage Reserve pairing of limited-release wines with small gourmet bites. All visits are by appointment only, with same-day tastings often possible. ⊠ 2000 Denmark St. ⊹ At Bundschu Rd.,

off 8th St. E ☎ 707/938–5277 ⊕ www.gunbun.com ⌲ Tastings from $30, tours from $55 (includes tasting).

★ Hamel Family Wines

WINERY/DISTILLERY | Seeking respite from foggy San Francisco summers, Pam and George Hamel Jr. purchased a vineyard mostly for the scenery, got bitten by the wine bug, and the next generation, sons John and George III, went all-in, too. The family now owns four biodynamic, mostly dry-farmed (no irrigation) vineyards. Collector-worthy Cabernet Sauvignon, the flagship Isthmus red blend, and carefully crafted Zinfandel and Sauvignon Blanc account for the bulk of production. John, who makes the wines, also supervises the farming (George III tackles the business side), striving for "purity of fruit" that, he says, requires little of him post-harvest. He's too modest. His choices during fermentation and aging beget magnificent wines. Appointment-only private tastings take place at the family's steel-and-glass Estate House, where guests indoors or on the broad stone terrace enjoy valley and Sonoma Mountain views. ∎ TIP→ **Despite its Sonoma address, the estate is closer to Glen Ellen.** ⊠ 15401 Sonoma Hwy./Hwy. 12 ⊹ At Madrone Rd., 5 miles north of Sonoma Plaza ☎ 707/996–5800 ⊕ hamelfamilywines.com ⌲ Tastings $75–$150 ⊘ Closed weekends.

Hanson of Sonoma Distillery

WINERY/DISTILLERY | The Hanson family makes grape-based organic vodkas, one traditional, the rest infused with cucumbers, ginger, mandarin oranges, Meyer lemons, or habanero and other chili peppers. A surprise to many visitors, the Hansons make a blended white wine before distilling it into vodka. The family pours its vodkas, along with single-malt whiskey, in an industrial-looking tasting room heavy on the steel, with wood reclaimed from Deep South smokehouses adding a rustic note. In good weather some sessions take place on the

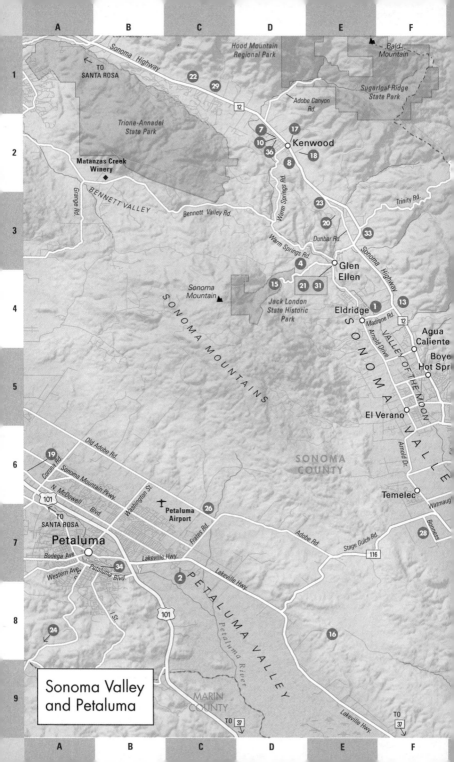

landscaped shore of a small pond. Per state law, there's a limit to the amount poured, but it's sufficient to get to know the product. ⊠ *22985 Burndale Rd.* ⊹ *At Carneros Hwy. (Hwy. 121)* ☎ *707/343–1805* ⊕ *hansonofsonoma.com* ✉ *Tastings from $25, tours from $50 (includes tasting).*

★ **Jeff Cohn Cellars**

WINERY/DISTILLERY | Rhône-style wines with complex layers and textures have long been the siren song of winemaker Jeff Cohn. The whites include a Viognier from the Napa Valley's Stagecoach Vineyard on which Cohn collaborates with noted French winemaker Yves Gangloff, and the Syrahs, from several Sonoma County vineyards, are superb. Cohn, who's known to crack wise, also makes Zinfandel and Petite Sirah, endeavoring to avoid making them "over-the-freakin'-top." Painted on an interior wall of his downtown Sonoma tasting room, a storefront space with a fireplace for cool days and an outdoor patio for warmer ones, is the motto for Cohn's wine making and hospitality: "What are we going to do today? We're going to make magic!" He's wildly successful at both, often earning high-90s scores for his wines and effusive praise from his guests. ⊠ *535 1st St. W* ⊹ *100 feet south of W. Napa St.* ☎ *707/938–8343* ⊕ *www.jeffcohncellars. com* ✉ *Tastings from $35.*

Patz & Hall

WINERY/DISTILLERY | Sophisticated single-vineyard Chardonnays and Pinot Noirs are the trademark of this respected winery that hosts tastings at a fashionable single-story former residence 3 miles southeast of Sonoma Plaza. A Wine Country adage holds that great wines are made in the vineyard—the all-star fields represented here include Hyde, Durell, and Gap's Crown—but winemaker James Hall routinely surpasses peers with access to the same fruit, proof that discernment and expertise (Hall is

a master at oak aging) play a role, too. In good weather you can sample wines on the vineyard-view patio behind the house. Tastings, one focusing on current releases, the other on older wines, are by appointment only. ⊠ *21200 8th St. E* ⊹ *Near Peru Rd.* ☎ *707/265–7700* ⊕ *www.patzhall.com* ✉ *Tastings from $45.*

Prohibition Spirits Tasting Room & Bar Shop

WINERY/DISTILLERY | Zesty limoncello was the first claim to fame of this distillery whose nearly three dozen artisanal offerings also include other "cellos" (try the fig if it's being poured), gins, brandies, liqueurs, and bottled cocktails. You can sample six at the tasting room, down an alley due east of Sonoma Plaza. In addition to the alcoholic beverages, the shop sells bar paraphernalia, cocktail-related books, a few snacks, and coffee aged in bourbon barrels. Reservations are recommended, especially on weekends. ⊠ *Mercato Courtyard, 452 1st St E* ⊹ *East of Sonoma Plaza* ☎ *707/933–7507* ⊕ *www.prohibition-spirits.com* ☺ *Tastings from $25.*

Ram's Gate Winery

WINERY/DISTILLERY | Stunning views, ultra-chic architecture, and wines made from grapes grown by acclaimed producers make a visit to Ram's Gate an event. The welcoming interior spaces—think Restoration Hardware with a dash of high-style whimsy—open up to outdoor tasting areas and views of the entire western Carneros. In fine weather cooling breezes waft through the site as guests sip sophisticated wines, mostly Pinot Noirs and Chardonnays but also Pinot Blanc, Sauvignon Blanc, rosé, sparkling brut rosé, Cabernet Sauvignon, and Syrah. With grapes sourced from Sangiacomo, Hudson, and other illustrious vineyards, the wine-making team focuses on creating balanced wines that express what occurred in nature that year. Appointments are necessary for all tastings, one

Did You Know?

Howard Backen, one of the Wine Country's most acclaimed architects, designed Ram's Gate Winery.

of which involves a three-course culinary pairing. ✉ *28700 Arnold Dr./Hwy. 121* ☎ *707/721–8700* ⊕ *www.ramsgatewinery.com* 🍷 *Tastings from $50* ☏ *Closed Tues. and Wed.*

Robledo Family Winery

WINERY/DISTILLERY | It's truly a family affair at this winery founded by Reynaldo Robledo Sr., a migrant worker from Michoacán, Mexico, and María de La Luz Robledo. Son and winemaker Everardo Robledo and most of his eight siblings are involved in the winery and vineyard-management company Reynaldo and Maria established. Everardo's lush reds—particularly Tempranillo, Zinfandel, and Cabernet Sauvignon from grapes grown on 350-plus estate acres in several counties—stand out among the wines poured in a modest interior space or on a covered patio that juts into a Pinot Noir vineyard. Los Braceros, a blend, pays tribute to temporary workers from Mexico, including Reynaldo's father and grandfather, who contributed to California agriculture as part of the Bracero Program (1942–1964). Over these wines, preceded perhaps by Sauvignon Blanc, Chardonnay, Pinot Noir, or Merlot, guests hear inspiring multigenerational tales, sometimes first-hand from a family member. ■TIP→ **Picnickers and pets are welcome here.** ✉ *21901 Bonness Rd.* ✛ *Off Hwy. 116 or E. Bonness Rd.* ☎ *707/939–6903* ⊕ *www.robledofamilywinery.com* 🍷 *Tastings from $25.*

★ Sangiacomo Family Wines

WINERY/DISTILLERY | Several dozen wineries produce vineyard-designate Chardonnays and Pinot Noirs from grapes grown by the Sangiacomo family, whose Italian ancestors first started farming in Sonoma in 1927. The family didn't establish its own label until 2016, but its cool-climate wines and a Napa Valley Cabernet are already earning critical plaudits. Chardonnay vines and the Carneros District's western hills form the backdrop for tastings, usually outdoors, at the 110-acre Home Ranch, the first of a dozen-plus vineyards the Sangiacomos acquired or lease. At appointment-only visits you're apt to encounter one or more third-generation members, all of whom enjoy meeting guests and sharing their family's legacy. ■TIP→ **On Fridays, the winery hosts Sunset on the Terrace, with wines served by the glass or bottle from 3:30 pm until sundown.** ✉ *21545 Broadway* ✛ *2½ miles south of Sonoma Plaza* ☎ *707/934–8445* ⊕ *www.sangiacomowines.com* 🍷 *Tastings from $30.*

★ Scribe

WINERY/DISTILLERY | Andrew and Adam Mariani established Scribe in 2007 on land first planted to grapes in 1858 by Emil Dresel, a German immigrant. Dresel's claims to fame include cultivating Sonoma's first Riesling and Sylvaner, an achievement the brothers honor by growing both varietals on land he once farmed. Using natural wine-making techniques, they craft bright, terroir-driven wines from those grapes, along with Chardonnay, Pinot Noir, Syrah, and Cabernet Sauvignon. In restoring their property's 1915 Mission Revival–style hacienda, the brothers preserved various layers of history—original molding and light fixtures, for instance, but also fragments of floral-print wallpaper and 1950s newspapers. Now a tasting space with a patio whose views extend west across the southern Sonoma Valley, the hacienda served during Prohibition as a bootleggers' hideout, and its basement harbored a speakeasy. Tastings, which include meze plates whose ingredients come from Scribe's farm, are by appointment only. ✉ *2100 Denmark St.* ✛ *Off Napa Rd.* ☎ *707/939–1858* ⊕ *scribewinery.com* 🍷 *Tastings from $70.*

Sojourn Cellars

WINERY/DISTILLERY | Stellar fruit sources and a winemaker with a wisely light touch have earned Sojourn Cellars high ratings from critics for its Chardonnay, Pinot Noir, and Cabernet Sauvignon

Sonoma Mission was the last of California's 21 missions.

wines. The initial releases of this winery founded in 2001 were Cabernets, but it's best known these days for well-balanced Sonoma Coast and Russian River Valley Pinot Noirs. The Chardonnays hail from the Sonoma Coast, the five Cabernets from the Napa and Sonoma valleys. In part because winemaker Erich Bradley uses oak in such a consistent way, the informative tastings (by appointment only) at Sojourn's bungalow just east of Sonoma Plaza focus on the subtle variations caused by climate, terrain, and clone type depending on the grape sources. Angelina Mondavi of the famous wine clan purchased Sojourn in 2020, but so far is keeping the team mostly intact. ⊠ 141 E. Napa St. ⊹ ½ block east of Sonoma Plaza ☎ 707/938–7212 ⊕ www.sojourncellars.com ☜ Tasting $35.

Sonoma Mission

RELIGIOUS SITE | The northernmost of the 21 missions established by Franciscan friars in California, Sonoma Mission was founded in 1823 as Mission San Francisco Solano. These days it serves as the centerpiece of **Sonoma State Historic Park,** which includes several other sites in Sonoma and nearby Petaluma. Some early mission structures fell into ruin, but all or part of several remaining buildings date to the era of Mexican rule over California. The **Sonoma Barracks,** a half block west of the mission at 20 East Spain Street, housed troops under the command of General Mariano Guadalupe Vallejo, who controlled vast tracts of land in the region. **General Vallejo's Home,** a Victorian-era structure, is a few blocks west. ⊠ 114 E. Spain St. ⊹ At 1st St. E ☎ 707/938–9560 ⊕ www.parks.ca.gov ☜ $3, includes same-day admission to other historic sites.

Sonoma Plaza

PLAZA | Dating to the mission era, Sonoma Plaza is surrounded by 19th-century adobes, atmospheric hotels, and the swooping marquee of the Depression-era Sebastiani Theatre. A statue on the plaza's northeastern side marks the spot where California proclaimed its independence from Mexico on June 14, 1846.

Despite its historical roots, the plaza is not a museum piece. On summer days it's a hive of activity, with children blowing off steam in the playground, couples enjoying picnics from gourmet shops, and groups listening to live music at the small amphitheater. The stone **city hall** is also here. If you're wondering why the 1906 structure looks the same from all angles, here's why: its four sides were purposely made identical so that none of the plaza's merchants would feel that city hall had turned its back to them. ⊠ *North end of Broadway/Hwy. 12* ✥ *Bordered by E. Napa St., 1st St. E, E. Spain St., and 1st St. W.*

Sonoma TrainTown Railroad
AMUSEMENT PARK/WATER PARK | FAMILY | A quarter-scale train at this fun, well-run attraction geared to kids under 10 chugs for 4 miles through tunnels and past a lake, a waterfall, and a miniature town with a petting zoo. Back near the entrance are a turntable and a round-house, amusement rides, and a combination snack bar and souvenir stand. ⊠ *20264 Broadway* ✥ *Near Napa Rd.* ☎ *707/938–3912* ⊕ *www.traintown.com* ⊠ *Free to main park area, $8 for train ride; additional fee for amusement rides* ⊘ *Closed rainy days and Mon.–Thurs. Sept.–May.*

★ Three Sticks Wines
WINERY/DISTILLERY | Pinot Noir artiste Bob Cabral of Three Sticks oversees Pinots and Chardonnays made by Ryan Prichard, himself a rising Wine Country star. Their grapes come from prized estate vineyards, including Durell and Gap's Crown, of winery founder Bill Price. Three Sticks also produces Rhône-style wines that bear the Casteñeda label in honor of the restored 1842 Vallejo-Casteñeda Adobe, where they're poured. San Francisco–based designer Ken Fulk transformed the structure, Sonoma's longest-occupied residence, into a showcase both lavish and refined. Seated private tastings unfold at a long elm table inside the adobe or at a cast-stone table under a willow-covered arbor. In either setting an appointment-only tasting here feels special. ⊠ *143 W. Spain St.* ✥ *At 1st St. W* ☎ *707/996–3328* ⊕ *www.threestickswines.com* ⊠ *Tastings from $60.*

Walt Wines
WINERY/DISTILLERY | This sister winery to Hall St. Helena specializes in Pinot Noir from Sonoma County, Mendocino County, California's Central Coast, and Oregon's Willamette Valley and also produces Chardonnay. Just north of Sonoma Plaza, the tasting room occupies a mid-1930s Tudor-inspired home whose backyard tables sit beneath canary palms and a tall, double-trunk redwood tree. One tasting focuses on current releases, another on older vintages. To see how the wines pair with food, make a reservation for Root 101, a showcase for single-vineyard Pinots that includes small bites. ⊠ *380 1st St. W* ✥ *At W. Spain St.* ☎ *707/933–4440* ⊕ *www.waltwines.com* ⊠ *Tastings from $30.*

★ Westwood Estate
WINERY/DISTILLERY | This winery's organic and biodynamic vineyard in the northern Sonoma Valley's Annadel Gap occupies a zone hospitable to cool-climate grapes such as Pinot Noir, along with Syrah and other Rhône varietals. Consulting winemaker Philippe Melka and director of winemaking Maayan Koschitzky fashion the fruit grown here into exciting, thought-provoking wines. Because the estate ones come from the same vineyard (up to half of which may need replanting due to 2020 fire damage), a focus at tastings is on which Pinot Noir or Rhône clones the wines derive from and how the team brings out the best in each. Hosts at tastings also pour wines from the grapes of other vineyards for further comparison. Appointments at Westwood's salon south of Sonoma Plaza are always needed on Tuesday. Walk-ins are welcome on other days as space indoors or on the patio permits,

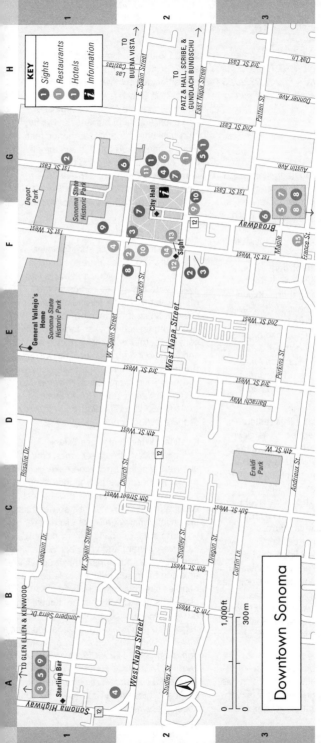

Downtown Sonoma

161

Sights ▶

1 Bedrock Wine Co. **G2**
2 Corner 103 .... **F2**
3 Jeff Cohn Cellars **F2**
4 Prohibition Spirits
   Tasting Room &
   Bar Shop. **G2**
5 Sojourn Cellars **G2**
6 Sonoma Mission **G2**
7 Sonoma Plaza **F2**
8 Three Sticks Wines **F2**
9 Walt Wines **F1**
10 Westwood Estate **G2**

Restaurants ▶

1 Cafe La Haye **G2**
2 El Dorado Kitchen **F2**
3 El Molino Central **A1**
4 Girl & the Fig **F1**
5 Kivelstadt Wine Garden
   and Eatery **F3**
6 LaSalette Restaurant **G2**
7 Layla Restaurant **F3**
8 Lou's Luncheonette **F3**
9 Oso Sonoma **F2**
10 Sunflower Caffé **F2**
11 Sweet Scoops **G2**
12 Tasca Tasca Portuguese
   Tapas Restaurant
   & Wine Bar **F2**
13 Taub Family Outpost **F2**
14 Valley Bar + Bottle **F2**
15 Wit & Wisdom Tavern **F3**

Hotels ▶

1 Auberge Sonoma **G2**
2 Cottage Inn & Spa **G1**
3 El Dorado Hotel **F2**
4 El Pueblo Inn **A1**
5 Fairmont Sonoma
   Mission Inn & Spa **A1**
6 Inn at Sonoma **F3**
7 Ledson Hotel **G2**
8 MacArthur Place
   Hotel & Spa **F3**
9 Sonoma Creek Inn **A1**

but it's best to book ahead on weekends. ✉ *Vine Alley Complex, 11 E. Napa St., No. 3* ✥ *Near Broadway* ☎ *707/933–7837* 🌐 *www.westwoodwine.com* 🎟 *Tasting $50.*

🍴 Restaurants

★ Cafe La Haye

$$$ | **AMERICAN** | In a postage-stamp-size open kitchen (the dining room, its white walls adorned with contemporary art, is nearly as compact), chef Jeffrey Lloyd turns out understated, sophisticated fare emphasizing seasonably available local ingredients. Meats, pastas, and seafood get deluxe treatment without fuss or fanfare—and the daily risotto special is always worth trying. **Known for:** Napa-Sonoma wine list with French complements; signature butterscotch pudding; owner Saul Gropman on hand to greet diners. [$] *Average main: $27* ✉ *140 E. Napa St.* ✥ *East of Sonoma Plaza* ☎ *707/935–5994* 🌐 *www.cafelahaye.com* 🕒 *Closed Sun. and Mon. No lunch.*

El Dorado Kitchen

$$$ | **MODERN AMERICAN** | This restaurant owes its visual appeal to its clean lines and handsome decor, but the eye inevitably drifts westward to the open kitchen, where longtime chef Armando Navarro and his team craft dishes full of subtle surprises. The menu might include cod ceviche or fried calamari with spicy marinara sauce as starters and pan-roasted salmon or paella awash with seafood and dry-cured Spanish chorizo sausage among the entrées. **Known for:** subtle tastes and textures; truffle-oil fries with Parmesan; bar menu's pizzas and burger. [$] *Average main: $29* ✉ *El Dorado Hotel, 405 1st St. W* ✥ *At W. Spain St.* ☎ *707/996–3030* 🌐 *eldoradokitchen.com.*

El Molino Central

$ | **MEXICAN** | The goodness at Karen Waikiki's roadside restaurant, which has more tables outside than in, starts with (until 11 am) breakfast chilaquiles Merida served with soft-scrambled eggs and spicy roasted tomato. Stars at lunch and dinner include tamales (chicken mole and Niman Ranch pork), tacos filled with beer-battered fish or crispy beef, and enchiladas and burritos. **Known for:** high-quality ingredients; authentic techniques; handmade tortillas and tamales from organic stone-ground heritage corn. [$] *Average main: $16* ✉ *11 Central Ave., Boyes Hot Springs* ✥ *At Hwy. 12* ☎ *707/939–1010* 🌐 *www.elmolinocentral.com.*

★ Girl & the Fig

$$ | **FRENCH** | At this hot spot for inventive French cooking inside the historic Sonoma Hotel bar, you can always find a dish with the signature figs on the menu, whether it's a fig-and-arugula salad or an aperitif blending sparkling wine with fig liqueur. Also look for duck confit, a burger with matchstick fries, and wild flounder meunière. **Known for:** Rhône-wines emphasis; artisanal cheese platters; Sunday brunch. [$] *Average main: $26* ✉ *Sonoma Hotel, 110 W. Spain St.* ✥ *At 1st St. W* ☎ *707/938–3634* 🌐 *www.thegirlandthefig.com.*

Kivelstadt Wine Garden and Eatery

$$ | **AMERICAN** | "The beer garden concept but with wine" is how winemaker Jordan Kivelstadt describes his roadhouse operation in southern Sonoma. Conventional wine tastings of Kivelstadt's sometimes unconventional wines take place here, with the outdoor space a lively combination restaurant and wine bar where local families and tourists mix it up while enjoying tri-tip sandwiches, salads, and heartier fare that might include glazed ribs and smoked half chicken. **Known for:** one-stop wine tasting and dining; vegan/vegetarian options; outdoor area good for travelers with pets and children. [$] *Average main: $18* ✉ *22900 Broadway* ✥ *At Hwy. 121/Carneros Hwy.* ☎ *707/938–7001* 🌐 *kivelstadtcellars.com/eatery* 🕒 *Closed Tues. and Wed. No dinner (but check website).*

El Dorado Kitchen's chefs craft flavorful dishes full of subtle surprises.

★ LaSalette Restaurant

$$$ | **PORTUGUESE** | Born in the Azores and raised in Sonoma, chef-owner Manuel Azevedo serves cuisine inspired by his native Portugal in this warmly decorated spot. The wood-oven-roasted fish is always worth trying, and there are usually boldly flavored pork dishes, along with stews, salted cod, and other hearty fare. **Known for:** authentic Portuguese cuisine; sophisticated spicing; local and Portuguese wine flights. [$] *Average main: $29* ✉ *452 1st St. E* ✥ *Near E. Spain St.* ☎ *707/938–1927* 🌐 *www.lasaletterestaurant.com* 🕒 *Closed Wed.*

★ Layla Restaurant

$$$ | **MODERN AMERICAN** | The large windows, open-truss ceiling, and palette of soft whites and beiges of MacArthur Place resort's destination restaurant lend it the feel of a jazzed-up 19th-century mansion's solarium. The meticulously plated Mediterranean-inspired cuisine—dishes like salmon with rainbow-chard risotto, grass-fed local New York strip with confit onions and blue cheese, and enticing vegetarian and vegan selections—is totally of the moment, though, both in conception and the ingredients' short interval from farm to table. **Known for:** sophisticated setting and service; craft cocktails on outdoor terrace; wine list. [$] *Average main: $30* ✉ *MacArthur Place Hotel & Spa, 29 E. MacArthur St.* ✥ *At Broadway* ☎ *707/933–3191* 🌐 *www.macarthurplace.com/food-drink/layla-restaurant.*

Lou's Luncheonette

$ | **SOUTHERN** | Down-home Southern cuisine with modern twists remains the mission of this retro-yet-au-courant roadside restaurant—originally the Fremont Diner and briefly Boxcar Fried Chicken—whose vineyard-view outdoor patio's vibe is nearly always rollicking. Local families and tourists savor the signature spicy Nashville fried chicken, the multiple burgers and barbecue dishes, and a sloppy-good variation on a po'boy, often accompanying them with a side of deviled eggs, hush puppies, or chicken biscuits with pepper jelly. **Known for:**

small-batch brews; Nashville fried-chicken special; barbecued pork by the pound. $ *Average main: $16* ⊠ *2698 Fremont Dr.* ✛ *At Hwy. 121/12* ☎ *707/938–7370* ⊕ *lousluncheonette.com* ☉ *Closed Mon. and Tues. (sometimes other days, so call first). No dinner (subject to change).*

Oso Sonoma

$$$ | MODERN AMERICAN | Chef David Bush, who achieved national recognition for his food pairings at St. Francis Winery, owns this barlike small-plates restaurant inside an 1890s storefront, erected as a livery stable, that incorporates materials reclaimed from the building's prior incarnations. Starters often include oysters, ceviche, and deviled eggs with Dungeness crab and homemade yellow curry, meant to be enjoyed before moving on to braised-pork-shoulder tacos, shrimp and cheesy grits, or an achiote chicken sandwich. **Known for:** bar menu between lunch and dinner; smart beer and wine selections; Sonoma Plaza location. $ *Average main: $31* ⊠ *9 E. Napa St.* ✛ *At Broadway* ☎ *707/931–6926* ⊕ *www. ososonoma.com.*

Sunflower Caffé

$ | AMERICAN | Whimsical art and brightly painted walls set a jolly tone at this casual eatery whose assets include sidewalk seating with Sonoma Plaza views and the verdant patio out back. Omelets and waffles are the hits at breakfast, with the grilled cheese sandwich and pork *banh mi,* the latter served on a sourdough hero roll with Sriracha aioli, two favorites for lunch. **Known for:** combination café, gallery, and wine bar; local cheeses and hearty soups; no-tipping policy. $ *Average main: $15* ⊠ *421 1st St. W* ✛ *At W. Spain St.* ☎ *707/996–6645* ⊕ *www.sonomasunflower.com* ☉ *Closed Tues. and Wed. No dinner.*

Sweet Scoops

$ | AMERICAN | The scent of waffle cones baking draws patrons into this family-run parlor serving artisanal ice cream made fresh daily. Butter brickle, peaches and cream, and salted caramel are among the 180 alternating flavors that include sorbets and sometimes sherbets, and always vegan options. **Known for:** ice-cream sandwiches; peppy decor and staffers; husband and wife owners. $ *Average main: $5* ⊠ *408 1st St. E* ✛ *Near E. Spain St.* ☎ *707/721–1187* ⊕ *www. sweetscoopsicecream.com.*

Tasca Tasca Portuguese Tapas Restaurant & Wine Bar

$ | PORTUGUESE | Sonoma dining—or nibbling, given the portion sizes—received a boost when Azores-born chef Manuel Azevedo opened this retro-contempo tavern dedicated to small Portuguese bites. Dividing his menu into five parts—Cheese, Garden, Sea, Land, Sweet—Azevedo, who also owns the nearby restaurant LaSalette, serves everything from hearty *caldo verde* stew, pork sliders, smoked duck breast, and salted codfish cakes to São Jorge cheese topped with marmalade. **Known for:** Portuguese wines; dessert mousses and sorbets; good for lunch. $ *Average main: $16* ⊠ *122 W. Napa St.* ✛ *Near 1st St. W* ☎ *707/996–8272* ⊕ *www.tascatasca.com.*

Taub Family Outpost

$$ | AMERICAN | Its varied initiatives and location across from Sonoma Plaza's southwest corner ensure steady traffic to this combination all-day restaurant, gourmet marketplace, wine shop, café, bar, and wine-tasting space whose updated-country-store decor suits its 1912 building's Mexican period/Old West flourishes. Items that might appear on the menu range from the healthful (ancient-grain burgers; smoked-beet salad) to the sinfully delicious (grilled cheese with bacon; fried chicken) and in-between (prosciutto with honeydew melon). **Known for:** coffee and cocktails; wines from many lands; patio dining. $ *Average main: $22* ⊠ *497 1st St. W* ✛ *At W. Napa St.* ☎ *707/721–1107* ⊕ *taubfamilyoutpost. com* ☉ *Closed Mon.*

★ **Valley Bar + Bottle**

$$$ | MODERN AMERICAN | Former Scribe Winery colleagues and a chef and a sommelier with NYC cred revamped a 19th-century adobe (though inside you'd never know) and opened this chipper wine shop, bar, and restaurant whose culinary philosophy revolves around "simple food driven by seasonal produce and our personal histories." Sustainably grown seafood and meats find their way into summer dishes that might include halibut with corn and cherry tomatoes and winter ones like brick chicken with charred leeks and crisp-on-the-bottom rice. **Known for:** shrimp rolls and other small plates; organically and biodynamically farmed wines by iconoclastic producers; spacious back patio. $ *Average main: $29* ⊠ *487 1st W* ✛ *At W. Napa St.* ☎ *707/934–8403* ⊕ *www.valleybarandbottle.com.*

★ **Wit & Wisdom Tavern**

$$$ | MODERN AMERICAN | A San Francisco culinary star with establishments worldwide, Michael Mina debuted his first Wine Country restaurant in 2020, its interior of charcoal grays, browns, and soft whites dandy indeed, if by evening vying with outdoor spaces aglow with fire pits and lighted water features. Seasonal regional ingredients—Pacific Coast fish, pasture-raised meats, freshly plucked produce—go into haute-homey dishes, prepared open-fire, that include pizzas, handmade pastas, and the signature lobster potpie with brandied lobster cream and black truffle. **Known for:** shellfish and duck-wing apps; extensive local wines; large outdoor patio. $ *Average main: $35* ⊠ *The Lodge at Sonoma, 1325 Broadway* ✛ *At Leveroni Rd.* ☎ *707/931–3405* ⊕ *www.witandwisdomsonoma.com.*

 Hotels

Auberge Sonoma

$$$ | RENTAL | If traveling in a group or you just prefer lodgings that feel more like home, consider the two-bedroom suites at this charmer just off Sonoma Plaza. **Pros:** good value for couples traveling together; close to Sonoma Plaza shops, restaurants, and tasting rooms; owners operate similar nearby lodgings if these are full. **Cons:** two-night minimum (three on summer weekends); lacks pool and other amenities; more or less self-serve. $ *Rooms from: $379* ⊠ *151 E. Napa St.* ☎ *707/939–5670 voice mail* ⊕ *www.aubergesonoma.com* ⇆ *3 suites* ❑ *No meals.*

★ **Cottage Inn & Spa**

$$ | B&B/INN | Delivering romance, relaxation, and Zen-like tranquility is the innkeepers' goal at this courtyard complex 1½ blocks north of Sonoma Plaza. **Pros:** convenient to plaza; quiet location; four suites with double Jacuzzi tubs. **Cons:** books up far ahead late spring–early fall; some bathrooms only have a shower; lacks amenities such as room service, restaurant, pool, or gym. $ *Rooms from: $235* ⊠ *310 1st St. E* ☎ *707/996–0719* ⊕ *www.cottageinnandspa.com* ⇆ *9 rooms* ❑ *Free breakfast.*

El Dorado Hotel

$$ | HOTEL | Guest rooms in this remodeled 1843 building strike a rustic-contemporary pose with their Restoration Hardware furnishings, but the Mexican-tile floors hint at Sonoma's mission-era past. **Pros:** stylish for the price; on-site El Dorado Kitchen restaurant; central location. **Cons:** rooms are small, though patios and balconies keep them from feeling claustrophobic; street noise audible in some rooms; parking can be problematic. $ *Rooms from: $275* ⊠ *405 1st St. W* ☎ *707/996–3030* ⊕ *www.eldoradosonoma.com* ⇆ *27 rooms* ❑ *No meals.*

El Pueblo Inn

$$ | HOTEL | A giant pepper tree and a few palms tower over the garden courtyard of this updated 1959 motel whose landscaping, festive pool area, and thoughtful service make a stay here worth considering. **Pros:** festive pool area; expanded continental breakfast buffet; helpful hosts. **Cons:** rates can spike in high season; street noise an issue in some rooms; several blocks west of Sonoma Plaza. [$] *Rooms from: $249* ✉ *896 W. Napa St.* ✣ *Off Hwy. 12 near Riverside Dr.* ☎ *707/996–3651* 🌐 *www.elpuebloinn.com* 🛏 *54 rooms* 🍴 *Free breakfast.*

Fairmont Sonoma Mission Inn & Spa

$$$ | **RESORT** | The draw at this mission-style resort is the extensive spa with its array of massages and treatments, some designed for couples. **Pros:** full-service hotel; enormous spa and other wellness services; Santé restaurant's haute-modern cuisine. **Cons:** smallish standard rooms; lacks intimacy of similarly priced options; hefty resort fee, though it does include perks. [$] *Rooms from: $332* ✉ *100 Boyes Blvd./Hwy. 12* ✣ *2½ miles north of Sonoma Plaza* ☎ *707/938–9000* 🌐 *www.fairmont.com/sonoma* 🛏 *226 rooms* 🍴 *No meals.*

Inn at Sonoma

$$ | **B&B/INN** | Little luxuries delight at this well-run inn ¼-mile south of Sonoma Plaza whose guest rooms, softly lit and done in pastels, have comfortable beds topped with feather comforters and plenty of pillows. **Pros:** last-minute specials are a great deal; afternoon wine, cheese, and freshly baked cookies; good soundproofing blocks out Broadway street noise. **Cons:** on a busy street rather than right on the plaza; pet-friendly rooms book up quickly; some rooms on the small side. [$] *Rooms from: $259* ✉ *630 Broadway* ☎ *707/939–1340* 🌐 *www.innatsonoma.com* 🛏 *27 rooms* 🍴 *Free breakfast.*

★ **Ledson Hotel**

$$$ | **B&B/INN** | With just six rooms the Ledson feels intimate, and the furnishings and amenities—down beds, mood lighting, gas fireplaces, whirlpool tubs, and balconies for enjoying breakfast or a glass of wine—stack up well against Wine Country rooms costing more, especially in high season. **Pros:** convenient Sonoma Plaza location; spacious, individually decorated rooms; whirlpool tub in all rooms. **Cons:** two people maximum occupancy in all rooms; children must be at least 12 years old; front rooms have plaza views but pick up some street noise. [$] *Rooms from: $350* ✉ *480 1st St. E* ☎ *707/996–9779* 🌐 *www.ledsonhotel.com* 🛏 *6 rooms* 🍴 *No meals.*

★ **MacArthur Place Hotel & Spa**

$$$$ | **HOTEL** | Guests at this 7-acre boutique property five blocks south of Sonoma Plaza bask in ritzy seclusion in plush accommodations set amid landscaped gardens. **Pros:** verdant garden setting; restaurant among Sonoma's best; great for a romantic getaway. **Cons:** a bit of a walk from the plaza; some traffic noise audible in street-side rooms; pricey in high season. [$] *Rooms from: $459* ✉ *29 E. MacArthur St.* ☎ *707/938–2929, 800/722–1866* 🌐 *www.macarthurplace.com* 🛏 *64 rooms* 🍴 *Free breakfast.*

Sonoma Creek Inn

$ | **B&B/INN** | The exterior of this property between Sonoma and Glen Ellen says "motel," but the design sensibility and customer service are more quaint country inn, with the rates splitting the difference. **Pros:** clean, well-lighted bathrooms; good for travelers on a budget; popular with bicyclists. **Cons:** office not staffed 24 hours; 10-minute drive from Sonoma Plaza; a few rooms cramped. [$] *Rooms from: $169* ✉ *239 Boyes Blvd.* ✣ *Off Hwy. 12* ☎ *707/939–9463, 888/712–1289* 🌐 *www.sonomacreekinn.com* 🛏 *16 rooms* 🍴 *No meals.*

🍸 Nightlife

Sigh!

WINE BARS—NIGHTLIFE | From the oval bar and walls the color of a fine Blanc de Blancs to retro chandeliers that mimic champagne bubbles, everything about this sparkling-wine bar's frothy space screams "have a good time." That owner Jayme Powers and her posse are trained in the fine art of *sabrage* (opening a bottle of sparkling with a saber) only adds to the festivity. ■TIP→ **Sigh! opens at noon, so it's a good daytime stop, too.** ✉ *120 W. Napa St.* ✛ *At 1st St. W* ☎ *707/996–2444* ⊕ *www.sighsonoma. com.*

Starling Bar Sonoma

BARS/PUBS | Chat up the locals at this neighborhood hangout with a welcoming vibe and bartenders slinging the classics and craft cocktails, some of whose ingredients are grown out back. Noteworthy drinks include the bacon bourbon sour and the Hawaiian salted plum margarita. ■TIP→ **The Starling is always open from Thursday through Monday; call ahead on other days.** ✉ *19380 Hwy. 12* ✛ *At W. Spain St.* ☎ *707/938–7442* ⊕ *www.star-lingsonoma.com.*

Swiss Hotel

BARS/PUBS | Head to the hotel's frozen-in-time wood-paneled watering hole for a blast of Glariffee, a cold and potent cousin to Irish coffee that a relation of Ernest Hemingway supposedly had a hand in creating. The only person who knows the recipe keeps it locked in a safe deposit box. ✉ *18 W. Spain St.* ✛ *At 1st St. W* ☎ *707/938–2884* ⊕ *swisshotel-sonoma.com.*

Performing Arts

Sebastiani Theatre

FILM | This theater, built on Sonoma Plaza in 1934 by Italian immigrant and entrepreneur Samuele Sebastiani, schedules first-run films, as well as occasional musical and theatrical performances. ✉ *476 1st St. E* ✛ *Near W. Spain St.* ☎ *707/996–2020* ⊕ *www.sebastianitheatre.com.*

🛍 Shopping

FOOD AND WINE

Sonoma's Best

WINE/SPIRITS | A casual roadside operation with a deli serving up breakfast burritos, panini on freshly made local bread, and good coffee, Sonoma's Best earns its moniker with its well-curated adjoining wine shop. At tastings that, like the retail bottles, are reasonably priced, knowledgeable staff members provide an excellent introduction to Sonoma County wines and wine making. ■TIP→ **Four unpretentious cottages behind the store are available for overnight stays.** ✉ *1190 E. Napa St., At 8th St. E* ☎ *707/470–9356* ⊕ *www.sonomas-best.com.*

HOUSEHOLD ITEMS

Chateau Sonoma

HOUSEHOLD ITEMS/FURNITURE | The fancy furniture, lighting fixtures, and objets d'art at this upscale shop make it a dangerous place to enter: within minutes you may find yourself reconsidering your entire home's aesthetic. The owner's keen eye for French style makes a visit here a pleasure. ✉ *453 1st St. W* ✛ *Between W. Napa and W. Spain Sts.* ☎ *707/309–1993* ⊕ *www.chateausonoma.com.*

★ The Passdoor

HOUSEHOLD ITEMS/FURNITURE | A cross between a design gallery and museum gift shop, Passdoor stocks high-quality artworks; glassware and ceramics; jewelry; and creative home-decor items. ✉ *452 1st St. E* ✛ *100 ft north of Sebastiani Theatre* ☎ *707/634–0015* ⊕ *www. thepassdoor.net.*

🏃 Activities

BICYCLING

Wine Country Cyclery

BICYCLING | You can rent comfort/hybrid, tandem, and road bikes by the hour or the day at this shop west of the plaza. ✉ *262 W. Napa St.* ✛ *At 3rd St. W* ☎ *707/996–6800* ⊕ *winecountrycyclery. com* 🖃 *From $12 per hr, $36 per day.*

SPAS

Willow Stream Spa at Fairmont Sonoma Mission Inn & Spa

FITNESS/HEALTH CLUBS | By far the Wine Country's largest spa, the Fairmont resort's 40,000-square-foot facility provides every amenity you could want, including pools and hot tubs fed by local thermal springs. Each of the three signature treatments achieves a specific objective. Starting with a lavender bubble bath, followed by a botanical body wrap and a massage, the Couples Lavender Kur focuses on pampering, whereas the Neroli Blossom Kur—a body polish, a full-body massage, a moisture mask, and a facial and scalp massage—is all about restoring balance. For clients in need of a detox, the Wine Country Kur begins with exfoliation, a soak, and a wrap, concluding with a grape-seed oil massage. ⊠ *100 Boyes Blvd./Hwy. 12* ✛ *2½ miles north of Sonoma Plaza* ☎ *707/938–9000* ⊕ *www. fairmont.com/sonoma/willow-stream* ⊠ *Treatments from $79.*

Glen Ellen

7 miles north of Sonoma.

Craggy Glen Ellen epitomizes the difference between the Napa and Sonoma valleys. Whereas small Napa towns like St. Helena get their charm from upscale boutiques and restaurants lined up along well-groomed sidewalks, Glen Ellen's crooked streets are shaded with stands of old oak trees and occasionally bisected by the Sonoma and Calabazas creeks. Tucked among the trees of a narrow canyon, where Sonoma Mountain and the Mayacamas pinch in the valley floor, Glen Ellen looks more like a town of the Sierra foothills gold country than a Wine Country village.

Wine has been part of Glen Ellen since the 1840s, when a French immigrant, Joshua Chauvet, planted grapes and later built a winery and the valley's first distillery. Machinery at the winery was powered by steam, and boilers were fueled with wood from local oaks. Other valley farmers followed Chauvet's example, and grape growing took off, although Prohibition took its toll on most of these

operations. Today dozens of wineries in the area beg to be visited, but sometimes it's hard not to succumb to Glen Ellen's slow pace and lounge poolside at your lodging or linger over a leisurely picnic. The renowned cook and food writer M. F. K. Fisher, who lived and worked in Glen Ellen for 22 years until her death in 1992, would surely have approved. Hunter S. Thompson, who lived here for a spell before he became famous, might not: he found the place too sedate. Glen Ellen's most famous resident, however, was Jack London, who personified the town's rugged spirit.

Getting Here and Around

To get to Glen Ellen from Sonoma, drive west on Spain Street. After about a mile, take Highway 12 north for 7 miles to Arnold Drive, which deposits you in the middle of town. Many of Glen Ellen's restaurants and inns are along a half-mile stretch of Arnold Drive. Sonoma Transit buses serve Glen Ellen from Sonoma and Kenwood.

◉ Sights

Abbot's Passage Winery & Mercantile
WINERY/DISTILLERY | For her passion project, sixth-generation vintner Katie Bundschu, who's also involved in her family's historic Gundlach Bundschu winery, focuses on wines made from organic grapes grown in other family-owned, mostly Sonoma County vineyards. Most of the wines are old-style field blends in which different types of grapes from the same vineyard are fermented and aged together rather than separately, as is more common these days. The wines impress with their balance, approachability, and rich flavors. You can sample them 2½ miles south of downtown Glen Ellen at a garden estate whose grape-growing history dates back nearly as far as the Bundschu family's. ⊠ *777 Madrone Rd., Sonoma* ✛ *Off Arnold Dr. or Hwy. 12*

Benziger tram tours take to the fields to show biodynamic farming techniques in action.

☎ 707/939–3017 ⊕ www.abbotspassage. com ✉ Tastings from $40 ☉ Closed Mon.–Wed. (check website for expanded hours).

Benziger Family Winery

WINERY/DISTILLERY | One of the best-known Sonoma County wineries sits on a sprawling estate in a bowl with 360-degree sun exposure. Hosts conducting popular tram tours explain the benefits of the vineyard's natural setting and how biodynamic farming yields healthier, more flavorful fruit. The eco-friendly agricultural practices include extensive plantings to attract beneficial insects and the deployment of sheep to trim vegetation between the vines while simultaneously tilling the soil with their hooves and fertilizing to boot. Known for Chardonnay, Cabernet Sauvignon, Merlot, Pinot Noir, and Sauvignon Blanc, the winery is a beautiful spot for an alfresco tasting, whether you take the tour or not. All visits are by appointment; in summer and early fall, reserve a tram tour at least a day or two ahead. ⊠ 1883 London Ranch Rd. ✛ Off Arnold Dr. ☎ 888/490–2739 ⊕ www.benziger.com ✉ Tasting $30, tram tour and tasting $60 ☉ Closed Tues. and Wed.

★ Jack London State Historic Park

NATIONAL/STATE PARK | The pleasures are pastoral and intellectual at author Jack London's beloved Beauty Ranch, where you could easily spend the afternoon hiking some of the 30-plus miles of trails that loop through meadows and stands of oaks, redwoods, and other trees. Manuscripts and personal artifacts depicting London's travels are on view at the House of Happy Walls Museum, which provides an overview of the writer's life, literary passions, humanitarian and conservation efforts, and promotion of organic farming. A short hike away lie the ruins of Wolf House, which burned down just before London was to move in. Also open to visitors are a few outbuildings and the restored wood-framed cottage where London penned many of his later works. He's buried on the property. ■ TIP➜ The park's Broadway Under the Stars series, a hot summer ticket, is expected to resume in 2021. ✉ *2400 London Ranch Rd.* ✛ *Off Arnold Dr.* ☎ *707/938–5216* ⊕ *www. jacklondonpark.com* 🚗 *Parking $10 ($5 walk-in or bike), includes admission to museum; cottage $4.*

★ **Lasseter Family Winery**

WINERY/DISTILLERY | Immaculately groomed grapevines dazzle the eye at John and Nancy Lasseter's secluded winery, and it's no accident: Phil Coturri, Sonoma Valley's premier organic vineyard manager, tends them. Even the landscaping, which includes an insectary to attract beneficial bugs, is meticulously maintained. Come harvesttime, the wine-making team oversees gentle processes that transform the fruit into wines of purity and grace, among them a Sémillon–Sauvignon Blanc blend, two rosés, and Bordeaux and Rhône reds. Evocative labels illustrate the tale behind each wine. In good weather, guests enjoy these well-told stories at tastings on the winery's outdoor patio, whose views include the vineyard and the Mayacamas Mountains. All visits are by appointment. ✉ *1 Vintage La.* ✛ *Off Dunbar Rd.* ☎ *707/933–2814* ⊕ *www.lasseterfamilywinery.com* 🚗 *Tastings from $25.*

Laurel Glen Vineyard

WINERY/DISTILLERY | As a longtime wine-industry marketing director, Bettina Sichel knew the potential pitfalls of winery ownership, but when she discovered a uniquely situated volcanic-soiled Sonoma Mountain vineyard for sale, she plunged in enthusiastically. Because her 14 acres of Cabernet Sauvignon vines face east, the mountain shelters the grapes from the hot late-afternoon sun and excessively cool Pacific influences. Sichel's impressive wine-making team includes Phil Coturri, an organic farming expert *Wine Spectator* magazine calls the "Wizard of Green," and winemaker Randall Watkins. By appointment at Sichel's tasting room in downtown Glen Ellen, you can taste the impressive estate Cabernet, along with another Cabernet, a rosé from the vineyard's oldest vines, and a Russian River Valley Sauvignon Blanc. ✉ *13750 Arnold Dr.* ✛ *At London Ranch Rd.* ☎ *707/933–9877* ⊕ *www.laurelglen.com* 🚗 *Tastings $40–$50.*

Loxton Cellars

WINERY/DISTILLERY | Back when tasting rooms were low-tech and the winemaker often poured the wines, the experience at Loxton Cellars unfolded pretty much the way it does today. The personable Australia-born owner, Chris Loxton, who's on hand many days, crafts a Sonoma Coast Chardonnay, Zinfandels, Syrahs, a Cabernet Sauvignon, and a Grenache, Syrah, and Petite Sirah blend. All are quite good, and some regulars swear by the late-harvest Zinfandel and seductively smooth Syrah Port. Tastings require an appointment, but the winery generally accommodates weekday walk-ins if guests call ahead. ■**TIP**➔ **To learn more about Loxton's wine-making philosophy and practices, book a Vineyard Walkabout (Saturday only) that's followed by a seated tasting.** ✉ *11466 Dunbar Rd.* ✛ *At Hwy. 12* ☎ *707/935–7221* ⊕ *www.loxtonwines. com* 🚗 *Tastings from $20.*

★ **Schermeister Winery**

WINERY/DISTILLERY | "I baby my wines big time," says Robert Schermeister, frequently visiting the grapes during growing season, fussing over the pick date "to nail it perfectly," personally handling all the lab work, and fermenting with native yeasts, a trickier process than employing commercial ones. His obsession pays off in aromatic Viognier and Chardonnay whites, deep-flavored Pinot Noirs and Syrahs, and a rosé of cofermented Cabernet Sauvignon and Cabernet Franc. A small niche within a historic Glen Ellen building serves as a tasting room, where you're likely to see Robert or his wife, Laura. Either will gladly tell you about how they got together (short version: she was his website designer, and after a false start he charmed her over a bottle

Jack London Country

The rugged, rakish author and adventurer Jack London is perhaps best known for his travels to Alaska and his exploits in the Pacific, which he immortalized in tales such as *The Call of the Wild*, *White Fang*, and *South Sea Tales*. But he loved no place so well as the hills of eastern Sonoma County, where he spent most of his thirties and where he died in 1916 at the age of 40.

Between 1905 and 1916 London bought seven parcels of land totaling 1,400 acres, which he dubbed Beauty Ranch. When he wasn't off traveling, he dedicated most of his time to cultivating the land and raising livestock. He also maintained a few acres of wine grapes for his personal use.

Dreams and Mysteries
In 1913 London rhapsodized about his beloved ranch near Glen Ellen, writing, "The grapes on a score of rolling hills are red with autumn flame. Across Sonoma Mountain wisps of sea fog are stealing. The afternoon sun smolders in the drowsy sky. I have everything to make me glad I am alive. I am filled with dreams and mysteries."

Much of Beauty Ranch is now preserved as Jack London State Historic Park, worth visiting for its museum and other glimpses into London's life and for trails that skirt vineyards and meander through Douglas firs, coastal redwoods, oaks, and madrones. London and his wife, Charmian, spent two years constructing their dream home, Wolf House, before it burned down one hot August night in 1913, days before they were scheduled to move in. A look at the remaining stone walls and fireplaces gives you a sense of the building's grand scale. Within, a fireproof basement vault was to hold London's manuscripts. Elsewhere in the park stands the unusually posh pigsty that London's neighbors called the Pig Palace.

Legacy Vineyards
Parts of Beauty Ranch are still owned by London's descendants, from whom Kenwood Vineyards leases and farms legacy vineyards producing Cabernet Sauvignon, Merlot, Syrah, and Zinfandel. The wines from Beauty Ranch are among the winery's best.

of his Pinot Noir) and their life in the Napa Valley on Mt. Veeder. ■ TIP→ This small winery, which also has a patio facing Sonoma Creek, usually produces fewer than a thousand cases annually but is highly regarded. ⊠ *Jack London Village, 14301 Arnold Dr., Studio 28 ✛ ¾ mile south of downtown Glen Ellen* ☏ *707/934–8953* ⊕ *schermeister.com* ✆ *Tastings from $25* ⊙ *Closed Mon.–Wed.*

Sonoma Botanical Garden
GARDEN | Rare East Asian trees and plants thrive in this 25-acre woodland garden a little over a mile north of downtown Glen

Ellen. There's also a heritage rose garden near the entrance. The colors throughout are most vibrant in spring, but year-round a visit here makes for a pleasant break from wine touring. ⊠ *12841 Hwy. 12 ✛ ¼ mile north of Arnold Dr.* ☏ *707/996–3166* ⊕ *www.sonomabg.org* ✆ *$12* ⊙ *Closed Tues.*

🍴 Restaurants

Fig Cafe
$$ | FRENCH | The compact menu at this cheerful bistro focuses on California and French comfort food—pot roast and duck

confit, for instance, as well as thin-crust pizza. Steamed mussels are served with crispy fries, which also accompany the Chef's Burger (top sirloin with Gruyère), two of the many dependable dishes that have made this restaurant a downtown Glen Ellen fixture. **Known for:** daily three-course prix-fixe specials; Rhône-oriented wine list; fig pizza, fig salad in season. [$] *Average main: $22* ✉ *13690 Arnold Dr.* ✣ *At O'Donnell La.* ☎ *707/938–2130* 🌐 *www.thefigcafe.com* 🕓 *No lunch.*

★ Glen Ellen Star

$$$ | ECLECTIC | Chef Ari Weiswasser honed his craft at The French Laundry, Daniel, and other bastions of culinary finesse, but at his Wine Country outpost he prepares haute-rustic cuisine, much of it emerging from a wood-fired oven that burns a steady 600°F. Crisp-crusted, richly sauced Margherita and other pizzas thrive in the torrid heat, as do tender whole fish entrées and vegetables roasted in small iron skillets. **Known for:** outdoor dining area; prix-fixe Wednesday "neighborhood night" menu with free corkage; Weiswasser's sauces, emulsions, and spices. [$] *Average main: $30* ✉ *13648 Arnold Dr.* ✣ *At Warm Springs Rd.* ☎ *707/343–1384* 🌐 *glenellenstar.com* 🕓 *No lunch.*

★ Les Pascals

$ | FRENCH | A bright-yellow slice of France in downtown Glen Ellen, this combination pâtisserie, boulangerie, and café takes its name from its husband-and-wife owners, Pascal and Pascale Merle. Pascal whips up croissants, breads, turnovers, and sweet treats like Napoleons, galettes, and eclairs, along with quiches, potpies, and other savory fare; Pascale creates an upbeat environment for customers to enjoy them. **Known for:** memorable French onion soup; shaded back patio; high-test French and Italian coffee drinks. [$] *Average main: $10* ✉ *13758 Arnold Dr.* ✣ *Near London Ranch Rd.* ☎ *707/934–8378* 🌐 *www.lespascalspatisserie.com* 🕓 *Closed Wed. No dinner.*

The Mill at Glen Ellen

$$ | MODERN AMERICAN | The redwood-timbered main dining space of this comfort-food haven recalls the 19th-century heyday of the former sawmill (later a grist mill) it occupies, though when the weather's nice most patrons take their meals on a plant-filled outdoor deck with timeless Sonoma Creek views. Culinary influences that range from Latin America to Southeast Asia underlie dishes that might include fire-roasted achiote half chicken, wild poached salmon, and potato patties with red lentils and chutney. **Known for:** steak and Impossible burgers; exotic desserts; owner-chefs of local renown. [$] *Average main: $22* ✉ *Jack London Village, 14301 Arnold Dr.* ✣ *¾ mile south of downtown* ☎ *707/721–1818* 🌐 *www.themillatglenellen.com* 🕓 *Closed Mon.*

Yeti Restaurant

$$ | INDIAN | Glen Ellen's finer restaurants emphasize seasonal local produce, but instead of riffs on French, Italian, or Cal-modern, the farm-to-table creations at this casual space (open kitchen, paper lanterns, wooden tables and chairs) fuse Indian and Himalayan cuisine. Start with samosas or tomato-based Himalayan pepper pot soup from Nepal—so warming on a chilly day—then proceed to curries, sizzling tandooris, or chicken, prawn, or vegetable biryanis of ethereally aromatic saffron basmati rice. **Known for:** deck overlooking Sonoma Creek; international beer selection; ample wines by the glass. [$] *Average main: $21* ✉ *Jack London Village, 14301 Arnold Dr.* ✣ *¾ mile south of downtown* ☎ *707/996–9930* 🌐 *www.yetirestaurant.com.*

🛏 Hotels

Beltane Ranch

$$$ | B&B/INN | On a slope of the Mayacamas range with gorgeous Sonoma Valley views, this working ranch, vineyard, and winery contains charmingly old-fashioned rooms. **Pros:** bountiful breakfasts; relaxed hospitality; ranch setting. **Cons:** downstairs rooms get some noise from upstairs rooms; ceiling fans instead of air-conditioning; may feel too remote or low-key for some guests. $ *Rooms from: $355* ✉ *11775 Sonoma Hwy./Hwy. 12* ☎ *707/833–4233* ⊕ *www.beltaneranch. com* ➦ *5 rooms* ⦿ *Free breakfast.*

★ Gaige House + Ryokan

$$$ | B&B/INN | There's no other place in Sonoma or Napa quite like the Gaige House + Ryokan, which blends the best elements of a traditional country inn, a boutique hotel, and a longtime expat's classy Asian hideaway. **Pros:** short walk to Glen Ellen restaurants, shops, and tasting rooms; freshly baked cookies; full breakfasts, afternoon wine and appetizers. **Cons:** sound carries in the main house; the least expensive rooms are on the small side; oriented more toward couples than families with children. $ *Rooms from: $302* ✉ *13540 Arnold Dr.* ☎ *707/935–0237, 800/935–0237* ⊕ *www. thegaigehouse.com* ➦ *23 rooms* ⦿ *Free breakfast.*

★ Olea Hotel

$$$ | B&B/INN | Husband-and-wife team Ashish and Sia Patel operate this down-home country casual yet sophisticated boutique lodging. **Pros:** beautiful style; complimentary wine; filling two-course breakfasts. **Cons:** minor road noise in some rooms; fills up quickly on weekends; weekend minimum-stay requirement. $ *Rooms from: $309* ✉ *5131 Warm Springs Rd.* ⊹ *West off Arnold Dr.* ☎ *707/996–5131* ⊕ *www.oleahotel.com* ➦ *15 rooms* ⦿ *Free breakfast.*

Kenwood

4 miles north of Glen Ellen.

Tiny Kenwood consists of little more than a few restaurants, shops, tasting rooms, and a historic train depot, now used for private events. But hidden in this pretty landscape of meadows and woods at the north end of Sonoma Valley are several good wineries, most just off Sonoma Highway. Varietals grown here at the foot of the Sugarloaf Mountains include Sauvignon Blanc, Chardonnay, Zinfandel, and Cabernet Sauvignon.

Getting Here and Around

To get to Kenwood from Glen Ellen, head northeast on Arnold Drive and north on Highway 12. Sonoma Transit buses serve Kenwood from Glen Ellen and Sonoma.

⊙ Sights

B. Wise Vineyards Tasting Lounge

WINERY/DISTILLERY | The stylish roadside tasting room of this producer of small-lot reds sits on the valley floor, but owner Brion Wise's winery and vineyards occupy prime acreage high in the Moon Mountain District AVA. The winery made its name crafting big, bold Cabernets, later introducing Pinot Noirs from Sonoma County and Oregon's Willamette Valley. The uniformly excellent lineup also includes Chardonnay, a rosé of Pinot Noir that quickly sells out, and the Cabernet-heavy blend Trios, whose grapes, all from the estate, include Merlot, Petit Verdot, Syrah, and Tannat. There's also a Napa Valley version of Trios. ■TIP➔ **A tasting here may whet your appetite for a visit to the estate, done by appointment only.** ✉ *9077 Sonoma Hwy.* ⊹ *At Shaw Ave.* ☎ *707/282–9169* ⊕ *www.bwisevineyards. com* ⊠ *Tastings from $25.*

Deerfield Ranch Winery

WINERY/DISTILLERY | Winemaker Robert Rex of Deerfield produces "clean wines"—low in histamines and sulfites—the better to eliminate the headaches and allergic reactions some red-wine drinkers experience. Rex accomplishes this with no loss of flavor or complexity: his wines are bold and fruit-forward, with a long finish. To sip ones that include several Bordeaux-style reds, Pinot Noir, and Chardonnay, guests walk deep into a 23,000-square-foot cave for a seated tasting in a relaxed, loungelike space. ⊠ 10200 Sonoma Hwy./Hwy. 12 ☎ 707/833–5215 ⊕ www.deerfieldranch.com ⊠ Tastings $25–$45.

★ En Garde Winery

WINERY/DISTILLERY | Sommeliers, critics, and collectors extol the Pinot Noirs and Cabernet Sauvignons of Csaba Szakál, En Garde's Hungarian-born winemaker and owner. Striving to create what he describes as "aromatic, complex, lush, and juicy" wines, Szakál selects top Sonoma County vineyards for the Pinots and the Napa Valley's Diamond Mountain, Mt. Veeder, and other high-elevation sites for the Cabernets. Not afraid to heavy up the oak on the Cabernets, he nevertheless achieves elegance as well. The winemaker is equally precise about hiring staffers for his modest highway's-edge tasting room along Kenwood's brief commercial strip. Well-acquainted with his goals and methods, they provide a wealth of knowledge about wine making and California viticulture. If you're lucky, Szakál himself will be around to discuss his wines (he loves to), which also include Chardonnay, Viognier, and rosé of Pinot Noir. Visits are by reservation, with same-day appointments sometimes possible. ⊠ 9077 Sonoma Hwy. ⊕ At Shaw Ave. ☎ 707/282–9216 ⊕ www.engardewinery.com ⊠ Tastings $25–$40.

Kenwood Vineyards

WINERY/DISTILLERY | Some of the best Kenwood wines—Cabernet Sauvignon, Zinfandel, and a red blend—are made from Sonoma Mountain AVA grapes the winery farms on the author Jack London's old vineyard. Kenwood, established in 1970, is best known for these wines and its widely distributed Sauvignon Blanc. Newer to the brand since its purchase by France's Pernod Ricard are the top-of-the-line The Barn Chardonnay and The Barn Pinot Noir, whose labels depict the 1906 barn, still in use, erected by the property's original vintners. Tastings are by appointment, though early on weekdays you might be able to drop in last-minute. ⊠ 9592 Sonoma Hwy./Hwy. 12 ☎ 707/282–4228 ⊕ www.kenwoodvineyards.com ⊠ Tastings from $28.

Kunde Family Winery

WINERY/DISTILLERY | Founded by its namesake family more than a century ago, this Sonoma Valley operation prides itself on producing 100% estate wines from its 1,850-acre property, which rises 1,400 feet from the valley floor. Kunde's whites, the winery's best offerings, include several Chardonnays and a Sauvignon Blanc, with Cabernet Sauvignon, Merlot, and a Zinfandel from 1880s vines among the reds. Reservations are required; call ahead for same-day visits. ■TIP→ The Mountain Top Tasting, a vineyard tour by luxury van to a tree-shaded ridge, ends with a sampling of reserve wines. ⊠ 9825 Sonoma Hwy./Hwy. 12 ☎ 707/833–5501 ⊕ www.kunde.com ⊠ Tastings from $40 ⊙ Closed Tues. and Wed.

Ledson Winery & Vineyards

WINERY/DISTILLERY | The Normandy-style castle visible from the highway was intended as winery owner Steve Ledson's family home when construction began in 1989, but this 16,000-square-foot space has always been a production facility and hospitality center. Pourers stationed amid a warren of tasting rooms introduce guests to the several dozen mostly single-varietal wines Ledson makes, everything from Zinfandel and Cabernet Sauvignon to Rhône varietals such as

Syrah and Mourvèdre. ■TIP→ **The on-site Marketplace sells salads, sandwiches, artisanal cheeses, and other edibles you can enjoy on the picnic grounds (no outside food, though).** ⊠ *7335 Sonoma Hwy./Hwy. 12* ☎ *707/537–3810* ⊕ *www.ledson.com* 🍷 *Tastings from $30.*

St. Francis Winery

WINERY/DISTILLERY | Nestled at the foot of Mt. Hood, St. Francis has earned national acclaim for its pairings of wines and small bites. With its red-tile roof and bell tower and views of the Mayacamas Mountains to the east, the winery's California Mission–style visitor center occupies one of Sonoma County's most scenic locations. The charm of the surroundings is matched by the mostly red wines, among them rich, earthy Zinfandels from the Dry Creek, Russian River, and Sonoma valleys. The five-course pairings might include Chardonnay with lobster bisque or Cabernet Sauvignon with wine-braised beef ribs. ⊠ *100 Pythian Rd.* ✦ *Off Hwy. 12* ☎ *707/538–9463, 888/675–9463* ⊕ *www.stfranciswinery. com* 🍷 *Tastings from $20* ☉ *Closed Tues. and Wed.*

VJB Cellars

WINERY/DISTILLERY | This Tuscan-inspired courtyard marketplace with tasting spaces and food shops is a fine spot to sip wines, enjoy a pizza or a deli sandwich, and just relax. Mostly from Italian varietals, the wines are, like the complex, less rustic than in the old country and clearly adapted for contemporary American tastes. This isn't always a bad thing, and the best wines—the Barbera, the Sangiovese, and the Montepulciano—are lively and clean on the palate. Reservations are required for seated tastings. ■TIP→ **For gourmet dolci, check out the Wine Truffle Boutique, which sells Italian gelato and artisanal truffles and other confections.** ⊠ *60 Shaw Ave.* ✦ *Off Hwy. 12* ☎ *707/833–2300* ⊕ *www.vjbcellars.com* 🍷 *Tastings from $15.*

🍽 Restaurants

Palooza Gastropub & Wine Bar

$$ | **AMERICAN** | Palooza pleases with 16 beers on tap, jazzed-up pub grub, casual decor, and an often-packed covered outdoor patio. Pulled-pork sandwiches, falafel wraps, pan-seared salmon, fish and fries, blue-cheese-and-bacon burgers, and Chicago-style hot dogs are among the popular items, with fish tacos and shredded-kale and apple-spinach salads for those seeking lighter fare. **Known for:** many local brews; mostly Sonoma Valley wines; beer-battered fried pickles, mozzarella-ball appetizers. $ *Average main: $18* ⊠ *8910 Sonoma Hwy./Hwy. 12* ☎ *707/833–4000* ⊕ *www.paloozafresh. com* ☉ *Closed Tues.*

Salt & Stone

$$$ | **MODERN AMERICAN** | The menu at this upscale roadhouse with a sloping wood-beamed ceiling focuses on seafood and meat—beef, lamb, chicken, duck, and other options—with many dishes in both categories grilled. Start with the classics, perhaps a martini and oysters Rockefeller, before moving on to well-plated contemporary entrées that might include crispy-skin salmon or duck breast, a fish stew, or grilled rib-eye. **Known for:** mountain-view outdoor seating area; weekend brunch; weekday happy hour 2:30–5:30 except holidays. $ *Average main: $29* ⊠ *9900 Sonoma Hwy.* ✦ *At Kunde Winery Rd.* ☎ *707/833–6326* ⊕ *www. saltstonekenwood.com* ☉ *No lunch Tues. and Wed.*

Tips Roadside

$$ | **AMERICAN** | The owners of a local-fave tri-tip food trolley seen at many events opened this comfort-food restaurant in a 90-year-old building originally a gas station and later an inn. In addition to tri-tip, the New Orleans–inspired menu consists of small bites like white-cheddar grits and barbecued shrimp and larger bites that include smoke-braised short ribs, fried chicken, and vegetarian homemade

A Great Day in Sonoma Valley

The drive through the Sonoma Valley from Sonoma in the south to Kenwood in the north takes half an hour, but you can easily fill a day touring the wineries and historic sites along the way. Make winery appointments at least two days ahead, especially at Scribe and St. Francis.

Breakfast and History

To hit the highlights, start in the town of Sonoma. Have breakfast at **Sunflower Caffé** or **Taub Family Outpost,** both across the street from the Sonoma Plaza to the west. From your breakfast spot, head east on East Napa Street, south on 8th Street East, and east on Denmark Street, a drive of just under 3 miles to reach **Scribe,** where grapes were first planted in 1858. If you can't get an appointment at Scribe, **Buena Vista Winery** (1857), the birthplace of modern California wine making, and **Gundlach Bundschu** (1858), still owned by members of the Bundschu family, are two other historic options.

Wine, Food, and Wine

Enjoy your tasting, then backtrack to East Napa Street and head west. The road eventually becomes Highway 12, which you'll take west and north to photogenic **St. Francis Winery** for the 1 pm wine and food pairing (reserve a few days ahead). From St. Francis, head back south 2 miles on Highway 12 to **En Garde Winery** (look for it on the right). Stop at this roadside tasting room for Cabernet Sauvignon, Pinot Noir, and Chardonnay.

Literary Stroll

From En Garde, continue south on Highway 12 and take Arnold Drive into the picturesque town of Glen Ellen. Turn right on London Ranch Road and wind your way uphill for a few minutes to reach **Jack London State Historic Park.** Take a short stroll through the grounds and observe the historic buildings near the parking area before the park closes at 5 pm. Backtrack down London Ranch road for an early dinner at **Glen Ellen Star** or return to Sonoma on Highway 12.

gnocchi with smoked-tomato sauce. **Known for:** open-air dining with mountain views; lunch served almost until dinner time; brunch beignets with Meyer lemon sauce. $ *Average main: $22 ✉ 8445 Sonoma Hwy./Hwy. 12 ✣ At Adobe Rd. ☎ 707/509–0078 🌐 www.tipsroadside.com ⏲ Closed Mon. and Tues. (but check).*

Hotels

★ **Kenwood Inn and Spa**

$$$ | **B&B/INN** | Fluffy feather beds, custom Italian furnishings, and French doors in most cases opening onto terraces or balconies lend this inn's uncommonly spacious guest rooms a romantic air—more than a few guests are celebrating honeymoons or anniversaries. **Pros:** large rooms; lavish furnishings; romantic setting. **Cons:** far from nightlife; expensive in high season; geared more to couples than families with children. $ *Rooms from: $381 ✉ 10400 Sonoma Hwy./Hwy. 12 ☎ 707/833–1293, 800/353–6966 🌐 www.kenwoodinn.com 🛏 29 rooms 🍴 Free breakfast.*

⚡ Activities

SPAS

★ Spa at Kenwood Inn

FITNESS/HEALTH CLUBS | A pretty setting, expert practitioners, and rejuvenating therapies using products from iS Clinical, Intraceuticals, Naturopathica, and Vital Body Therapeutics CBD make a visit to this spa, completely remodeled in 2020, an ethereal experience. Done in soft whites and chocolate-brown accents that play off the greenery outside, the intimate space holds three individual treatment rooms, a room for couples, and a private outdoor terrace (also good for couples) with its own tub and shower. The Cielo Bliss Detox Massage, one of the signature treatments, incorporates CBD. For the Himalayan Salt Stone Massage, the practitioners gently rub smooth warm stones from the Himalayas over the body to melt away tension. A 20-minute hands-and-feet massage done poolside includes a mimosa; Arabica coffee and volcanic pumice go into the Espresso & Mud Detoxifying Body Treatment. Facials and bath cures are among the spa's other services. ⊠ *10400 Sonoma Hwy./Hwy. 12* ☎ *707/833–1293, 800/353–6966* ⊕ *www.kenwoodinn.com/spa* ⊠ *Treatments from $149.*

Petaluma

14 miles west of Sonoma; 39 miles north of San Francisco.

The first thing you should know about Petaluma is that this is a farm town—with 62,500 residents, a large one—and the residents are proud of it. Recent years have seen an uptick in the quality of Petaluma cuisine, fueled in part by the proliferation of local organic and artisanal farms and boutique wine production. With the 2018 approval of the Petaluma Gap AVA, the town even has its name on a wine appellation.

Petaluma's agricultural history reaches back to the mid-1800s, when General Mariano Vallejo established Rancho de Petaluma as his vast agrarian empire's headquarters. From the late 1800s into the 1960s Petaluma marketed itself as the "Egg Capital of the World," and with production totals that peaked at 612 million eggs in 1946, the point was hard to dispute. Although a poultry processor remains one of Petaluma's largest employers, the town has diversified. The adobe, an informative stop, albeit one whose presentation may recall grade-school field trips, was once the area's *only* employer. These days its visitation figures are dwarfed by Lagunitas Brewing Company, whose free tour, when offered, is a hoot. At McEvoy Ranch, which started out making gourmet olive oil before branching into wine, you can taste both products and tour parts of the farm.

Getting Here and Around

Petaluma lies west of Sonoma and southwest of Glen Ellen and Kenwood. From Highway 12 or Arnold Drive, take Watmaugh Road west to Highway 116 west. Sonoma Transit buses serve Petaluma from the Sonoma Valley. From San Francisco take U.S. 101 (or Golden Gate Transit Bus 101) north.

Visitor Information

CONTACTS Visit Petaluma. ⊠ *210 Lakeville St.* ☎ *707/769–0429* ⊕ *visitpetaluma. com.*

◉ Sights

Adobe Road Winery

WINERY/DISTILLERY | An upbeat atmosphere prevails in the downtown Petaluma tasting areas of this winery founded by former race-car driver Kevin Buckler and his wife, Debra. To produce its portfolio of mostly small-lot wines, Adobe Road sources grapes from top-tier growers, among them Beckstoffer for Napa Valley Cabernet Sauvignon and Malbec, and Sangiacomo for Chardonnay, Pinot Noir, and Syrah from the Petaluma Gap AVA. The Cabernet and Malbec shine, as does a red blend of both. ■TIP→ **The Bucklers are developing a combination tasting room, winery, and car museum along the waterfront near the current space; the new facility, at C and 1st streets, is scheduled to open by 2022.** ⊠ *6 Petaluma Blvd. N, Petaluma ✛ At B St.* ☎ *707/774–6699* ⊕ *www.adoberoadwines.com* 🍷 *Tastings from $20.*

Keller Estate

WINERY/DISTILLERY | This boutique winery's guests discover why "wind to wine" is the Petaluma Gap AVA's slogan. The steady Pacific Ocean and San Pablo Bay breezes that mitigate the midday heat give the grapes thick "sailor's skin," heightening their tannins and flavor, says Ana Keller, whose parents began planting vineyards here in 1989 on former dairy fields. Keller Estate concentrates on Chardonnay, Pinot Noir, and Syrah wines, many of which receive high marks from critics. Tastings, which often begin with a brief stroll of the grounds, usually take place alfresco on a stone terrace shaded by umbrellas and flowering pear trees. The winery requires reservations for all visits. ⊠ *5875 Lakeville Hwy., Petaluma ✛ At Cannon La.* ☎ *707/765–2117* ⊕ *www.kellerestate.com* 🍷 *Tasting $40* ☉ *Closed Sun.–Wed. (check with winery for updates).*

Lagunitas Brewing Company

WINERY/DISTILLERY | These days owned by Heineken International, Lagunitas began as a craft brewery in Marin County in 1993 before moving to Petaluma in 1994. In addition to its large facility, the company operates a taproom, the Schwag Shop for gifts, and an outdoor beer garden that in good weather bustles even midday.

Guides leading the brewery tour, which when offered includes a beer flight, provide an irreverent version of the company's rise to international acclaim. An engaging tale involves the state alcohol board's sting operation commemorated by Undercover Investigation Shut-down Ale, one of several small-batch brews made here. ■TIP→ **The taproom closes on Monday and Tuesday, but the gift shop stays open and tours may take place.** ⊠ *1280 N. McDowell Blvd., Petaluma ✛ ½ mile north of Corona Rd.* ☎ *707/769–4495* ⊕ *lagunitas.com/taproom/petaluma* 🍷 *Tour free* ☉ *Taproom closed Mon. and Tues.*

★ McEvoy Ranch

WINERY/DISTILLERY | The late Nan McEvoy's retirement project after departing as board chair of the *San Francisco Chronicle,* the ranch produces organic extra virgin olive oil as well as Pinot Noir and other wines, the estate ones from the Petaluma Gap AVA. Relaxing tastings of oils or wines unfold on a pond's-edge flagstone patio with views of alternating rows of Syrah grapes and mature olive trees. Two wine tastings include a simple lunch; the Taste of the Season spread involves wine served with artisanal cheeses, charcuterie, and other items. Walkabout Ranch Tours of four guests or more take in vineyards, gardens, and a Chinese pavilion. All visits require an appointment. ⊠ *5935 Red Hill Rd., Petaluma ✛ 6½ miles south of downtown* ☎ *866/617–6779* ⊕ *www.mcevoyranch. com* 🍷 *Tastings from $25 (olive oil), $35 (wine); tours from $55.*

Petaluma Adobe State Historic Park

NATIONAL/STATE PARK | A 10-foot cactus fence lines the blacktop path from the parking lot to the Petaluma Adobe, the largest extant 19th-century residential adobe in the United States. History buffs won't want to miss this landmark, which was, from 1836 to 1846, the headquarters of General Mariano Vallejo's vast

(66,000 acres at its peak) agricultural domain. Exhibits explain Vallejo's role as Mexico's head honcho before California joined the United States and depict daily life for native peoples and Spanish and Mexican settlers. ✉ *3325 Adobe Rd., Petaluma* ⊹ *Near Casa Grande Rd.* ☎ *707/762–4871* ⊕ *www.parks.ca.gov/ petalumaadobeshp* 🎟 *$3, includes same-day admission to Sonoma Mission and other historical sites.*

Sonoma Portworks

WINERY/DISTILLERY | In the mid-1990s Bill Reading got the bright idea to create the world's first chocolate wine. The concept went nowhere, but a later experiment adding dark-chocolate essences to port proved a winner—and became the first Sonoma Portworks product, Deco Port, these days made from Zinfandel, Grenache, and Alicante Bouschet. Reading followed this up by adding hazelnut essences to what's now called Duet Sherry. Individual ports made from Petite Sirah and Petit Verdot are among the additional offerings. You can taste these crowd-pleasing wines where they're made, in a warehouselike space on downtown's southern edge. ✉ *613 2nd St., Petaluma* ⊹ *Near H St.* ☎ *707/769–5203* ⊕ *portworks.com* 🎟 *Tasting $10* ☉ *Closed Tues. and Wed.*

🍴 Restaurants

Brewsters Beer Garden

$$ | **AMERICAN** | **FAMILY** | Succulent fried chicken and barbecued ribs whose meat glides off the bone are among the hits at this open-air, partially covered restaurant where diners sit at sturdy oak picnic or high-top tables. Many of the ingredients come from top artisanal protein and produce purveyors; most of the two dozen beers on tap are by craft producers. **Known for:** easygoing atmosphere; full bar; good wine selection. $ *Average main: $21* ✉ *229 Water St. N, Petaluma*

⊹ *Near E. Washington St.* ☎ *707/ 981–8330* ⊕ *brewstersbeergarden.com.*

★ Central Market

$$ | **MODERN AMERICAN** | A participant in the Slow Food movement, Central Market serves creative, upscale Cal-Mediterranean dishes—many of whose ingredients come from the restaurant's organic farm—in a century-old building with an exposed brick wall and an open kitchen. The menu, which changes daily depending on chef Tony Najiola's inspiration and what's ripe and ready, might include smoked duck wings as a starter, a slow-roasted-beets salad, pizzas, stews, two or three pasta dishes, and wood-grilled fish and meat. **Known for:** chef's tasting menus; superior wine list; historic setting. $ *Average main: $26* ✉ *42 Petaluma Blvd. N, Petaluma* ⊹ *Near Western Ave.* ☎ *707/778–9900* ⊕ *www. centralmarketpetaluma.com* ☉ *Closed Mon. and Tues. No lunch.*

★ Pearl Petaluma

$$ | **MEDITERRANEAN** | Regulars of this southern Petaluma "daytime café" with indoor and outdoor seating rave about its eastern Mediterranean–inflected cuisine—then immediately downplay their enthusiasm lest this unassuming gem become more popular. The menu changes often, but mainstays include *shakshuka* (a tomato-based stew with baked eggs) and a lamb burger dripping with tzatziki. **Known for:** weekend brunch; fun beverage lineup, both alcoholic and non; menu prices include gratuity. $ *Average main: $20* ✉ *500 1st St., Petaluma* ⊹ *At G St.* ☎ *707/559–5187* ⊕ *pearlpetaluma. com* ☉ *Closed Tues. No dinner.*

★ Stockhome

$$ | **SCANDINAVIAN** | The Petaluma-based owners of a San Francisco Scandinavian fine-dining landmark run this hip-homey counter-service homage to Swedish street food, whose influences, it turns out, include Middle Eastern cuisine. Seasonal ingredients, for the most part locally produced and raised, find their way into kebabs, Swedish meatballs, Wiener schnitzel, gravlax, herring done "grandma's way," and *korv kiosk* (grilled frankfurters or sausages), all prepared with élan. **Known for:** vegetarian and vegan options; artisanal beer, wine, and hard cider selection; Swedish desserts and candy. [$] *Average main: $21* ✉ *220 Western Ave., Petaluma* ✥ *At Liberty St.* ☎ *707/981–8511* 🌐 *www.stockhomerestaurant.com* 🕒 *Closed Mon. and Tues.*

Hotels

Hampton Inn Petaluma

$ | **HOTEL** | The former Carlson-Currier Silk Mill, its oldest section dating to 1892, houses this atypical Hampton Inn, some of whose guest rooms have 14-foot ceilings and exposed-brick walls. **Pros:** original architectural details in some rooms; classy breakfast area; reasonable rates. **Cons:** traffic noise (ask for a historic room away from the road); some standard rooms are small; no pool, nondescript neighborhood. [$] *Rooms from: $199* ✉ *450 Jefferson St., Petaluma* ☎ *707/397–0000* 🌐 *www.hampton.com* 🛏 *75 rooms* 🍴 *Free breakfast.*

Hotel Petaluma

$ | **HOTEL** | Reasonable rates and vintage allure make this 1923 art-deco property, the recipient of a top-to-bottom renovation completed in 2018, a smart choice for budget travelers seeking a convenient downtown location and a touch of style. **Pros:** downtown location; solid value; ground-floor Shuckery restaurant for seafood. **Cons:** public spaces grander than the mostly small rooms; hallway sound carries into rooms; lacks parking lot, fitness center, and other amenities. [$] *Rooms from: $190* ✉ *205 Kentucky St., Petaluma* ☎ *707/559–3393* 🌐 *www.hotelpetaluma.com* 🛏 *57 rooms* 🍴 *No meals.*

Nightlife

★ Ernie's Tin Bar

BARS/PUBS | Ramshackle Ernie's shares a corrugated tin building with a frozen-in-time roadside garage, with part of the bar actually in the garage. Mounted stag heads and a toothy wild boar watch over this rural-neighborhood hangout with a long, narrow bar, a patio outside, and Pliny the Elder and another 20 or so brews on tap. Signs everywhere ban cellphone use, though patrons and even staffers occasionally flout them. ✉ *5100 Lakeville Hwy., Petaluma* ✥ *At Stage Gulch Rd. (Hwy. 116)* ☎ *707/762–2075.*

La Dolce Vita Wine Lounge

WINE BARS—NIGHTLIFE | Sahar Gharai's downtown wine bar highlights boutique producers worldwide. You can sip by the glass or order a themed flight, perhaps of whites and reds from Italy or comparing Sauvignon Blancs from France, New Zealand, and Mendocino. The kitchen turns out small bites, pizzas, soups, and sandwiches. Two good times to come are at happy hour (3–5 pm) and when classic movies screen (check website or Facebook). ✉ *151 Petaluma Blvd. S, Suite 117, Petaluma* ✥ *Between C and D Sts.* ☎ *707/763–6363* 🌐 *www.ldvwine.com* ☞ *Closed Sun. and Mon.*

Performing Arts

Mystic Theatre & Music Hall

CONCERTS | In keeping with its roots as a vaudeville house, the Mystic, which opened in 1911, books all sorts of acts and events, from indie bands and comedians to folk and alternative acts and old-school rockers. The space holds about 500 people. ✉ *23 Petaluma Blvd. N, Petaluma* ✥ *Near Western Ave.* ☎ *707/775–6048* 🌐 *www.mystictheatre.com.*

NORTHERN SONOMA, RUSSIAN RIVER, AND WEST COUNTY

6

⊙ Sights   🍽 Restaurants   🛏 Hotels   🛍 Shopping   🍸 Nightlife
★★★★★   ★★★★★   ★★★★☆   ★★★★☆   ★★★☆☆

WELCOME TO NORTHERN SONOMA, RUSSIAN RIVER, AND WEST COUNTY

TOP REASONS TO GO

★ **Back-roads biking:** The region's ultrascenic back roads include gentle hills and challenging terrain you can traverse with a guide or on your own.

★ **Diverse dining:** Area chefs tickle diners' palates with diverse offerings—everything from haute-French and Peruvian cuisine to playful variations on American standards.

★ **Hillside Cabs and old-vine Zins:** Alexander Valley hillside Cabernet Sauvignon and Dry Creek Valley old-vine Zinfandel grapes—as far as the eye can see in spots—thrive in the high heat here.

★ **Hip Healdsburg shopping:** Healdsburg wins the shopping wars fair and square, with more captivating galleries, design-oriented shops, and clothing stores than anywhere in the Wine Country.

★ **Pinot aplenty and Chardonnay, too:** Russian River Valley and Sonoma Coast wineries large and small produce some of California's most celebrated Pinot Noirs and Chardonnays.

1 Healdsburg. Its hotels, wineries, restaurants, and shops make this town a tourist hub.

2 Geyserville. Mostly rural Geyserville has a small, engaging downtown.

3 Windsor. Workaday Windsor hosts Russian River Brewing.

4 Forestville. West of Healdsburg, Forestville nestles among redwoods.

5 Guerneville. This lively town has been a vacation retreat for a century-plus.

6 Jenner. The cliffs here overlook the estuary where the Russian River empties into the Pacific.

7 Bodega Bay. Harbor seals bask on Bodega Bay's windswept beaches.

8 Occidental. Redwoods tower over this small burg east of Bodega Bay.

9 Sebastopol. East of Occidental, Sebastopol contains restaurants, shops, and wineries.

10 Graton. Sebastopol surrounds this hamlet.

11 Santa Rosa. Sonoma County's largest city and commercial core straddles U.S. 101.

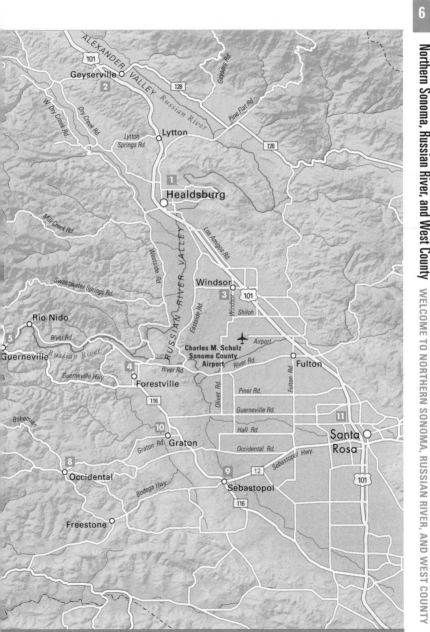

Sonoma County's northern and western reaches are a study in contrasts. Trendy hotels, restaurants, shops, and tasting rooms have transformed Healdsburg into a hot spot. Within a few miles, though, the chic yields to the bucolic, with only an occasional horse ranch, apple or peach orchard, or stand of oaks to interrupt the rolling vineyard hills.

Each of northern and western Sonoma County's regions claims its own micro-climates, soil types, and most-favored varietals, but—except for urban Santa Rosa—all have something in common: peace and quiet. This area is less crowded than the Napa Valley and southern Sonoma. Healdsburg, in particular, is hardly a stranger to overnight visitors, but you'll find less company in many of the region's tasting rooms. The Russian River, Dry Creek, and Alexander valleys are the grape-growing stars, along with the Sonoma Coast, but smaller appellations like Fort Ross–Seaview also merit investigation.

MAJOR REGIONS

Healdsburg's walkable downtown, swank hotels, and remarkable restaurant scene make it the most convenient base for exploring Northern Sonoma County. The wineries here and in Geyserville to the north produce some of the country's best Pinot Noirs, Cabernet Sauvignons, Zinfandels, and Chardonnays.

In the smaller West County towns of Forestville, Guerneville, Sebastopol, Graton, and Occidental, high-style lodgings and fine dining are in shorter supply. Each town has a few charmers, however, along with wineries worth seeking out. The western reaches of Sonoma County, extending all the way to the Pacific Ocean and the towns of Jenner and Bodega Bay, are more sparsely populated, although more and more vineyards are popping up where orchards or ranches once stood.

As the county's—and Wine Country's—largest city, workaday Santa Rosa may lack sex appeal, but it does contain the Charles M. Schulz Museum, Safari West, and other nonwine attractions, and dining and lodging options here and just to the north in Windsor tend to be more affordably priced than in the smaller towns.

Planning

When to Go

High season runs from early June through October, but even then weekday mornings find many wineries blissfully uncrowded. Summers are warm and nearly always pleasant on the coast, and though inland the temperatures often reach 90°F, this is nothing a rosé of Pinot Noir can't cure. Fall brings harvest fairs and other celebrations. Things slow down during winter, but with smaller crowds come more intimate winery visits. Roads along the Russian River are prone to flooding during heavy rains, as are a few in the Alexander Valley. Spring, when the grapevines are budding but the crowds are still thin, is a good time to visit.

Getting Here and Around

SMART (Sonoma-Marin Area Rail Transit) commuter trains can be helpful if you're visiting the restaurants and tasting rooms of downtown Petaluma and Santa Rosa, but until the tracks are extended to Healdsburg (several years off) it's of minimal use to wine tourists. It's possible to tour by bus, but travel by car remains the best option. One alternative is to book a group or private tour.

BUS

Sonoma County Transit provides transportation to all the main towns in this region. Except for the routes from Santa Rosa to Healdsburg and Sebastopol, service isn't always frequent. *For more information about arriving by bus, see the Bus section in the Travel Smart chapter. For more information about local bus service, see the Bus sections for the individual towns in this chapter.*

CAR

Driving a car is by far the easiest way to get to and experience this region. From San Francisco, the quickest route to Northern Sonoma is north on U.S. 101 to Santa Rosa and Healdsburg. Highway 116 (aka Gravenstein Highway) heads west from U.S. 101, taking you through Sebastopol and the hamlets of Graton and Forestville before depositing you along the Russian River near Guerneville. Traffic can be slow on U.S. 101, especially around Petaluma and Santa Rosa during rush hour and on summer weekends. Parking can be difficult in downtown Healdsburg

on busy summer and early fall weekends, when you may have to park in a lot, feed a meter, or walk a few blocks.

Restaurants

Each year at the Sonoma County Harvest Festival and seasonally at local farmers' markets, the remarkable output of Northern Sonoma's farms and ranches is on display. Local chefs often scour the markets for seafood, meats, cheeses, and produce, and many restaurants have their own gardens. With all these fresh ingredients at hand, it should come as no surprise that farm-to-table cuisine predominates here, especially among the high-profile restaurants. Wood-fired pizzas are another local passion, as is modern Italian fare. Gourmet delis and grocery stores in several towns are excellent sources for picnic fare. Except in the region's most expensive restaurants, it's fine to dress casually.

Hotels

Healdsburg's hotels and inns set this region's standard for bedding down in style, with plush rooms that top $1,000 a night in a few cases. In the more affordable category are traditional bed-and-breakfast inns and small hotels, and there are even some inns and motels with down-to-earth prices. These last lodgings book up well in advance for high season, which is why Santa Rosa—just 15 miles away and home to decent chain and independent inns and hotels—is worth checking out year-round. Several secluded West County inns provide an elegant escape. Smaller properties throughout the region have two-night minimums on weekends (three nights on holiday weekends), though in winter this is negotiable.

What It Costs in U.S. Dollars			
$	$$	$$$	$$$$
RESTAURANTS			
under $17	$17–$26	$27–$36	over $36
HOTELS			
under $201	$201–$300	$301–$400	over $400

Planning Your Time

With hundreds of wineries separated by miles of highway—Sonoma County is as big as Rhode Island—you could wander for weeks here and still not cover everything. To get a taste of what makes this region special, plan on a minimum of two or three days to hit the highlights. Healdsburg and the Russian River Valley are the must-sees, but it's worth venturing beyond them to the Alexander and Dry Creek valleys. If you still have time, head west toward the coast.

Appellations

Covering about 329,000 acres, the **Northern Sonoma AVA,** itself within the larger Sonoma County "appellation of origin," a geopolitical designation, and the even larger multicounty **North Coast AVA,** is divided into smaller subappellations. Three of the most important meet at Healdsburg: the Russian River Valley AVA, which runs southwest along the river; the Dry Creek Valley AVA, which runs northwest of town; and the Alexander Valley AVA, which extends to the east and north. Also in this far northern area are smaller AVAs whose names you're more likely to see on wine labels than at the few visitable wineries within the appellations themselves: Knights Valley, Chalk Hill, Fountaingrove, Rockpile, and Pine Mountain–Cloverdale Peak.

The cool climate of the low-lying **Russian River Valley AVA,** which extends from Healdsburg west to Guerneville, is perfect for Pinot Noir and Chardonnay. Because of the low elevation, sea fog pushes far inland, dropping temperatures at night (good for maintaining acidity), yet in summer it burns off, giving grapes sufficient sun to ripen fully. The namesake river does its part by depositing layers of gravel that force the vines' roots to push deep down in search of water and nutrients. In the process, the plants absorb trace minerals that add complexity to the grapes' flavors. Three decades ago this area had as many ranches and apple orchards as vineyards. Now one of Sonoma's most-recognized growing regions, it has a significant subappellation of its own in the Forestville-Sebastopol area, the **Green Valley of the Russian River Valley AVA.**

The **Dry Creek Valley AVA** is a small region—only about 16 miles long and 2 miles wide. The valley's well-drained, gravelly floor is planted with Chardonnay grapes to the south, where an occasional sea fog creeps in from the Russian River and cools the vineyards. Sauvignon Blanc is found in the warmer north. The red decomposed soils of the benchlands bring out the best in Zinfandel—the grape for which Dry Creek is famous—but they also produce excellent Cabernet Sauvignon and Petite Sirah. And these soils are well suited to such white Rhône varietals as Viognier, Roussanne, and Marsanne, along with Grenache, Syrah, and Mourvèdre reds.

As recently as the 1980s the **Alexander Valley AVA** was mostly planted to walnuts, pears, plums, and bulk grapes, but these days fruit for premium wines, mainly Cabernet Sauvignon but also Sauvignon Blanc, Petite Sirah, and Zinfandel, have largely replaced them. Rhône varietals such as Grenache and Syrah, along with Sangiovese, Barbera, and other Italian grapes, also make great wines here, and certain cooler spots have proven hospitable to Chardonnay and Merlot.

Much of the **Sonoma Coast AVA,** which stretches the length of Sonoma County's coastline, lies within the Northern Sonoma AVA. The classic combination of hot summer days and cooling evening fog and breezes (in some spots even cooler than the Russian River Valley) inspired major Napa Valley wineries to invest in acreage here. The hunch paid off—Sonoma Coast Pinots and Chardonnays have become the darlings of national wine critics. Because the AVA encompasses such varied terrain—the southeastern portion edges into the comparatively warmer Sonoma Valley—some West County growers and vintners have proposed subappellations that express what they promote as the "true" Sonoma Coast geology and microclimates. One subappellation approved was the **Fort Ross–Seaview AVA,** whose hillside vineyards, mostly of Chardonnay and Pinot Noir, occupy land once thought too close to the Pacific Ocean to support grape growing. Far along in the approval process—and perhaps official by the time you read this—is the **West Sonoma Coast AVA,** which encompasses the entire Sonoma coast but not the inland areas of the larger AVA.

Mountains surround the idyllic **Bennett Valley AVA** on three sides. Entirely in the Sonoma Valley AVA *(see Chapter 5)* and overlapping two other AVAs, it bears a Santa Rosa address. Coastal breezes sneak through the wind gap at Crane Canyon, making this area ideal for such cooler-weather grapes as Pinot Noir and Chardonnay. Syrah, Cabernet Sauvignon, and Sauvignon Blanc also do well here.

Healdsburg

17 miles north of Santa Rosa.

Sonoma County's ritziest town and the star of many a magazine spread or online feature, Healdsburg is located at the intersection of the Dry Creek Valley, Russian River Valley, and Alexander Valley AVAs. Several dozen wineries bear a Healdsburg address, and around downtown's plaza you'll find fashionable boutiques, spas, hip tasting rooms, and art galleries, and some of the Wine Country's best restaurants.

Especially on weekends, you're apt to have plenty of company as you tour the downtown area. You could spend a day exploring the tasting rooms and shops surrounding Healdsburg Plaza, but be sure to allow time to venture into the surrounding countryside. With orderly rows of vines alternating with beautifully overgrown hills, this is the setting you dream about when planning a Wine Country vacation.

Getting Here and Around

To get to Healdsburg from San Francisco, cross the Golden Gate Bridge and continue north for 65 miles on U.S. 101. Take the Central Healdsburg exit and follow Healdsburg Avenue a few blocks north to Healdsburg Plaza. Wineries bearing Healdsburg addresses can be as far apart as 20 miles, so you'll find a car handy. The Dry Creek Valley AVA and most of the Russian River Valley AVA are west of U.S. 101; most of the Alexander Valley AVA is east of the freeway. Sonoma County Transit buses serve Healdsburg from Santa Rosa.

Westside wineries: To get to wineries along Westside Road, head south on Center Street, then turn right at Mill Street. After Mill Street crosses under U.S. 101, its name changes to Westside

Top Tastings and Tours

Tastings

Aperture Cellars, Healdsburg. Its tasting room's ingenious design a nod to the winemaker's father's photography, Aperture clicks with guests even before they sample single-vineyard Cabernets, arguably Sonoma County's best.

Robert Young Estate Winery, Geyserville. The "infinity lawn" of the Young family's hilltop hospitality center gives way to views across the Alexander Valley as captivating as the winery's Chardonnays and Bordeaux-style reds.

Setting

Flowers Vineyard & Winery, Healdsburg. Astonishing architecture blends harmoniously with nature at this showcase for cool-climate Chardonnays and Pinot Noirs.

Iron Horse Vineyards, Sebastopol. The vine-covered hills and valleys surrounding this sparkling wine producer provide such compelling views that the winery hosts all its tastings outside.

Ridge Vineyards, Healdsburg. Patrons of this longtime producer enjoy views of rolling vineyards while tasting intense Zinfandels and other well-rounded wines.

Food Pairing

Cāpo Creek Ranch, Healdsburg. Owner-winemaker and physician Dr. Mary Roy pulls out all the stops for a six-course extravaganza, with dishes like butter-poached lobster tail and a four-cheese tomato tart bringing out the best in her Rhône- and Bordeaux-style wines and Zinfandel.

Jordan Vineyard and Winery, Healdsburg. For seasonal terrace tastings during summer illustrating the versatility of the winery's Chardonnay and Cabernet Sauvignon, the executive chef plucks most of the ingredients from the estate's organic gardens.

Just Plain Fun

Davis Family Vineyards, Healdsburg. On weekends from late spring to early fall, you can "get your BLT on" with sandwiches paired with superlative Pinot Noir, Syrah, and other wines.

Road. After about ½ mile, veer south to continue on Westside Road to reach the Russian River Valley wineries.

Eastside wineries: The route to wineries on Old Redwood Highway and Eastside Road starts out less scenic. Follow Healdsburg Avenue south to U.S. 101. Hop on the freeway, exiting after a mile at Old Redwood Highway. Bear right as you exit, and continue south. Just past the driveway that serves Rodney Strong and J Vineyards, turn southwest to merge onto Eastside Road.

Dry Creek Valley and Alexander Valley wineries: To reach the wineries along Dry Creek Road and West Dry Creek Road, head north from the plaza on Healdsburg Avenue. After about a mile, turn west on Dry Creek Road. Roughly parallel to Dry Creek Road is West Dry Creek Road, accessible by the cross streets Lambert Bridge Road and Yoakim Bridge Road. For Alexander Valley wineries, continue north on Healdsburg Avenue past Dry Creek Road.

Visitor Information

Healdsburg Chamber of Commerce & Visitors Bureau

✉ *217 Healdsburg Ave.* ✛ *At Matheson St.* ☎ *707/433–6935* ⊕ *www.healdsburg. com.*

👁 Sights

★ Acorn Winery

WINERY/DISTILLERY | A throwback to the era when a hardworking couple forsook sensible careers and went all-in to become grape growers and vintners, this low-tech yet classy operation earns high praise for wines that include Cabernet Franc, Sangiovese, Zinfandel, and the rare-in-America Italian varietal Dolcetto. Betsy and Bill Nachbaur share their output in a garage-style, appointment-only tasting room amid their Alegría Vineyard. Each Acorn wine is a field blend of multiple grape varietals interplanted (grown side by side) and then crushed and fermented together. In the wrong hands, this old-school approach produces muddled, negligible wines, but these, made by Bill in consultation with local winemaker Clay Mauritson, soar. ■ TIP→ **Unlike many wineries these days, family- and dog-friendly Acorn invites guests to bring their own food and picnic beside the vineyard before or after a tasting.** ✉ *12040 Old Redwood Hwy.* ✛ *¼ mile south of Limerick La.* ☎ *707/433–6440* ⊕ *acornwinery.com* 🍷 *Tasting $30.*

Alley 6 Craft Distillery

WINERY/DISTILLERY | Krystle and Jason Jorgensen make small-batch rye and single-malt whiskey, plus gin, peach liqueur, apple brandy, and candy-cap bitters, at the couple's industrial-park distillery 2 miles north of Healdsburg Plaza. The rye derives its overlapping flavors from its "mash bill" of rye and malted barley aged in heavily charred American oak barrels that add further layers of spice and complexity. The Jorgensens pride themselves on crafting their spirits entirely on-site, from grain milling through bottling, a process they describe with enthusiasm at their apothecarylike tasting room, open on weekends (weekdays by appointment). ✉ *1401 Grove St., Unit D* ✛ *North of Dry Creek Rd.* ☎ *707/484–3593* ⊕ *www.alley6.com* 🍷 *Tastings from $10.*

★ Aperture Cellars

WINERY/DISTILLERY | As a youth, Jesse Katz tagged along with his photographer father, Andy Katz, to wineries worldwide, stimulating curiosity about wine that led to stints at august operations like the Napa Valley's Screaming Eagle and Bordeaux's Petrús. In 2009, still in his 20s, Katz started Aperture, a success from the get-go for his single-vineyard Cabernets and Bordeaux blends. Among the whites are Sauvignon Blanc and an old-vine Chenin Blanc that's one of California's best. Katz's wines, which benefit from rigorous farming and cellar techniques, are presented by appointment only in an ultracontemporary hospitality center that opened in 2020 about 2½ miles south of Healdsburg Plaza. One tasting explores Aperture's various wine-growing sites, the other the single-vineyard wines. The center's shutterlike windows and other architectural elements evoke Andy Katz's photography career; his images of the Russian River Valley and beyond hang on the walls. ✉ *12291 Old Redwood Hwy.* ✛ *¼ mile south of Limerick La.* ☎ *707/200–7891* ⊕ *www.aperture-cellars.com* 🍷 *Tastings from $50.*

★ Arista Winery

WINERY/DISTILLERY | Brothers Mark and Ben McWilliams own this winery specializing in small-lot Pinot Noirs that was founded in 2002 by their parents. The sons have raised the winery's profile in several ways, most notably by hiring winemaker Matt Courtney, who has earned high praise from *Wine Spectator* and other publications for his balanced,

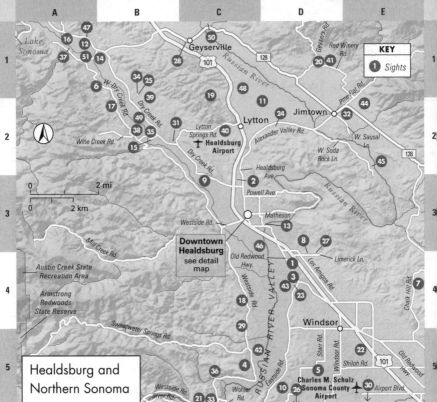

Healdsburg and Northern Sonoma

KEY

1 Sights

Sights ▼

richly textured Pinot Noirs. Courtney shows the same deft touch with Arista's Zinfandels, Chardonnays, and a Riesling. Appointment-only introductory tastings focus on Chardonnay, Pinot Noir, and the family's sustainable farming practices. The property's Japanese garden predates the winery. ⌧ *7015 Westside Rd.* ☎ *707/473–0606* ⊕ *www.aristawinery. com* 🍷 *Tastings from $50.*

BloodRoot Wines

WINERY/DISTILLERY | How about this for a marketing twist: the folks behind this winery that opened in 2020 produce outstanding wines using grapes from leading vineyards but reveal neither sources nor winemakers. The novel approach turned the debut lineup—Blanc de (Pinot) Gris sparkling wine, Chardonnay, two Pinots (plus a rosé thereof), Carignane, and Cabernet Sauvignon—into a who-made-what-from-where guessing game for local oenophiles, who also appreciated prices well below expected for wines so well crafted. (The Cabernet topped out at $55, and one of the Pinots was $25.) Hidden away in a tiny strip mall a block from Healdsburg Plaza, the storefront tasting space's country-cool decor hints at the panache behind this enterprise, whose servers appear to have been chosen for their ebullience; they're also generous with suggestions about other places to taste. ⌧ *118 North St.* ✛ *At Center St.* ☎ *707/387–7058* ⊕ *www.bloodrootwines.com* 🍷 *Tastings from $25* ⊙ *Closed Tues.*

Breathless Wines

WINERY/DISTILLERY | The mood's downright bubbly (pardon that pun) at the oasis-like garden patio of this sparkling-wine producer tucked away in an industrial park northwest of Healdsburg Plaza. Established by three sisters in memory of their mother, Breathless sources grapes from appellations in Sonoma, Napa, and Mendocino counties that find their way into sparklers and a few still wines. The small indoor tasting area, decorated flapper-era-style, was ingeniously fashioned out of shipping containers, though nearly everyone sips in the umbrella-shaded garden in fine weather. You can sample wine by the glass, flight, or bottle; all visits require an appointment, with same-day reservations sometimes possible. ■TIP→ **Splurge on the Sabrage Experience to learn how to open a bottle with a saber, a tradition supposedly initiated by Napoléon's soldiers.** ⌧ *499 Moore La.* ✛ *Off North St.* ☎ *707/395–7300* ⊕ *www.breathlesswines.com* 🍷 *Tastings from $13 per glass, $20 per flight* ⊙ *Closed Tues. and Wed. (sometimes changes).*

★ Cāpo Creek Ranch

WINERY/DISTILLERY | Halfway through a wine-and-food pairing at this serenely rustic Dry Creek Valley winery you may find yourself asking not only "How does she do it?"—"she" being Dr. Mary Roy, Cāpo Creek Ranch's proprietor, winemaker, chef, and hostess with the mostest—but also how does she make it look so easy? The answer might simply be that running a winery isn't likely to faze someone who raised six kids while operating a bustling radiological imaging center. Whatever the reason, in "retirement" Roy has created a magical showcase for her mostly Rhône-style whites and reds (the stars) along with Cabernet Sauvignon, estate old-vine Zinfandel, and numerous blends. Most tastings occur outdoors facing east toward the heritage-Zin vineyard, with the cave and the tasting room alternative possibilities. ■TIP→ **All tastings involve Roy's food, but a worthwhile splurge is the six-course Ultimate Food & Wine Pairing, which lives up to its name.** ⌧ *7171 W. Dry Creek Rd.* ✛ *1¼ miles south of Yoakam Bridge Rd.* ☎ *707/608–8448* ⊕ *www.capocreekranch.com* 🍷 *Tastings from $70.*

★ Cartograph Wines

WINERY/DISTILLERY | The husband-wife team behind Cartograph believes in Pinot Noirs emphasizing "balance, nuance, and complexity, rather than power and intensity." To that end they select vineyard sites based on climate and clone compatibility, harvest their grapes on the early side, and intervene as little as possible during the wine-making process. The resulting wines please on their own and pair well with food. Unlike many Sonoma County Pinot producers, Cartograph eschews Chardonnay for its still whites, opting instead for the Alsatian grapes Gewürztraminer and Riesling, both done in a refreshingly crisp and dry style. Chardonnay does, however, appear in the winery's two sparkling wines. All visits to the storefront space a block northeast of Healdsburg Plaza are by appointment (call for same-day). ⊠ *340 Center St.* ✢ *At North St.* ☎ *707/433–8270* ⊕ *www. cartographwines.com* ▨ *Tastings from $25* ⊗ *Closed Mon.*

Chalk Hill Estate

WINERY/DISTILLERY | At 1,300 acres it's one of Sonoma County's largest estates, and this is the most prominent winery of the Chalk Hill appellation. Most guests taste on the châteaulike production facility's terrace, basking in views of steep, woodsy, vineyard-studded hills. A subappellation of the Russian River Valley AVA, the Chalk Hill AVA is so far east—less than 10 miles from the northern Napa Valley as the crow flies—that it gets much warmer. Although even in summer you might detect the Russian River Valley's cooling Pacific breezes, the estate, which has 15 separate microclimates, isn't cool enough for Pinot Noir, so the winery grows it on land nearer the ocean. Many of Chalk Hill Estate's 300 vineyard acres are devoted to Chardonnay—the grape represents more than half of production—with Sauvignon Blanc, Cabernet Sauvignon, a few other Bordeaux varietals (the Malbec's quite good), and Syrah also planted. ⊠ *10300 Chalk Hill Rd.* ✢ *Take Old Redwood Hwy. east off U.S. 101 in Windsor to Pleasant Ave.* ☎ *707/657–1809* ⊕ *www.chalkhill. com* ▨ *Tastings from $30.*

Christopher Creek Winery

WINERY/DISTILLERY | Petite Sirah and Syrah made this winery's early reputation, but under this 11-acre property's current vineyard manager and winemaker, Pinot Noir, Bordeaux reds, and Rhône whites have come to the fore. The varied portfolio lends itself to three different experiences. The Estate Tasting involves the whites and reds that established the winery. Guests at a Legacy Tasting sip barrel samples of Pinot Noir and place orders for "futures" available after aging. The Ultimate Tasting Experience includes bottled wines, barrel tastings, cheese and charcuterie, and a reserve library wine. ■TIP➔ **Expect to linger over a rare small-production wine at Legacy and Ultimate tastings.** ⊠ *641 Limerick La.* ✢ *¼ mile east of Los Amigos Rd.* ☎ *707/433– 2001* ⊕ *www.christophercreek.com* ▨ *Tastings from $25.*

Comstock Wines

WINERY/DISTILLERY | Winemaker Chris Russi gained fans during previous stops at the Christopher Creek and Thomas George wineries, and with the high-quality fruit at his disposal here, his posse continues to expand. Elegant Zinfandels are a specialty, one of them from the characterful old vines that front the tasting room. Russi also does well with estate-grown Dry Creek Valley Merlot and purchased Sonoma Coast Pinot Noir, and the winery has branched into Rhône varietals with Sonoma Valley Grenache and Bennett Valley Syrah. Whites include Chardonnay, Viognier, a Blanc de Blanc sparkling wine, and Sauvignon Blanc. Comstock is the kind of place that encourages lingering, best done in fine weather behind the contemporary barn-like production facility, whose terrace's vineyard and hillside views enhance the pleasure of these refined wines. Tastings are by appointment only, with same-day visits sometimes possible. ⊠ *1290 Dry Creek Rd.* ✢ *1 mile west of U.S. 101 (Dry Creek Rd. exit)* ☎ *707/723–3011* ⊕ *www.*

The Russian River Valley AVA extends from Healdsburg west to Guerneville.

comstockwines.com ✉ *Tastings from* *$20* ☉ *Closed Tues.*

Copain Wines

WINERY/DISTILLERY | The reputation of this winery whose name means "friends" in French rests on its Chardonnays, Pinot Noirs, and Syrahs. Copain occupies an enviable slope in Northern Sonoma County—one that begs guests to sit, sip, and take in the Russian River Valley view—but for years most of its wines derived from grapes grown in hillside vineyards near the coast in Monterey and Mendocino counties. In recent years Russian River Valley and Sonoma Coast fruit has joined the mix. One appointment-only tasting focuses on single-vineyard current releases, another on older vintages. There's also an alfresco lunch option. ✉ *7800 Eastside Rd.* ✛ *Near Ballard Rd.* ☎ *707/837–1101* ⊕ *www.copainwines. com* ✉ *Tastings from $35.*

Davis Family Vineyards

WINERY/DISTILLERY | On weekends from late spring to early fall, this winery's garden-side outdoor tasting space becomes party central as guests heeding the invitation to "get your BLT on" enjoy sandwiches prepared in the colorful Black Piglet food truck. Pinot Noir and Rhône-style wines are the specialties here. Owner-winemaker Guy Davis crafts all the Pinots the same way—aiming to let vineyard conditions and the specific clones of Pinot Noir find expression in the bottle—and wine critics routinely praise the results of this humble approach. Other reds include the beautifully rendered estate Soul Patch Vineyard Syrah (great with the BLTs) and the powerful Cab 5 Bordeaux-style blend from the Rockpile AVA. On the lighter side Davis makes Chardonnay, a sparkling wine, rosé, and the flagship Cuvée Luke blend of Roussanne, Marsanne, and Viognier. All visits are by appointment. ✉ *52 Front St.* ✛ *At Hudson St.* ☎ *707/433–3858* ⊕ *www.davisfamilyvine-yards.com* ✉ *Tastings from $15.*

★ Dry Creek Peach & Produce

FARM/RANCH | If you happen by this farm stand in the summer, don't pass up the

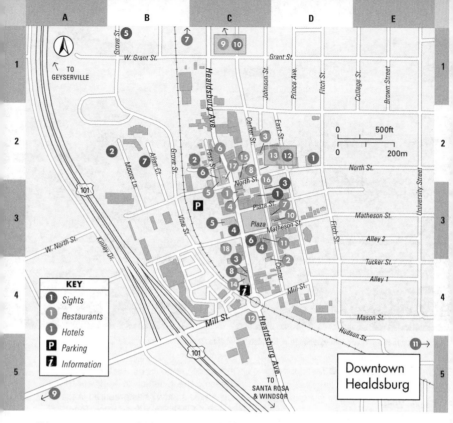

Downtown Healdsburg

chance to sample the tree-ripened white and yellow peaches, some of which may have been harvested moments before you arrived. You can buy peaches in small quantities, as well as organic peach jam. How good are these peaches? Customers include the famed Chez Panisse Restaurant in Berkeley. ■TIP➙ **The stand is typically open from July to mid-September between noon and 5 on Wednesday, Friday, and the weekend. Call ahead to confirm, though.** ⊠ *2179 Yoakim Bridge Rd. ⊕ Near Dry Creek Rd.* ☎ *707/433–8121* ⊕ *www. drycreekpeach.com* ⊗ *Closed mid-Sept.–June and Mon., Tues., and Thurs. July–mid-Sept.*

Dry Creek Vineyard

WINERY/DISTILLERY | Loire-style Sauvignon Blanc marketed as Fumé Blanc brought instant success to the Dry Creek Valley's first new winery since Prohibition, but this stalwart established in 1972 also does well with Zinfandel and Cabernet Sauvignon and other Bordeaux-style reds. Founder David Stare's other contributions include leading the drive to develop the Dry Creek Valley appellation and coining the term "old-vine Zinfandel." The winery's history and wine-making evolution are among the topics addressed at tastings—outdoors under the shade of a magnolia and several redwood trees or in the nautical-themed tasting room. ⊠ *3770 Lambert Bridge Rd. ⊕ Off Dry Creek Rd.* ☎ *707/433–1000, 800/864–9463* ⊕ *www.drycreekvineyard.com* ☚ *Tastings from $25.*

Ferrari-Carano Winery

WINERY/DISTILLERY | Known for its grand Italian villa and manicured gardens—not a stray blade of grass anywhere here—this winery produces Chardonnay, Sauvignon Blanc, Merlot, Zinfandel, and Cabernet Sauvignon. Although whites have traditionally been the specialty, the reds also garner attention—in particular the Bordeaux-style blend called Trésor—and some guests come just for the dessert wines. The villa's terrace and sycamore

grove host many tastings, which, like the ones that take place indoors, are by appointment. ⊠ *8761 Dry Creek Rd. ⊕ At Yoakim Bridge Rd.* ☎ *707/433–6700, 800/831–0381* ⊕ *www.ferrari-carano.com* ☚ *Tastings from $30.*

★ Flambeaux Wine

WINERY/DISTILLERY | A family with deep ties to New Orleans founded this winery named for the dancing torchbearers at Mardi Gras. Zinfandel and Cabernet Sauvignon that go into separate bottlings and jointly into a crisp summery rosé flourish in the iron-rich estate Flambeaux Vineyard, up a winding road on the Dry Creek Valley AVA's western slope. Ryan Prichard, also of Sonoma's Three Sticks Wines, has been making these wines plus a Sonoma Coast Chardonnay, a Cabernet Sauvignon from sourced grapes, and a few others since the first (2014) vintage. Most people sample these wines in Windsor at Grand Cru Custom Crush, where they're made, but for a more intimate introduction arrange a terrace tasting at the estate vineyard. The Crescent City hospitality and views across the valley to Geyser Peak uplift the experience all the more. ⊠ *1333 Jack Pine Rd. ⊕ Off W. Dry Creek Rd.* ☎ *707/637–9019* ⊕ *www.flambeauxwine. com* ☚ *Tastings $30 at Grand Cru, $50 at vineyard.*

★ Flowers Vineyard & Winery

WINERY/DISTILLERY | Steel, glass, and wood architecture that discreetly astonishes but ultimately yields to the surrounding gardens, redwoods, vineyards, and distant hills supplies a dramatic backdrop for tastings of this illustrious winery's Chardonnays and Pinot Noirs. Their grapes, grown far to the west in wild Pacific Coast terrain thought years ago too cool and harsh to produce fruit sufficiently ripe, undergo minimal cellar intervention during their transformation into wines recognized for their balance and vibrancy. Tastings take place indoors or out, in some cases accompanied by delicate small bites that illustrate how food-friendly these beautifully crafted wines are. ✉ *4035 Westside Rd.* ✛ *4 miles south of Healdsburg Plaza* ☎ *707/723–4800* ⊕ *flowerswinery.com* ☑ *Tastings from $55* ⊙ *Closed Tues. and Wed.*

Gary Farrell Vineyards & Winery

WINERY/DISTILLERY | Pass through an impressive metal gate and wind your way up a steep hill to reach this winery with knockout Russian River Valley views from the elegant two-tiered tasting room and terrace outside. In 2017 *Wine Enthusiast Magazine* named a Gary Farrell Chardonnay wine of the year, one among many accolades for this winery known for sophisticated single-vineyard Chardonnays and Pinot Noirs. Farrell departed in the early 2000s, but current winemaker Theresa Heredia acknowledges that her philosophy has much in common with his. For the Pinots, this means picking on the early side to preserve acidity and focusing on "expressing the site." The Elevation Tasting of single-vineyard wines provides a good introduction. All visits are by appointment; same-day reservations are possible during the week, but call ahead. ✉ *10701 Westside Rd.* ☎ *707/473–2909* ⊕ *www.garyfarrellwinery.com* ☑ *Tastings from $35.*

Hand Fan Museum

MUSEUM | A diverting stop across from Healdsburg Plaza, this small storefront museum displays antique fans from around the world. Nineteenth-century floral-themed specimens from Japan, France, and Austria show exquisite craft, with utilitarian 20th-century ones from the USA in a recent exhibition more about messaging both serious ("Drive with Care") and not ("Elvis for President"). Some fans are for sale. ✉ *309 Healdsburg Ave.* ✛ *Near Matheson St.* ☎ *707/431–2500* ⊕ *www.thehandfanmuseum.org* ☑ *Free* ⊙ *Closed Mon. and Tues. (occasionally other days, so check).*

J Vineyards & Winery

WINERY/DISTILLERY | A top sparkling-wine producer, J also makes Russian River Valley Pinot Gris, Chardonnay, Pinot Noir, and other still wines. Some tastings highlight wines whose grapes come from multiple vineyards, with others emphasizing smaller-lot single-vineyard and reserve wines. For a more indulgent experience, book yourself into the Bubble Room's five-course wine and food pairing. All tastings require a reservation. ✉ *11447 Old Redwood Hwy.* ✛ *At Eastside Rd.* ☎ *707/431–3646* ⊕ *www.jwine.com* ☑ *Tastings from $25.*

★ Jordan Vineyard and Winery

WINERY/DISTILLERY | Founders Tom and Sally Jordan erected the French-style château here in part to emphasize their goal of producing Sonoma County Chardonnays and Cabernet Sauvignons—one of each annually—to rival those from the Napa Valley and France itself. Their son John, now at the helm, has instituted numerous improvements, among them the replanting of many vines and a shift to all-French barrels for aging. Most tastings revolve around executive chef Todd Knoll's small bites, whose ingredients come mainly from Jordan's organic garden. The Library Tasting of current releases concludes with an older Cabernet for comparison. An enchanting themed lunch and wine pairing, Paris on the Terrace, unfolds on the château's terrace from spring to early fall, when the winery often hosts a three-hour Estate Tour & Tasting. The latter's pièce de résistance is the stop at a 360-degree vista point overlooking the 1,200-acre property's vines, olive trees, and countryside. Visits are strictly by appointment. ✉ *1474 Alexander Valley Rd.* ✛ *1½ miles east of Healdsburg Ave.* ☎ *800/654–1213, 707/431–5250* ⊕ *www.jordanwinery.com* ☑ *Tastings from $45* ⊙ *Closed Tues. and Wed. Dec.–Mar.*

The ivy-covered château at Jordan Vineyard looks older than its four-plus decades.

★ Kokomo Winery

WINERY/DISTILLERY | Since decamping for California, Hoosier winemaker Erik Miller, who named his winery after his Indiana hometown, has raked in awards for his single-vineyard wines, most notably Chardonnay, Merlot, Pinot Noir, and Zinfandel. A few years back, one of the Pinots scored 100 points at a prestigious local competition, capturing top honors not only for its varietal but also among all the reds entered. Fans of the Pauline's Vineyard Grenache Rosé snag most of the bottles within weeks of release. Some guests sit amid the potted plants fronting the industrial-parklike production facility, though the banter in the main tasting area, high rows of oak aging barrels its focal point, lures many inside. (The adjacent room for club members is a veritable party even midweek on some summer days.) Appointments are highly recommended; same-day visits are possible, but call first. ⊠ *4791 Dry Creek Rd.* ✛ *At Timber Crest Farms* ☎ *707/433–0200* ⊕ *www.kokomowines. com* 🍷 *Tasting $20.*

★ Limerick Lane Cellars

WINERY/DISTILLERY | The rocky, clay soils of this winery's northeastern sliver of the Russian River Valley combine with foggy mornings and evenings and hot, sunny afternoons to create the swoon-worthy Zinfandels produced here. The coveted 1910 Block Zinfandel comes from old-style head-trained vines planted more than a century ago. Fruit from this block adds richness and depth to the flagship Russian River Estate Zinfandel, whose grapes also come from two sets of nearby vines—one planted a decade ago, the other in the 1970s. Along with its Zins, you can taste Limerick Lane's Syrah and a Petite Sirah at a restored stone farm building with views of the vineyards and the Mayacamas Mountains. Tastings are by appointment; call ahead for same-day visits, which are easier on weekdays than weekends. ⊠ *1023 Limerick La.* ✛ *1 mile east of Old Redwood Hwy.* ☎ *707/433–9211* ⊕ *www.limericklanewines.com* 🍷 *Tastings from $25.*

MacRostie Estate House

WINERY/DISTILLERY | A driveway off Westside Road curls through undulating vineyard hills to the steel, wood, and heavy-on-the-glass tasting space of this longtime Chardonnay and Pinot Noir producer. Moments after you've arrived and a host has offered a glass of wine, you'll already feel transported to a genteel, rustic world. Hospitality is clearly a priority, but so, too, is seeking out top-tier grape sources—30 for the Chardonnays, 15 for the Pinots—among them Dutton Ranch, Sangiacomo, and owner Steve MacRostie's Wildcat. With fruit this renowned, current winemaker Heidi Bridenhagen downplays the oak and other tricks of her trade, letting the vineyard settings, grape clones, and vintage do the talking. Tastings, inside or on balcony terraces with views across the Russian River Valley, are all seated and by appointment. ⊠ *4605 Westside Rd.* ⊹ *Near Frost Rd.* ☎ *707/473–9303* ⊕ *macrostiewinery.com* 🏷 *Tastings from $35.*

★ **Mauritson Wines**

WINERY/DISTILLERY | Winemaker Clay Mauritson's Swedish ancestors planted grapes in what is now the Rockpile appellation in the 1880s, but it wasn't until his generation, the sixth, that wines bearing the family name first appeared. Much of the original homestead lies submerged under human-made Lake Sonoma, but the remaining acres produce the distinctive Zinfandels for which Mauritson is best known. Cabernet Sauvignon, other red Bordeaux grapes, Syrah, and Petite Sirah grow here as well, but the Zinfandels in particular illustrate how Rockpile's varied climate and hillside soils produce vastly different wines—from the soft, almost Pinot-like Westphall Ridge to the more structured and tannic Pritchett Peaks. The Mauritsons also grow grapes in Dry Creek Valley, where the winery and tasting room are located, and Alexander Valley. ⊠ *2859 Dry Creek Rd.* ⊹ *At Lytton Springs Rd.* ☎ *707/431–0804* ⊕ *www.mauritsonwines.com* 🏷 *Tasting $30.*

Medlock Ames Tasting Room

WINERY/DISTILLERY | Cofounders Chris Medlock James and Ames Morison converted a century-old country store into a contemporary venue for the small-lot wines Ames makes from organic grapes he grows at 55-acre Bell Mountain Ranch in the southeastern Alexander Valley. The winery, known for estate Cabernet Sauvignons from Bell Mountain, also produces Sauvignon Blanc, Chardonnay, rosé, and club-member exclusives that include Merlot and Malbec. Seated tastings, by appointment only, are on an open-air patio or amid a culinary garden, both with vineyard views. Book the Olive Grove Experience, which comes with a picnic of bread, cheese, salami, and chocolate, for the most leisurely pace. ■ TIP➔ **To see the Medlock Ames sustainable vineyard and winery practices up close, schedule a tour and tasting at the ranch, 6½ miles away on Chalk Hill Road.** ⊠ *3487 Alexander Valley Rd.* ⊹ *At Hwy. 128* ☎ *707/431–8845* ⊕ *www.medlockames.com* 🏷 *Tastings from $25 at tasting room, $75 at ranch.*

Moshin Vineyards

WINERY/DISTILLERY | If you've ever wondered how your college math professor might fare as a winemaker, slip over to this winery known for single-vineyard Pinot Noirs. Rick Moshin, formerly of San Jose State University's math department, started out small in 1989, but by the mid-2000s demand for his Pinots supported the construction of a four-tier, gravity-flow winery on his hillside property across Westside Road from the Russian River. When offered, cellar tours focus on the winery's layout and Moshin's penchant for picking grapes earlier than most of his neighbors to preserve acidity, which he believes helps his wines pair well with food. In the tasting room and outside, guests sip Pinot Noirs along with Chardonnay, Merlot, Sauvignon Blanc, Zinfandel, and other wines. All visits are by appointment. ⊠ *10295 Westside Rd.* ⊹ *Off Wohler Rd.* ☎ *707/433–5499* ⊕ *moshinvineyards.com* 🏷 *Tastings from*

$30, tours from $45 ⊘ *Closed Tues. and Wed.*

Papapietro Perry Winery

WINERY/DISTILLERY | The mood is almost always upbeat on the vineyard-view patio at Papapeitro Perry as regulars and first-timers sip some of the 10 Pinot Noirs—eight from Russian River Valley grapes and one each from Sonoma Coast and Mendocino County fruit. A Russian River Valley Chardonnay and a Dry Creek Zinfandel also grace the lineup. The house style with all the wines, which include a rosé of Pinot Noir, is to pick early and shoot for elegance rather than the "overexpression" that can result from using riper fruit. ■TIP→ **Papapietro Perry is one of several tasting rooms in the Family Wineries complex; Kokomo is another fun stop with exemplary wines.** ⊠ *4791 Dry Creek Rd.* ✛ *At Timber Crest Farms* ☎ *707/433–0422* ⊕ *www.papapietro-perry.com* ⊠ *Tastings from $25.*

Passalacqua Winery

WINERY/DISTILLERY | Healdsburg native and fourth-generation vintner Jason Passalacqua specializes in Dry Creek Valley Zinfandels and Cabernets. The vintage-style label of the Estate Zinfandel honors Passalacqua's great aunt Edith, who owned a downtown Healdsburg winery from Prohibition's end to the late 1950s. The Cabernets come from specific blocks in a 120-acre vineyard Jason's parents planted in southern Dry Creek in 1996. On most days hosts pour these wines—plus Sauvignon Blanc, Chardonnay, Valdiguié (a red grape from southern France), and a few others—on a multilevel redwood-shaded deck with vineyard and mountain views. All tastings are by appointment. ■TIP→ **The splurge here, offered part of the year, is an ATV tour of the Cabernet vineyard; though hefty, the price includes a tasting and six bottles of Cabernet per person.** ⊠ *3805 Lambert Bridge Rd.* ✛ *Near Dry Creek Rd.* ☎ *707/433–5550* ⊕ *passalacquawinery.com* ⊠ *Tastings from $35.*

Porter Creek Vineyards

WINERY/DISTILLERY | About as down-home as you can get—the easy-going tastings at this modest family farm take place in or just outside a small redwood-beamed structure—Porter Creek makes notably good wines, some from estate biodynamically grown Chardonnay and Pinot Noir grapes. Its vineyards climb up steep hillsides of volcanic soil that is said to impart a slight mineral note to the Chardonnay; cover crops planted between the vines provide erosion control in addition to nutrients. Winemaker Alex Davis— son of George Davis, who founded the winery—also makes two wines from old-vine grapes, Carignane from Mendocino County and Zinfandel from Sonoma County, and his lineup includes Viognier and Syrah. ⊠ *8735 Westside Rd.* ✛ *Look for sign at sharp bend in road* ☎ *707/433–6321* ⊕ *www.portercreekvineyards.com* ⊠ *Tasting $30.*

Preston Farm & Winery

WINERY/DISTILLERY | The long driveway at homespun Preston, flanked by vineyards and punctuated by the occasional olive tree, winds down to farmhouses encircling a large shady yard. Year-round, organic produce grown in the winery's gardens is sold at a small shop near the tasting room; house-made bread and olive oil are also available. Owners Lou and Susan Preston are committed to organic growing techniques and use only estate-grown grapes in their wines, which include a perky Sauvignon Blanc, Barbera, Petite Sirah, Grenache, Viognier, and Zinfandel. All visits are by appointment, with same-day visits often possible on weekdays (call ahead, though). ⊠ *9282 W. Dry Creek Rd.* ✛ *At Hartsock Rd. No. 1* ☎ *707/433–3372* ⊕ *www.prestonfarmandwinery.com* ⊠ *Tastings from $30.*

Quivira Vineyards

WINERY/DISTILLERY | Solar panels top the modern wooden barn at Quivira, which produces Sauvignon Blanc, Zinfandel,

The focus at Ridge Vineyards is on single-vineyard estate wines.

Grenache-based rosé, and other wines using organic and sustainable agricultural practices. The emphasis is on "growing wine"—farming grapes so meticulously that little manipulation is required in the winery. That said, winemaker Hugh Chappelle's mastery of technique is in evidence in wines such as the flagship Fig Tree Sauvignon Blanc, whose zesty yet refined characteristics derive from the combination of stainless steel and oak and acacia barrels used during fermentation and aging. Guided tours (as with all visits by appointment only) cover the farming and wine-making philosophies and offer a glimpse of the property's garden and animals. ⊠ *4900 W. Dry Creek Rd.* ⊹ *Near Wine Creek Rd.* ☎ *707/431–8333* ⊕ *www.quivirawine. com* ⊠ *Tastings $30–$40, tour $50.*

Reeve Wines

WINERY/DISTILLERY | A narrow driveway leads up a forested hill to the secluded hilltop tasting enclave where Kelly and Noah Dorrance present their expressive cool-climate whites and Pinot Noirs. With views of vineyards fanning magic carpet-like to the south, the outdoor tables here often spark daydreams accelerated by the dry Mendocino County Riesling and Sonoma Coast Chardonnay commencing many sessions. (If the day's brisk, the indoor space's country-chic sensibility—high wood-beamed ceilings, black walls, dried and fresh flowers, and handcrafted furniture, all courtesy of Kelly—inspires reveries as well.) You're here for winemaker Dorrance's Pinot Noirs, though, all terrific and in ways that illuminate the differences not only among clone types but also variations in vineyards' soils, elevations, and weather. Tastings are by appointment only; same-day guests should call ahead rather than arrive unannounced. ■TIP→ **If a visit leaves you yearning to contemplate the views (or wines) further, ask about overnight stays at Reeve's villa.** ⊠ *4551 Dry Creek Rd.* ⊹ *1¼ miles north of Lambert Bridge Rd.* ☎ *707/235–6345* ⊕ *www. reevewines.com* ⊠ *Tastings $35–$50* ⊗ *Closed Tues. and Wed. (but check).*

⭐ Ridge Vineyards

WINERY/DISTILLERY | Ridge stands tall among local wineries, and not merely because its 1971 Monte Bello Cabernet Sauvignon rated second-highest among California reds competing with French ones at the famous Judgment of Paris blind tasting of 1976. The winery built its reputation on Cabernets, Zinfandels, and Chardonnays of unusual depth and complexity, but you'll also find blends of Rhône varietals. Ridge makes wines using grapes from several California locales—including the Dry Creek Valley, Sonoma Valley, Napa Valley, and Paso Robles—but the focus is on single-vineyard estate wines such as the Lytton Springs Zinfandel from fruit grown near the tasting room. In good weather you can sit outside, taking in views of rolling vineyard hills while you sip. ⊠ *650 Lytton Springs Rd.* ✛ *Off U.S. 101* ☎ *408/867–3233* ⊕ *www.ridgewine.com/visit/lytton-springs* ☟ *Tastings from $20.*

Rochioli Vineyards and Winery

WINERY/DISTILLERY | Claiming one of the prettiest sites in the area, with patio tables overlooking the vineyards, this winery has an airy tasting room with an equally romantic view. Production is small, and fans on the winery's mailing list snap up most of the bottles, but Rochioli is still worth a stop to sample wines that might include the estate Sauvignon Blanc, Chardonnay, Pinot Noir, and Syrah. Because of the cool growing conditions in the Russian River Valley, the whites' flavors are intense and complex, and the Pinot Noir, which helped cement the Russian River's status as a varietal powerhouse, is consistently excellent. Tastings are by appointment only. ⊠ *6192 Westside Rd.* ☎ *707/433–2305* ⊕ *www.rochioliwinery.com* ☟ *Tastings from $25.*

Rodney Strong Vineyards

WINERY/DISTILLERY | The late Rodney Strong was among the first winemakers to plant Pinot Noir in the Russian River Valley. His namesake winery still makes Pinot Noirs, but it's known more for Cabernet Sauvignon. The large brand's main tasting room got a sprucing up in 2020, though from April through October many guests sit on an umbrella-shaded vineyard-view terrace sipping Cabs, Pinots, and other wines from several Sonoma County appellations. Some tastings also include Davis Bynum Pinot Noirs (like Strong, Bynum was a pioneer of this varietal here) or the Cabernet-heavy Bordeaux-style Rowen Wine blends from a hilly ranch in far northern Sonoma County. Appointments are recommended, with same-day visits often possible. ■TIP→ **The winery hosts summer outdoor concerts; Alanis Morissette, Rick Springfield, and Smokey Robinson have performed in recent years.** ⊠ *11455 Old Redwood Hwy.* ✛ *North of Eastside Rd.* ☎ *707/431–1533, 800/678–4763* ⊕ *www.rodneystrong.com* ☟ *Tastings from $30.*

Seghesio Family Vineyards

WINERY/DISTILLERY | After working nearly a decade at Italian Swiss Colony, then among California's largest wine producers, Edoardo Seghesio purchased land in 1895 and planted some of the Alexander Valley's earliest Zinfandel vines. Fruit from them goes into his namesake winery's highly rated Home Ranch Zinfandel, one of several Zins made here. Wines from Italian varietals are another emphasis, most notably Venom, from what the winery says is North America's oldest Sangiovese vineyard. The whites, from the Italian grapes Arneis and Vermentino, are exceptional, too. At appointment-only tastings, some of which take place on the broad lawn and patio fronting the property, you can learn about the winery's history, farming philosophy, and Sonoma County fruit sources. ⊠ *700 Grove St.* ✛ *Off W. Grant St.* ☎ *707/433–3579* ⊕ *www.seghesio.com* ☟ *Tastings from $25.*

The Russian River Valley's hot summer days and cool nights create ideal conditions for growing Chardonnay and Pinot Noir.

★ Silver Oak

WINERY/DISTILLERY | The views and architecture are as impressive as the wines at the Sonoma County outpost of the same-named Napa Valley winery. In 2018, six years after purchasing a 113-acre parcel with 73 acres planted to grapes, Silver Oak debuted its ultramodern, environmentally sensitive winery and glass-walled tasting pavilion. As in Napa, the Healdsburg facility produces just one wine each year: a well-balanced Alexander Valley Cabernet Sauvignon aged in American rather than French oak barrels. One tasting includes the current Alexander Valley and Napa Valley Cabernets plus an older vintage. Two or more wines of sister operation Twomey Cellars, which produces Sauvignon Blanc, Pinot Noir, and Merlot, begin a second offering that concludes with the current Cabernets. Hosts at a third pour current and older Cabernets from either Napa or Sonoma. Make a reservation for all visits. ⊠ *7300 Hwy. 128* ✢ *Near Chaffee Rd.* ☏ *707/942–7082* ⊕ *www.silveroak.com* ⊠ *Tastings from $40.*

Stuhlmuller Vineyards

WINERY/DISTILLERY | Chardonnay and Cabernet Sauvignons from estate-grown grapes are the specialty of this slightly off-the-beaten-path winery whose tasting room and production facility occupy a stained-redwood former barn. Standout wines include the Summit Chardonnay and the Estate Cabernet Sauvignon, the latter from Stuhlmuller's oldest vines. Another wine to look for is the Cooper Block Russian River Valley Pinot Noir from the Starr Ridge Vineyard. Some tastings (by appointment; same-day visits possible) take place in a room adjoining the aging cellar, but in good weather you can sip outdoors on a gravel patio near the vines. ■ TIP➔ **Picnickers are welcome at this dog-friendly winery.** ⊠ *4951 W. Soda Rock La.* ✢ *Off Alexander Valley Rd.* ☏ *707/431–7745* ⊕ *www.stuhlmullervineyards.com* ⊠ *Tastings from $20.*

Thumbprint Cellars

WINERY/DISTILLERY | With its exposed-brick walls, wine-bottle chandelier, plush booths, and curving bar, this tasting room on Healdsburg Plaza's southern edge has a hip feel. Owner-winemaker Scott Lindstrom-Drake, who believes in selecting good fruit and applying minimal manipulation during fermentation and aging, has received critical acclaim for his single-vineyard Cabernet Franc and Cabernet Sauvignon. He also makes Grenache, Malbec, and a few other single-varietal reds, along with Chardonnay, Viognier, and white, rosé, and red blends with alluring names such as Arousal, Four Play, and Three Some. ⊠ *102 Matheson St.* ✛ *At Healdsburg Ave.* ☎ *707/433–2393* ⊕ *www.thumbprintcellars.com* ⊠ *Tastings from $20.*

★ Tongue Dancer Wines

WINERY/DISTILLERY | Down a country lane less than 2 miles south of Healdsburg Plaza, James MacPhail's modest production facility seems well away from the upscale fray. MacPhail makes wines for The Calling, Sangiacomo, and other labels, but Tongue Dancer's Chardonnays and Pinot Noirs are his handcrafted labors of love. Made from small lots of grapes from choice vineyard sites, the wines impress, sometimes stun, with their grace, complexity, and balance. The flagship Sonoma Coast Pinot Noir, a blend from two or more vineyards, is poured at most tastings, in a mezzanine space above oak-aging barrels or on an outdoor patio. Either the winemaker or his co-owner and wife, Kerry Forbes-MacPhail—she's credited on bottles as the "Knowledgeable One" (and she is)—will host you. As James describes it, they aim to "create an approachable experience for guests we hope will leave as friends." Appointment-only visits are best made a day or more ahead. ⊠ *851 Magnolia Dr.* ✛ *Off Westside Rd.* ☎ *707/433–4780* ⊕ *tonguedancerwines.com* ⊠ *Tastings from $25* ⊙ *Closed Sun.*

Unti Vineyards

WINERY/DISTILLERY | There's a reason why Unti, known for Zinfandel and wines made from sometimes obscure Rhône and Italian varietals, often bustles even when business is slow elsewhere in Dry Creek: this is a fun, casual place. You'll often find sociable cofounder Mick Unti chatting up guests and pouring wine in or outside the rustic-not-trying-to-be-chic tasting room. Sessions might begin with Vermentino or Cuvée Blanc (the latter a blend of Vermentino and Grenache Blanc), perhaps followed by rosé, which, as with the whites, is aged in concrete. The Rhône reds, particularly two Syrahs and Cuvée Foudre (Grenache, Syrah, Mourvèdre), tend to garner more critical notice than the Italians—which include Sangiovese and Montepulciano singly and in the Segromigno blend—but all are well made. Appointments are necessary, with same-day ones usually possible on weekdays. ⊠ *4202 Dry Creek Rd.* ✛ *¾ mile north of Lambert Bridge Rd.* ☎ *707/433–5590* ⊕ *www.untivineyards.com* ⊠ *Tastings from $25* ⊙ *Closed Tues. and Wed.*

Young & Yonder Spirits

WINERY/DISTILLERY | The husband-and-wife team behind this artisanal distillery forsook gainful employment to produce small-batch vodka, gin, bourbon, and absinthe. A few blocks northwest of Healdsburg Plaza, the two and their crew serve flights and cocktails in a high-ceilinged space whose loungelike decor—dark walls, padded-leather and plush-velvet furniture, and cowskin rugs—hips up the industrial-park setting. The mood is consistently upbeat, the spirits skillfully crafted. ⊠ *449 Allan Ct.* ✛ *Off North St.* ☎ *707/473–8077* ⊕ *www.youngandyonder.com* ⊠ *Tastings from $10* ⊙ *Closed Mon.–Wed.*

★ Zichichi Family Vineyard

WINERY/DISTILLERY | Most winery owners would love to be in Steve Zichichi's shoes: wines from his flagship vineyard, some of whose vines were planted in the 1920s during Prohibition, are largely sold out before they're bottled. As a result, customers of this northern Dry Creek

Valley operation taste some wines while they're still aging in barrels and purchase "futures" available for shipping or pickup months or more later. The highlight, not always available for tasting, is the Old Vine Zinfandel. Zichichi makes another Zinfandel and a Petite Sirah from his main vineyard, and one of each from another Dry Creek property. There's also a 100% Cabernet from the Chalk Hill appellation. The amiably paced tastings, all by appointment, often take place on a porch overlooking the historic vines. ✉ *8626 W. Dry Creek Rd.* ✣ *At Yoakim Bridge Rd.* ☎ *707/433–4410* 🌐 *www.zichichifamilyvineyard.com* 🎫 *Tasting $20.*

🍴 Restaurants

Baci Café & Wine Bar
$$$ | **ITALIAN** | A neighborhood trattoria with cream-yellow walls, zinc-top tables, and colorful artwork and banners, Baci bustles with tourists during high season, but after things die down, locals continue dropping by for wood-fired pizzas, varied pasta options, and osso buco, saltimbocca, and other stick-to-your-ribs Italian standards. The Iranian-born chef, Shari Sarabi, applies a Pan-Mediterranean sensibility to area-sourced, mostly organic ingredients, and his dishes satisfy without being overly showy. **Known for:** wine selection by Lisbeth Holmefjord, the chef's sommelier wife; enthusiastic owners; many gluten-free dishes. [$] *Average main: $28* ✉ *336 Healdsburg Ave.* ✣ *At North St.* ☎ *707/433–8111* 🌐 *www.bacicafeandwinebar.com* 🕑 *Closed Tues. and Wed. No lunch.*

★ **Barndiva**
$$$$ | **AMERICAN** | Music plays quietly in the background while servers carry inventive seasonal cocktails at this restaurant that abandons the homey vibe of many Wine Country spots in favor of a more urban feel. Make a light meal out of yellowtail tuna crudo or homemade linguine, or settle in for the evening with pan-seared day scallops or a grass-fed strip loin. **Known for:** good cocktails; stylish cuisine; open-air patio. [$] *Average main: $38* ✉ *231 Center St.* ✣ *Near Matheson St.* ☎ *707/431–0100* 🌐 *www.barndiva.com* 🕑 *Closed Mon. and Tues. No lunch weekdays.*

Bravas Bar de Tapas
$$$ | **SPANISH** | Spanish-style tapas and an outdoor patio in perpetual party mode make this restaurant, headquartered in a restored 1920s bungalow, a popular downtown perch. Contemporary Spanish mosaics set a perky tone inside, but unless something's amiss with the weather, nearly everyone heads out back for flavorful croquettes, paella, jamón, *pan tomate* (tomato toast), grilled octopus, skirt steak, and crispy fried chicken. **Known for:** casual small plates; specialty cocktails, sangrias, and beer; sherries from dry to sweet. [$] *Average main: $28* ✉ *420 Center St.* ✣ *Near North St.* ☎ *707/433–7700* 🌐 *www.barbravas.com* 🕑 *Closed Mon. and Tues.*

Campo Fina
$$ | **ITALIAN** | Chef Ari Rosen serves up contemporary-rustic Italian cuisine at this converted storefront that once housed a bar notorious for boozin' and brawlin'. Sandblasted red brick, satin-smooth walnut tables, and old-school lighting fixtures (and a large back patio) strike a retro note for a menu built around pizzas and gems such as Rosen's variation on his grandmother's tomato-braised chicken with creamy-soft polenta. **Known for:** outdoor patio's boccie court out of an Italian movie set; lunch sandwiches; wines from California and Italy. [$] *Average main: $23* ✉ *330 Healdsburg Ave.* ✣ *Near North St.* ☎ *707/395–4640* 🌐 *www.campofina.com.*

Chalkboard
$$$ | **MODERN AMERICAN** | Unvarnished oak flooring, wrought-iron accents, and a vaulted ceiling create a polished yet rustic ambience for playfully ambitious small-plate cuisine. Starters such as pork-belly biscuits might seem frivolous, but the

silky flavor blend—maple glaze, pickled onions, and chili aioli playing off feathery biscuit halves—hints at the subtlety of subsequent plates. **Known for:** zesty artisanal cocktails; house-made pastas; decadent desserts. $ *Average main: $31* ⊠ *Hotel Les Mars, 29 North St.* ✛ *West of Healdsburg Ave.* ☎ *707/473–8030* ⊕ *www.chalkboardhealdsburg.com* ⊘ *Closed Mon. and Tues. No lunch (but check).*

Costeaux French Bakery

$ | **FRENCH** | Breakfast, served all day at this bright-yellow French-style bakery and café, includes the signature omelet (sun-dried tomatoes, bacon, spinach, and Brie) and French toast made from thick slabs of cinnamon-walnut bread. French onion soup and cranberry-turkey, French dip, and (on the cinnamon-walnut bread) Monte Cristo sandwiches are among the lunch favorites. **Known for:** breads, croissants, and fancy pastries; quiche and omelets; front patio. $ *Average main: $15* ⊠ *417 Healdsburg Ave.* ✛ *At North St.* ☎ *707/433–1913* ⊕ *www.costeaux. com* ⊘ *Closed Mon. and Tues. (check to be sure). No dinner.*

Downtown Bakery & Creamery

$ | **BAKERY** | To catch the Healdsburg spirit, hit the plaza in the early morning for a cup of coffee and a fragrant sticky bun or a too-darlin' *canelé,* a French-style pastry with a soft custard center surrounded by a dense caramel crust. Until 2 pm from Friday through Monday, you can also go the full breakfast route: pancakes, granola, poached farm eggs on polenta, or perhaps the mushroom-and-cheese pizza. **Known for:** morning coffee and pastries; lunchtime pizzas and calzones; fresh-fruit galettes. $ *Average main: $8* ⊠ *308A Center St.* ✛ *At North St.* ☎ *707/431–2719* ⊘ *Closed Mon. No dinner.*

★ Guiso Latin Fusion

$$$ | **LATIN AMERICAN** | Shortly after graduating from a local college's culinary program, chef Carlos Mojica opened this warmly lit Latin American–Caribbean restaurant with a handful of tables inside and out. Loyalists pine for small-plate fish tacos and *pupusas* (corn tortillas stuffed with cheese and pork or vegetables), a prelude to signature entrées like *pescado con coco* (fish in sweet coconut) and Caribbean-style paella that's light on the saffron rice, heavy on seafood, sausage, and heirloom chicken, and suffused with smoky-garlicky tomato broth. **Known for:** attentive service; distinctive flavors; neighborhood feel. $ *Average main: $35* ⊠ *117 North St.* ✛ *Near Center St.* ☎ *707/431–1302* ⊕ *guisolatinfusion.com* ⊘ *No lunch.*

Hazel Hill

$$$$ | **MODERN AMERICAN** | Even before diners settle in their seats, the Montage resort's glass-walled destination restaurant captures the imagination with exterior views of vineyards, oaks, and far-off Mt. St. Helena and interior haute-luxury touches like chandeliers of locally handblown Czech glass. The Cali-Continental connection comes full circle in dishes—Pacific oysters with Asian-pear mignonette, perhaps, or striped bass with a Provençal-style artichoke sauce—whose French flourishes elevate hyper-fresh seasonal ingredients. **Known for:** romantic/special-occasion feel; signature côte de boeuf rib eye for two with Pinot Noir jus; embrace of local wines on food-friendly international list. $ *Average main: $45* ⊠ *Montage Healdsburg, 100 Montage Way* ✛ *Off Healdsburg Ave.* ☎ *707/354–6900* ⊕ *www.montagehotels. com/healdsburg/dining.*

KINSmoke

$$ | **BARBECUE** | Beef brisket and St. Louis ribs are the hits at this saloon-like, order-at-the-counter joint whose house-made sauces include espresso barbecue, North Carolina mustard, and the sweet-and-sourish KIN blend. Along with the expected sides of potato salad, cornbread muffins, and baked beans (the latter bourbon-infused), the spiced

sweet-potato tater tots and Granny Smith–and-horseradish slaw stand out. **Known for:** upbeat crew; pulled smoked chicken with Alabama white sauce; beer selection and sensibly priced local wines. [$] *Average main: $17* ✉ *304 Center St.* ✣ *At Matheson St.* ☎ *707/473–8440* 🌐 *www.kinsmoke.com.*

★ Noble Folk Ice Cream and Pie Bar

$ | **BAKERY** | Seasonal pies including blood-orange custard with graham-cracker crust are the specialty of this white-walled, brightly lit pie palace with a few tables and barstool window seating. The bakers use heritage grains like buckwheat and farro in the crusts, filling them with local fruits and other ingredients, and, if desired, topping the ensemble with ice cream in flavors from Swiss chocolate and vanilla bean to Thai tea, salted caramel, cornflake-maple and other obscurities. **Known for:** trad and rad cupcakes; cookies and whoopie pies; macarons and brownie cubes. [$] *Average main: $9* ✉ *116 Matheson St.* ✣ *Near Center St.* ☎ *707/395–4426* 🌐 *www.thenoblefolk.com.*

Parish Café

$ | **AMERICAN** | A few blocks south of Healdsburg Plaza at the busy roundabout, Parish's chefs whip up beignets, gumbo, muffulettas, and heapin' po'boys—from fried oyster, shrimp or catfish to roast beef, turkey, or ham and cheese—along with other New Orleans delights. Borderline decadent breakfasts served inside a white-trimmed yellow house or on its patio include bananas Foster French toast, egg po'boys, and the crawfish and andouille omelet slathered in Creole sauce. **Known for:** beignets all day; regular and "king" po'boy portions; fried sides—pickles, okra, green tomatoes. [$] *Average main: $15* ✉ *60 Mill St.* ✣ *At Healdsburg Ave. roundabout* ☎ *707/431–8474* 🌐 *theparishcafe.com* ⏲ *Call or check website for days closed. No dinner.*

★ SingleThread Farms Restaurant

$$$$ | **ECLECTIC** | The seasonally oriented, multicourse Japanese dinners known as *kaiseki* inspired the prix-fixe vegetarian, meat, and seafood menu at the spare, elegant restaurant—redwood walls, walnut tables, mesquite-tile floors, muted-gray yarn-thread panels—of internationally renowned culinary artists Katina and Kyle Connaughton (she farms, he cooks). As Katina describes the endeavor, the microseasons of their nearby farm (ask about visiting it) plus SingleThread's rooftop garden of fruit trees and greens dictate Kyle's rarefied fare, prepared in a theatrically lit open kitchen. **Known for:** culinary precision; instinctive service; impeccable wine pairings. [$] *Average main: $295* ✉ *131 North St.* ✣ *At Center St.* ☎ *707/723–4646* 🌐 *www.singlethreadfarms.com* ⏲ *No lunch weekdays.*

Spoonbar

$$ | **MODERN AMERICAN** | Concrete walls and mid-century modern furnishings create an urbane setting for the h2hotel restaurant's contemporary California cuisine, and cantina doors make Spoonbar especially appealing in summer when a breeze wafts in. The seasonally changing selections might include herb-roasted salmon, dry-aged rib eye with truffle fries, or Moroccan-spiced chicken. **Known for:** craft cocktails; inventive sides and salads; seafood Sunday. [$] *Average main: $23* ✉ *h2hotel, 219 Healdsburg Ave.* ✣ *At Vine St.* ☎ *707/433–7222* 🌐 *spoonbar.com* ⏲ *Closed Mon. and Tues. No lunch.*

Taste of Tea

$$ | **JAPANESE** | At this storefront a block north of Healdsburg Plaza, Japanese-style prints and furniture offset the mildly industrial feel of enterprise whose satisfying offerings include tea flights, light cuisine, and a spa-like tea treatment involving a foot soak and a facial mask. Ramen cold or hot and rice bowls are the highlights, the former accompanied by shoyu-marinated egg, fish cake, tofu, and other ingredients as desired. **Known**

for: vegan variations on most dishes; milk tea and matcha drinks; retail tea shop. $ *Average main: $21* ✉ *109 North St.* ✛ *Near Healdsburg Ave.* ☎ *707/431–1995* ⊕ *www.thetasteoftea.com* ☉ *Closed Tues. and Wed.*

★ Valette

$$$ | **MODERN AMERICAN** | Northern Sonoma native Dustin Valette opened this homage to the area's artisanal agricultural bounty with his brother, who runs the high-ceilinged dining room, where the playful contemporary lighting tempers the austerity of the exposed concrete walls and butcher-block-thick wooden tables. Charcuterie is an emphasis, but also consider the signature day-boat scallops *en croûte* (in a pastry crust) or dishes that might include Szechuan-crusted duck breast or a variation on Niçoise salad with albacore poached in olive oil. **Known for:** "Trust me" (the chef) tasting menu; mostly Northern California and French wines; chef's nearby The Matheson for wine tasting, pairings, and rooftop dining. $ *Average main: $36* ✉ *344 Center St.* ✛ *At North St.* ☎ *707/473–0946* ⊕ *www.valettehealdsburg.com* ☉ *No lunch.*

Willi's Seafood & Raw Bar

$$$ | **SEAFOOD** | Willi's occupies a corner storefront with street-side outdoor seating and a compact dining room that curls around the full bar. After more than a decade the warm Maine lobster roll with garlic butter and fennel remains a hit among the small, mostly seafood-oriented plates, with the ceviches, barbecued local oysters, and bacon-wrapped scallops among its worthy rivals. **Known for:** gluten-, dairy-, nut-, and seed-free options; "Kale Caesar!" salad with toasted capers; crème brûlée and other desserts. $ *Average main: $30* ✉ *403 Healdsburg Ave.* ✛ *At North St.* ☎ *707/433–9191* ⊕ *www.willisseafood.net.*

Wurst Restaurant

$ | **AMERICAN** | "The Wurst is the best" is the motto at this glass-fronted fast-food joint with a menu of sausages and dogs with specific toppings like the Detroit Polish (with sauerkraut, beer mustard, and onion rings) or augmented with (choose two: caramelized onions, sweet peppers, hot peppers, or kraut). Burgers are another specialty, with the blue-cheese and blackened-barbecue ones from a local beef purveyor among the top sellers patrons enjoy at communal and single tables inside and on the front patio. **Known for:** onion rings and fries; Midwestern pop (soda) selection; turkey, falafel, and smash burgers. $ *Average main: $11* ✉ *22 Matheson St.* ✛ *Near Healdsburg Ave.* ☎ *707/395–0214* ⊕ *thewurst.com.*

🛏 Hotels

Camellia Inn

$$ | **B&B/INN** | In a well-preserved 1869 Italianate Victorian, this colorful bed-and-breakfast sits on a quiet residential street 2½ blocks from Healdsburg Plaza. **Pros:** large Roman-shaped backyard pool; late-afternoon wine-and-cheese sessions; within easy walking distance of restaurants. **Cons:** a few rooms have a shower but no bath; all rooms lack TVs; no fitness center. $ *Rooms from: $269* ✉ *211 North St.* ☎ *707/433–8182* ⊕ *www.camelliainn.com* ⚑ *9 rooms* ⦿ *Free breakfast.*

Duchamp Hotel

$$$$ | **B&B/INN** | This luxury property whose six standalone postmodern-minimalist cottages—polished concrete floors, blond-wood furniture, California kings, spacious bathrooms with walk-in showers—surround a courtyard with a 50-foot pool is such a well-kept secret that it's not even on the radar of many locals. **Pros:** sense of seclusion; five-minute walk to Healdsburg Plaza's restaurants, tasting rooms, and shops; rates often lower off-season. **Cons:** lacks room service and other hotel amenities;

minimalist aesthetic may be too austere for some guests; after 6 pm no one at front desk (though one owner lives nearby). [$] *Rooms from: $695* ✉ *421 Foss St.* ☎ *707/431–1300* 🌐 *duchamphotel.com* 🛏 *6 cottages* 🍴 *No meals.*

★ Harmon Guest House

$$$ | **HOTEL** | A boutique sibling of the h2hotel two doors away, this downtown delight debuted in late 2018 having already earned LEED Gold status for its eco-friendly construction and operating practices. **Pros:** rooftop bar's cocktails, food menu, and views; connecting rooms and suites; similarly designed sister property h2hotel two doors south. **Cons:** minor room-to-room noise bleed-through; room gadgetry may flummox some guests; minimum-stay requirements some weekends. [$] *Rooms from: $389* ✉ *227 Healdsburg Ave.* ☎ *707/922–5262* 🌐 *harmonguesthouse.com* 🛏 *39 rooms* 🍴 *Free breakfast.*

Healdsburg Inn

$$$ | **B&B/INN** | A sensible choice if you'll be dining in town during your stay, this inn across from Healdsburg Plaza occupies a 19th-century office building whose former tenants include a Wells, Fargo & Co. Express office and stagecoach stop. **Pros:** central location; freshly baked cookies; late-afternoon wine and hors d'oeuvres. **Cons:** garish room lighting; slightly impersonal feel for this type of inn; street noise audible in plaza-facing rooms. [$] *Rooms from: $319* ✉ *112 Matheson St.* ☎ *707/433–6991* 🌐 *www.healdsburginn.com* 🛏 *12 rooms* 🍴 *Free breakfast.*

Hotel Healdsburg

$$$$ | **RESORT** | Across the street from the tidy town plaza, this spare, sophisticated full-service hotel has an upscale restaurant, a gourmet pizzeria, a spa, a pool, and a fitness center. **Pros:** Charlie Palmer's Dry Creek Kitchen restaurant on first floor; several rooms overlook town plaza; most rooms have private balconies. **Cons:** exterior rooms get some street noise; some sound bleed-through between rooms; smallest rooms pricey. [$] *Rooms from: $449* ✉ *25 Matheson St.* ☎ *707/431–2800, 707/922–5256 reservations* 🌐 *www.hotelhealdsburg.com* 🛏 *55 rooms* 🍴 *Free breakfast.*

★ Hôtel Les Mars

$$$$ | **HOTEL** | This Relais & Châteaux property takes the prize for opulence with guest rooms, spacious and elegant enough for French nobility, furnished with 18th- and 19th-century antiques and reproductions, canopy beds dressed in luxe linens, and gas-burning fireplaces. **Pros:** large rooms; luxurious feel; just off Healdsburg's plaza. **Cons:** very expensive; minimum-stay requirement on weekends; no pool or spa. [$] *Rooms from: $526* ✉ *27 North St.* ☎ *707/433–4211* 🌐 *www.hotellesmars.com* 🛏 *16 rooms* 🍴 *Free breakfast.*

Hotel Trio Healdsburg

$$ | **HOTEL** | Named for the three major wine appellations—the Russian River, Dry Creek, and Alexander valleys—whose confluence it's near, this Residence Inn by Marriott 1¼ miles north of Healdsburg Plaza caters to families and extended-stay business travelers with spacious rooms equipped with full kitchens. **Pros:** cute robot room service; full kitchens; rooms sleep up to four or six. **Cons:** 30-minute walk to downtown; slightly corporate feel; pricey in high season. [$] *Rooms from: $242* ✉ *110 Dry Creek Rd.* ☎ *707/433–4000* 🌐 *www.hoteltrio.com* 🛏 *122 rooms* 🍴 *Free breakfast.*

h2hotel

$$$ | **HOTEL** | Eco-friendly touches abound at this hotel, from the plant-covered "green roof" to wooden decks made from salvaged lumber. **Pros:** stylish modern design; free bikes for use around town; relaxing pool and public areas. **Cons:** least expensive rooms lack bathtubs; fitness facility a block away at Hotel Healdsburg; can get pricey in high season. [$] *Rooms from: $379*

Some rooms at Montage Healdsburg face oak-laden hills, others a young Cabernet vineyard.

✉ 219 Healdsburg Ave. ☎ 707/922–5251 🌐 h2hotel.com 🛏 36 rooms 🍴 Free breakfast.

The Madrona

$$$$ | HOTEL | An 1881 mansion lauded in its early decades as Healdsburg's finest residence remains the centerpiece of this 8-acre estate of wooded and landscaped grounds that in 2021 began transformation into a high-style boutique property. **Pros:** secluded and romantic; 1¼ miles from Healdsburg Plaza; destination restaurant. **Cons:** renovations to continue through 2021 (building by building to minimize noise); geared more toward couples than families; two-night minimum on weekends. *[$] Rooms from: $600 ✉ 1001 Westside Rd. ☎ 707/433–4231 🌐 www.madronamanor.com 🛏 22 rooms 🍴 No meals.*

★ Montage Healdsburg

$$$$ | RESORT | Its bungalowlike guest rooms deftly layered into oak- and Cabernet-studded hills a few miles north of Healdsburg Plaza, this architectural sensation that opened fully in 2021 significantly upped Sonoma County's ultraluxury game. **Pros:** vineyard views from spa, restaurant, and swimming pool; outdoor living spaces with daybeds and fire pits; recreational options on-property or nearby. **Cons:** expensive year-round; hefty resort fee; car trip required for off-property visits. *[$] Rooms from: $845 ✉ 100 Montage Way ☎ 707/979–9000 🌐 www.montagehotels.com/healdsburg 🛏 130 bungalows 🍴 No meals.*

★ River Belle Inn

$$ | B&B/INN | An 1875 Victorian with a storied past and a glorious colonnaded wraparound porch anchors this boutique property along the Russian River. **Pros:** riverfront location near a dozen-plus tasting rooms; cooked-to-order full breakfasts; attention to detail. **Cons:** about a mile from Healdsburg Plaza; minimum-stay requirement on weekends; lacks on-site pool, fitness center, and other amenities. *[$] Rooms from: $280 ✉ 68 Front St. ☎ 707/955–5724 🌐 www.*

riverbelleinn.com 🛏 *12 rooms* 🍴 *Free breakfast.*

★ **SingleThread Farms Inn**
$$$$ | B&B/INN | A remarkable Relais & Châteaux property a block north of Healdsburg Plaza, SingleThread is the creation of husband-and-wife team Kyle and Katina Connaughton, who operate the ground-floor destination restaurant and the four guest rooms and a suite above it. **Pros:** multicourse breakfast; spacious bathrooms with luxurious touches; rooftop garden. **Cons:** expensive year-round; no pool or fitness center; no spa. [$] *Rooms from: $950* ✉ *131 North St.* ☎ *707/723–4646* 🌐 *www.singlethread-farms.com* 🛏 *5 rooms* 🍴 *Free breakfast.*

Nightlife

Duke's Spirited Cocktails
BARS/PUBS | Fruity and savory "farm-to-bar" cocktails, many powered by local artisanal spirits and organically farmed ingredients, are among the specialties of this bar on Healdsburg Plaza's northern periphery. The old-school-in-a-fresh-setting vibe suits the inventive libations, but the owner-mixologists who run this happening hangout fashion the classics with equal aplomb. ✉ *111 Plaza St.* ✥ *Near Healdsburg Ave.* ☎ *707/431–1060* 🌐 *www.drinkatdukes.com.*

Performing Arts

Raven Performing Arts Theater
ARTS CENTERS | The Raven Players theater group is the resident company of this venue that also presents comedy and, most years in June, Healdsburg Jazz Festival performances. ✉ *115 North St.* ✥ *At Center St.* ☎ *707/433–6335* 🌐 *www.raventheater.org.*

Shopping

ART GALLERIES

★ **Gallery Lulo**
ART GALLERIES | A collaboration between a local artist and jewelry maker and a Danish-born curator, this gallery presents changing exhibits of jewelry, sculpture, and objets d'art. ✉ *303 Center St.* ✥ *At Plaza St.* ☎ *707/433–7533* 🌐 *www.gallerylulo.com.*

Paul Mahder Gallery
ART GALLERIES | At 9,000 square feet this is one of California's largest art galleries, with contemporary paintings, sculptures, and photographs. It's also the GrapeSeed tasting room (wines by Matt Smith from Italian varietals are the highlight); patrons sip amid the fine art. The gallery claims its moss wall art in the back is North America's largest. ✉ *222 Healdsburg Ave.* ✥ *200 feet north of roundabout* ☎ *707/473–9150* 🌐 *www.paulmahdergallery.com* 🕒 *Closed Tues.*

BOOKS

Copperfield's Books
BOOKS/STATIONERY | In addition to magazines and best-selling books, this store, part of a local indie chain, stocks a wide selection of discounted and remaindered titles, including many cookbooks. ✉ *104 Matheson St.* ✥ *Near Healdsburg Ave.* ☎ *707/433–9270* 🌐 *www.copperfields-books.com/healdsburg.*

CRAFTS

★ **JAM JAR Goods**
CRAFTS | Local artisans that include the two owners—one a painter, the other a jewelry maker—create many of the crafts, clothing, and other items, some vintage, sold at this smartly curated shop a block north of the plaza. ✉ *126 North St.* ✥ *At Center St.* ☎ *707/508–6664* 🌐 *jamjargoods.com* 🕒 *Closed Mon. and Tues.*

FOOD AND WINE

Dry Creek General Store

FOOD/CANDY | For breakfasts, sandwiches, bread, cheeses, and picnic supplies, stop by the general store, established in 1881 and still a popular spot for locals to hang out on the porch or in the bar. Beer and wine are also for sale, along with artisanal sodas, ciders, and juices. ✉ *3495 Dry Creek Rd.* ✛ *At Lambert Bridge Rd.* ☎ *707/433–4171* ⊕ *www.drycreekgeneralstore1881.com.*

Oakville Grocery

WINE/SPIRITS | The Healdsburg branch of this Napa-based store is filled with wine, condiments, and deli items, and sells sandwiches and picnic fixings. A terrace with ample seating makes a good place for an impromptu meal, but you might want to lunch early or late to avoid the crowds. ✉ *124 Matheson St.* ✛ *At Center St.* ☎ *707/433–3200* ⊕ *www.oakvillegrocery.com.*

🏃 Activities

BICYCLING

Getaway Adventures / Wine Country Bikes

TOUR—SPORTS | This shop several blocks southeast of Healdsburg Plaza is perfectly located for setting up single or multi-day treks into the Dry Creek and Russian River valleys by bike, kayak, or both. Private and group tours might include wineries, organic farms, and other stops. If you prefer to explore on your own, you can rent equipment. ✉ *61 Front St.* ✛ *At Hudson St.* ☎ *800/499–2453* ⊕ *getawayadventures.com* ☞ *Daily rentals from $39 per day, full-day tours from $139.*

BOATING

Russian River Adventures

BOATING | This outfit open from mid-April through mid-November rents inflatable canoes for self-guided, full- and half-day trips down the Russian River. Pack a swimsuit, pick up a picnic lunch, and shove off. You'll likely see wildlife on the shore and can stop at fun swimming holes and even swing on a rope above the water. The fee includes a shuttle ride back to your car. The full-day trip is dog-friendly. ✉ *20 Healdsburg Ave.* ✛ *At S. University St.* ☎ *707/433–5599, 800/280–7627* ⊕ *www.russianriveradventures.com* ☞ *From $75.*

HIKING

Healdsburg Ridge Open Space Preserve

PARK—SPORTS-OUTDOORS | The preserve's easy to navigate trails wind past oaks, manzanitas, Douglas firs, and redwoods on the way to an overlook with postcard views of the Russian River. ✉ *Bridle Path and Arabian Way* ✛ *2 miles north from plaza on Healdsburg Ave., then east ¾ mile on Parkhill Farms Blvd.* ☎ *707/431–3317* ⊕ *www.ci.healdsburg.ca.us/741/open-space.*

SPAS

★ A Simple Touch Spa

FITNESS/HEALTH CLUBS | Skilled in Swedish, deep-tissue, sports, and other massage modalities, this soothing but unpretentious day spa's therapists routinely receive post-session raves. The most popular treatment involves heated basalt stones applied to the client's body, followed by a massage of choice. Foot reflexology, reiki, and facials are among the other specialties. ■**TIP➜ Couples can enjoy any of the massages performed side-by-side by two therapists.** ✉ *239 Center St., Suite C* ✛ *Near Matheson St.* ☎ *707/433–6856* ⊕ *asimpletouchspa.com* ☞ *Treatments $55–$300.*

The Spa Hotel Healdsburg

FITNESS/HEALTH CLUBS | Taking a page from its restaurant's farm-to-table approach, the Hotel Healdsburg's spa also sources many of its treatments' ingredients from area farms. Swedish-style massage techniques are central to the Healdsburg

Three AVAs in a Single Day

Cover three AVAs in a single day on a scenic loop drive past vineyards and wineries that begins in downtown Healdsburg. Make tasting reservations at least a day ahead, more for a summer weekend or if food is involved. Before departing, have breakfast at **Costeaux French Bakery.** Plan on having lunch at Dry Creek General Store either before or after your tasting in the Dry Creek Valley AVA. It's near both wineries mentioned below.

Russian River Valley AVA

A few blocks south of Healdsburg Plaza (past the roundabout), stay to the right to briefly hop on U.S. 101, after 1 mile taking Exit 502/Old Redwood Highway. Continue south 1½ miles on Old Redwood to Eastside Road and turn right (southwest). After 5¼ miles make a right on Wohler Road. Before long you'll cross the rusting, highly photogenic Wohler Bridge. At Westside Road, turn north (right) to reach **Arista Winery,** which makes several Russian River Valley Chardonnays and Pinot Noirs. After tasting there, continue north on Westside Road about 6½ miles. If you can't get an appointment at Arista, try Rochioli Vineyards and Winery.

Dry Creek Valley AVA

A sign along Westside Road indicates your passage into the Dry Creek Valley AVA. Turn northwest at Kinley Road, follow it 1½ miles to Dry Creek Road, and turn west (left). In 2½ miles you'll reach **Mauritson Wines,** where you can sip the type of Zinfandels that made Dry Creek famous. Another good option in the AVA, Dry Creek Vineyard, is about ¾ mile farther along Dry Creek Road, at Lambert Bridge Road.

Alexander Valley AVA

From Dry Creek Road, head east on Lytton Springs Road to reach the Alexander Valley. After passing under the freeway, head north and east on Lytton Station Road, east on Alexander Valley Road, and southeast (right) on Highway 128. After ¾ mile, you'll arrive at **Silver Oak,** which makes a quintessential Alexander Valley Cabernet. If you're still game for more tasting, follow Highway 128 west to downtown Geyserville's **Locals Tasting Room,** which (for no charge) pours the wines of numerous small producers.

Enjoy dinner at **Diavola Pizzeria & Salumeria** or **Catelli's** in Geyserville (reservations recommended on weekends), or take the scenic route back to Healdsburg, south on Geyserville Avenue, briefly east (left) onto Lytton Springs Road, and south on Healdsburg Avenue.

Signature Massage, which also involves aromatic oils. Deep-tissue and hot-stone massages are among the other modalities. The signature facial uses biodynamic botanicals and concludes with a cool-stone facial massage. ✉ *327 Healdsburg Ave.* ✛ *At Matheson St.* ☎ *707/433–4747* ⊕ *www.hotelhealdsburg.com/spa* ▦ *Treatments $55–$310.*

Geyserville

8 miles north of Healdsburg.

Several high-profile Alexander Valley AVA wineries, including the splashy Francis Ford Coppola Winery, can be found in the town of Geyserville, a small part of which stretches west of U.S. 101 into northern Dry Creek. Not long ago this was a dusty farm town, and downtown Geyserville retains its rural character, but the restaurants, shops, and tasting rooms along the short main drag hint at Geyserville's growing sophistication.

Getting Here and Around

From Healdsburg, the quickest route to downtown Geyserville is north on U.S. 101 to the Highway 128/Geyserville exit. Turn right at the stop sign onto Geyserville Avenue and follow the road north to the small downtown. Sonoma County Transit buses serve Geyserville from Healdsburg.

Visitor Information

Geyserville Chamber of Commerce
✉ *Geyserville* ☎ *707/276–6067*
⊕ *visitgeyserville.com.*

Sights

Crux Winery
WINERY/DISTILLERY | A 1,000-case-a-year winery that produced its first ten vintages in a garage, Crux validates the notion that superior fruit and an idiosyncratic perspective can trump high-tech equipment and a textbook approach. With its relatively small output—mostly Rhône-style wines now made in the bare-bones industrial space where appointment-only tastings take place—Steven Gower and Brian Callahan's operation is hardly a powerhouse. If you're looking to tap into the passion that drives Sonoma County's grassroots "handmade wines" scene, though, you'll likely find a stop here enlightening. Viognier, Grenache, Syrah, and a GSM (Grenache, Syrah, Mourvèdre) blend, all soulful and distinctive, are the ones to seek out, but there's not a bad sip in the bunch. Gower and Callahan own adjacent vineyards in the Russian River Valley's "middle reach," an area warmer than where Pinot Noir and Chardonnay thrive. The two grow six varietals (including non-Rhône Zinfandel) and purchase grapes, too. ✉ *18850 Hassett La., Building C* ⊹ *Off Lytton Station Rd.* ☎ *707/837–8061* ⊕ *cruxwinery.com* ▧ *Tasting $25.*

David Coffaro Estate Vineyard
WINERY/DISTILLERY | One of the Dry Creek Valley's least pretentious wineries, David Coffaro specializes in red blends and single-varietal wines from grapes grown on a 20-acre estate. Zinfandel and Petite Sirah are strong suits, but Coffaro and his team also make wines using Lagrein, Aglianico, and other less familiar grapes, which also find their way into his unique blends, including the Rhône-style Terre Melange, with Peloursin and Carignane added to the usual Grenache, Syrah, and Mourvèdre mix. ✉ *7485 Dry Creek Rd.* ⊹ *Near Yoakim Bridge Rd.* ☎ *707/433–9715* ⊕ *www.coffaro.com* ▧ *Tasting free.*

Francis Ford Coppola Winery
WINERY/DISTILLERY | The fun at what the film director has called his "wine wonderland" is all in the excess. You may find it hard to resist having your photo snapped standing next to Don Corleone's desk from *The Godfather* or beside other memorabilia from Coppola films (including some directed by his daughter, Sofia). A bandstand reminiscent of one in *The Godfather Part II* is the centerpiece of a large pool area where you can rent a changing room, complete with shower, and spend the afternoon lounging poolside, perhaps ordering food from the

adjacent café. A more elaborate restaurant, Rustic, overlooks the vineyards. As for the wines, the excess continues in the cellar, where Coppola's team produces several dozen varietal bottlings and blends. ⊠ 300 Via Archimedes ✛ Off U.S. 101 ☎ 707/857–1400 ⊕ www.franciscopolawinery.com ⍟ Tastings from $35.

★ Garden Creek Ranch Vineyards and Winery

WINERY/DISTILLERY | During private tastings at this hilly 100-acre property, you may find yourself swept away by husband-and-wife Justin and Karin Miller's passion for their land and determination to craft collector-worthy wines from its grapes. Justin has lived his whole life on the ranch, which his father purchased in 1963; Karin's Swedish-born parents owned vineyards nearby. Just as his father became an early Alexander Valley adopter of Cabernet Sauvignon, well before many of his peers, Justin embraced sustainable practices before many others. He grows several white grapes—Chardonnay, Grenache Blanc, Marsanne, Roussanne, and the rare-in-California Scheurebe. Cabernet Sauvignon and other Bordeaux varietals go into the flagship Tesserae red blend. Justin and Karin jointly make their small label's wines, only releasing the red after several years in bottle. Supple upon release, it's built to last. ■TIP➔ **The two-hour appointment-only tasting (book well ahead) includes a vineyard tour; there's also a 2½-hour Cabernet library session.** ⊠ 2335 Geysers Rd. ✛ Off Hwy. 128 ☎ 707/433–8345 ⊕ gardencreekvineyards.com ⍟ Tastings from $100 ⊗ Closed Sun.–Tues.

★ Locals Tasting Room

WINERY/DISTILLERY | If you're serious about wine, Carolyn Lewis's tasting room is worth the trek 8 miles north of Healdsburg Plaza to downtown Geyserville. Connoisseurs who appreciate Lewis's ability to spot up-and-comers head here regularly to sample the output of a dozen or so small wineries, most without tasting rooms of their own. There's no fee for tasting—extraordinary for wines of this quality—and the extremely knowledgeable staff are happy to pour you a flight of several wines so you can compare, say, different Cabernet Sauvignons. ⊠ 21023A Geyserville Ave. ✛ At Hwy. 128 ☎ 707/857–4900 ⊕ www.localstastingroom.com ⍟ Tasting free.

★ Robert Young Estate Winery

WINERY/DISTILLERY | Panoramic Alexander Valley views unfold at Scion House, the stylish yet informal knoll-top tasting space of this longtime Geyserville grower. The first Youngs began farming this land in the mid-1800s, raising cattle and growing wheat, prunes, and other crops. In the 1960s the late Robert Young, of the third generation, began cultivating grapes, eventually planting two Chardonnay clones now named for him. Grapes from them go into the Area 27 Chardonnay, among the best whites. The reds—small-lot Cabernet Sauvignons plus individual bottlings of Cabernet Franc, Malbec, Merlot, and Petit Verdot—shine even brighter. Tastings at Scion House, named for the fourth generation, whose members built on Robert Young's legacy and established the winery, are by appointment. Call ahead for same-day reservations. ■TIP➔ **Cab fanatics should consider the Ultimate Cabernet Lovers Experience of top-tier estate wines.** ⊠ 5120 Red Winery Rd. ✛ Off Hwy. 128 ☎ 707/431–4811 ⊕ www.ryew.com ⍟ Tastings from $30 ⊗ Closed Tues.

Trattore Farms

WINERY/DISTILLERY | The tectonic shifts that created the Dry Creek Valley reveal themselves at this winery atop one of several abruptly rolling hills tamed only partially by grapevines and olive trees. Food offerings vary by day and time of year but might include cheeses, charcuterie, panini, and wood-fired pizzas. The main events, though, are the views and the Rhône-style wines, among them a Marsanne-Roussanne white blend and reds that range from Grenache to the Proprietor's Reserve GSM (Grenache, Syrah, Mourvèdre). The Zinfandel, Petite Sirah, and Grenache grapes for the dense and powerful Stone Soup blend come from the estate's rockiest section. You'll get a feel for the rollicking terrain on the fun (by appointment only) Get Your Boots Dirty vineyard, olive orchard, and mill tour in a Kawasaki 4x4. Reservations for tastings are recommended, especially on weekends. ■ TIP→ **To fully enjoy those valley views, book a seated outdoor tasting.** ✉ *7878 Dry Creek Rd.* ✥ *¾ mile north of Yoakim Bridge Rd.* ☎ *707/431–7200* 🌐 *www.trattorefarms.com* 🎫 *Tastings from $30.*

Trentadue Winery

WINERY/DISTILLERY | Sangiovese, Zinfandel, and La Storia Cuvée 32 (a "Super Tuscan"–style blend of Sangiovese, Merlot, and other grapes) are among the strong suits of this Alexander Valley stalwart established in 1959 by the late Leo and Evelyn Trentadue, credited with planting the first vines in the Geyserville area since the Prohibition era. The diverse lineup also includes Sauvignon Blanc, a Sangiovese rosé, Merlot, Cabernet Sauvignon, Petite Sirah, Zinfandel, and dessert wines (enough for a full port flight), all moderately priced. Tastings take place inside an ivy-covered villa, in a courtyard, and under an arbor. All tastings require an appointment, with same-day visits usually possible. ✉ *19170 Geyserville Ave.* ✥ *Off U.S. 101* ☎ *707/433–3104* 🌐 *www.trentadue.com* 🎫 *Tastings from $15.*

★ **Zialena**

WINERY/DISTILLERY | Sister-and-brother team Lisa and Mark Mazzoni (she runs the business, he makes the wines) debuted their small winery's first vintage in 2014, but their Italian American family's wine-making heritage stretches back more than a century. Named for the siblings' great aunt Lena, known for her hospitality, Zialena specializes in estate-grown Zinfandel and Cabernet Sauvignon, some of whose lush mouthfeel derives from techniques Mark absorbed while working for the international consultant Philippe Melka. The Zin and Cab grapes, along with those for the Chardonnay and seductive rosé of Sangiovese, come from the 120-acre Mazzoni Vineyard, from which larger labels like Jordan also source fruit. Tastings are by appointment only, with same-day visits often possible. ✉ *21112 River Rd.* ✥ *Off Hwy. 128* ☎ *707/955–5992* 🌐 *www.zialena.com* 🎫 *Tastings from $15.*

🍴 Restaurants

★ **Catelli's**

$$ | **ITALIAN** | Cookbook author and *Iron Chef* judge Domenica Catelli teamed up with her brother Nicholas to revive their family's American-Italian restaurant, a Geyserville fixture. Contemporary abstract paintings, reclaimed-wood furnishings, and muted gray and chocolate-brown walls signal the changing times, but you'll find good-lovin' echoes of traditional cuisine in the sturdy meat sauce that accompanies the signature lasagna paper-thin noodles and ricotta-and-herb-cheese filling. **Known for:** three-meat ravioli and other pasta dishes; festive back patio; organic gardens. [$] *Average main: $24* ✉ *21047 Geyserville Ave.* ✥ *At Hwy. 128* ☎ *707/857–3471* 🌐 *www.mycatellis.com* ⏲ *Closed Mon. and Tues.*

Diavola Pizzeria & Salumeria

$$ | **ITALIAN** | A dining area with hardwood floors, a pressed-tin ceiling, and exposed-brick walls provides a fitting setting for the rustic cuisine at this Geyserville mainstay. Chef Dino Bugica studied with artisanal cooks in Italy before opening this restaurant specializing in wood-fired pizzas and house-cured meats, with a few salads and meaty main courses rounding out the menu. **Known for:** talented chef; smoked pork belly, pancetta, and spicy Calabrese sausage; casual setting.

$ *Average main: $23* ✉ *21021 Geyserville Ave.* ✣ *At Hwy. 128* ☎ *707/814–0111* 🌐 *www.diavolapizzeria.com.*

Hotels

Geyserville Inn
$$ | HOTEL | Clever travelers give the Healdsburg hubbub and prices the heave-ho but still have easy access to outstanding Dry Creek and Alexander Valley wineries from this modest, motel-like inn with a boutique-hotel sensibility. **Pros:** outdoor pool; vineyard-view decks from second-floor rooms in back; picnic area. **Cons:** rooms facing pool or highway can be noisy; weekend two-night minimum requirement; not for party types. $ *Rooms from: $209* ✉ *21714 Geyserville Ave.* ☎ *707/857–4343, 877/857–4343* 🌐 *www.geyservilleinn.com* 🛏 *41 rooms* 🍴 *No meals.*

Nightlife

Geyserville Gun Club Bar & Lounge
BARS/PUBS | Two doors down from Diavola pizzeria (same ownership), this long, skinny bar in Geyserville's Odd Fellows Building wows locals and tourists with Sazeracs, Gibsons, and other classic cocktails and a bar menu of international comfort food. Hardwood floors, exposed brick, taxidermied animals, and contemporary lighting set the mood at this cool spot. ✉ *21025 Geyserville Ave.* ✣ *At Hwy. 128* ☎ *707/814–0036* 🌐 *www.geyservillegunclub.com.*

Windsor

6 miles south of Healdsburg.

Founded in 1855 but not incorporated until 1992, Windsor lies between Healdsburg to the north and Santa Rosa to the south. Heavily rural into the mid-20th century and known for oak trees and wine-grape, prune, and beer-hops farms, the town, with a population of 27,500, consists these days of suburban-style developments straddling U.S. 101 and a small downtown, with vineyards still in abundance.

Many wineries in Santa Rosa's orbit, among them La Crema and Martinelli, actually bear a Windsor address. Russian River Brewing Company, home of Pliny the Elder and other exalted brews, opened a combination brewery, pub, and tasting space here in 2018.

Getting Here and Around

To get to Windsor from Santa Rosa, head north on U.S. 101; from Healdsburg take the highway south. Sonoma County Transit serves Windsor from both towns. Once here, a car or ride share will be most convenient.

Visitor Information

Windsor Chamber of Commerce and Visitors Center
✉ *9001 Windsor Rd.* ✣ *At Emily Rose Circle, Windsor* ☎ *707/838–7285* 🌐 *www.windsorchchamber.com/visitors.*

Sights

Bricoleur Vineyards
WINERY/DISTILLERY | According to cofounders Mark and Beth Hanson, the French word *bricoleur* loosely translates to "flying by the seat of the pants," the feeling the two experienced when they purchased a 40-acre estate southwest of Windsor's town green and set about establishing a winery and lavish hospitality center. The Hansons enlisted Wine Country veterans Cary Gott (Davis Estates and other startups) and chef Shane McAnely (formerly of Healdsburg's Chalkboard restaurant) to develop wine-making and culinary programs—and voilà! (well, almost) a star was born. The Windsor property produces Chardonnay and Pinot Noir, with vineyards in

Alexander Valley (Zinfandel, Carignane) and Fountaingrove (Sauvignon Blanc, Viognier, and Grenache for rosé) supplying additional varietals. By appointment, hosts pour Gott's self-assured wines in a 10,000-square-foot barn, a courtyard shaded by London plane trees, an open-air pavilion, and other settings with vineyard, garden, or Russian River Valley views (sometimes all three). ✉ *7394 Starr Rd., Windsor* ✣ *1¾ miles south of Windsor River Rd.* ☎ *707/857–5700* 🌐 *www.bricoleurvineyards.com* 🎫 *Tastings from $45* 🕓 *Closed Tues. and Wed.*

★ **Grand Cru Custom Crush**

WINERY/DISTILLERY | Wineries without production equipment of their own often make wine at communal "custom-crush" facilities. Most such places don't have tasting rooms open to the public, but by appointment at Grand Cru you can reserve a Vintners' Selection of several wineries' offerings or book a private tasting with one label. If you go the latter route, **Black Kite, Butcher,** and **Maritana** for Pinot Noir and Chardonnay are worth seeking out, as are **Edaphos** for wines from rare white and red grapes and **Flambeaux** for estate Dry Creek Valley Zinfandel and Cabernet Sauvignon. Vintners or winemakers often host their winery's tastings. ■ TIP→ **Some visitors pair a stop here with beer tasting and lunch at Russian River Brewing Company, a block away.** ✉ *1200 American Way, Windsor* ✣ *From U.S. 101 Exit 496, head west on Shiloh Rd. and north on Conde La.* ☎ *707/687–0904* 🌐 *www.grandcrucustomcrush.com* 🎫 *Tastings from $25.*

La Crema Estate at Saralee's Vineyard

WINERY/DISTILLERY | The high-profile brand's multistory tasting space occupies a restored early-1900s redwood barn used over the years for hops, hay storage, and as a stable. With its cool Russian River Valley maritime climate, the celebrated Saralee's Vineyard, named for a former owner, fits the preferred La Crema profile for growing Chardonnay and Pinot Noir. You can sample wines from set flights, or staffers will customize a flight based on your preferences. ✉ *3575 Slusser Rd., Windsor* ✣ *¾ mile north of River Rd.* ☎ *707/525–6200* 🌐 *www.lacrema.com* 🎫 *Tastings from $30.*

★ **Martinelli Winery**

WINERY/DISTILLERY | In a century-old hop barn with the telltale triple towers, Martinelli has the feel of a traditional country store, but sophisticated wines are made here. The winery's reputation rests on its complex Pinot Noirs, Syrahs, and Zinfandels, including the Jackass Hill Vineyard Zin, made with grapes from vines planted mostly in the 1880s. Noted winemaker Helen Turley set the Martinelli style—fruit-forward, easy on the oak, reined-in tannins—in the 1990s, and the current team continues this approach. Tastings held (weather permitting) on a vineyard's-edge terrace survey the current releases. All visits are by appointment, best made online. ■ TIP→ **Call the winery directly about library or collector flights.** ✉ *3360 River Rd., Windsor* ✣ *East of Olivet Rd.* ☎ *707/525–0570, 800/346–1627* 🌐 *www.martinelliwinery.com* 🎫 *Tastings from $25* 🕓 *Closed days may vary; check with winery.*

🍴 Restaurants

Russian River Brewing Company Windsor

$ | **AMERICAN** | The makers of Pliny the Elder and the Younger operate this cavernous brewpub with a vast lawn and outdoor patio on the site of their state-of-the-art brewing facility. Choose among 20 beers on tap to wash down beer-compatible pub grub—chicken wings with Pliny sauce, a malted-bacon burger with cheddar fondue, fish-and-chips, pulled-pork sliders and sandwiches, and a few salads. **Known for:** year-round and seasonal beers; beers to go; casual atmosphere. [$] *Average main: $16* ✉ *700 Mitchell La., Windsor* ✣ *At Conde La. (Shilo Rd. Exit west off U.S. 101)* ☎ *707/545–2337* 🌐 *russianriverbrewing.com.*

Forestville

9 miles southwest of Windsor.

To experience the Russian River AVA's climate and rusticity, follow the river's westward course to the town of Forestville, home to a highly regarded restaurant and inn and a few wineries producing Pinot Noir from the Russian River Valley and well beyond.

Getting Here and Around

To reach Forestville from U.S. 101 near Windsor, take Exit 494/River Road and head west. From Healdsburg, follow Westside Road to River Road and then continue west. Sonoma County Transit buses serve Forestville.

◉ Sights

★ Hartford Family Winery
WINERY/DISTILLERY | Pinot Noir lovers appreciate the subtle differences in the wines Hartford's team crafts from grapes grown in several Sonoma County AVAs, along with fruit from nearby Marin and Mendocino counties and Oregon. The winery also produces highly rated Chardonnays and old-vine Zinfandels. If the weather's good, enjoy a flight on the patio outside the opulent main winery building. At private library tastings, guests sip current and older vintages. All visits are by appointment; call ahead on the same day. ⊠ *8075 Martinelli Rd.* ✛ *Off Hwy. 116 or River Rd.* ☎ *707/887–8030* ⊕ *www.hartfordwines.com* ⊠ *Tastings from $25* ⊘ *Closed Tues. and Wed.*

Joseph Jewell Wines
WINERY/DISTILLERY | Pinot Noirs from the Russian River Valley and Humboldt County to the north are the strong suit of this winery sourcing from prestigious vineyards like Bucher and Hallberg Ranch. Owner-winemaker Adrian Manspeaker, a Humboldt native, spearheaded the foray into Pinot Noir grown in the coastal redwood country. His playfully rustic storefront tasting room in downtown Forestville (visits by appointment) provides the opportunity to experience what's unique about the varietal's next Northern California frontier. There are plenty of whites here, too—Sauvignon Blanc, two Chardonnays, Pinot Gris, and Vermentino—plus rosé of Pinot, and Zinfandel from 1970s vines. ∎ TIP➔ **In 2021 the winery expects to begin offering outdoor tastings and vineyard tours at Raymond Burr Vineyards in Healdsburg.** ⊠ *6542 Front St.* ✛ *Near 1st St.* ☎ *707/820–1621* ⊕ *www.josephjewell.com* ⊠ *Tastings from $25* ⊘ *Closed Mon.–Wed.*

Russian River Vineyards
WINERY/DISTILLERY | Live music on summer and fall Fridays and Saturdays attracts an eclectic clientele to this winery specializing in single-vineyard Russian River Valley Pinot Noirs, but it's worth a stop anytime. In good weather, most guests sip wine in the courtyard under pergolas, shade trees, and umbrellas as woodpeckers pilfer acorns from nearby oaks, caching their booty in the redwood roof of the property's hop-barn-style structure. The countrified setting, complete with rusting vintage autos, has been known to induce "couch lock," causing patrons to while away hours sipping wine and nibbling on gourmet food boards, sandwiches, and salads, with some folks even settling in with a book. (Bottle service makes this option all the more tempting.) Appointments are preferred, but walk-ins are usually welcome. ⊠ *5700 Hwy. 116 N* ✛ *¾ mile south of town* ☎ *707/887–2300* ⊕ *www.russianrivervineyards.com* ⊠ *Tastings from $25.*

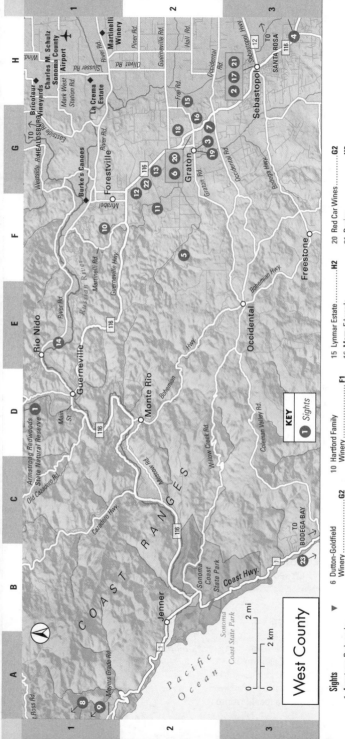

West County

KEY

1 Sights

Sights

1 Armstrong Redwoods State Natural Reserve ...**D1**

2 The Barlow **H3**

3 Bowman Cellars **G2**

4 California Carnivores ...**H3**

5 Chenoweth Wines **F2**

6 Dutton-Goldfield Winery **G2**

7 Emeritus Vineyards **G2**

8 Fort Ross State Historic Park **A1**

9 Fort Ross Vineyard & Winery **A1**

10 Hartford Family Winery **F1**

11 Iron Horse Vineyards ...**F2**

12 Joseph Jewell Wines ...**G2**

13 Kobler Estate Winery ...**G2**

14 Korbel Champagne Cellars **E1**

15 Lynmar Estate **H2**

16 Merry Edwards Winery **G2**

17 Patrick Amiot Junk Art. **H3**

18 Paul Hobbs Winery **G2**

19 Paul Mathew Vineyards **G2**

20 Red Car Wines **G2**

21 Region. **H3**

22 Russian River Vineyards. **G2**

23 Sonoma Coast Vineyards. **B3**

🍴 Restaurants

Backyard

$$$ | **MODERN AMERICAN** | The couple behind this casually rustic modern American restaurant, who met while working at Thomas Keller restaurants in Yountville, regard Sonoma County's farms and gardens as their "backyard." Dinner entrées, which change seasonally, usually include buttermilk fried chicken with buttermilk biscuits, coleslaw, and honey butter. **Known for:** husband-and-wife chef-owners; ingredients from high-quality local purveyors; poplar-shaded outdoor front patio. [$] *Average main: $28* ✉ *6566 Front St./Hwy. 116* ✥ *At 1st St.* ☎ *707/820–8445* 🌐 *backyardforestville.com* 🕒 *Closed Tues.–Thurs.*

★ **The Farmhouse Inn Restaurant**

$$$$ | **FRENCH** | Longtime executive chef Steve Litke produces three-, four-, and five-course French-inspired prix-fixe meals at the inn's romantic, softly lit destination restaurant inside a restored 19th-century farmhouse. The signature "Rabbit Rabbit Rabbit," which involves rabbit prepared three ways, is both rustic and refined, as are dishes that may include wild Alaskan halibut with Chardonnay beurre blanc; the sommelier's set wine pairings, from a list that favors Sonoma County producers but roams the globe, are flawless. **Known for:** sophisticated cuisine; romantic dining; nonalcoholic artisanal-juice pairings with advance notice. [$] *Average main: $99* ✉ *7871 River Rd.* ✥ *At Wohler Rd.* ☎ *707/887–3300, 800/464–6642* 🌐 *www.farmhouseinn.com* 🕒 *Closed Tues. and Wed. No lunch.*

Twist Eatery

$ | **AMERICAN** | A lunch-only spot on Forestville's blink-and-you'll-miss-it main drag, Twist serves sandwiches like moms of yore made, only better: Cajun meat loaf with sharp cheddar, chicken salad with crunch from cashews and spice from serrano peppers, and a local-favorite BLT when tomatoes are in season. The sandwich of grilled yams, eggplant, red peppers, and other seasonal ingredients on a focaccia roll with sun-dried tomatoes and goat cheese wows the no-meat-for-me set. **Known for:** all-day egg scrambles; gluten-free options; good beers, wines, and soft drinks. [$] *Average main: $15* ✉ *6536 Front St.* ✥ *Near Railroad Ave.* ☎ *707/820–8443* 🌐 *www.twisteatery.com* 🕒 *Closed Sun. and Mon. (sometimes Tues.). No dinner.*

🛏 Hotels

★ **The Farmhouse Inn**

$$$$ | **B&B/INN** | With a farmhouse-meets-modern-loft aesthetic, this low-key but upscale getaway with a pale-yellow exterior contains spacious rooms filled with king-size four-poster beds, whirlpool tubs, and hillside-view terraces. **Pros:** fantastic restaurant; luxury bath products; full-service spa. **Cons:** mild road noise audible in rooms closest to the street; two-night minimum on weekends; pricey, especially during high season. [$] *Rooms from: $518* ✉ *7871 River Rd.* ☎ *707/887–3300, 800/464–6642* 🌐 *www.farmhouseinn.com* 🛏 *25 rooms* 🍽 *Free breakfast.*

🏃 Activities

Burke's Canoe Trips

CANOEING/ROWING/SKULLING | You'll get a real feel for the Russian River's flora and fauna on a leisurely 10-mile paddle downstream from Burke's to Guerneville. A shuttle bus returns you to your car at the end of the journey, which is best taken from late May through mid-October and, in summer, on a weekday—summer weekends can be crowded and raucous. ✉ *8600 River Rd.* ✥ *At Mirabel Rd.* ☎ *707/887–1222* 🌐 *www.burkescanoetrips.com* 🎟 *$75 per canoe.*

Guerneville

7 miles northwest of Forestville; 15 miles southwest of Healdsburg.

Guerneville's tourist demographic has evolved over the years—Bay Area families in the 1950s, lesbians and gays starting in the 1970s, and these days a mix of both groups, plus techies and outdoorsy types—with coast redwoods and the Russian River always central to the town's appeal. The area's most famous winery is Korbel Champagne Cellars, established nearly a century and a half ago. Even older are the shady stands of trees that make Armstrong Redwoods State Natural Reserve such a perfect respite from wine tasting on hot summer days.

Getting Here and Around

To get to Guerneville from Healdsburg, follow Westside Road south to River Road and turn west. From Forestville, head west on Highway 116; alternatively, you can head north on Mirabel Road to River Road and then head west. Sonoma County Transit serves Guerneville.

Visitor Information

Guerneville Visitor Center
✉ *16209 1st St.* ✥ *At Armstrong Woods Rd.* ☎ *707/869–9000* 🌐 *www.russianriver.com.*

Sights

★ **Armstrong Redwoods State Natural Reserve**
NATIONAL/STATE PARK | **FAMILY** | Here's your best opportunity in the western Wine Country to wander amid *Sequoia sempervirens,* also known as coast redwood trees. The oldest example in this 805-acre state park, the Colonel Armstrong Tree, is thought to be more than 1,400 years old. A half mile from the parking lot, the tree is easily accessible, and you can hike a long way into the forest before things get too hilly. ■ **TIP→ During hot summer days, Armstrong Redwoods's tall trees help the park keep its cool.** ✉ *17000 Armstrong Woods Rd.* ✥ *Off River Rd.* ☎ *707/869–2958 for visitor center, 707/869–2015 for park headquarters* 🌐 *www.parks.ca.gov* 🎟 *$8 per vehicle, free to pedestrians and bicyclists.*

Korbel Champagne Cellars
WINERY/DISTILLERY | The brothers Korbel (Joseph, Francis, and Anton) planted Pinot Noir grapes in the Russian River Valley in the 1870s, pioneering efforts duly noted during tastings at the well-known brand's Guerneville facility. Korbel makes still wines, but the core business is producing dry to sweet bubblies using the French *méthode champenoise,* for which the second fermentation takes place in the bottle. ■ **TIP→ If it's open when you visit, stroll through the rose garden, home to more than 250 varieties.** ✉ *13250 River Rd.* ✥ *West of Rio Nido* ☎ *707/824–7000* 🌐 *www.korbel.com/winery* 🎟 *Tastings free–$10.*

🍴 Restaurants

Big Bottom Market
$ | **MODERN AMERICAN** | Foodies love this culinary pit stop and grocery for its breakfast biscuits, clever sandwiches, and savory salads to go or eat here. Everything from butter and jam and mascarpone and honey to barbecue pulled pork with pickles and slaw accompanies the biscuits, whose mix made Oprah's Favorite Things list, and the sandwiches include the Colonel Armstrong (curried chicken salad with currants and cashews on brioche). **Known for:** biscuits and heartier breakfast fare; Wine Country lunches; excellent for a quick bite. [$] *Average main: $13* ✉ *16228 Main St.* ✥ *Near Church St.* ☎ *707/604–7295* 🌐 *www.bigbottommarket.com* 🕒 *Closed Tues. No dinner.*

On a hot summer day the shady paths of Armstrong Redwoods State Natural Reserve provide cool comfort.

★ boon eat+drink

$$ | **MODERN AMERICAN** | A casual storefront restaurant on Guerneville's main drag, boon eat+drink has a menu built around salads, smallish shareable plates, and entrées that might include a vegan bowl, chili-braised pork shoulder, and local cod with beluga lentils. Like many of chef-owner Crista Luedtke's dishes, the signature polenta lasagna—creamy ricotta salata cheese and polenta served on greens sautéed in garlic, all of it floating upon a spicy marinara sauce—deviates significantly from the lasagna norm but succeeds on its own merits. **Known for:** adventurous culinary sensibility; Sonoma County wine selection; local organic ingredients. [$] *Average main: $23* ✉ *16248 Main St.* ✣ *At Church St.* ☎ *707/869–0780* 🌐 *eatatboon.com* 🕑 *Closed Mon. and Tues.*

Pat's International

$$ | **ECLECTIC** | On Main Street for several generations, Pat's got a new lease on life when a pop-up chef known for gooey-delicious, highly addictive Korean fried chicken (aka "Korean Fried Crack") bought the place and broadened its menu to include chicken pozole, huevos rancheros, and other international comfort food items. The setting—diner with counter and booths on one side, "dining room" with fake grass and picnic tables on the other, and plenty of cabinlike wood paneling all around—is peppy ersatz retro. **Known for:** playful ambience; artful spin on American classics; KFT (with tofu), noodle bowls, and other nonmeat options. [$] *Average main: $20* ✉ *16236 Main St.* ✣ *Near Church St.* ☎ *707/604–4007* 🌐 *patsinternational.com* 🕑 *Closed Wed.*

Hotels

AutoCamp Russian River

$$$ | **B&B/INN** | **FAMILY** | Guests at this spot along the Russian River camp (well, sort of) in luxury under the redwoods in cute-as-a-button Airstream trailers decked out with top-notch oh-so-contemporary beds, linens, and bath products, with smaller "Happier Camper" and tent options

(not year-round) only for two. **Pros:** retro feel; comfortable down beds; campfire and barbecue pit for each Airstream. **Cons:** lacks room service and other hotel amenities; fee for housekeeping; tents late spring–mid-fall only, with two-guest maximum including children. $ *Rooms from: $324* ✉ *14120 Old Cazadero Rd.* ☎ *888/405–7553* ⊕ *autocamp.com* ⇌ *24 trailers* ⦿ *No meals.*

boon hotel+spa

$$ | HOTEL | Redwoods, Douglas firs, and palms supply shade and seclusion at this lushly landscaped resort ¾ mile north of downtown Guerneville. **Pros:** filling breakfasts; pool area and on-site spa; complimentary bikes. **Cons:** lacks amenities of larger properties; pool rooms too close to the action for some guests; can be pricey in high season. $ *Rooms from: $213* ✉ *14711 Armstrong Woods Rd.* ☎ *707/869–2721* ⊕ *boonhotels.com* ⇌ *15 rooms* ⦿ *Free breakfast.*

Cottages on River Road

$ | B&B/INN | FAMILY | Redwoods on a steep slope tower above this tidy roadside complex of single and duplex cottages separated by a grassy lawn. **Pros:** family business run with care; affordable rates; five two-bedroom cottages good for families and groups. **Cons:** books up far in advance in summer; lacks upscale amenities; some road noise audible (ask for a cottage under the trees). $ *Rooms from: $159* ✉ *14880 River Rd.* ✛ *1¼ miles east of town* ☎ *707/869–3848* ⊕ *www.cottagesonriverroad.com* ⇌ *19 cottages* ⦿ *Free breakfast.*

Nightlife

El Barrio

BARS/PUBS | Mescal and classic tequila margaritas are the mainstays of this bar—a festive spot to begin or end the evening or to park yourself while waiting for a table at owner Crista Luedtke's nearby boon eat+drink. El Pepino (mescal with muddled cucumbers and agave) and more fanciful creations, some featuring "bourbons and browns," also await at this serape-chic watering hole. ✉ *16230 Main St.* ✛ *Near Church St.* ☎ *707/604–7601* ⊕ *www.elbarriobar.com* ⌖ *Closed Tues.*

Jenner

10 miles north of Bodega Bay.

The Russian River empties into the Pacific Ocean at Jenner, a wide spot in the road where houses dot a mountainside high above the sea. Facing south, the village looks across the river's mouth to Sonoma Coast State Park's Goat Rock Beach. North of the village, Fort Ross State Historic Park provides a glimpse into Russia's early-19th-century foray into California. South of the fort a winery named for it grows Chardonnay and Pinot Noir above the coastal fog line. North of the fort lie more beaches and redwoods to hike and explore.

Getting Here and Around

Jenner is north of Bodega Bay on Highway 1; from Guerneville head west on Highway 116 (River Road). Mendocino Transit Authority (⊕ *mendocinotransit. org*) buses serve Jenner from Bodega Bay and other coastal towns.

⊙ Sights

Fort Ross State Historic Park

NATIONAL/STATE PARK | FAMILY | With its reconstructed Russian Orthodox chapel, stockade, and officials' quarters, Fort Ross looks much the way it did after the Russians made it their major California coastal outpost in 1812. Russian settlers established the fort on land they leased from the native Kashia people. The Russians hoped to gain a foothold in the Pacific coast's warmer regions and to produce crops and other supplies for their Alaskan fur-trading operations. In 1841, with the local marine mammal population depleted and farming having proven unproductive, the Russians sold their holdings to John Sutter, later of gold-rush fame. The land, privately ranched for decades, became a state park in 1909. One original Russian-era structure remains, as does a cemetery. The rest of the compound has been reconstructed to look much as it did during Russian times. An excellent small museum documents the history of the fort, the Kashia people, and the ranch and state-park eras. No dogs are allowed past the parking lot and picnic area. ✉ *19005 Hwy. 1* ✣ *11 miles north of Jenner village* ☎ *707/847–3437* 🌐 *www.fortross.org* 🎟 *$8 per vehicle.*

Fort Ross Vineyard & Winery

WINERY/DISTILLERY | The Russian River and Highway 116 snake west from Guerneville through redwood groves to the coast, where Highway 1 twists north past rocky cliffs to this windswept ridge-top winery. Until recently many experts deemed the weather this far west too chilly even for cool-climate varietals, but Fort Ross Vineyard and other Fort Ross–Seaview AVA wineries are proving that Chardonnay and Pinot Noir can thrive above the fog line. The sea air and rocky soils here produce wines generally less fruit-forward than their Russian River Valley counterparts but equally sophisticated and no less vibrant. With its rustic-chic, barnlike tasting room and outdoor patio overlooking the Pacific, Fort Ross provides an appealing introduction to its region's wines. Tastings include a cheese and charcuterie plate (vegetarian option possible). Appointments are required; for same-day visits call before 11 am. ✉ *15725 Meyers Grade Rd.* ✣ *Off Hwy. 1, 6 miles north of Jenner* ☎ *707/847–3460* 🌐 *www.fortrossvineyard.com* 🎟 *Tastings from $55* 🕒 *Closed Tues. and Wed.*

🍴 Restaurants

River's End

$$$ | **AMERICAN** | The hot tip at this low-slung cliff's-edge restaurant is to come early or reserve a window table, where the Russian River and Pacific Ocean views alone, particularly at sunset, might make your day (even more so if you're a birder). Seafood is the specialty—during the summer the chef showcases local king salmon—but filet mignon, duck, elk, a vegetarian napoleon, and pasta with prawns are often on the dinner menu. **Known for:** majestic setting; international wine list; burgers, fish-and-chips for lunch. [$] *Average main: $34* ✉ *11048 Hwy. 1* ✣ *1½ miles north of Hwy. 116* ☎ *707/865–2484* 🌐 *www.ilovesunsets.com.*

🛏 Hotels

★ **Timber Cove Resort**

$$$ | **RESORT** | Restored well beyond its original splendor, this resort anchored to a craggy oceanfront cliff is by far the Sonoma Coast's coolest getaway. **Pros:** dramatic sunsets; grand public spaces; patio dining at Coast Kitchen restaurant. **Cons:** some service lapses; pricey ocean-view rooms; far from nightlife. [$] *Rooms from: $360* ✉ *21780 Hwy. 1* ☎ *707/847–3231* 🌐 *www.timbercoveresort.com* 🔑 *46 rooms* 🍽 *No meals.*

Bodega Bay

23 miles west of Santa Rosa.

Pockets of modernity notwithstanding, this commercial fishing town retains the workaday vibe of its cinematic turn in Alfred Hitchcock's *The Birds* (1963). Little from the film's era remains save the windswept bay and ocean views. (For the ocean ones, drive west from Highway 1, Eastshore to Bay Flat to Westshore.) To the east in the town of Bodega, the film's schoolhouse still stands, at Bodega Lane off Bodega Highway.

Getting Here and Around

To reach Bodega Bay, exit U.S. 101 at Santa Rosa and take Highway 12 west (called Bodega Highway west of Sebastopol) 23 miles to the coast. A scenic alternative is to take U.S. 101's East Washington Street/Central Petaluma exit and follow signs west to Bodega Bay; just after you merge onto Highway 1, you'll pass through down-home Valley Ford. Mendocino Transit Authority (🌐 *mendocinotransit.org*) buses serve Bodega Bay.

Sights

Sonoma Coast Vineyards

WINERY/DISTILLERY | This winery with an ocean-view tasting room makes small-lot wines from grapes grown close to the Pacific. The Petersen Vineyard Chardonnay and Antonio Mountain Pinot Noir stand out among cool-climate bottlings that also include Sauvignon Blanc, rosé of Pinot Noir, and a Blanc de Noirs sparkler. ✉ *555 Hwy. 1* ☎ *707/921–2860* 🌐 *www.sonomacoastvineyards.com* 🎟 *Tastings from $10 glass.*

Beaches

★ **Sonoma Coast State Park**

BEACH—SIGHT | The park's gorgeous sandy coves stretch for 17 miles from Bodega Head to 4 miles north of Jenner. **Bodega Head** is a popular whale-watching perch in winter and spring, and **Rock Point, Duncan's Landing,** and **Wright's Beach,** at about the halfway mark, have good picnic areas. Rogue waves have swept people off the rocks at Duncan's Landing Overlook, so don't stray past signs warning you away. Calmer **Shell Beach,** about 2 miles north, is known for beachcombing, tidepooling, and fishing. Walk part of the bluff-top **Kortum Trail** or drive about 2½ miles north of Shell Beach to **Blind Beach.** Near the mouth of the Russian River just north of here at **Goat Rock Beach,** you'll find harbor seals; pupping season is from March through August. Bring binoculars and walk north from the parking lot to view the seals. During summer, lifeguards are on duty at some beaches, but strong rip currents and heavy surf keep most visitors onshore. **Amenities:** parking (fee); toilets. **Best for:** solitude; sunset; walking. ✉ *Park Headquarters/Salmon Creek Ranger Station, 3095 Hwy. 1* ✣ *2 miles north of Bodega Bay* ☎ *707/875–3483* 🌐 *www.parks.ca.gov* 🎟 *$8 per vehicle.*

Restaurants

Fisherman's Cove

$ | **SEAFOOD** | Brave the lines at this seafood shack that doubles as a bait-and-tackle store to feast on crab sandwiches on sourdough, catch-of-the-day fish tacos, and fresh Tomales Bay oysters raw or barbecued (the latter with sauces that include piquant chorizo butter). The family owners place a premium on quality and sustainably produced ingredients, so you'll pay top dollar, but most patrons find the offerings well worth the price. **Known for:** indoor and outdoor seating; hearty clam chowder and Portuguese fish stew; vegetarian options including salads and beer-batter avocado and fries. [$] *Average main: $16* ✉ *1850 Bay Flat Rd.* ✣ *Follow Eastshore Rd. west from Hwy. 1* ☎ *707/377–4238* 🌐 *www.fishermanscovebodegabay.com* 🕒 *No dinner.*

★ **Ginochio's Kitchen**

$ | **ECLECTIC** | The eye-level bay perspective steals the show at this low-slung self-described barbecue and Italian restaurant whose outdoor seating areas fill up quickly in good weather. For breakfast the kitchen turns out oh-so-moist caramel-bacon monkey bread and burritos with scrambled eggs and brisket; lunchtime brings Italian-style scallop-and-clam chowder, fish tacos, pulled-pork sandwiches, and, in season, Dungeness crab sandwiches awash in molten Havarti cheese. **Known for:** Alicia's Crackling Nachos with or without meat; 14-hour cherrywood-smoked beef and brisket; wine list favoring small Sonoma County producers. [$] *Average main: $12* ✉ *1410 Bay Flat Rd.* ✥ *Off Eastshore Rd. west off Hwy. 1* ☎ *707/377–4359* 🌐 *ginochi-oskitchen.com* ⏲ *No dinner.*

Spud Point Crab Company

$ | **SEAFOOD** | Crab sandwiches, New England or Manhattan clam chowder, and homemade crab cakes with roasted red-pepper sauce star on this food stand's brief menu. Place your order and enjoy your meal to go or, when possible, at one of the marina-view picnic tables outside. **Known for:** family operation; opens at 9 am; seafood cocktails, superb chowder. [$] *Average main: $10* ✉ *1910 Westshore Rd.* ✥ *West off Hwy. 1, Eastshore Rd. to Bay Flat Rd.* ☎ *707/875–9472* 🌐 *www.spudpointcrabco.com* ⏲ *No dinner.*

★ **Terrapin Creek Cafe & Restaurant**

$$$ | **MODERN AMERICAN** | Intricate but not fussy cuisine based on locally farmed ingredients and *fruits de mer* has made this casual yet sophisticated restaurant with an open kitchen a West County darling. Start with raw oysters, rich potato-leek soup, or (in season) Dungeness crab before moving on to halibut or other fish pan-roasted to perfection. **Known for:** intricate cuisine of chefs Liya and Andrew Truong; Bay Area food-lovers' choice; great starters and salads. [$] *Average main: $34* ✉ *1580 Eastshore Rd.* ✥ *Off Hwy. 1* ☎ *707/875–2700* 🌐 *www.terrapincreekcafe.com* ⏲ *Closed Mon.–Wed. No lunch Thurs.*

Hotels

Bodega Bay Lodge

$$$ | **HOTEL** | Looking out to the ocean across a wetland, the lodge's shingle-and-river-rock buildings contain Bodega Bay's finest accommodations. **Pros:** spacious rooms with ocean views; on-site Drakes Sonoma Coast restaurant for seafood; fireplaces and patios or balconies in most rooms. **Cons:** pricey in-season; parking lot in foreground of some rooms' views; fairly long drive to other fine dining. [$] *Rooms from: $349* ✉ *103 Coast Hwy. 1* ☎ *707/875–3525* 🌐 *www.bodegabaylodge.com* 🛏 *83 rooms* 🍴 *No meals.*

Bodega Harbor Inn

$ | **HOTEL** | As humble as can be, this is among the few places on this stretch of the coast with rooms for a little more than $100 a night. **Pros:** budget choice; rooms for larger groups; ocean views from public areas and some rooms. **Cons:** older facility; nondescript rooms; behind a shopping center. [$] *Rooms from: $124* ✉ *1345 Bodega Ave.* ☎ *707/875–3594* 🌐 *www.bodegaharborinn.com* 🛏 *16 rooms* 🍴 *No meals.*

Activities

Bodega Bay Sailing Adventures

WHALE-WATCHING | Part salty dog and part jolly entertainer, Captain Rich conducts three-hour Bodega Bay tours on his 33-foot sailboat. Whales are often sighted from winter into spring, and sea lions and harbor seals commonly appear. The sunset tour is fun. ✉ *1418 Bay Flat Rd.* ✥ *Meeting place near sportfishing center* ☎ *707/318–2251* 🌐 *www.bodegabaysailing.com* 🎟 *From $95.*

Occidental

11 miles south of Guerneville; 14 miles east of Bodega Bay.

A village surrounded by redwood forests, orchards, and vineyards, Occidental is a former logging hub with a bohemian vibe. The small downtown, which contains several handsome Victorian-era structures, has a whimsically decorated bed-and-breakfast inn, two good restaurants, and a handful of art galleries and shops worth poking around.

Getting Here and Around

From Guerneville, head west on Highway 116 for 4 miles to the town of Monte Rio, then turn south on Church Street and travel past the old Rio Theater and over the bridge spanning the Russian River. By this point the road is signed as the Bohemian Highway, which takes you into town, where the road's name changes to Main Street. From Bodega Bay, head south and then east on Highway 1, continuing east on Bodega Highway at the town of Bodega; at Freestone, head north on the Bohemian Highway. Public transit is not a convenient way to travel here.

🍴 Restaurants

★ Hazel
$$ | MODERN AMERICAN | Pizza and pastries are the specialties of this tiny restaurant whose owner-chefs, Jim and Michele Wimborough, forsook their fancy big-city gigs for the pleasures of small-town living. Jim's mushroom pizza, adorned with feta, mozzarella, and truffle oil, and the pie with sausage and egg are among the headliners, with Michele's chocolate pot de crème among the enticements for dessert. **Known for:** flavorful seasonal cuisine; roasted chicken with lemon vinaigrette entrée; outdoor seating area.

$ *Average main: $24* ⊠ *3782 Bohemian Hwy.* ✛ *At Occidental Rd.* ☎ *707/874–6003* ⊕ *www.restauranthazel.com* ⊘ *Closed Mon. and Tues. No lunch.*

Howard Station Cafe
$ | AMERICAN | The mile-long list of morning fare at Occidental's neo-hippie go-to breakfast and weekend brunch spot includes huevos rancheros, omelets, eggs Benedict, waffles, pancakes, French toast, and "healthy alternatives" such as oatmeal, house-made granola, and quinoa and brown rice bowls with kale and eggs. Soups, salads, burgers, and monstrous sandwiches are on the menu for lunch at this laid-back space with seating inside a 19th-century gingerbread Victorian and outside on its wooden porch. **Known for:** mostly organic ingredients; juice bar; vegetarian and gluten-free items. $ *Average main: $13* ⊠ *3611 Main St./Bohemian Hwy.* ✛ *At 2nd St.* ☎ *707/874–2838* ⊕ *www.howardstation-cafe.com* ⊘ *No dinner.*

🛏 Hotels

The Inn at Occidental
$$ | B&B/INN | Quilts, folk art, and original paintings and photographs fill this colorful and friendly inn up the hill from tiny Occidental's shops and restaurants. **Pros:** whimsical decor; most rooms have private decks and jetted tubs; full gourmet breakfast. **Cons:** not for those with minimalist tastes; not for kids; no pool. $ *Rooms from: $219* ⊠ *3657 Church St.* ☎ *707/874–1047* ⊕ *www.innatoccidental. com* ⇆ *17 rooms* ⦿ *Free breakfast.*

🏃 Activities

Sonoma Canopy Tours
ZIPLINING | Zip through the trees with the greatest of ease—at speeds up to 25 mph—at this ziplining center 2½ miles north of Occidental. Friendly guides prepare guests well for their 2½-hour natural high. ■ TIP➔ **Participants must be at least**

10 years old and weigh between 70 and 250 pounds. ⊠ *6250 Bohemian Hwy.* ⊹ *2½ miles north of Occidental* ☎ *888/494–7868* ⊕ *www.sonomacanopytours.com* 🎫 *From $99.*

Sebastopol

6 miles east of Occidental; 7 miles southwest of Santa Rosa.

A stroll through downtown Sebastopol—a town formerly known more for Gravenstein apples than for grapes but these days a burgeoning wine hub—reveals glimpses of the distant and recent past and perhaps the future, too. Many hippies settled here in the 1960s and 70s and, as the old Crosby, Stills, Nash & Young song goes, they taught their children well: the town remains steadfastly, if not entirely, countercultural.

Sebastopol has long had good, if somewhat low-profile, wineries, among them Iron Horse, Lynmar Estate, and Merry Edwards. With the replacement in 2016 of the town's beloved Fosters Freeze location with a vaguely industrial-chic venue for California coastal cuisine and the evolving cluster of artisanal producers at The Barlow, the site of a former apple cannery, the town always seems poised for a Healdsburg-style transformation. Then again, maybe not—stay tuned (in, not out).

Getting Here and Around

Sebastopol can be reached from Occidental by taking Graton Road east to Highway 116 and turning south. From Santa Rosa, drive west on Highway 12. Sonoma County Transit buses serve Sebastopol.

Visitor Information

Sebastopol Visitor Center
⊠ *265 S. Main St.* ⊹ *At Willow St.* ☎ *707/823–3032* ⊕ *www.sebastopol.org.*

◉ Sights

The Barlow
MARKET | A multibuilding complex on a former apple-cannery site, The Barlow celebrates Sonoma County's "maker" culture with tenants who produce or sell wine, beer, spirits, crafts, clothing, art, and artisanal food and herbs. The anchor wine tenant, Kosta Browne, receives only club members and allocation-list guests, but other tasting rooms are open to the public, and Region wine bar promotes small Sonoma County producers. Crooked Goat Brewing makes and sells ales, Golden State Cider pours apple-driven beverages, and you can have a nip of vodka, gin, sloe gin, or wheat and rye whiskey at Spirit Works Distillery. Over at Fern Bar, the zero-proof (as in nonalcoholic) cocktails entice as much as the traditional ones. The bar serves food, as do Sushi Koshō, Blue Ridge Kitchen (Southern-influenced comfort fare), and a few other spots. ⊠ *6770 McKinley St.* ⊹ *At Morris St., off Hwy. 12* ☎ *707/824–5600* ⊕ *www.thebarlow.net* 🎫 *Complex free; fees for tasting.*

★ **Chenoweth Wines**
WINERY/DISTILLERY | Distinguished producers like Patz & Hall and Kosta Browne make wines from grapes farmed by the Chenoweth family, whose ancestors settled in the redwood-studded hills northwest of Sebastopol in the mid-1800s. In 2000, Charlie Chenoweth converted apple orchards to vineyards, in recent years reserving some of the grapes for his wife, Amy, to craft the namesake Chardonnay, rosé of Pinot Noir, and Pinot Noirs. Uniformly excellent, they alone warrant a visit to the 600-acre property,

Iron Horse produces sparklers that make history.

but the down-home hospitality and hardworking but fun-loving family vibe elevate the experience exponentially. For lofty Russian River Valley perspectives few other wineries can supply, book the ATV Tasting Tour, stopping for sips where the wines' grapes are grown. As with the other appointment-only sessions, the gregarious Amy sometimes hosts these herself. ■TIP→ **If you can't make it to the ranch, Region in The Barlow pours some Chenoweth wines.** ✉ *5550 Harrison Grade Rd.* ⊹ *Off Green Valley Rd.* ☎ *707/829–3367* ⊕ *www.chenowethwines.com* 🍷 *Tastings from $45* ⊙ *Closed Fri., Sun., and Mon.*

★ Dutton-Goldfield Winery

WINERY/DISTILLERY | An avid cyclist whose previous credits include developing the wine-making program at Hartford Court, Dan Goldfield teamed up with fifth-generation farmer Steve Dutton to establish this small operation devoted to cool-climate wines. Goldfield modestly strives to take Dutton's meticulously farmed fruit and "make the winemaker unnoticeable," but what impresses the most about these wines, which include Chardonnay, Gewürztraminer, Riesling, Pinot Noir, and Zinfandel, is their sheer artistry. Among the ones to seek out are the Angel Camp Pinot Noir, from Anderson Valley (Mendocino County) grapes, and the Morelli Lane Zinfandel, from fruit grown on the remaining 1.8 acres of an 1880s vineyard Goldfield helped revive. One tasting focuses on current releases, another on single-vineyard Pinot Noirs. ✉ *3100 Gravenstein Hwy. N/Hwy. 116* ⊹ *At Graton Rd.* ☎ *707/827–3600* ⊕ *www.duttongoldfield.com* 🍷 *Tastings from $30.*

Emeritus Vineyards

WINERY/DISTILLERY | Old-timers recall the superb apples grown at Hallberg Ranch, since a 2000 replanting an elite Pinot Noir vineyard. Owner Brice Jones coveted this land for its temperate climate and layer of Goldridge sandy loam soil atop a bed of Sebastopol clay loam. Along with dry-farming (no irrigation), this soil combination forces vine roots to work hard to obtain water, yielding berries concentrated with flavor. Emeritus sells grapes to boutique and larger wineries, reserving much of the remainder for the flagship Emeritus Hallberg Ranch Pinot Noir. Less than 10 miles away, the winery farms the 30-acre Pinot Hill Vineyard, whose wines are often even denser and more complex. You can sample the Pinots at a structure whose floor-to-ceiling windows are retracted in good weather to create an extended open-air space steps from the vines. Tastings are by appointment, with same-day visits usually possible. ⊠ 2500 Gravenstein Hwy. N ✛ At Peachland Ave. ☎ 707/823–9463 ⊕ www.emeritusvineyards.com ☞ Tastings from $25, tour and tasting $50.

★ Iron Horse Vineyards

WINERY/DISTILLERY | A meandering one-lane road leads to this winery known for its sparkling wines and estate Chardonnays and Pinot Noirs. The sparklers have made history: Ronald Reagan served them at his summit meetings with Mikhail Gorbachev; George H. W. Bush took some along to Moscow for treaty talks; and Barack Obama included them at official state dinners. Despite Iron Horse's brushes with fame, a casual rusticity prevails at its outdoor tasting area (large heaters keep things comfortable on chilly days), which gazes out on acres of rolling, vine-covered hills. Tastings are by appointment only. ⊠ 9786 Ross Station Rd. ✛ Off Hwy. 116 ☎ 707/887–1507 ⊕ www.ironhorsevineyards.com ☞ Tasting $30.

Kobler Estate Winery

WINERY/DISTILLERY | Find out what makes small family-owned wineries tick at this operation producing fewer than 1,000 cases annually. In northern Sebastopol almost to Forestville, Michael Kobler farms 4½ acres of Viognier and Syrah. His son Brian, who cut his teeth at

large outfits like Korbel and Clos du Bois, makes wines from these grapes, along with Chardonnay and Pinot Noir purchased from Bacigalupi and other respected growers. Keeping it all in the family, Brian's outgoing brother Mike hosts guests for tastings on a vineyard's-edge patio outside the family's 1870 Victorian farmhouse. Visits are by appointment. If you can't get one, try Region wine bar in downtown Sebastopol, which always pours a white and a red. ⊠ 4630 Gravenstein Hwy. N/Hwy. 116 ✛ ¼-mile north of Guerneville Rd. ☎ 707/329–5474 ⊕ koblerestatewinery. com ☞ Tasting $15, vineyard tour and tasting $30.

Lynmar Estate

WINERY/DISTILLERY | *Elegant* and *balanced* describe Lynmar's landscaping and contemporary architecture, but the terms also apply to the wine-making philosophy. Expect handcrafted Chardonnays and Pinot Noirs with long, luxurious finishes, especially on the Pinots. The attention to refinement and detail extends to the tasting spaces, where well-informed pourers serve patrons enjoying garden and vineyard views. Consistently performing well is the Quail Hill Vineyard Pinot Noir, a blend of some or all of the 14 Pinot Noir clones grown in the vineyard outside. Also exceptional are the Pinnacle Tier wines: a Chardonnay (La Sereinité) and three Pinot Noirs (Five Sisters, Anisya's Blend, and Lynn's Blend). Most wines can be bought only by belonging to the allocation list or at the winery. Tastings are by appointment only. ⊠ 3909 Frei Rd. ✛ Off Hwy. 116 ☎ 707/829–3374 ⊕ www.lynmarestate. com ☞ Tastings from $60 ⊗ Closed Mon.–Wed.

Merry Edwards Winery

WINERY/DISTILLERY | Winemaker Merry Edwards has long extolled the Russian River Valley as "the epicenter of great Pinot Noir." The winery that bears her

Patrick Amio's "junk art" sculptures liven up three blocks in Sebastopol.

name, since 2019 owned by the Roederer Estate sparkling-wine house, produces single-vineyard and blended wines that express the unique characteristics of the soils, climates, and grape clones from which they derive. (Edwards's research into Pinot Noir clones has been so extensive that one is named after her.) Edwards preferred the Russian River as a growing site, believing that the warmer-than-average daytime temperatures encouraged more intense fruit, with the evening fogs mitigating the extra heat's potentially adverse effects. The winery also makes a Sauvignon Blanc that's lightly aged in old oak, and there's a late-harvest Sauvignon Blanc dessert wine. ⊠ *2959 Gravenstein Hwy. N/Hwy. 116* ✛ *Near Oak Grove Ave.* ☎ *707/823–7466* ⊕ *www.merryedwards. com* ⊠ *Tasting $25.*

Patrick Amiot Junk Art

PUBLIC ART | The whimsical sculptures of local junk artist Patrick Amiot and his wife, Brigitte Laurent (he creates them,

she paints them), can be seen all over Sonoma County, but you can see many works on **Florence Avenue** three blocks west of Main Street. Amiot reclaims old car parts, abandoned appliances, and the like, refashioning them into everything from pigs, dogs, and people to mermaids and Godzilla. ⊠ *Florence Ave.* ✛ *between Bodega Ave. (Hwy. 12) and Healdsburg Ave.* ⊕ *www.patrickamiot.com.*

Paul Hobbs Winery

WINERY/DISTILLERY | Wine critics routinely bestow high-90s scores on the Chardonnays, Pinot Noirs, and Cabernet Sauvignons produced at this appointment-only winery set amid gently rolling vineyards in northwestern Sebastopol. Owner-winemaker Paul Hobbs's university thesis investigated the flavors that result from various oak-barrel toasting levels. He continued his education at Robert Mondavi Winery, Opus One, and other storied establishments before striking out on his own in 1991. Tastings take place in a space designed by winery specialist Howard Backen's architectural firm. Guests on a Signature Tasting visit the winery and sip several wines; the Vineyard Designate Experience includes the tour plus small bites paired with limited-edition single-vineyard wines. ✉ *3355 Gravenstein Hwy. N* ✣ *Near Holt Rd.* ☎ *707/824–9879* 🌐 *www.paulhobbswinery.com* 🎫 *Tastings from $65* 🕙 *Closed weekends and holidays.*

Red Car Wines

WINERY/DISTILLERY | Some ex-movie folks started Red Car as the new millennium dawned, naming it for Los Angeles's old streetcars and producing wines out of Southern California before moving operations to Sonoma County. Coastal, cool-climate wines are the specialty. The Estate Vineyard Chardonnay, Pinot Noir, and Syrah, among the best, come from grapes grown in the far-coastal Fort Ross–Seaview AVA. Other wines that consistently shine include the Sonoma Coast Chardonnay, the rosé of Pinot Noir ("hits the mark year after year," enthused one critic), and Heaven and Earth Pinot Noir. The tasting room's hip country-casual decor pairs well with the upbeat rock playlist and the hosts' low-key vibe, though on a sunny afternoon the shaded outdoor patio is the place to be. ■ TIP→ **Red Car shares a parking lot with Dutton-Goldfield, making this an excellent two-for-one stop.** ✉ *8400 Graton Rd.* ✣ *At Gravenstein Hwy. (Hwy. 116)* ☎ *707/829–8500* 🌐 *redcarwine.com* 🎫 *Tastings from $25.*

Region

WINERY/DISTILLERY | "Drink your region" is the motto of this combination wine bar and shop whose self-serve stations dispense the wines of multiple small Sonoma County producers in 1-, 2-, and 5-ounce pours. Each week a different operation takes center stage, with vintners, winemakers, or staffers from the featured winery discussing wines during meet-the-makers happy hours. AldenAlli, named for the wives of its two principals, Kosta Browne cofounder Dan Kosta and celeb chef Emeril Legasse, is among the labels represented, along with Chenoweth, Eric Kent, Trombetta, Young Hagen, and other local brands worth learning about. (If you've never heard of them, there's your reason to check this place out.) ■ TIP→ **Region, which encourages appointments but strives to accommodate same-day guests, opens at 1 pm and closes at 8.** ✉ *The Barlow, 180 Morris St., Suite 170* ✣ *At McKinley St.* ☎ *707/329–6724* 🌐 *drinkyourregion.com* 🎫 *Tastings from $7 for a 5-oz pour.*

🍴 Restaurants

Blue Ridge Kitchen

$$$ | MODERN AMERICAN | Artfully plated Southern-inspired cuisine piques the palate at this farm-to-table restaurant inside a vast industrial-looking space whose garagelike doors open up to unite the dining/bar area and spacious patio. Dishes that might include ahi tuna tartare, truffle fries, and Mt. Lassen trout owe as much to California as Carolina (fried chicken with collard greens), and options like lobster croque madame with country ham and specials like shrimp and grits straddling both coasts. **Known for:** smash burgers and po'boys; vegan roasted cauliflower steak; Mississippi mud pie ("kinda"). [$] *Average main: $28* ✉ *The Barlow, 6770 McKinley St., No. 150* ✣ *Off Morris St.* ☎ *707/222–5040* 🌐 *brkitchen.com.*

★ **Fern Bar**

$$ | MODERN AMERICAN | The mixologists at this self-proclaimed "bar-focused restaurant" whip up "garden-to-glass" craft cocktails meant for pairing with neo-comfort food whose ingredients, especially the produce, are primarily cultivated in West Sonoma County. The menu divides the entrées between "veggie style" (falafel, posole, "umami bomb" mushrooms with shiitake ersatz cream and sticky rice) and "animal style" (fried chicken, noodles with cumin lamb, smash burgers)—so there's something for everyone, including vegans and those in search of gluten- and dairy-free sustenance. **Known for:** creative artisanal cocktails; hip yet inviting 21st-century tavern feel; live-music lineup. $ *Average main: $18* ⊠ *The Barlow, 6780 Depot St., Suite 120* ✛ *Near McKinley St.* ☎ *707/861–9603* ⊕ *fernbar.com* ☾ *No lunch Mon.–Wed.*

★ Gravenstein Grill

$$$ | **MODERN AMERICAN** | Tablecloths, cut flowers, and the soft glow of liquid paraffin candles and strings of lights overhead draw most diners to this casual-elegant restaurant's expansive outdoor patio. Chef Bob Simontacchi relies on local sources for the organic, sustainable ingredients in vegan, vegetarian, and omnivore dishes like roasted beets with sweet potato and coconut-cream purée, bone-in pork chop with apples, wild-caught petrale sole, and a town-fave Sonoma-beef burger. **Known for:** patio atmosphere; artisanal wines, beers, and ciders; dessert and dessert-wine pairings. $ *Average main: $27* ⊠ *8050 Bodega Ave.* ✛ *At Pleasant Hill Ave. N* ☎ *707/634–6142* ⊕ *www.gravensteingrill. com* ☾ *Closed Mon. and Tues. (sometimes open on Tues.).*

★ Handline Coastal California

$ | **MODERN AMERICAN** | **FAMILY** | Sebastopol's former Foster's Freeze location, now a 21st-century fast-food palace, won design awards for its rusted-steel frame and translucent panel-like windows. The menu, a paean to coastal California cuisine, includes oysters raw and grilled, fish tacos, ceviche, tostadas, three burgers (beef, vegetarian, and fish), and, honoring the location's previous incarnation, chocolate and vanilla soft-serve ice cream. **Known for:** upscale comfort food; outdoor patio; sustainable seafood and other ingredients. $ *Average main: $14* ⊠ *935 Gravenstein Hwy. S* ✛ *Near Hutchins Ave.* ☎ *707/827–3744* ⊕ *www. handline.com.*

Khom Loi

$$ | **THAI** | Two restaurateurs with separate Sebastopol businesses (Handline and Ramen Gaijin) parlayed the success of a nouveau-Thai pop-up into a 2021 storefront eatery with an open kitchen. Early favorites such as whole fish; citrus salad with pomelo, green apple, toasted coconut, and dried shrimp; and green curry with clam and brined peppercorn captivate even before the first bite with their fragrant aromas, colorful presentation, and obviously fresh locally cultivated ingredients. **Known for:** casual vibe; patio seating area; wines from local producers. $ *Average main: $19* ⊠ *7385 Healdsburg Ave.* ✛ *At Florence Ave.* ☎ *707/329–6917* ⊕ *www.khomloisonoma.com* ☾ *Closed Mon. and Tues. No lunch (check for updates).*

★ Pascaline Patisserie & Café

$ | **CAFÉ** | Delicate pastries and quiches, croques monsieur, and other bistro bites have made locals as passionate about this Highway 116 café as its executive and pastry chefs, who previously worked at establishments in Paris, San Francisco, and elsewhere, are about their cuisine and hospitality. Pastel-green walls, a wood-burning stove, and tables from reclaimed wood lend the small interior space a French-country feel; on sunny days the best seating is on the wooden deck outside. **Known for:** kouign-amann French pastry; French-style coffee; joyous atmosphere. $ *Average main: $12* ⊠ *4552 Gravenstein Hwy. N* ✛ *Almost to Forestville* ☎ *707/823–3122* ⊕ *pascalinepatisserieandcafe.com* ☾ *No dinner.*

Ramen Gaijin

$$ | **JAPANESE** | Inside a tall-ceilinged, brick-walled, vaguely industrial-looking space with reclaimed wood from a coastal building backing the bar, the chefs at Ramen Gaijin turn out richly flavored ramen bowls brimming with crispy pork belly, woodear mushrooms, seaweed, and other well-proportioned ingredients.

Izakaya (Japanese pub grub) dishes like *donburi* (meat and vegetables over rice) are another specialty, like the ramen made from mostly local proteins and produce. **Known for:** artisanal cocktails, beer, wine, and cider; gluten-free, vegetarian dishes; karage (fried chicken) and other small plates. $ *Average main: $18* ⊠ *6948 Sebastopol Ave.* ✛ *Near Main St.* ☎ *707/827–3609* ⊕ *www.ramengaijin. com* ⊘ *Closed Sun. and Mon. No lunch.*

Sushi Koshō

$$$ | **JAPANESE** | Hailed by local food writers as Sonoma County's best sushi restaurant, this industrial-looking high-ceilinged spot pushes the envelope with crowd-pleasers like the 15-spice spare ribs with hoisin barbecue sauce and salmon tartare tacos with crispy wonton shells. The chefs present sushi classics with style and precision as well, the intricacy enticing as much as the freshness of the mostly local ingredients. **Known for:** sake selection; beer, wine, and mocktails; outdoor seating area with firepit. $ *Average main: $29* ⊠ *The Barlow, 6750 McKinley St.* ✛ *Off Morris St.* ☎ *707/827–6373* ⊕ *www.koshosushi. com* ⊘ *Closed Mon. and Tues.*

🛏 Hotels

Fairfield Inn & Suites Santa Rosa Sebastopol

$ | **HOTEL** | A safe West County bet that often has availability when other inns and hotels are full, the three-story Fairfield, a bit south of Sebastopol's core, is a competently run chain hotel. **Pros:** convenient to West County wineries and Santa Rosa; good-size outdoor pool and spa; frequent Internet specials. **Cons:** hardly a unique Wine Country experience; occasional service letdowns; sometimes overpriced during high season. $ *Rooms from: $151* ⊠ *1101 Gravenstein Hwy. S* ☎ *707/829–6677* ⊕ *www.winecountryhi.com* ⇌ *82 rooms* ⦿ *Free breakfast.*

Graton

½ mile west of Sebastopol.

Steps from Sebastopol and near Occidental, tiny Graton has a one-block main drag one can stroll in two minutes—although it's possible to while away a few hours at the artist-run gallery, nostalgia-inducing antiques shop, tasting rooms, and two notably fine restaurants.

Getting Here and Around

To reach Graton from Sebastopol, head west from Highway 116 a half-mile on Graton Road. Sonoma County Transit buses pass through Graton.

◉ Sights

Bowman Cellars

WINERY/DISTILLERY | Winemaker Alex Bowman learned his craft as a lad, making hobby wines with his father, an electrical contractor with deep West County roots. By his late 20s the wine-making bug had bitten Alex hard, inspiring him to make wines "for real." His debut wine won a double-gold ribbon at the local county fair, prompting him to draw on the experience of several wine-industry relatives to establish Bowman Cellars with his wife, Katie, whose family has long owned a roadside produce market in Sebastopol. The two pour their wines (reservations required, same-day possible) in a casual tasting room that's fronted by a patio twice as large. Alex shows a light but knowing touch with Russian River Valley Chardonnay and Pinot Noir, the winery's two stars. ⊠ *9010 Graton Rd.* ✛ *At Edison St.* ☎ *707/827–3391* ⊕ *bowmancellars.com* ⊠ *Tastings $15–$35* ⊘ *Closed Mon.–Wed.*

Paul Mathew Vineyards

WINERY/DISTILLERY | With experience that includes stints as a winery tour guide, cellar rat, sales rep, vineyard developer, and finally winemaker, owner Mat Gustafson knows how to make and market his single-vineyard wines. Gustafson specializes in spare, low-alcohol, food-friendly Russian River Valley Pinots and makes Chardonnay, Gewürztraminer, and Viognier whites along with Grenache, Cabernet Franc, and Syrah reds. On a hot summer day his rosé of Pinot Noir and sparkling brut rosé make for delightful sipping in the picnic area behind the appointment-only tasting room, which occupies a century-old Edwardian storefront. ✉ *9060 Graton Rd.* ✣ *At Ross Rd.* ☎ *707/861–9729* 🌐 *www.paulmathewvineyards.com* 🎫 *Tasting $40* 🕘 *Closed Mon.–Wed.*

🍴 Restaurants

★ Underwood Bar & Bistro

$$ | MODERN AMERICAN | The same people who operate the Willow Wood Market Cafe across the street run this restaurant with a Continental atmosphere and a seasonal menu based on smaller and larger dishes. The offerings might include anything from hoisin-glazed ribs, crispy duck confit, and salmon with farro risotto to Thai staples like green papaya salad and Chiang Mai pork-belly curry. **Known for:** French onion soup; old-style cocktails, ports, and cognacs; outdoor patio with heaters. [$] *Average main: $24* ✉ *9113 Graton Rd.* ✣ *About ½ mile west of Hwy. 116* ☎ *707/823–7023* 🌐 *www.underwoodgraton.com* 🕘 *Closed Mon. No lunch Sun.*

Willow Wood Market Cafe

$$ | MODERN AMERICAN | This café across the street from the Underwood Bar & Bistro serves simple, tasty soups, salads, and sandwiches. Sunday brunch is elaborate, but even breakfast—specialties include hot, creamy polenta and housemade granola—is modern-American down-home solid. **Known for:** casual setting; outdoor back patio; ragouts on polenta. [$] *Average main: $19* ✉ *9020 Graton Rd.* ✣ *About ½ mile west of Hwy. 116* ☎ *707/823–0233* 🌐 *willowwoodgraton.com* 🕘 *No dinner Sun.*

Santa Rosa

6 miles east of Sebastopol; 55 miles north of San Francisco.

Urban Santa Rosa isn't as popular with tourists as many Wine Country destinations—which isn't surprising, seeing as there are more office parks than wineries within its limits. Nevertheless, this hardworking town is home to a couple of interesting cultural offerings and a few noteworthy restaurants and vineyards. The city's chain motels and hotels can come in handy if everything else is booked up, especially since Santa Rosa is roughly equidistant from Sonoma, Healdsburg, and the western Russian River Valley, three heavily visited wine-tasting destinations.

Getting Here and Around

To get to Santa Rosa from Sebastopol, drive east on Highway 12. From San Francisco, cross the Golden Gate Bridge and continue north on U.S. 101. Santa Rosa's hotels, restaurants, and wineries are spread over a wide area; factor in extra time when driving around the city, especially during morning and evening rush hour. To get here from downtown San Francisco, take Golden Gate Transit Bus 101. Several Sonoma County Transit buses serve the city and surrounding area.

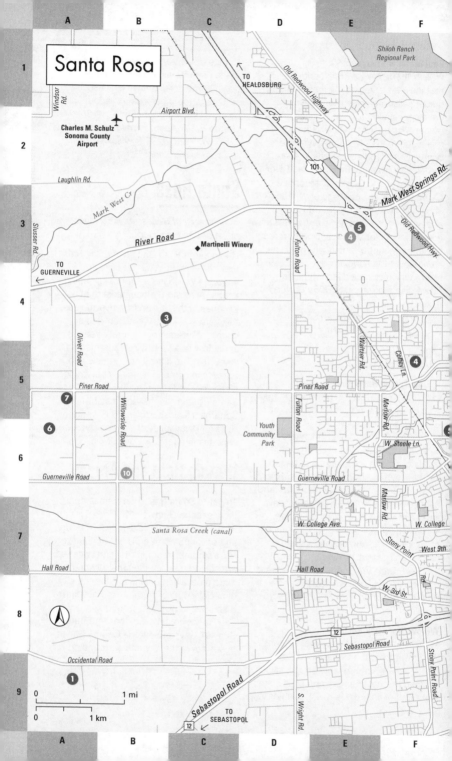

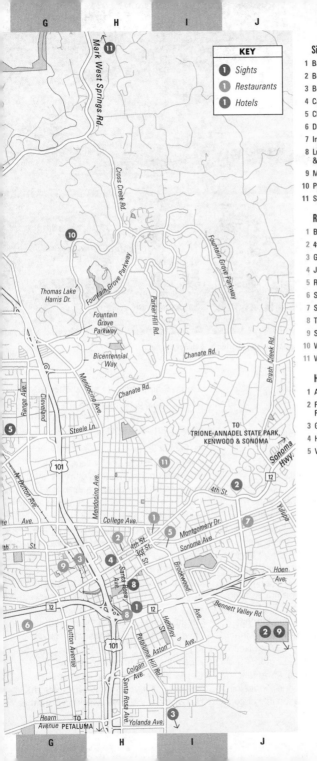

KEY

1 *Sights*

1 *Restaurants*

1 *Hotels*

Sights ▼

1	Balletto Vineyards	**A9**
2	Belden Barns	**J8**
3	Benovia Winery	**B4**
4	Carol Shelton Wines	**F5**
5	Charles M. Schulz Museum	**F6**
6	DeLoach Vineyards	**A6**
7	Inman Family Wines	**A5**
8	Luther Burbank Home & Gardens	**H7**
9	Matanzas Creek Winery	**J8**
10	Paradise Ridge Winery	**G3**
11	Safari West	**H1**

Restaurants ▼

1	Bird & The Bottle	**H7**
2	4th Street Social Club	**H7**
3	Grossman's Noshery and Bar	**H7**
4	John Ash & Co	**E3**
5	Rosso Pizzeria & Wine Bar	**I7**
6	Sazon Peruvian Cuisine	**G8**
7	SEA Thai Bistro	**J7**
8	The Spinster Sisters	**H8**
9	Stark's Steak & Seafood	**G7**
10	Walter Hansel Wine & Bistro	**B6**
11	Willi's Wine Bar	**I6**

Hotels ▼

1	Astro Motel	**H8**
2	Flamingo Conference Resort & Spa	**J6**
3	Gables Wine Country Inn	**I9**
4	Hotel E	**H7**
5	Vintners Resort	**E3**

A familiar-looking hat provides shade at the Charles M. Schulz Museum.

Visitor Information

Visit Santa Rosa

✉ 9 4th St. ✛ At Wilson St. ☎ 800/404–7673 ⊕ visitsantarosa.com.

◉ Sights

Balletto Vineyards

WINERY/DISTILLERY | A few decades ago Balletto was known more for quality produce than grapes, but the new millennium saw vineyards emerge as the core business. About 90% of the fruit from the family's 650-plus acres goes to other wineries, with the remainder destined for Balletto's estate wines. The house style is light on the oak, high in acidity, and low in alcohol content, a combination that yields exceptionally food-friendly wines. Sipping a Pinot Gris, rosé of Pinot Noir, or brut rosé sparkler on the outdoor patio can feel transcendent on a warm day, though the Chardonnays and Pinot Noirs, starting with the very reasonably priced Teresa's Unoaked Chard and flagship Estate Pinot, steal the show. ✉ 5700 Occidental Rd. ✛ 2½ miles west of Hwy. 12 ☎ 707/568–2455 ⊕ www.ballettovineyards.com ☙ Tastings from $15.

★ Belden Barns

WINERY/DISTILLERY | Experiencing the enthusiasm this winery's owners radiate supplies half the pleasure of a visit to Lauren and Nate Belden's Sonoma Mountain vineyard, where at elevation 1,000 feet they grow fruit for their all-estate lineup. Grüner Veltliner, a European white grape, isn't widely planted in California, but the crisp yet softly rounded wine they produce from it makes a case for an increase. Critics also hail the Grenache, Pinot Noir, Syrah, and a nectarlike late-harvest Viognier, but you're apt to like anything poured. Tastings take place in a high-ceilinged former milking barn whose broad doorway frames a view of grapevines undulating toward a hilltop. The Beldens tailor visits to guests' interests but will nearly always whisk you into the vineyard, past a 2-acre organic garden, and over to a wishing tree whose results Lauren swears by. ■TIP→ **The tasting fee here is a two-bottle purchase per adult.** ✉ *5561 Sonoma Mountain Rd.* ⊹ *10 miles south of downtown off Bennett Valley Rd.; 5½ miles west of Glen Ellen off Warm Springs Rd.* ☎ *415/577–8552* ⊕ *www.beldenbarns.com* ✉ *Tastings from $50 (for two bottles).*

★ Benovia Winery

WINERY/DISTILLERY | Winemaker Mike Sullivan's Chardonnays and Pinot Noirs would taste marvelous even in a toolshed, but guests at Benovia's unassumingly chic Russian River Valley ranch house will never know. Appointment-only tastings of his critically acclaimed wines take place in the brown-hued living room or on the open-air patio. From either vantage point, the views of the estate Martaella Vineyard all the way to Mt. St. Helena draw the eye. Opting for a minimalistic approach in two Chardonnays from Martinelli family grapes, Sullivan subtly emphasizes the minerality in a wine from the Three Sisters Vineyard in the coastal Fort Ross–Seaview AVA. By contrast, he lets a hint of California ripeness express itself in La Pommeraie, from Zio Tony Ranch in the warmer Russian River Valley. The same scenario plays out with the estate Tilton Hill and Cohn Pinot Noirs, the former from cooler Freestone, the latter from fruit grown farther inland. ✉ *3339 Hartman La.* ⊹ *Off Piner Rd.* ☎ *707/921–1040* ⊕ *benoviawinery.com* ✉ *Tastings from $30.*

Carol Shelton Wines

WINERY/DISTILLERY | It's winemaker Carol Shelton's motto that great wines start in the vineyard, but you won't see any grapevines outside her winery—it's in an industrial park 4 miles north of downtown Santa Rosa. What you will find, and experience, are well-priced Zinfandels from grapes grown in vineyards Shelton, ever the viticultural sleuth, locates from Mendocino to Southern California's Cucamonga Valley. With coastal, hillside, valley, inland, and desert's-edge fruit, the Zins collectively reveal the range and complexity of this varietal that so arouses Shelton's passion. Although Zinfandel gets most of the attention, Shelton also makes Cabernet Sauvignon, Carignane, and Petite Sirah reds, and whites that include Chardonnay, Viognier, and the Rhône-style Coquille Blanc blend. ✉ *3354-B Coffey La.* ⊹ *Off Piner Rd.* ☎ *707/575–3441* ⊕ *www.carolshelton. com* ✉ *Tasting $10.*

Charles M. Schulz Museum

MUSEUM | FAMILY | Fans of Snoopy and Charlie Brown will love this museum dedicated to the late Charles M. Schulz, who lived his last three decades in Santa Rosa. Permanent installations include a re-creation of the cartoonist's studio, and temporary exhibits often focus on a particular theme in his work. ✉ *2301 Hardies La.* ⊹ *At W. Steele La.* ☎ *707/579–4452* ⊕ *www.schulzmuseum.org* ✉ *$12* ⊘ *Closed Tues.*

DeLoach Vineyards

WINERY/DISTILLERY | Best known for Russian River Valley Pinot Noirs, DeLoach also produces Chardonnays, old-vine Zinfandels, and a few other wines. Grapes for some reds are fermented in open-top wooden vats similar to those used in France for centuries to intensify a wine's flavor. On a self-guided tour of the winery's ½-acre Theater of Nature culinary garden, you can learn the role biodynamic farming plays in creating DeLoach wines. All visits are by appointment. ■TIP→ **Boxed lunches from the affiliated Oakville Grocery in Healdsburg can be ordered when booking.** ✉ *1791 Olivet Rd.* ⊹ *Off Guerneville Rd.* ☎ *707/526–9111* ⊕ *www.deloachvineyards.com* ✉ *Tastings from $20.*

Luther Burbank Home & Gardens showcases the results of its namesake's many botanical experiments.

Inman Family Wines

WINERY/DISTILLERY | "The winemaker is in," reads a driveway sign when owner Kathleen Inman, who crafts her winery's Chardonnay, Pinot Noir, and other western Russian River Valley wines, is present. She's often around, and it's an extra treat to learn directly from the source about her farming, fermenting, and aging methods. Her restrained, balanced wines complement sophisticated cuisine so well that top-tier restaurants include them on their lists. Inman shows equal finesse with rosé of Pinot Noir, sparkling wines, and Pinot Gris. Her zeal to recycle is in evidence everywhere, most conspicuously in the tasting room, where redwood reclaimed from an on-site barn was incorporated into the design, and crushed wine-bottle glass was fashioned into the bar. Tastings, some held on an outdoor patio, are by appointment only. ⊠ *3900 Piner Rd.* ✛ *At Olivet Rd.* ☎ *707/293–9576* ⊕ *www. inmanfamilywines.com* ⊠ *Tastings from $20* ☉ *Closed Tues. and Wed.*

Luther Burbank Home & Gardens

GARDEN | Renowned horticulturist Luther Burbank lived and worked on these grounds and made significant advances using modern selection and hybridization techniques. The 1.6-acre garden and greenhouse showcase the results of some of Burbank's experiments to develop spineless cactus and such flowers as the Shasta daisy. ■**TIP**➔ **Use your cell phone on a free self-guided garden tour, or from April through October take a docent-led tour (required to see the house).** ⊠ *204 Santa Rosa Ave.* ✛ *At Sonoma Ave.* ☎ *707/524–5445* ⊕ *www.lutherburbank.org* ⊠ *Gardens free, tour $10* ☉ *No house tours Nov.–Mar.*

Matanzas Creek Winery

WINERY/DISTILLERY | The visitor center at Matanzas Creek sets itself apart with an understated Japanese aesthetic, extending to a tranquil fountain, a koi pond, and a vast field of lavender. The winery makes Sauvignon Blanc, Chardonnay, Merlot, Pinot Noir, and Cabernet Sauvignon under the Matanzas Creek name, and three equally well-regarded wines—a Bordeaux red blend, a Chardonnay, and a Sauvignon Blanc—bearing the Journey label. The winery, owned by Jackson Family Wines, encourages guests to enjoy a picnic on the property with a bottle of Matanzas wine. Visits and picnicking are by appointment. Same-day reservations are usually possible except on summer weekends, but call ahead. ■ TIP→ An ideal time to visit is from late June to mid-August, when lavender perfumes the air. ⊠ 6097 Bennett Valley Rd. ☎ 707/528–6464, 800/590–6464 ⊕ www.matanzascreek.com ⊠ Tastings from $30.

Paradise Ridge Winery

WINERY/DISTILLERY | Among the few winery casualties of the 2017 Wine Country wildfires, Paradise Ridge has bounced back nimbly, again receiving guests for visits that charm all the more for the 156-acre hillside estate's Russian River Valley views and walk-through outdoor sculpture grove. The Blanc de Blanc bubblies, Sauvignon Blancs, and Chardonnays receive as much critical attention as the reds, whose standouts include The Convict Rockpile Zinfandel. ■ TIP→ Paradise Ridge stays open late on summer and early-fall Wednesdays, when locals and tourists (reserve well ahead) sip wines by the glass or bottle, catch the sunset, listen to local bands, and sample food from area vendors. ⊠ 4545 Thomas Lake Harris Dr. ⊹ Off Fountaingrove Pkwy. ☎ 707/528–9463 ⊕ www.prwinery.com ⊠ Tastings from $25.

Safari West

NATURE PRESERVE | FAMILY | An unexpected bit of wilderness in the Wine Country, this preserve with African wildlife covers 400 acres. Begin your visit with a stroll around enclosures housing lemurs, cheetahs, giraffes, and rare birds like the brightly colored scarlet ibis. Next, climb with your guide onto open-air vehicles that spend about two hours combing the expansive property, where more than 80 species—including gazelles, cape buffalo, antelope, wildebeests, and zebras—inhabit the hillsides. ■ TIP→ If you'd like to extend your stay, lodging in swank Botswana-made tent cabins is available. ⊠ 3115 Porter Creek Rd. ⊹ Off Mark West Springs Rd. ☎ 707/579–2551, 800/616–2695 ⊕ www.safariwest.com ⊠ $93–$103 Sept.–May, $108–$128 June–Aug.

🍴 Restaurants

Bird and the Bottle

$$$ | ECLECTIC | The owners of Willi's Seafood, Bravas Bar de Tapas, and other Sonoma County favorites operate this "modern tavern" serving global bar bites and comfort food in a multiroom, nostalgic yet contemporary space that evokes home, hearth, and good cheer. Shrimp wontons, matzo-ball soup, Cobb salad, crispy pork belly, and skirt steak all go well with the astute menu of cocktails, wines, and artisanal beers, ciders, and spirits. **Known for:** small bites and full meals; happy hour (Sun.–Thurs.); neighborhood feel. $ *Average main: $28* ⊠ 1055 4th St. ⊹ Near College Ave. ☎ 707/568–4000 ⊕ birdandthebottle.com.

4th Street Social Club

$ | VEGETARIAN | Zesty plant-based comfort food receives top billing at this loungelike downtown restaurant whose vegan and vegetarian owners also serve dishes with animal protein so families and friends with varied preferences can dine together. The nimble chefs reinterpret ingredients like watermelon into poke, carrots into salmonlike smoky-good lox (served with vegan cream cheese), and jackfruit into convincing faux pulled pork (for barbecued sliders) and "chikn" nuggets with cornmeal batter. **Known for:** 70-foot-long mural of goddess Athena by painter/tattoo artist Evan Lovett; "design your own" mimosa flights; best for lunch or when in mood for a light meal. $ *Average main: $15* ⊠ 643 4th St. ⊹ At D St.

Rare zebras are among the animals on view at Santa Rosa's Safari West.

☎ *707/978–3882* 🌐 *4thstreetsocialclub.com* 🕒 *Closed Mon.–Wed. (but check).*

Grossman's Noshery and Bar

$$ | **DELI** | The menu at this homage to Jewish delicatessens plays the greatest hits—blintzes, latkes, lox, chopped liver, and knishes, plus pastrami, corned beef, and Reuben sandwiches—but mashes things up with chicken shawarma kebabs, fish-and-chips, and other atypical deli dishes. It's all executed with panache, and the retro-eclectic decor (black-and-white ceramic tile floors, colorful tropical-bird-print wallpaper, chunky stone fireplace) feels nostalgic yet of the moment. **Known for:** baked goods; happy-hour (daily 3–5) frozen vodka shots; picnic-table seating beside the building. [$] *Average main: $18* ✉ *Hotel La Rose, 308½ Wilson St.* ✣ *Near 4th St.* ☎ *707/595–7707* 🌐 *grossmanssr.com.*

John Ash & Co

$$$ | **MODERN AMERICAN** | A dress-up multiroom special-occasion establishment that debuted in 1980, John Ash bills itself as Sonoma County's first farm-to-table restaurant, but its legacy extends even further: the namesake founder, no longer involved, was among several pioneering Wine Country chefs who tailored their cuisine to the region's wines. Though eclipsed as a destination restaurant by rivals in Healdsburg and elsewhere, this remains a worthy stop for well-crafted dishes like mushroom ravioli in porcini cream, pan-seared dayboat scallops, and chicken cordon bleu. **Known for:** raw and cooked oysters and other apps; happy hour (3–5 pm) beverages and small bites; Sonoma-centric wine list. [$] *Average main: $34* ✉ *Vintners Resort, 4350 Barnes Rd.* ✣ *At River Rd.* ☎ *707/527–7687* 🌐 *vintnersresort.com/dining/john-ash-co* 🕒 *No lunch.*

Rosso Pizzeria & Wine Bar

$$ | **PIZZA** | Ask local wine pourers where to get the best pizza, and they'll often recommend Rosso, a sprawling strip-mall restaurant whose chefs hold center stage in the large open kitchen. Two perennial Neapolitan-style pizza

favorites are the Moto Guzzi, with house-smoked mozzarella and spicy Caggiano sausage, and the Funghi di Limone, with oven-roasted mixed mushrooms and Taleggio and fontina cheese. **Known for:** wine selection; fried chicken with caramelized pancetta glaze; salumi and salads. $ *Average main: $20 ⊠ Creekside Center, 53 Montgomery Dr. ✢ At Brookwood Ave.* ☎ 707/544–3221 ⊕ *www. rossopizzeria.com* ⊗ *Closed Sun.*

Sazon Peruvian Cuisine
$$ | PERUVIAN | Join Peruvian locals enjoying a taste of back home at this strip-mall restaurant whose name means "flavor" or "seasoning." Several ceviche appetizers—including one with ponzu sauce for a Japanese twist—show the range of tastes the lead chef and owner, José Navarro, conjures up, as does the *arroz con mariscos,* a velvety, turmeric-laced seafood paella. **Known for:** skillfully spiced Peruvian food; small and large plates for sharing family-style; deli annex with salads and sandwiches. $ *Average main: $21 ⊠ 1129 Sebastopol Rd. ✢ At Roseland Ave.* ☎ 707/523–4346 ⊕ *www. sazonsr.com.*

SEA Thai Bistro
$$ | ASIAN | The initials in this upscale strip-mall bistro's name stand for "Southeast Asian," reflecting the cuisines beyond Thailand's the chef prepares. Glass chandeliers of jellyfish and schools of fish glow softly above patrons who sit at dark-wood tables, the rectangular onyx bar, or on the patio, enjoying comfort food like spring rolls and "street fair" rice noodles with chicken, bacon, and vegetables before moving on to distinctively spiced entrées. **Known for:** culinary mashups like Thai bruschetta with prawns, avocado, and peanut sauce; many seafood dishes; beer and wine list. $ *Average main: $22 ⊠ 2350 Midway Dr. ✢ At Farmers La.* ☎ 707/528–8333 ⊕ *www.seathaibistrobar.com.*

The Spinster Sisters
$$$ | MODERN AMERICAN | The versatile chef of this concrete-and-glass hot spot anchoring the SOFA Santa Rosa Arts District satisfies her diverse devotees with an eclectic menu of American standards and playful variations on international cuisines. The lockdown era prompted a pivot to family takeout meals, though a return to normal may see a reprise of longtime favorites like kimchi-and-bacon deviled eggs, wilted kale salad, and, for dinner, grilled ahi tuna and hanger steak. **Known for:** thought-provoking flavors; dessert pastries; local and international wines. $ *Average main: $29 ⊠ 401 S. A St. ✢ At Sebastopol Ave.* ☎ 707/528–7100 ⊕ *thespinstersisters.com* ⊗ *Closed Sun.–Tues. (but check).*

Stark's Steak & Seafood
$$$ | STEAKHOUSE | The low lighting, well-spaced tables, and gas fireplaces at Stark's create a congenial setting for dining on steak, seafood from the raw bar, and sustainable fish. With entrées that include a 20-ounce, dry-aged rib eye and a 32-ounce porterhouse for two, there's not a chance that meat eaters will depart unsated, and nonsteak options like tamarind barbecue prawns and halibut with cherry-tomato confit surpass those at your average temple to beef. **Known for:** thick steaks; high-quality seafood; steak-house atmosphere. $ *Average main: $33 ⊠ 521 Adams St. ✢ At 7th St.* ☎ 707/546–5100 ⊕ *www.starkssteakhouse.com* ⊗ *No lunch weekends.*

★ Walter Hansel Wine & Bistro
$$$ | FRENCH | Tabletop linens and lights softly twinkling from this ruby-red roadhouse restaurant's low wooden ceiling raise expectations the Parisian-style bistro cuisine consistently exceeds. A starter of cheeses or lobster bisque in a puff pastry awakens the palate for entrées like chicken cordon bleu, steak au poivre, or what this place does best: seafood dishes that might include scallops in

Many rooms at Vintners Resort have vineyard views.

white-truffle cream sauce or subtly sauced wild Alaskan halibut. **Known for:** romantic setting for classic cuisine; prix-fixe option; vegan and vegetarian dishes. [$] *Average main: $35* ✉ *3535 Guerneville Rd.* ✣ *At Willowside Rd., 6 miles northwest of downtown* ☎ *707/546–6462* 🌐 *walterhanselbistro.com* ⏲ *Closed Mon. and Tues. No lunch.*

★ **Willi's Wine Bar**

$$$ | **ECLECTIC** | Among the few restaurants to perish in the Wine Country's 2017 wildfires, Willi's relocated to a Santa Rosa strip mall, still serving up inventive globe-trotting small plates paired with international wines. Dishes like pork-belly pot stickers represent Asia, with Tunisian roasted local carrots and Moroccan-style lamb chops among the Mediterranean-inspired foods. **Known for:** patio seating; inspired wine selection; 2-ounce pours so you can pair a new wine with each dish. [$] *Average main: $33* ✉ *1612 Terrace Way* ✣ *Near Town and Country Dr.* ☎ *707/526–3096* 🌐 *starkrestaurants.com.*

Hotels

★ **Astro Motel**

$ | **HOTEL** | **FAMILY** | The Sixties are back splashier than ever at this tastefully and whimsically restored motel diagonally next to a park and across from the Luther Burbank Home & Gardens. **Pros:** vintage mid-century modern furnishings; well-designed rooms; nearby Spinster Sisters restaurant (same owners) anchors neighborhood arts district. **Cons:** no pool, gym, spa, or other amenities; about a mile from Railroad Square Historic District; surrounding area mildly scruffy. [$] *Rooms from: $199* ✉ *323 Santa Rosa Ave.* ☎ *707/200–4655* 🌐 *theastro.com* 🛏 *34 rooms* 🍴 *No meals.*

Flamingo Conference Resort & Spa

$ | **HOTEL** | If Don Draper from *Mad Men* popped into this 1950s motel-hotel hybrid 2¼ miles northeast of downtown Santa Rosa, he'd feel right at home. **Pros:** movie star Jayne Mansfield partied here in the 60s; retro vibe; renovations to bring new look in 2021. **Cons:** 30-minute walk to downtown; standard rooms can feel cramped; feels more conference hotel than resort. $ *Rooms from: $152* ✉ *2777 4th St.* ☎ *707/545–8530, 800/848–8300* ⊕ *www.flamingoresort.com* ⇆ *170 rooms* ⦿ *No meals.*

★ Gables Wine Country Inn

$$ | **B&B/INN** | Guests at this circa-1887 Gothic Victorian inn set on 3½ bucolic acres slip back in time inside high-ceilinged, period-decorated pastel-painted rooms, some with four-poster beds and all with comfortable mattresses and high-quality sheets. **Pros:** Victorian style and hospitality; three-course gourmet breakfasts; country vibe yet 4 miles from downtown. **Cons:** period look may not work for all guests; slightly off the beaten path; weekend minimum-stay requirement April–mid-November. $ *Rooms from: $249* ✉ *4257 Petaluma Hill Rd.* ☎ *707/585–7777* ⊕ *www.thegablesinn. com* ⇆ *8 rooms* ⦿ *Free breakfast.*

Hotel E

$$ | **HOTEL** | This downtown hotel's developer renovated a four-story 1908 Beaux Arts former bank into a boutique property within walking distance of restaurants, bars, and shops and less than a 10-minute drive to vineyards and tasting rooms. **Pros:** appealing room decor; convenient to downtown restaurants; lobby doubles as wine bar. **Cons:** lacks small-town Wine Country feel; no on-site parking (valet service provided); some rooms are smallish (but thoughtfully organized). $ *Rooms from: $239* ✉ *37 Old Courthouse Sq.* ☎ *707/481–3750* ⊕ *hotelesantarosa.com* ⇆ *39 rooms* ⦿ *No meals.*

★ Vintners Resort

$$$$ | **HOTEL** | With a countryside location, a reserved sense of style, and spacious rooms with comfortable beds, the Vintners Resort further seduces with a slew of amenities and a scenic vineyard landscape. **Pros:** John Ash & Co. restaurant; vineyard jogging path; personalized service. **Cons:** occasional noise from adjacent events center; trips to downtown Santa Rosa or Healdsburg require a car; pricey on summer and fall weekends. $ *Rooms from: $415* ✉ *4350 Barnes Rd.* ☎ *707/575–7350, 800/421–2584* ⊕ *www. vintnersresort.com* ⇆ *78 rooms* ⦿ *No meals.*

ⓨ Nightlife

BREWPUBS

Russian River Brewing Company

BREWPUBS/BEER GARDENS | It's all about Belgian-style ales, "aggressively hopped California ales," and barrel-aged beers at this famous brewery's Santa Rosa pub. The legendary lineup includes Pliny the Elder (and Younger, but only in February), Blind Pig IPA, Supplication sour (aged 12 months in used Pinot Noir barrels), and many more. ■ TIP➔ **A second, larger pub (more seats, more beers) operates out of RRBC's production facility in Windsor.** ✉ *725 4th St.* ✛ *Near D St.* ☎ *707/545–2337* ⊕ *www.russianriverbrewing.com.*

ⓝⓔⓦ Performing Arts

Luther Burbank Center for the Arts

ARTS CENTERS | This cultural hub, configured theater-style or open-floor depending on the performance, books acts and ensembles as varied as Celtic Thunder, Anjelah Johnson, Amy Grant, and John Cleese. ✉ *50 Mark West Springs Rd.* ✛ *East off U.S. 101* ☎ *707/546–3600* ⊕ *www.lutherburbankcenter.org.*

ⓡ Activities

BALLOONING

Up & Away Ballooning

BALLOONING | The flights of this longtime Wine Country outfit depart from Charles M. Schulz Sonoma County Airport. If the balloon you're in gets high enough and the day is sunny, you'll have ocean views to go with those vineyard vistas. ✉ *Santa Rosa* ☎ *707/836–0171* ⊕ *www.up-away. com* 💲 *$275 per person.*

Index

Photo Credits

Front Cover: ivanastar [Description: Sonoma Valley Under Bright Sun.]. **Back cover, from left to right:** FloridaStock/Shutterstock, Kent Sorensen/Shutterstock, cheng cheng/Shutterstock. **Spine:** Juancat/Shutterstock. **Interior, from left to right:** Ljupco Smokovski/Shutterstock (1). Rebecca Gosselin Photography (2). **Chapter 1: Experience Napa and Sonoma:** Courtesy of Inglenook (6-7). Michael Warwick/Shutterstock (8). I8V-Israel Valencia All Rights Reserved (9). Courtesy of the Napa Valley Wine Train (9). Longmeadow Ranch (10). Courtesy of Wine Country Botanicals (10). Mariana Marakhovskaia/Shutterstock (10). Photo courtesy of Sonoma County Tourism. (10). Joseph Phelps Vineyards (11). Nat and Cody Gantz 2018/Hanson of Sonoma Distillery (11). CIA at Copia (12). Valentina_G/Shutterstock (12). Donum Estate (12). Courtesy of Sonoma County/Smugmug (12). Zack Frank/Shutterstock (13). Photo courtesy of Sonoma County Tourism. (13). Lisovskaya Natalia/Shutterstock (16). Jeff Bramwell (16). Steven Freeman 2016. All rights reserved. (16). Courtesy of Sonoma County/Smugmug (16). Richard Ault (17). Robert McClenahan (17). New Africa/Shutterstock (17). Tubay Yabut Photography (17). 2016 Natalie and Cody Gantz (18). Garrett Rowland (18). HARMON GUESTHOUSE (18). Ernie's Tin Bar (18). El Barrio Bar (19). Courtesy of Sonoma County Tourism (19). Christophe Genty Photography/Goose & Gander (19). Courtesy of Sky & Vine Rooftop Bar (19). Jay Jeffers (20). Courtesy of Makers Market (20). Carlos Yudica/Shutterstock (20). McEvoy Ranch (20). Zeljko Radojko/Shutterstock (20). McEvoy Ranch (21). Nikovfrmoto | Dreamstime.com (21). Natalia Svistunova/Shutterstock (21). Napa Soap Company (21). Napa Wine Candles (21). Sara sanger 2017 (22). Infinity Visuals (23). **Chapter 3: Visiting Wineries and Tasting Rooms:** Courtesy of Three Sticks Wines (45). Megan Reeves Photography (49). Courtesy of Napa Valley Balloons, Inc. (50). Andy Dean Photography / Shutterstock (56). **Chapter 4: Napa Valley:** Courtesy of the Napa Valley Wine Train (65). Avis Mandel (74). Di Rosa (77). Robert Holmes (78). Courtesy of the Napa Valley Wine Train (80). Victor M. Samuel (93). cheng cheng/Shutterstock(94). OPENKITCHENPhotography (96). Far Niente+Dolce+Nickel & Nickel (107). Jason Tinacci. (108). Olaf Beckman (114). Scott Chebagia (122). Courtesy of Long Meadow Ranch (127). Smcfeeters | Dreamstime.com (133). TIM CARL (139). Tim Carl. (140). **Chapter 5: Sonoma Valley and Petaluma:** Wildly Simple Productions (143). Rocco Ceselin/Ram's Gate Winery (157). Julie Vader/Shutterstock (159). Leo Gong (163). Benziger Family Winery (169). **Chapter 6: Northern Sonoma, Russian River, and West County:** Eric Wolfinger (181). Joe Becerra/Shutterstock (193). Matt Armendariz (197). Robert Holmes (200). Warren H. White (202). Christian Horan Photography (209). Sonoma County Tourism (222). Laurence G. Sterling/Iron Horse Vineyards (229). Patrick Amiot/Sonoma County/Smugmug (231). Joe Shlabotnik/Flickr (238). Jeffrey M. Frank/Shutterstock (240). R. Mabry Photography 2017/Safari West (242). Vintners Resort/Sonoma County/Smugmug (244). **About Our Writers:** All photos are courtesy of the writers.

*Every effort has been made to trace the copyright holders, and we apologize in advance for any accidental errors. We would be happy to apply the corrections in the following edition of this publication.

Notes